D1074564

BATMAN/TEENAGE MUTANT NINJA TURTLES II

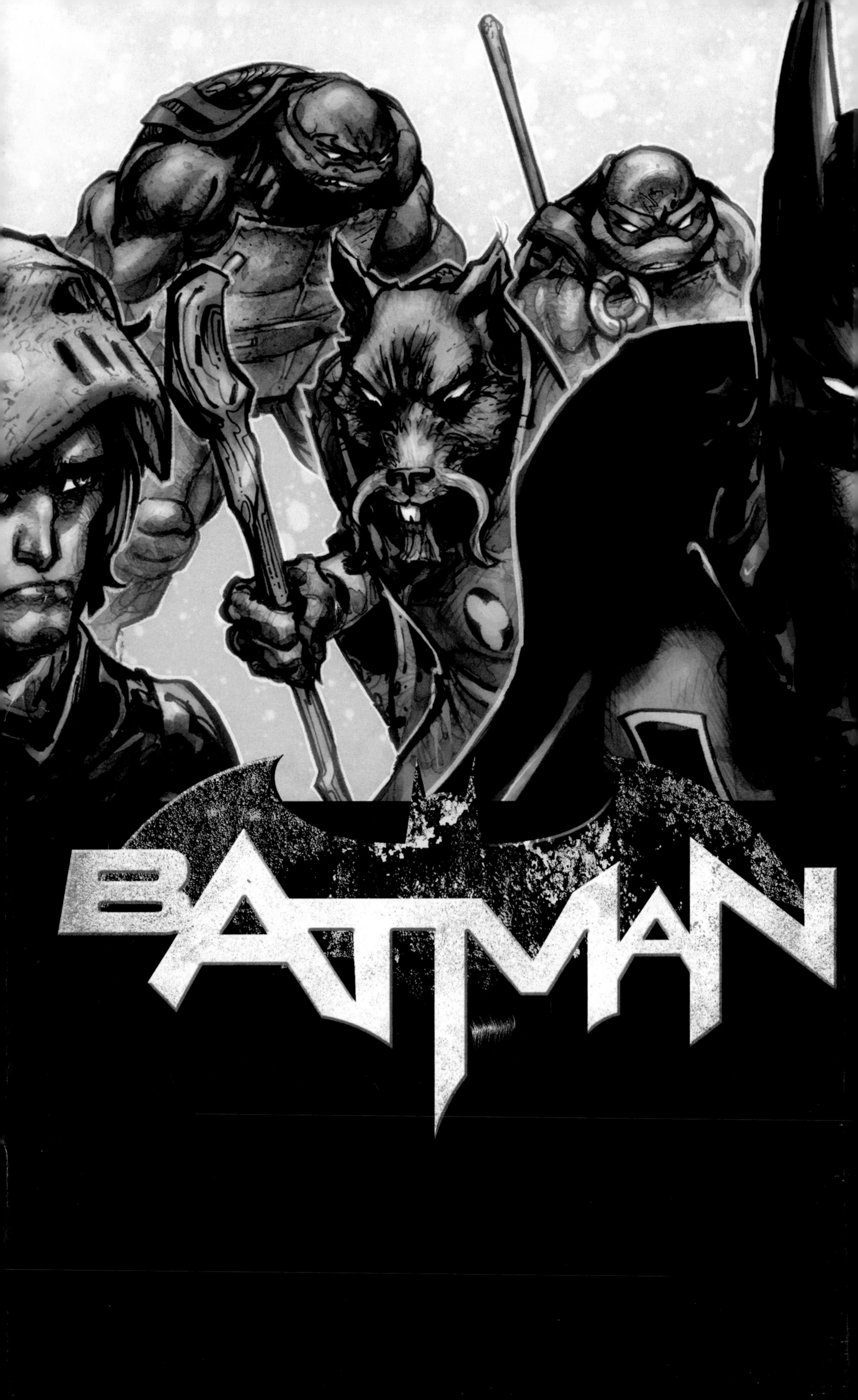

BATMAN

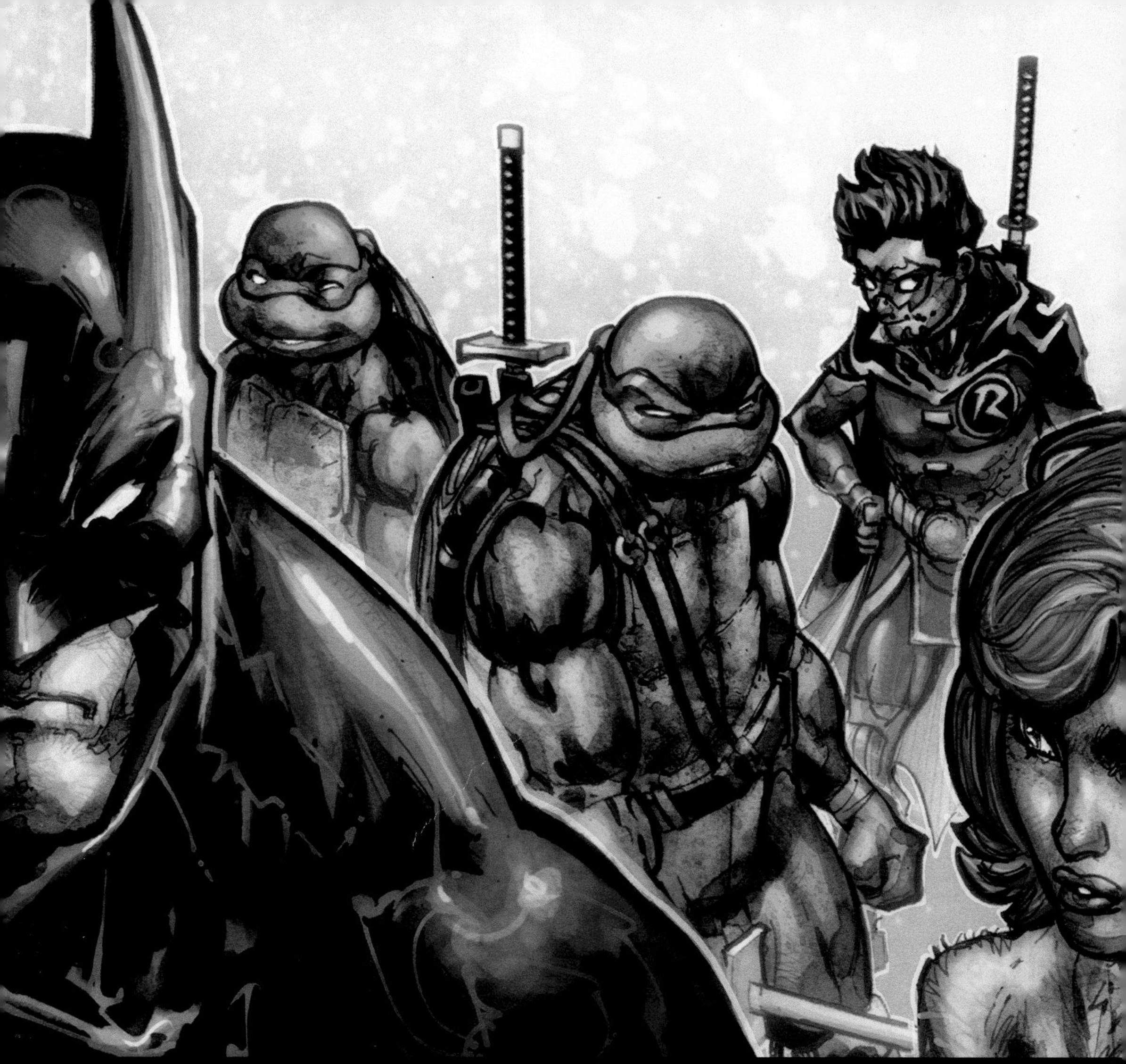

TEENAGE MUTANT NINJA TURTLES II

JAMES TYNION IV (plot, dialogue #1-2)
RYAN FERRIER (dialogue #3-6) Writers

FREDDIE E. WILLIAMS II Artist

JEREMY COLWELL Colorist

TOM NAPOLITANO Letterer

FREDDIE E. WILLIAMS II and JEREMY COLWELL
Series and Collection Cover Artists

BATMAN created by BOB KANE with BILL FINGER

TEENAGE MUTANT NINJA TURTLES
created by KEVIN EASTMAN and PETER LAIRD

JIM CHADWICK Editor – Original Series
LIZ ERICKSON Assistant Editor – Original Series
JEB WOODARD Group Editor – Collected Editions
ERIKA ROTHBERG Editor – Collected Edition
STEVE COOK Design Director – Books
LOUIS PRANDI Publication Design

BOB HARRAS Senior VP – Editor-in-Chief, DC Comics
PAT McCALLUM Executive Editor, DC Comics

DIANE NELSON President
DAN DiDIO Publisher
JIM LEE Publisher
GEOFF JOHNS President & Chief Creative Officer
AMIT DESAI Executive VP – Business & Marketing Strategy,
Direct to Consumer & Global Franchise Management
SAM ADES Senior VP & General Manager, Digital Services
BOBBIE CHASE VP & Executive Editor, Young Reader & Talent Development
MARK CHIARELLO Senior VP – Art, Design & Collected Editions
JOHN CUNNINGHAM Senior VP – Sales & Trade Marketing
ANNE DePIES Senior VP – Business Strategy, Finance & Administration
DON FALLETTI VP – Manufacturing Operations
LAWRENCE GANEM VP – Editorial Administration & Talent Relations
ALISON GILL Senior VP – Manufacturing & Operations
HANK KANALZ Senior VP – Editorial Strategy & Administration
JAY KOGAN VP – Legal Affairs
JACK MAHAN VP – Business Affairs
NICK J. NAPOLITANO VP – Manufacturing Administration
EDDIE SCANNELL VP – Consumer Marketing
COURTNEY SIMMONS Senior VP – Publicity & Communications
JIM (SKI) SOKOLOWSKI VP – Comic Book Specialty Sales & Trade Marketing
NANCY SPEARS VP – Mass, Book, Digital Sales & Trade Marketing
MICHELE R. WELLS VP – Content Strategy

BATMAN/TEENAGE MUTANT NINJA TURTLES II

DC Comics, 2900 West Alameda Ave., Burbank, CA 91505
Printed by LSC Communications, Kendallville, IN, USA. 7/6/18.
First Printing.
ISBN: 978-1-4012-8031-4

Library of Congress Cataloging-in-Publication Data is available.

HUFF-HUFF

I NEED THE POLICE!

9-1-1, WHAT'S YOUR EMERGENCY?

THE LIGHTS...THE LIGHTS WENT OUT...

I WAS IN THE SUBWAY, AND THE LIGHTS CUT OUT, AND I COULDN'T SEE ANYTHING...

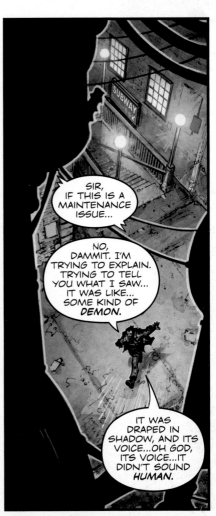

SIR, IF THIS IS A MAINTENANCE ISSUE...

NO, DAMMIT. I'M TRYING TO EXPLAIN. TRYING TO TELL YOU WHAT I SAW... IT WAS LIKE... SOME KIND OF DEMON.

IT WAS DRAPED IN SHADOW, AND ITS VOICE...OH GOD, ITS VOICE...IT DIDN'T SOUND HUMAN.

IT TOLD ME TO RUN. IT TOLD ME THAT IT WAS SAVING ME... AND THEN...AND THEN...

IT SAID SOMETHING THAT SENT A CHILL RIGHT DOWN MY SPINE. I DIDN'T UNDERSTAND...

I CAN STILL HEAR WHAT IT SAID TO ME, RINGING OUT...

WHAT DID IT SAY?

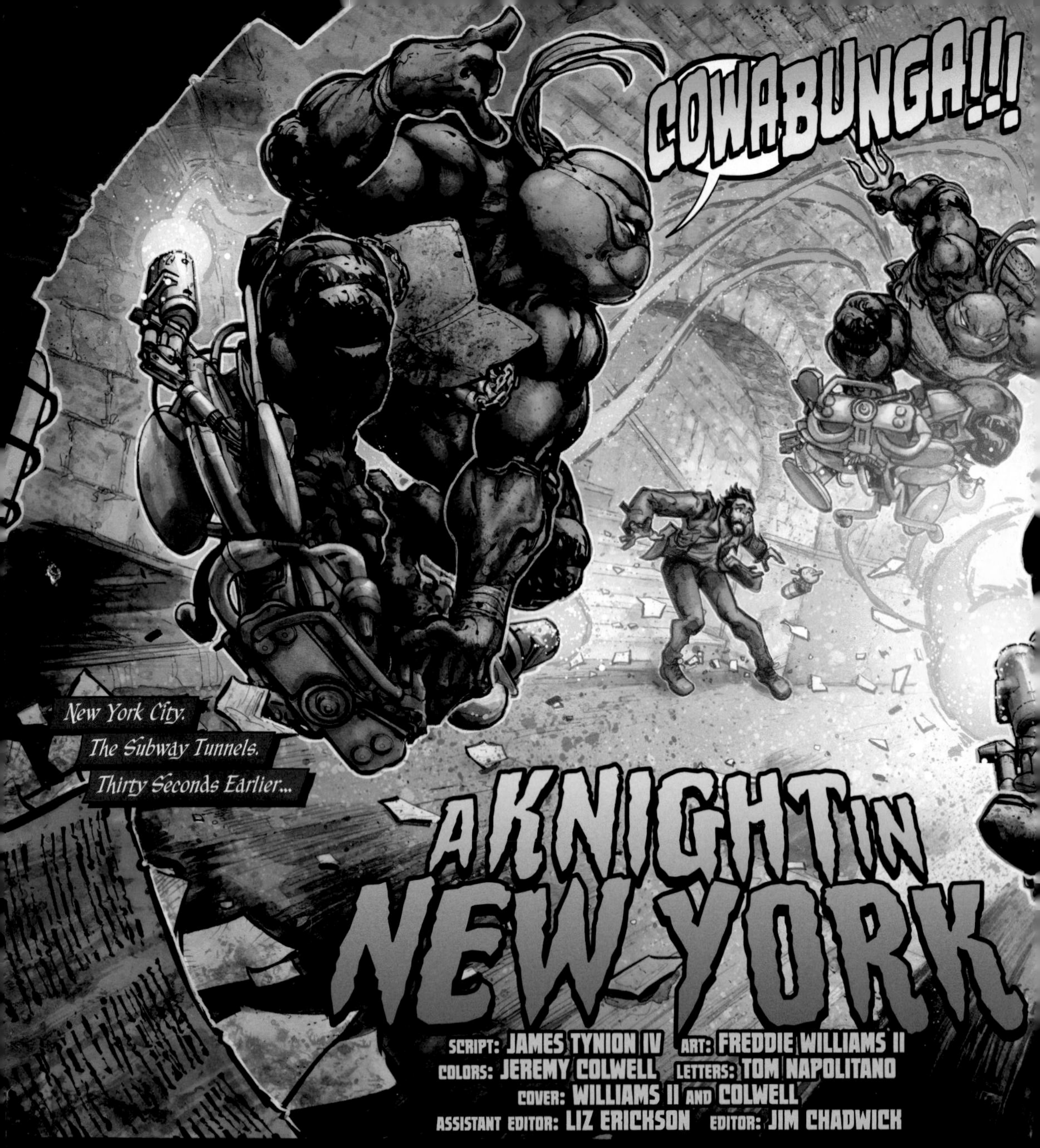
COWABUNGA!!!
New York City.
The Subway Tunnels.
Thirty Seconds Earlier...
A KNIGHT IN NEW YORK
SCRIPT: JAMES TYNION IV ART: FREDDIE WILLIAMS II
COLORS: JEREMY COLWELL LETTERS: TOM NAPOLITANO
COVER: WILLIAMS II AND COLWELL
ASSISTANT EDITOR: LIZ ERICKSON EDITOR: JIM CHADWICK

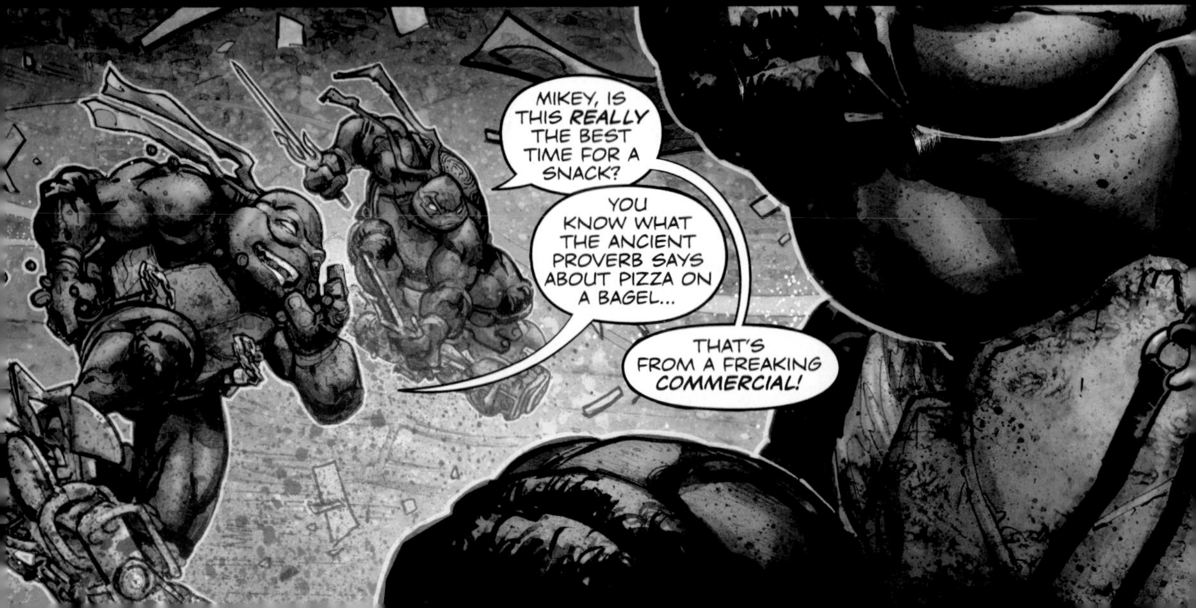
MIKEY, IS THIS REALLY THE BEST TIME FOR A SNACK?
YOU KNOW WHAT THE ANCIENT PROVERB SAYS ABOUT PIZZA ON A BAGEL...
THAT'S FROM A FREAKING COMMERCIAL!

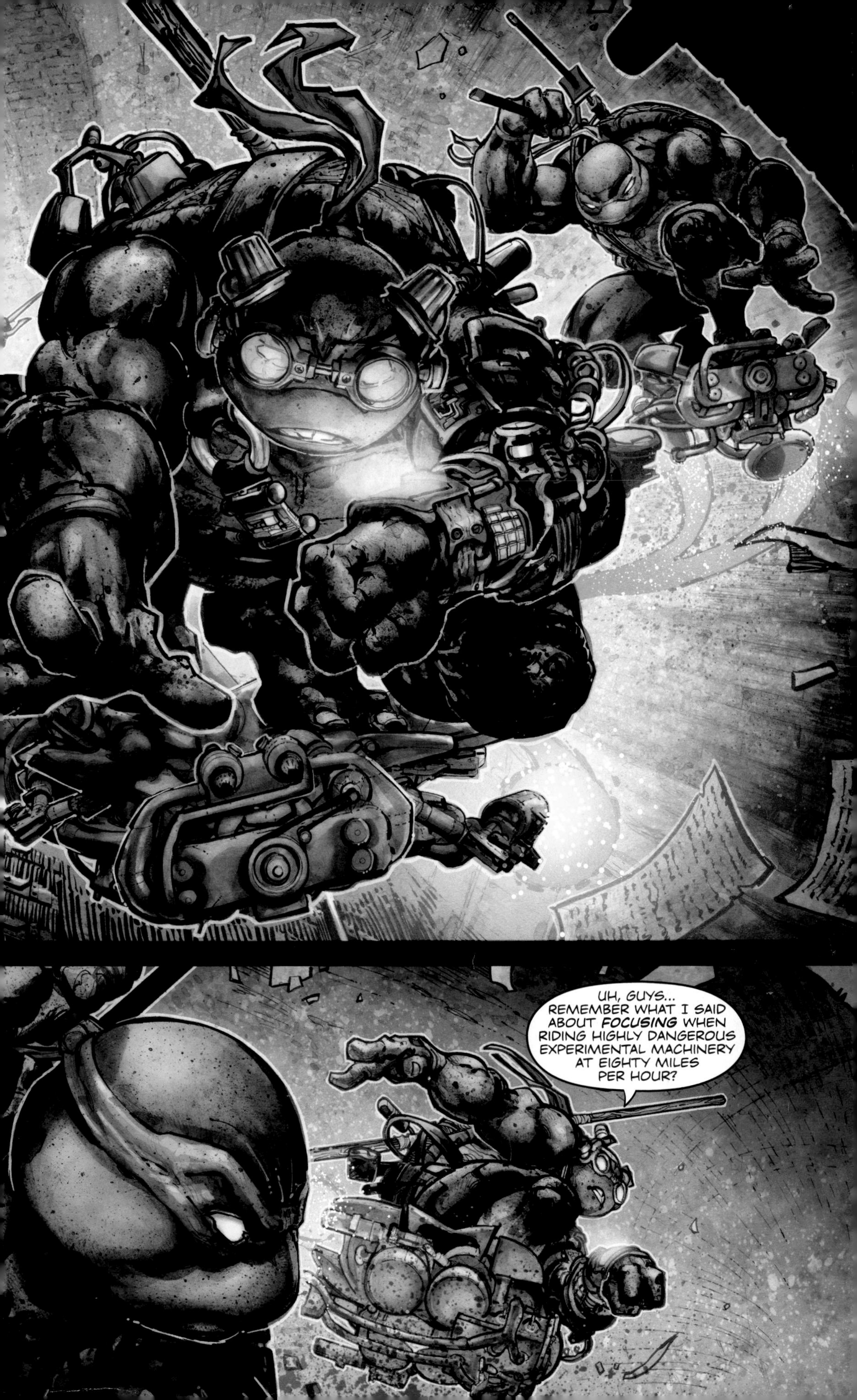
UH, GUYS... REMEMBER WHAT I SAID ABOUT FOCUSING WHEN RIDING HIGHLY DANGEROUS EXPERIMENTAL MACHINERY AT EIGHTY MILES PER HOUR?

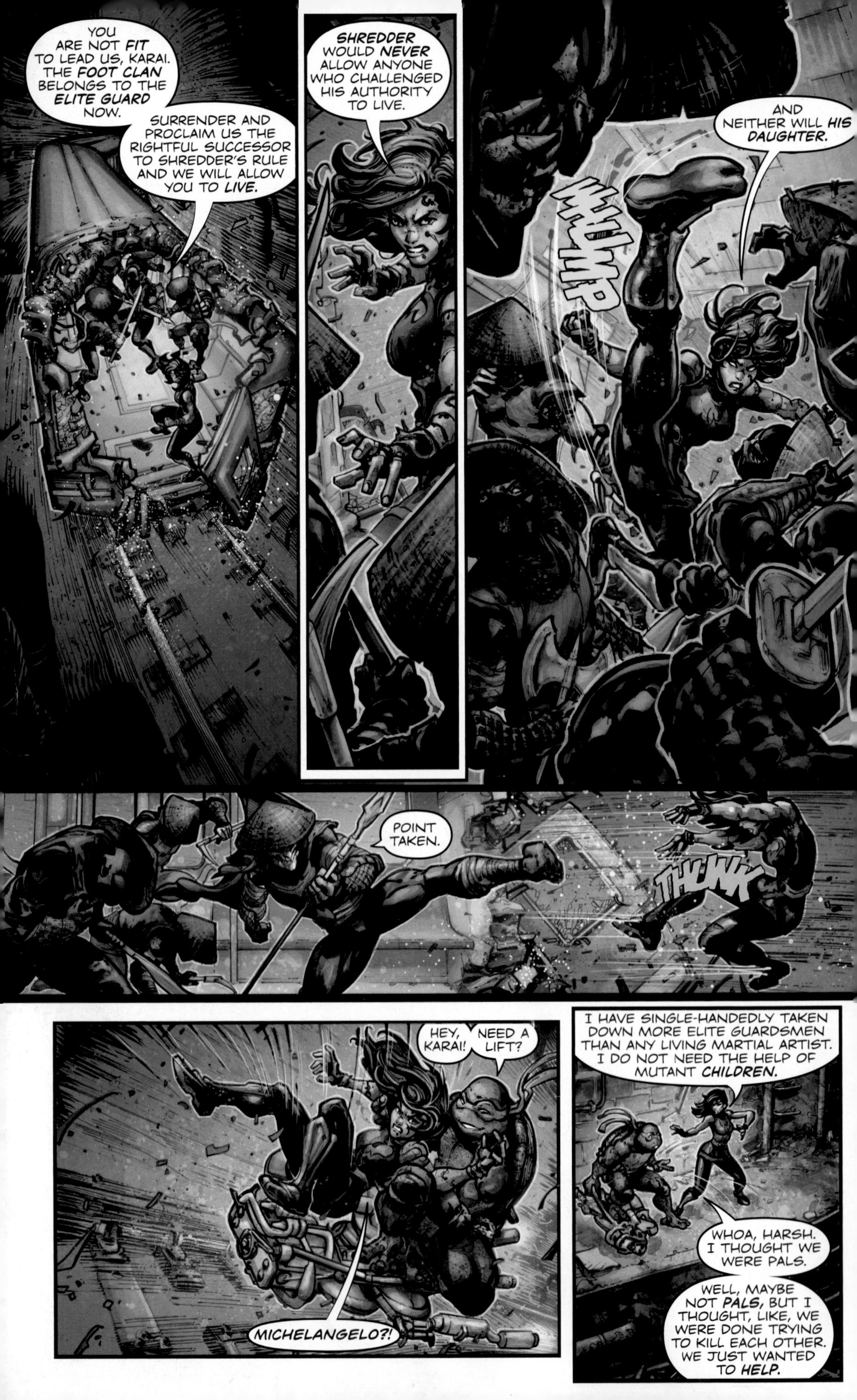
YOU ARE NOT FIT TO LEAD US, KARAI. THE FOOT CLAN BELONGS TO THE ELITE GUARD NOW.
SURRENDER AND PROCLAIM US THE RIGHTFUL SUCCESSOR TO SHREDDER'S RULE AND WE WILL ALLOW YOU TO LIVE.
SHREDDER WOULD NEVER ALLOW ANYONE WHO CHALLENGED HIS AUTHORITY TO LIVE.
AND NEITHER WILL HIS DAUGHTER.
WHUMP
POINT TAKEN.
THUNK
HEY, KARAI!
NEED A LIFT?
MICHELANGELO?!
I HAVE SINGLE-HANDEDLY TAKEN DOWN MORE ELITE GUARDSMEN THAN ANY LIVING MARTIAL ARTIST. I DO NOT NEED THE HELP OF MUTANT CHILDREN.
WHOA, HARSH. I THOUGHT WE WERE PALS.
WELL, MAYBE NOT PALS, BUT I THOUGHT, LIKE, WE WERE DONE TRYING TO KILL EACH OTHER. WE JUST WANTED TO HELP.

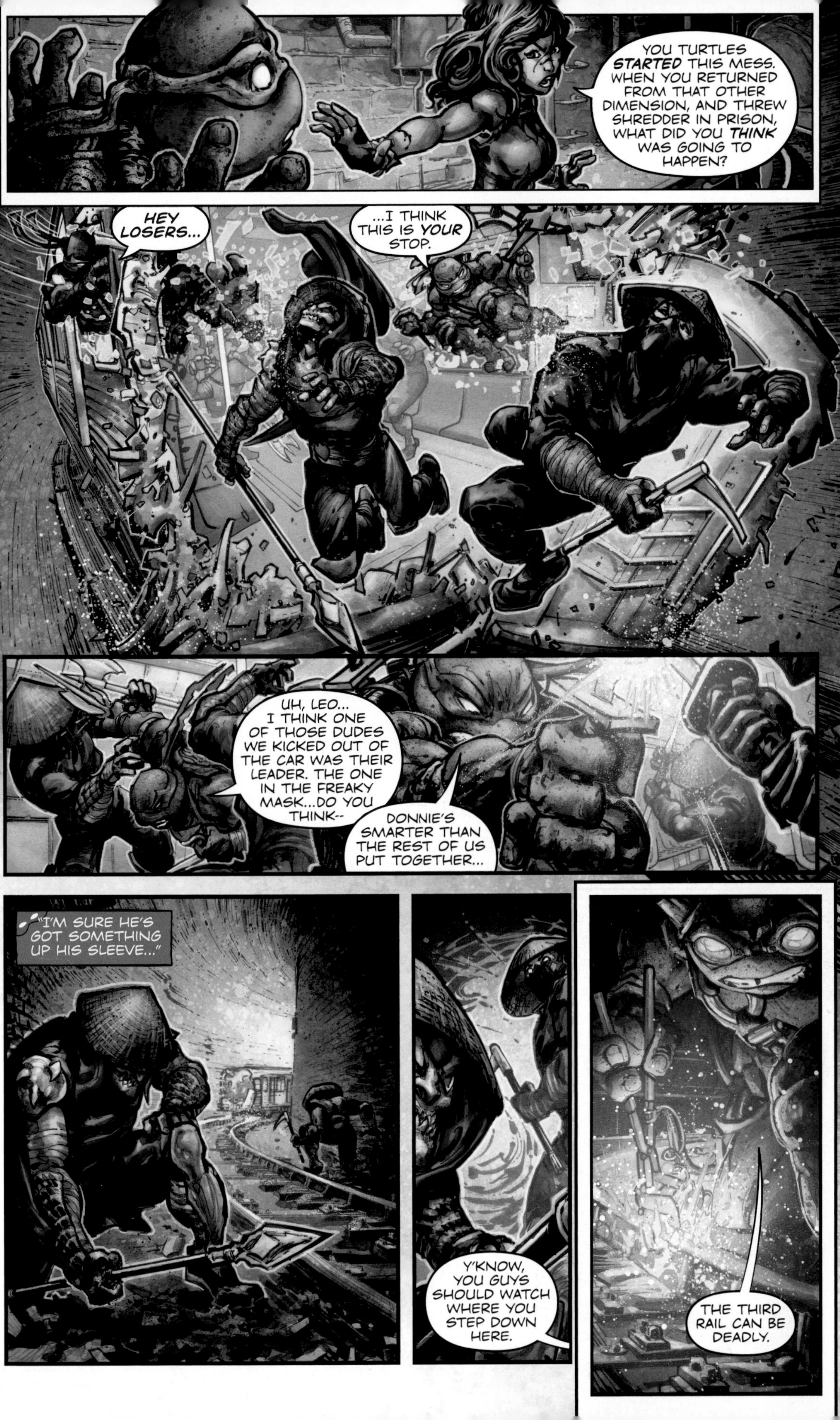
YOU TURTLES STARTED THIS MESS. WHEN YOU RETURNED FROM THAT OTHER DIMENSION, AND THREW SHREDDER IN PRISON, WHAT DID YOU THINK WAS GOING TO HAPPEN?
HEY LOSERS...
...I THINK THIS IS YOUR STOP.
UH, LEO... I THINK ONE OF THOSE DUDES WE KICKED OUT OF THE CAR WAS THEIR LEADER. THE ONE IN THE FREAKY MASK...DO YOU THINK--
DONNIE'S SMARTER THAN THE REST OF US PUT TOGETHER...
"I'M SURE HE'S GOT SOMETHING UP HIS SLEEVE..."
Y'KNOW, YOU GUYS SHOULD WATCH WHERE YOU STEP DOWN HERE.
THE THIRD RAIL CAN BE DEADLY.

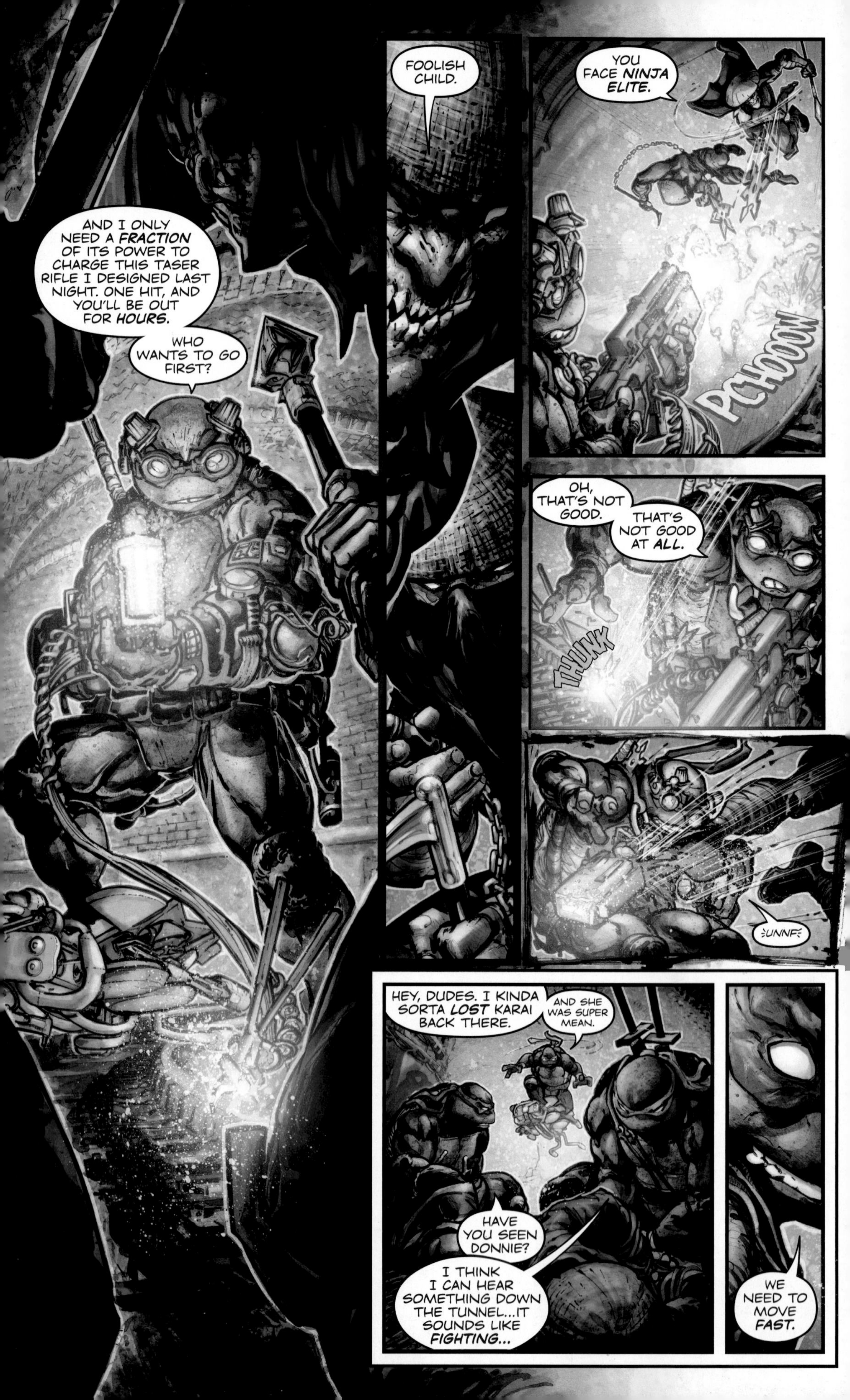

AND I ONLY NEED A FRACTION OF ITS POWER TO CHARGE THIS TASER RIFLE I DESIGNED LAST NIGHT. ONE HIT, AND YOU'LL BE OUT FOR HOURS.
WHO WANTS TO GO FIRST?
FOOLISH CHILD.
YOU FACE NINJA ELITE.
PCHOOOW
OH, THAT'S NOT GOOD.
THAT'S NOT GOOD AT ALL.
THUNK
UNNF
HEY, DUDES. I KINDA SORTA LOST KARAI BACK THERE.
AND SHE WAS SUPER MEAN.
HAVE YOU SEEN DONNIE?
I THINK I CAN HEAR SOMETHING DOWN THE TUNNEL...IT SOUNDS LIKE FIGHTING...
WE NEED TO MOVE FAST.

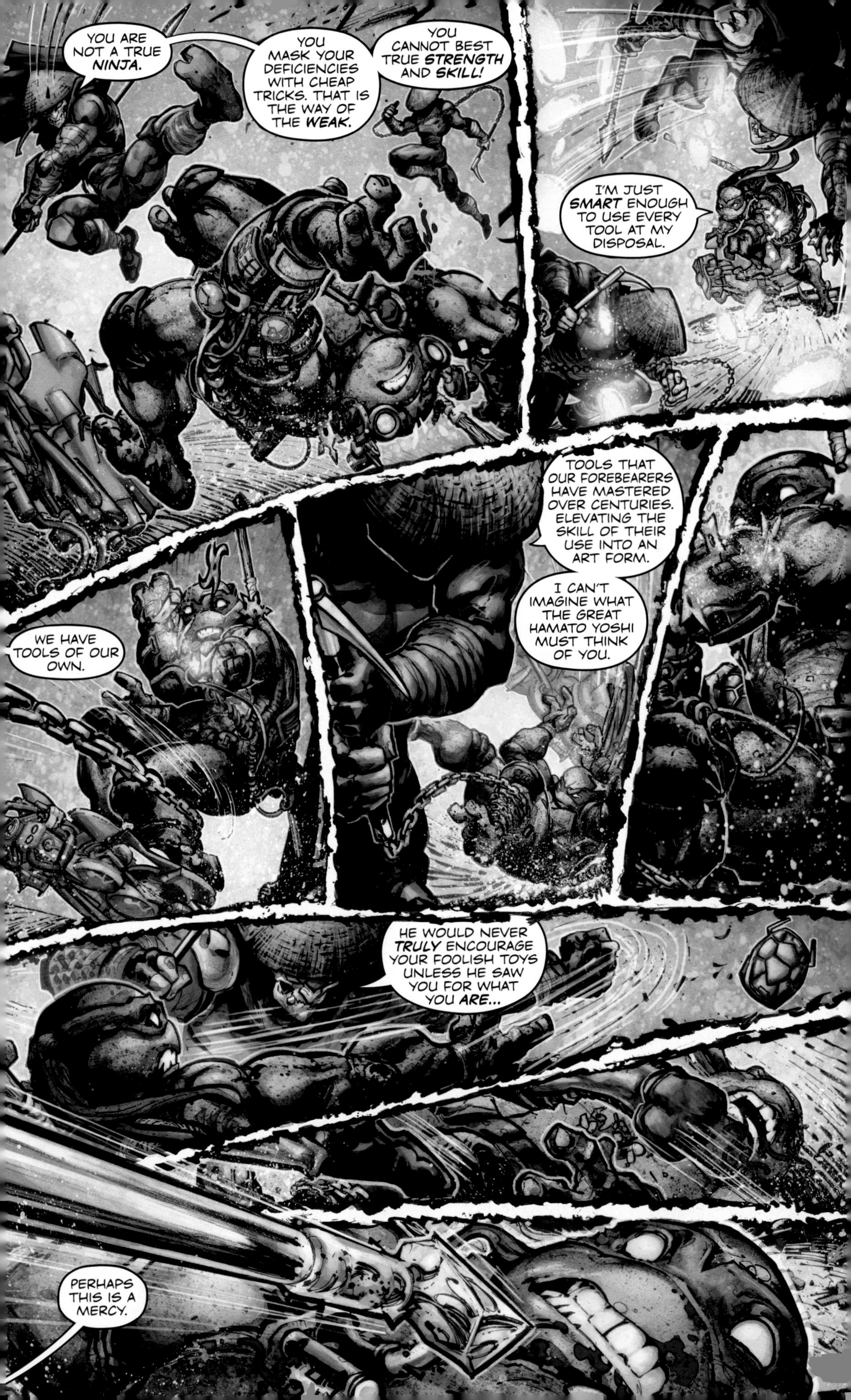
YOU ARE NOT A TRUE NINJA.
YOU MASK YOUR DEFICIENCIES WITH CHEAP TRICKS. THAT IS THE WAY OF THE WEAK.
YOU CANNOT BEST TRUE STRENGTH AND SKILL!
I'M JUST SMART ENOUGH TO USE EVERY TOOL AT MY DISPOSAL.
WE HAVE TOOLS OF OUR OWN.
TOOLS THAT OUR FOREBEARERS HAVE MASTERED OVER CENTURIES. ELEVATING THE SKILL OF THEIR USE INTO AN ART FORM.
I CAN'T IMAGINE WHAT THE GREAT HAMATO YOSHI MUST THINK OF YOU.
HE WOULD NEVER TRULY ENCOURAGE YOUR FOOLISH TOYS UNLESS HE SAW YOU FOR WHAT YOU ARE...
PERHAPS THIS IS A MERCY.

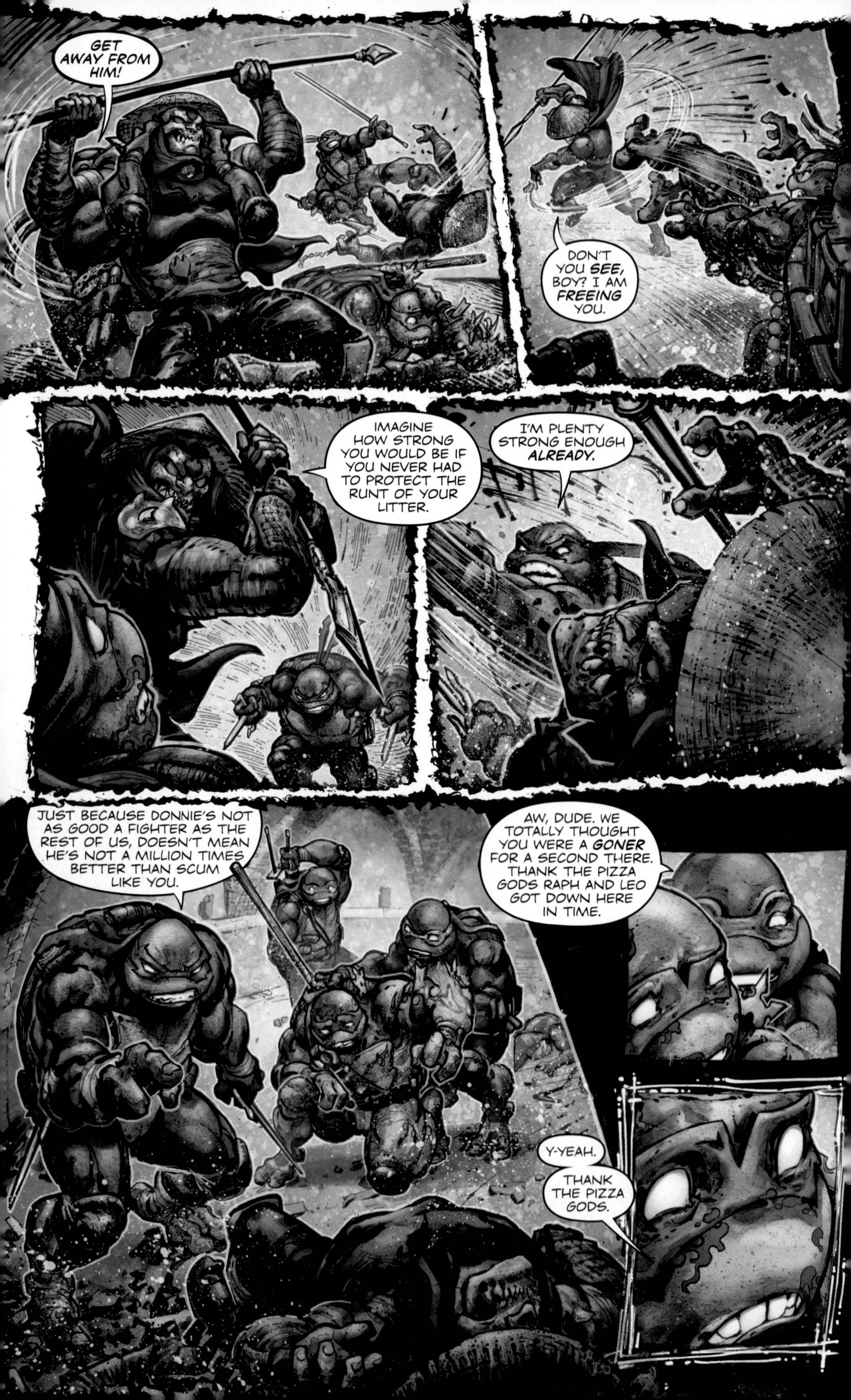
GET AWAY FROM HIM!
DON'T YOU **SEE,** BOY? I AM **FREEING** YOU.
IMAGINE HOW STRONG YOU WOULD BE IF YOU NEVER HAD TO PROTECT THE RUNT OF YOUR LITTER.
I'M PLENTY STRONG ENOUGH ***ALREADY.***
JUST BECAUSE DONNIE'S NOT AS GOOD A FIGHTER AS THE REST OF US, DOESN'T MEAN HE'S NOT A MILLION TIMES BETTER THAN SCUM LIKE YOU.
AW, DUDE. WE TOTALLY THOUGHT YOU WERE A ***GONER*** FOR A SECOND THERE. THANK THE PIZZA GODS RAPH AND LEO GOT DOWN HERE IN TIME.
Y-YEAH.
THANK THE PIZZA GODS.

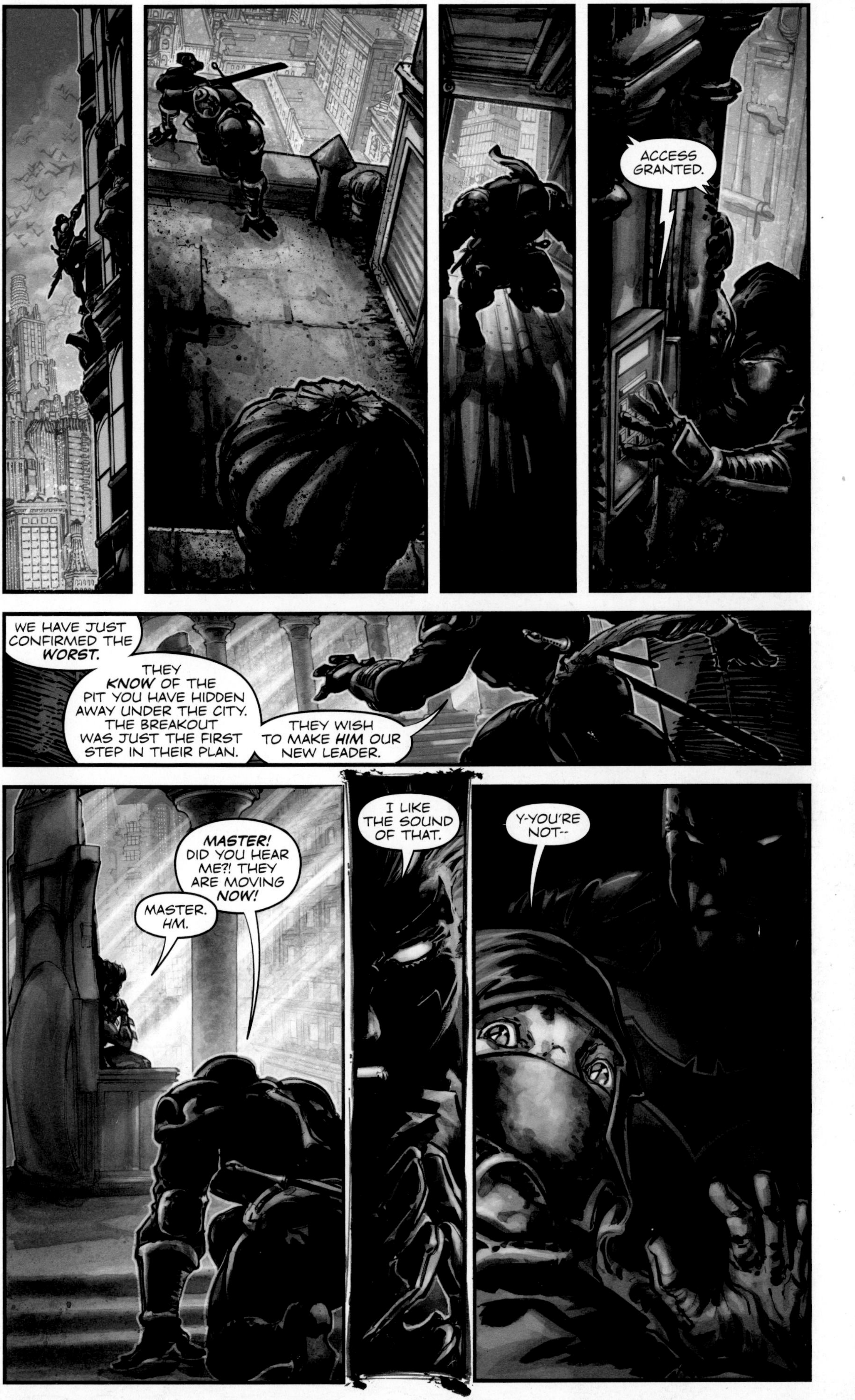
ACCESS GRANTED.
WE HAVE JUST CONFIRMED THE **WORST.**
THEY **KNOW** OF THE PIT YOU HAVE HIDDEN AWAY UNDER THE CITY. THE BREAKOUT WAS JUST THE FIRST STEP IN THEIR PLAN.
THEY WISH TO MAKE **HIM** OUR NEW LEADER.
MASTER. HM.
MASTER! DID YOU HEAR ME?! THEY ARE MOVING **NOW!**
I LIKE THE SOUND OF THAT.
Y-YOU'RE NOT--

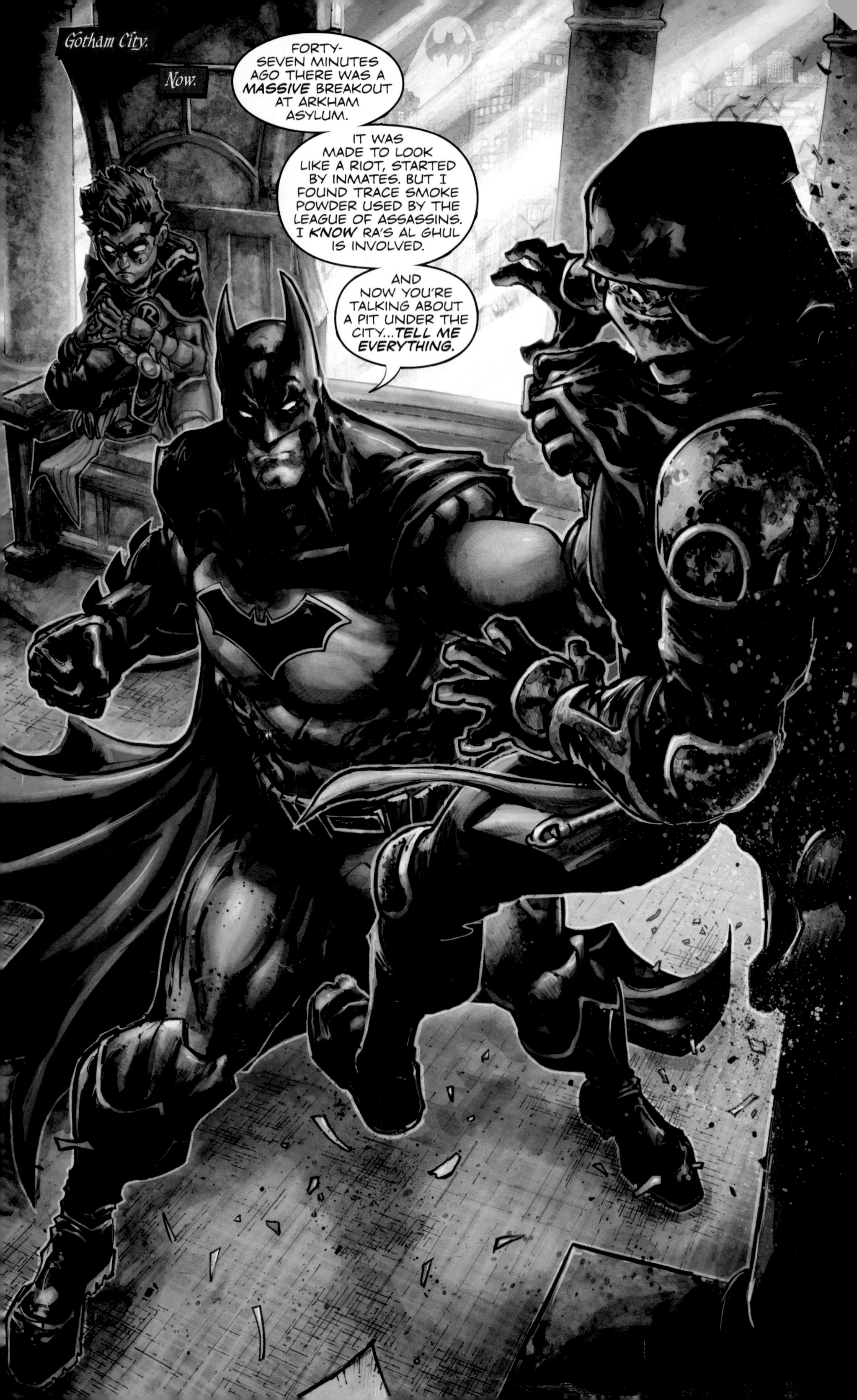
Gotham City.
Now.
FORTY-SEVEN MINUTES AGO THERE WAS A MASSIVE BREAKOUT AT ARKHAM ASYLUM.
IT WAS MADE TO LOOK LIKE A RIOT, STARTED BY INMATES. BUT I FOUND TRACE SMOKE POWDER USED BY THE LEAGUE OF ASSASSINS. I KNOW RA'S AL GHUL IS INVOLVED.
AND NOW YOU'RE TALKING ABOUT A PIT UNDER THE CITY...TELL ME EVERYTHING.

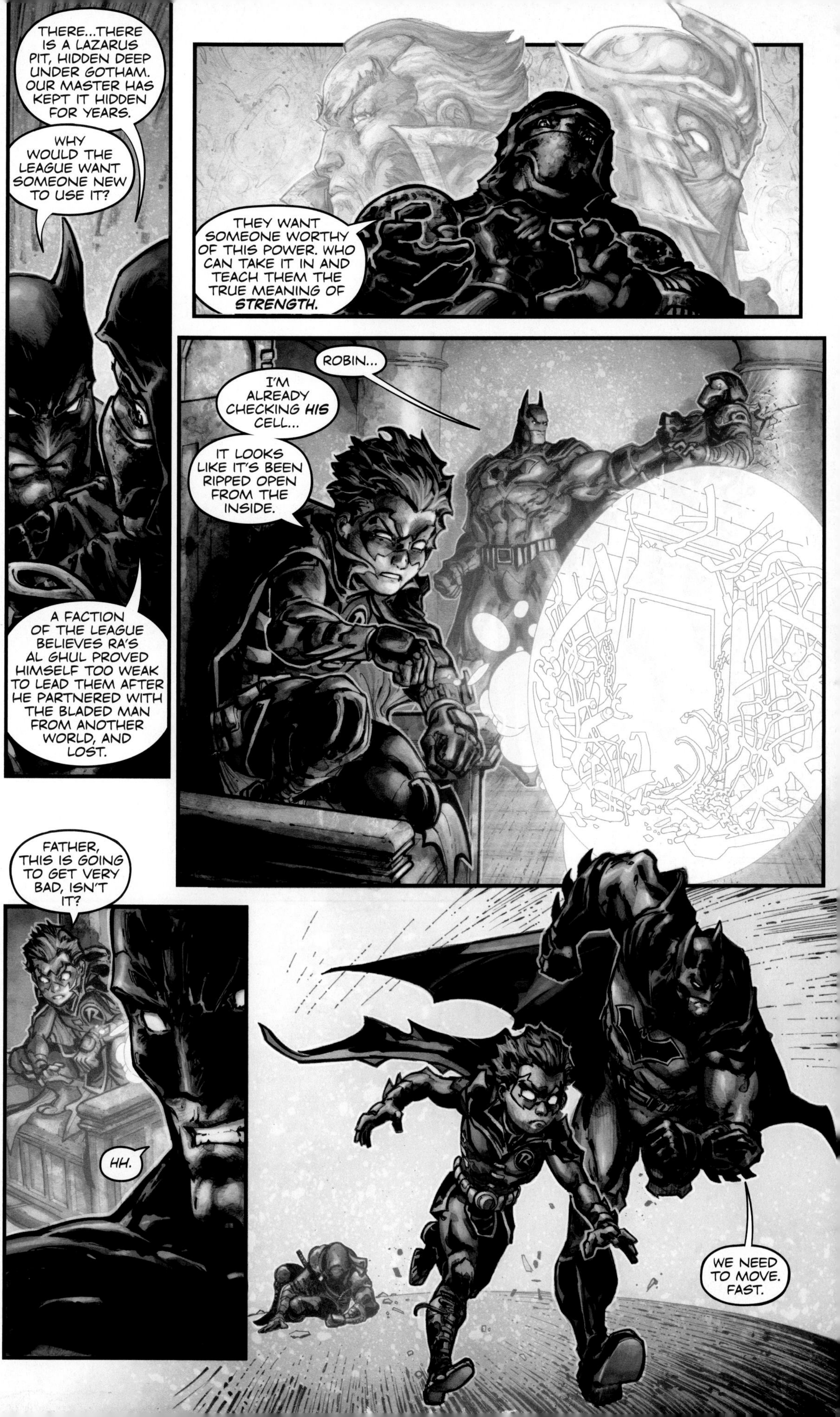
THERE...THERE IS A LAZARUS PIT, HIDDEN DEEP UNDER GOTHAM. OUR MASTER HAS KEPT IT HIDDEN FOR YEARS.
WHY WOULD THE LEAGUE WANT SOMEONE NEW TO USE IT?
THEY WANT SOMEONE WORTHY OF THIS POWER. WHO CAN TAKE IT IN AND TEACH THEM THE TRUE MEANING OF STRENGTH.
A FACTION OF THE LEAGUE BELIEVES RA'S AL GHUL PROVED HIMSELF TOO WEAK TO LEAD THEM AFTER HE PARTNERED WITH THE BLADED MAN FROM ANOTHER WORLD, AND LOST.
ROBIN...
I'M ALREADY CHECKING HIS CELL...
IT LOOKS LIKE IT'S BEEN RIPPED OPEN FROM THE INSIDE.
FATHER, THIS IS GOING TO GET VERY BAD, ISN'T IT?
HH.
WE NEED TO MOVE. FAST.

CASEY, ARE YOU SURE YOU KNOW WHAT YOU'RE DOING?

I'VE BEEN STITCHING UP MY DAD AFTER BAR FIGHTS SINCE I WAS SIX YEARS OLD, APRIL. I KNOW MY WAY AROUND SOME STITCHES.

SO THAT'S WHERE YOUR DAD GOT THOSE FRANKENSTEIN SCARS.

YEAH, WELL, SCARS BUILD CHARACTER. WE'LL GET YOU GOOD AND GRIZZLED UP, DONNIE. HOW DOES THAT SOUND?

FINE.

I'M GUESSING IT DIDN'T GO WELL?

FROM WHAT WE UNDERSTOOD, TONIGHT WAS SUPPOSED TO BE A **MEDIATION** BETWEEN KARAI'S WING OF THE FOOT CLAN AND THE ELITE GUARD.

LOOKS LIKE THAT BROKE DOWN BEFORE WE EVEN GOT **CLOSE**.

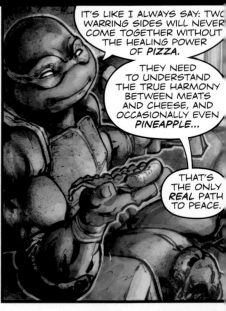

IT'S LIKE I ALWAYS SAY: TWO WARRING SIDES WILL NEVER COME TOGETHER WITHOUT THE HEALING POWER OF *PIZZA*.

THEY NEED TO UNDERSTAND THE TRUE HARMONY BETWEEN MEATS AND CHEESE, AND OCCASIONALLY EVEN *PINEAPPLE*...

THAT'S THE ONLY *REAL* PATH TO PEACE.

I DON'T REMEMBER THE STREETS *EVER* FEELING THIS DANGEROUS BEFORE.

WELL, ALL STITCHED UP AND READY TO TACKLE A FEW MORE ELITE GUARDS, RIGHT, DONNIE?

YOU'RE LOOKING AT THE WRONG TURTLE. THEY TOOK THE GUARDS DOWN.

I'M JUST THE ONE WHO GOT HIS *SHELL* HANDED TO HIM.

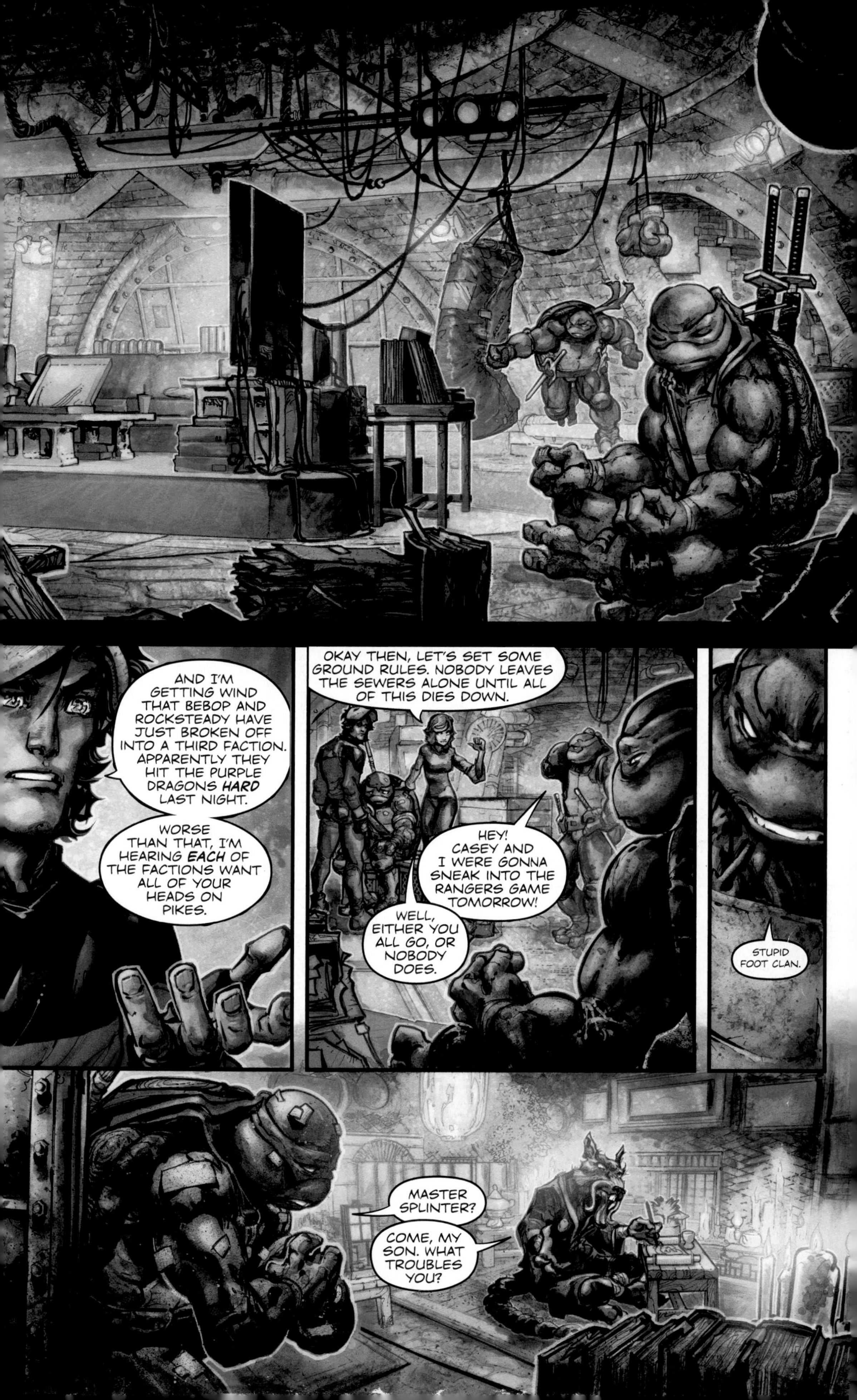
AND I'M GETTING WIND THAT BEBOP AND ROCKSTEADY HAVE JUST BROKEN OFF INTO A THIRD FACTION. APPARENTLY THEY HIT THE PURPLE DRAGONS HARD LAST NIGHT.
WORSE THAN THAT, I'M HEARING EACH OF THE FACTIONS WANT ALL OF YOUR HEADS ON PIKES.
OKAY THEN, LET'S SET SOME GROUND RULES. NOBODY LEAVES THE SEWERS ALONE UNTIL ALL OF THIS DIES DOWN.
HEY! CASEY AND I WERE GONNA SNEAK INTO THE RANGERS GAME TOMORROW!
WELL, EITHER YOU ALL GO, OR NOBODY DOES.
STUPID FOOT CLAN.
MASTER SPLINTER?
COME, MY SON. WHAT TROUBLES YOU?

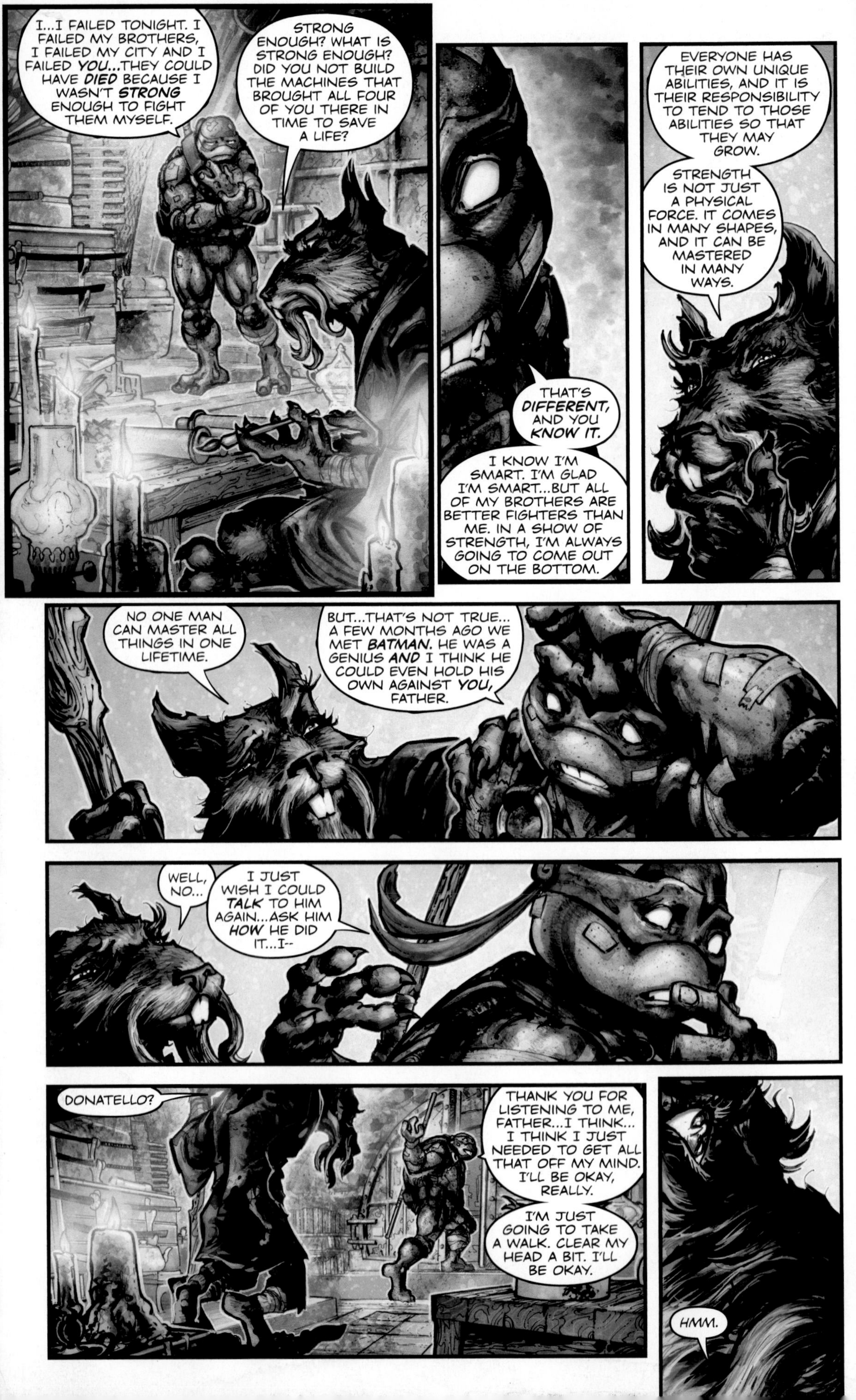

I...I FAILED TONIGHT. I FAILED MY BROTHERS, I FAILED MY CITY AND I FAILED *YOU*...THEY COULD HAVE *DIED* BECAUSE I WASN'T *STRONG* ENOUGH TO FIGHT THEM MYSELF.
STRONG ENOUGH? WHAT IS STRONG ENOUGH? DID YOU NOT BUILD THE MACHINES THAT BROUGHT ALL FOUR OF YOU THERE IN TIME TO SAVE A LIFE?
THAT'S *DIFFERENT,* AND YOU *KNOW IT.*
I KNOW I'M SMART. I'M GLAD I'M SMART...BUT ALL OF MY BROTHERS ARE BETTER FIGHTERS THAN ME. IN A SHOW OF STRENGTH, I'M ALWAYS GOING TO COME OUT ON THE BOTTOM.
EVERYONE HAS THEIR OWN UNIQUE ABILITIES, AND IT IS THEIR RESPONSIBILITY TO TEND TO THOSE ABILITIES SO THAT THEY MAY GROW.
STRENGTH IS NOT JUST A PHYSICAL FORCE. IT COMES IN MANY SHAPES, AND IT CAN BE MASTERED IN MANY WAYS.
NO ONE MAN CAN MASTER ALL THINGS IN ONE LIFETIME.
BUT...THAT'S NOT TRUE... A FEW MONTHS AGO WE MET *BATMAN.* HE WAS A GENIUS *AND* I THINK HE COULD EVEN HOLD HIS OWN AGAINST *YOU,* FATHER.
WELL, NO...
I JUST WISH I COULD *TALK* TO HIM AGAIN...ASK HIM *HOW* HE DID IT...I--
DONATELLO?
THANK YOU FOR LISTENING TO ME, FATHER...I THINK... I THINK I JUST NEEDED TO GET ALL THAT OFF MY MIND. I'LL BE OKAY, REALLY.
I'M JUST GOING TO TAKE A WALK. CLEAR MY HEAD A BIT. I'LL BE OKAY.
HMM.

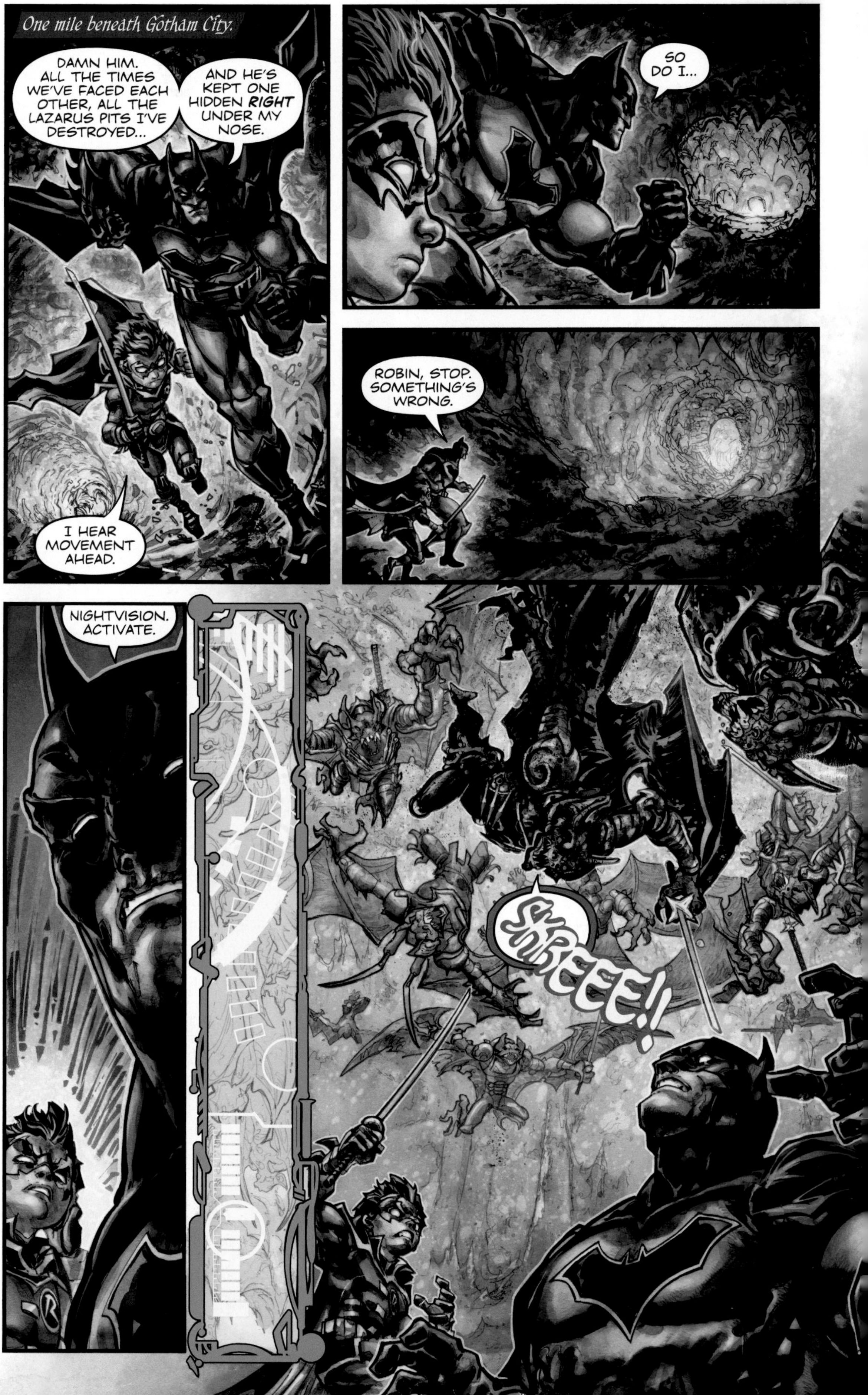
One mile beneath Gotham City.
DAMN HIM. ALL THE TIMES WE'VE FACED EACH OTHER, ALL THE LAZARUS PITS I'VE DESTROYED...
AND HE'S KEPT ONE HIDDEN **RIGHT** UNDER MY NOSE.
I HEAR MOVEMENT AHEAD.
SO DO I...
ROBIN, STOP. SOMETHING'S WRONG.
NIGHTVISION. ACTIVATE.
SKREEEE!!

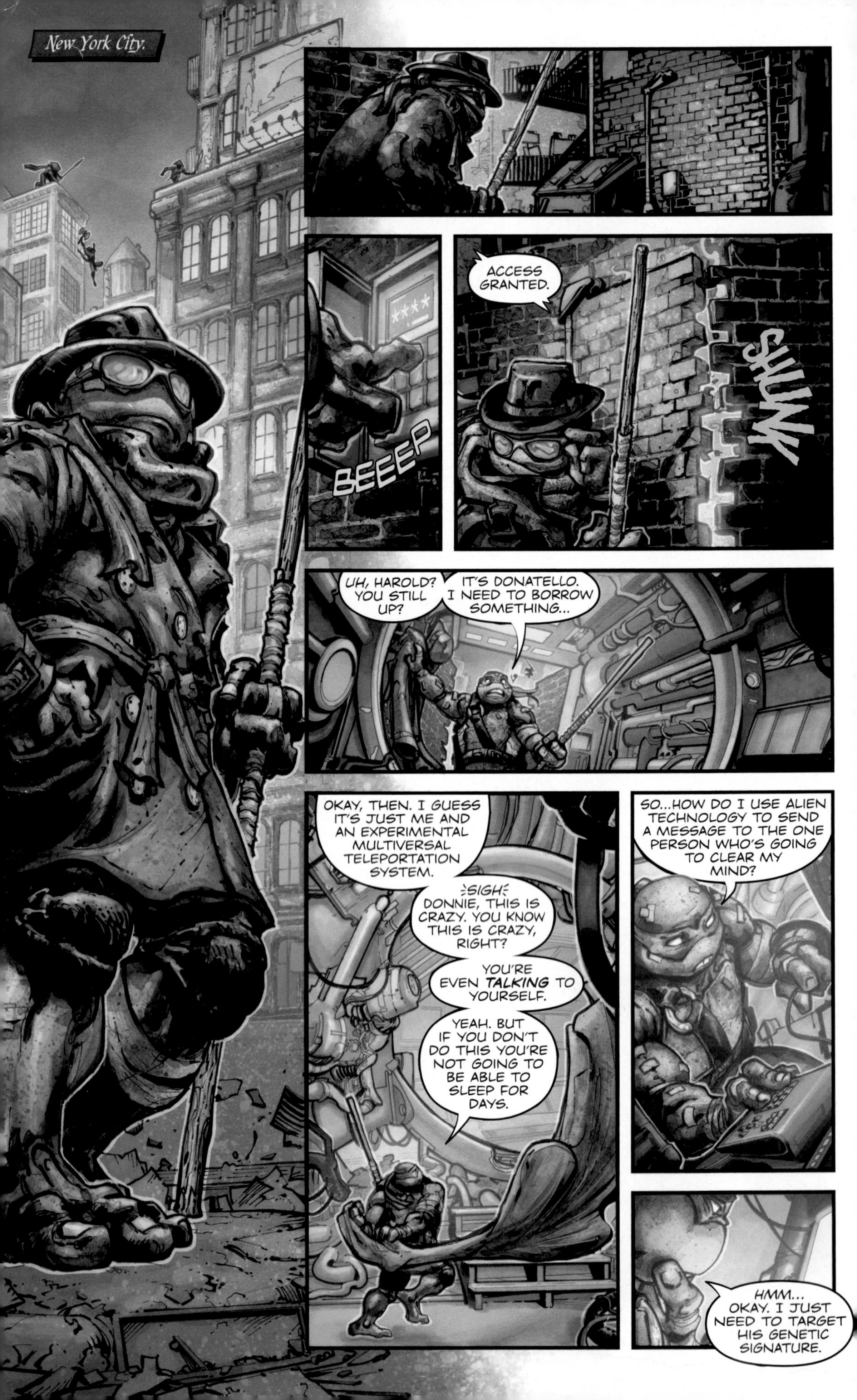
New York City.
ACCESS GRANTED.
BEEEP
SHUNK
UH, HAROLD? YOU STILL UP?
IT'S DONATELLO. I NEED TO BORROW SOMETHING...
OKAY, THEN. I GUESS IT'S JUST ME AND AN EXPERIMENTAL MULTIVERSAL TELEPORTATION SYSTEM.
SIGH
DONNIE, THIS IS CRAZY. YOU KNOW THIS IS CRAZY, RIGHT?
YOU'RE EVEN TALKING TO YOURSELF.
YEAH. BUT IF YOU DON'T DO THIS YOU'RE NOT GOING TO BE ABLE TO SLEEP FOR DAYS.
SO...HOW DO I USE ALIEN TECHNOLOGY TO SEND A MESSAGE TO THE ONE PERSON WHO'S GOING TO CLEAR MY MIND?
HMM... OKAY. I JUST NEED TO TARGET HIS GENETIC SIGNATURE.

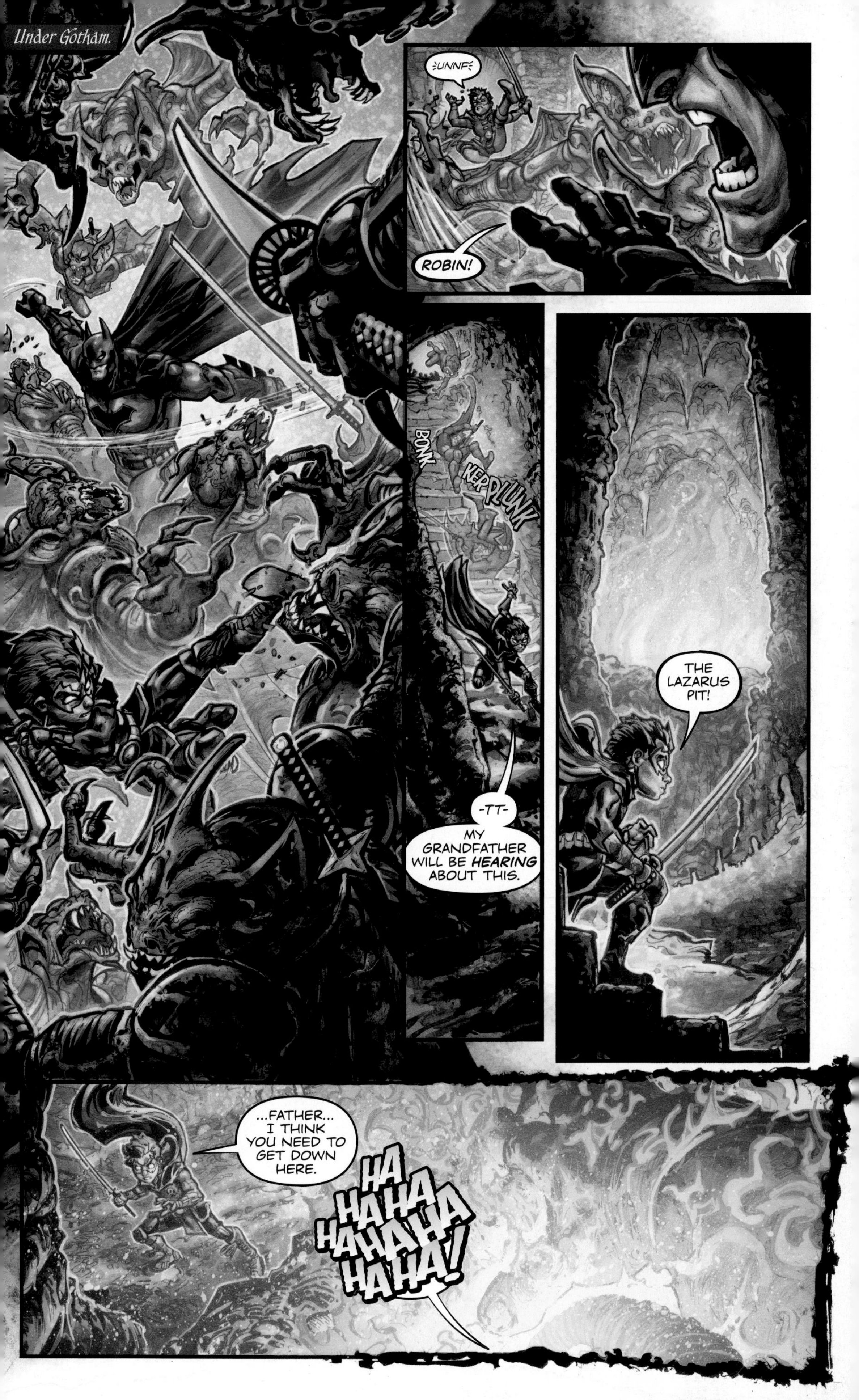
Under Gotham.
UNNF
ROBIN!
BONK
KERPLUNK
-TT-
MY GRANDFATHER WILL BE HEARING ABOUT THIS.
THE LAZARUS PIT!
...FATHER... I THINK YOU NEED TO GET DOWN HERE.
HA HA HA HA HA HA HA HA HA!

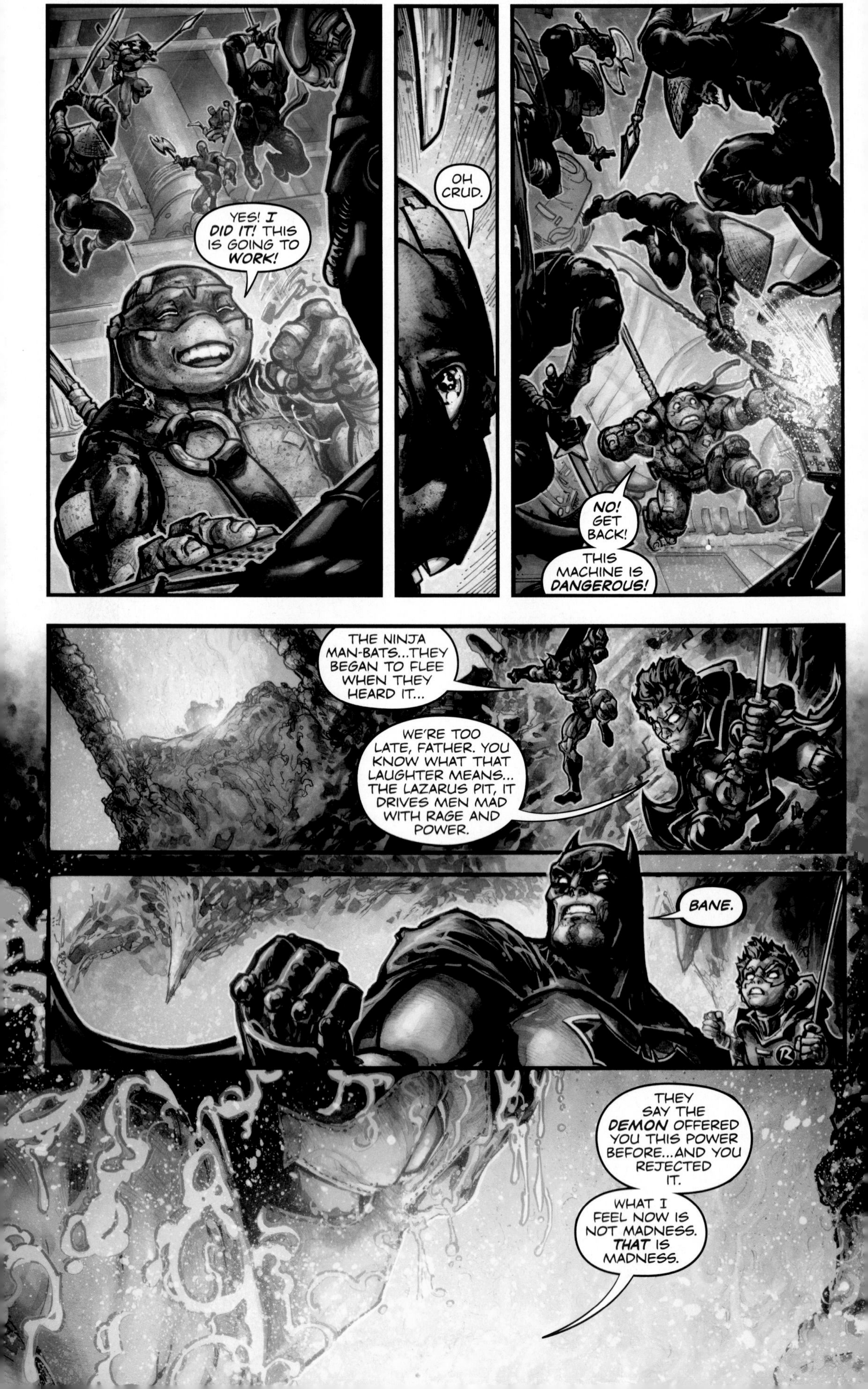
YES! I DID IT! THIS IS GOING TO WORK!
OH CRUD.
NO! GET BACK!
THIS MACHINE IS DANGEROUS!
THE NINJA MAN-BATS...THEY BEGAN TO FLEE WHEN THEY HEARD IT...
WE'RE TOO LATE, FATHER. YOU KNOW WHAT THAT LAUGHTER MEANS... THE LAZARUS PIT, IT DRIVES MEN MAD WITH RAGE AND POWER.
BANE.
THEY SAY THE DEMON OFFERED YOU THIS POWER BEFORE...AND YOU REJECTED IT.
WHAT I FEEL NOW IS NOT MADNESS. THAT IS MADNESS.

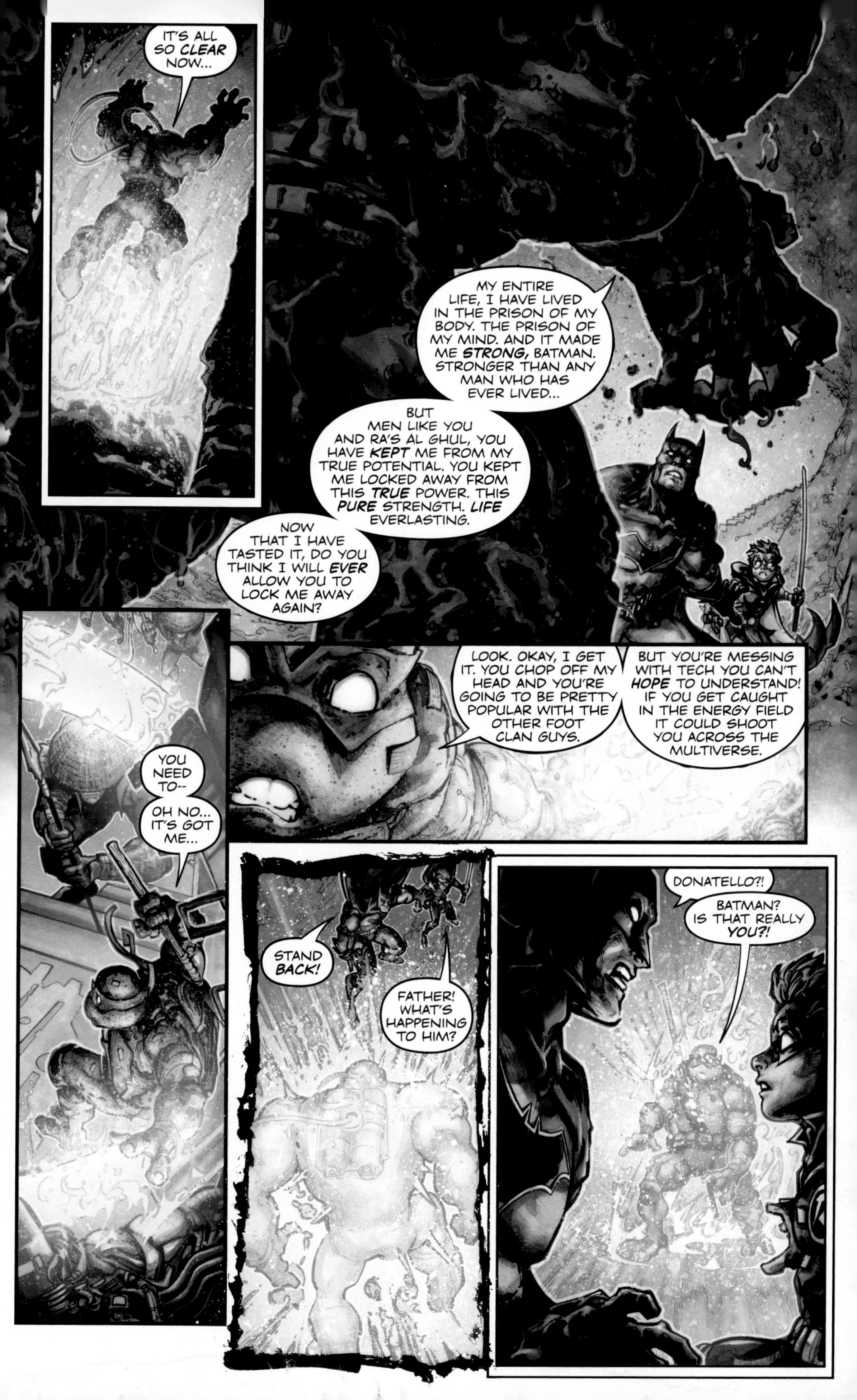
IT'S ALL SO CLEAR NOW...
MY ENTIRE LIFE, I HAVE LIVED IN THE PRISON OF MY BODY. THE PRISON OF MY MIND. AND IT MADE ME STRONG, BATMAN. STRONGER THAN ANY MAN WHO HAS EVER LIVED...
BUT MEN LIKE YOU AND RA'S AL GHUL, YOU HAVE KEPT ME FROM MY TRUE POTENTIAL. YOU KEPT ME LOCKED AWAY FROM THIS TRUE POWER. THIS PURE STRENGTH. LIFE EVERLASTING.
NOW THAT I HAVE TASTED IT, DO YOU THINK I WILL EVER ALLOW YOU TO LOCK ME AWAY AGAIN?
LOOK. OKAY, I GET IT. YOU CHOP OFF MY HEAD AND YOU'RE GOING TO BE PRETTY POPULAR WITH THE OTHER FOOT CLAN GUYS.
BUT YOU'RE MESSING WITH TECH YOU CAN'T HOPE TO UNDERSTAND! IF YOU GET CAUGHT IN THE ENERGY FIELD IT COULD SHOOT YOU ACROSS THE MULTIVERSE.
YOU NEED TO--
OH NO... IT'S GOT ME...
STAND BACK!
FATHER! WHAT'S HAPPENING TO HIM?
DONATELLO?!
BATMAN? IS THAT REALLY YOU?!

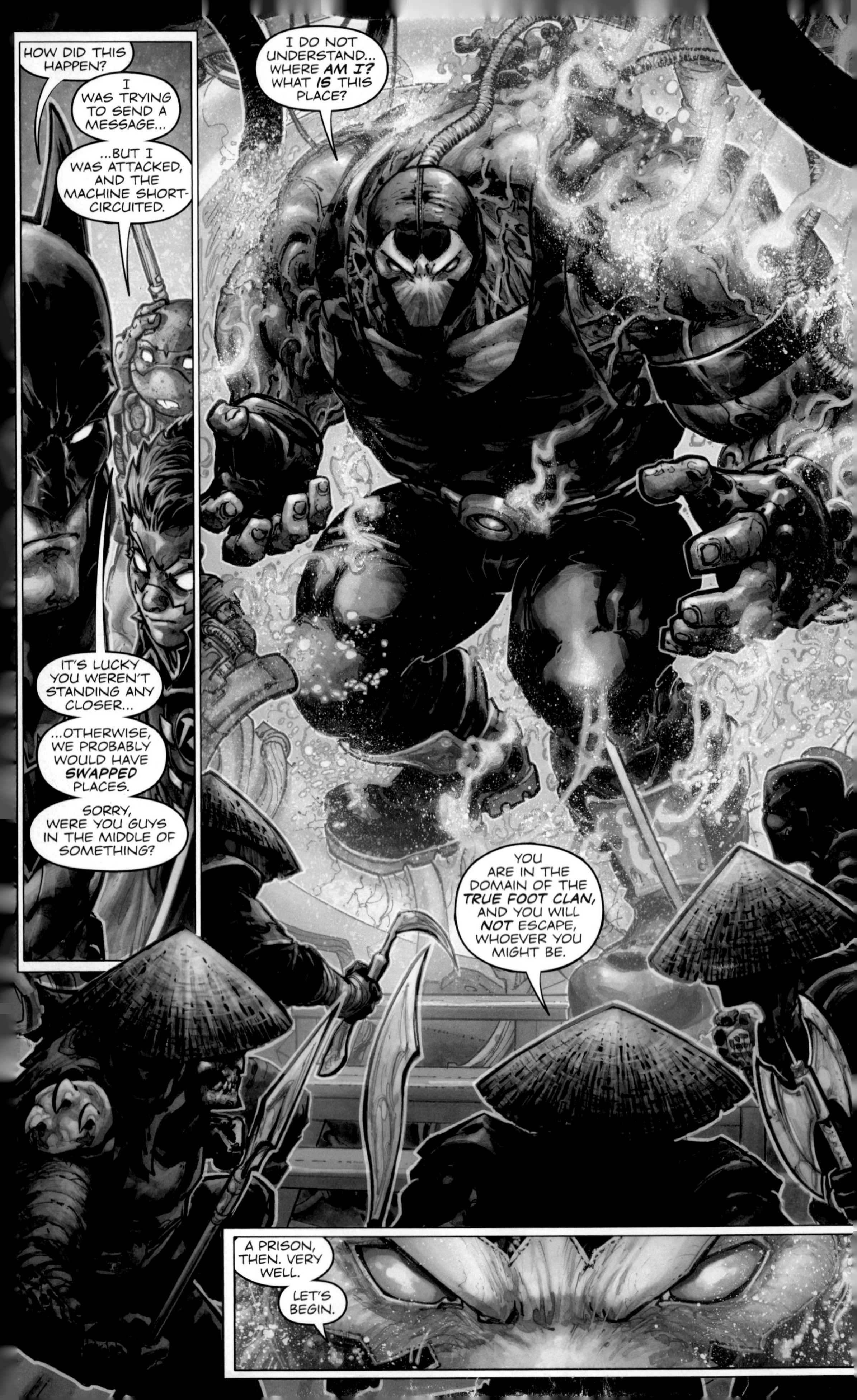
HOW DID THIS HAPPEN?
I WAS TRYING TO SEND A MESSAGE...
...BUT I WAS ATTACKED, AND THE MACHINE SHORT-CIRCUITED.
IT'S LUCKY YOU WEREN'T STANDING ANY CLOSER...
...OTHERWISE, WE PROBABLY WOULD HAVE SWAPPED PLACES.
SORRY, WERE YOU GUYS IN THE MIDDLE OF SOMETHING?
I DO NOT UNDERSTAND... WHERE AM I? WHAT IS THIS PLACE?
YOU ARE IN THE DOMAIN OF THE TRUE FOOT CLAN, AND YOU WILL NOT ESCAPE, WHOEVER YOU MIGHT BE.
A PRISON, THEN. VERY WELL.
LET'S BEGIN.

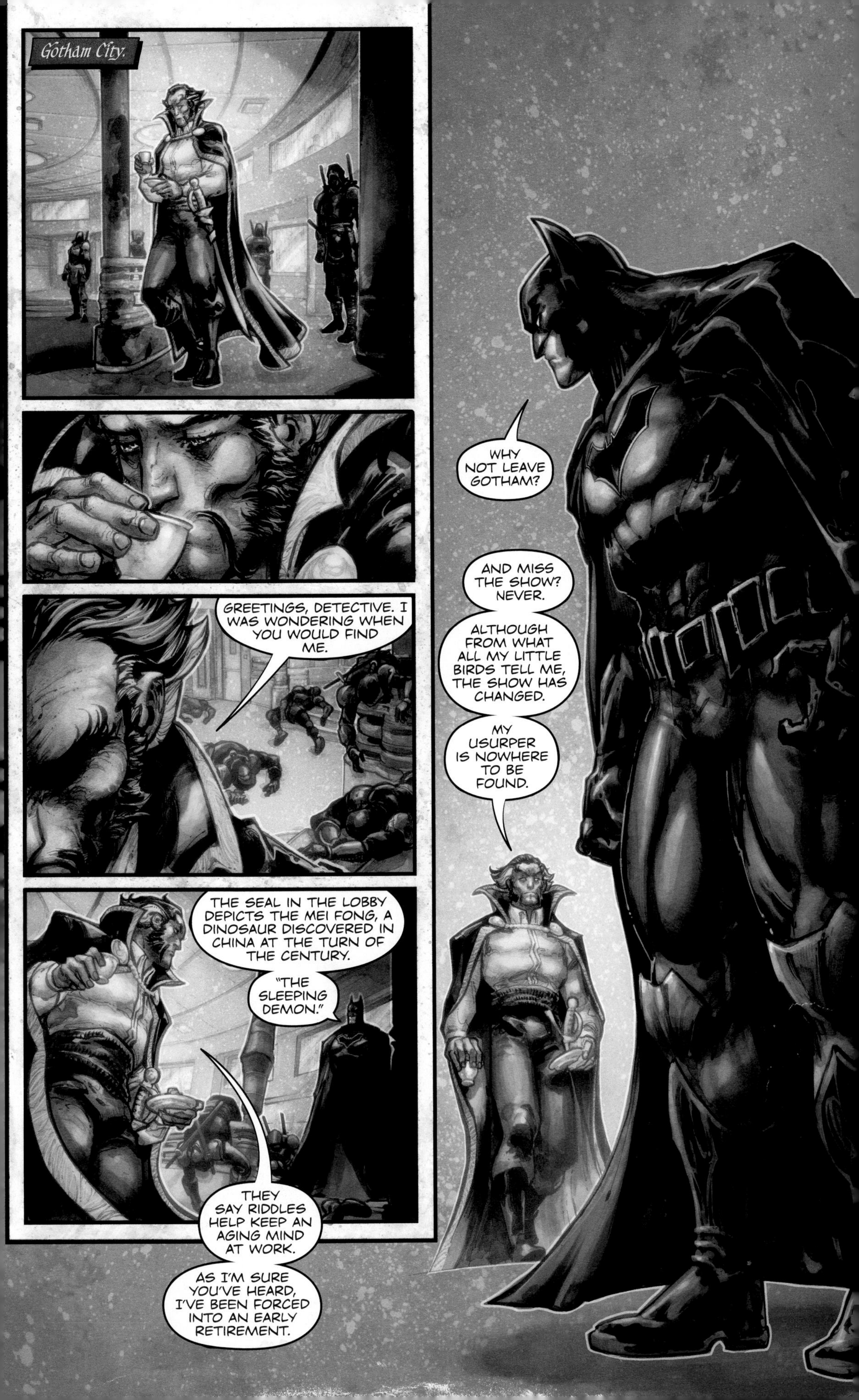
Gotham City.
GREETINGS, DETECTIVE. I WAS WONDERING WHEN YOU WOULD FIND ME.
THE SEAL IN THE LOBBY DEPICTS THE MEI FONG, A DINOSAUR DISCOVERED IN CHINA AT THE TURN OF THE CENTURY.
"THE SLEEPING DEMON."
THEY SAY RIDDLES HELP KEEP AN AGING MIND AT WORK.
AS I'M SURE YOU'VE HEARD, I'VE BEEN FORCED INTO AN EARLY RETIREMENT.
WHY NOT LEAVE GOTHAM?
AND MISS THE SHOW? NEVER.
ALTHOUGH FROM WHAT ALL MY LITTLE BIRDS TELL ME, THE SHOW HAS CHANGED.
MY USURPER IS NOWHERE TO BE FOUND.

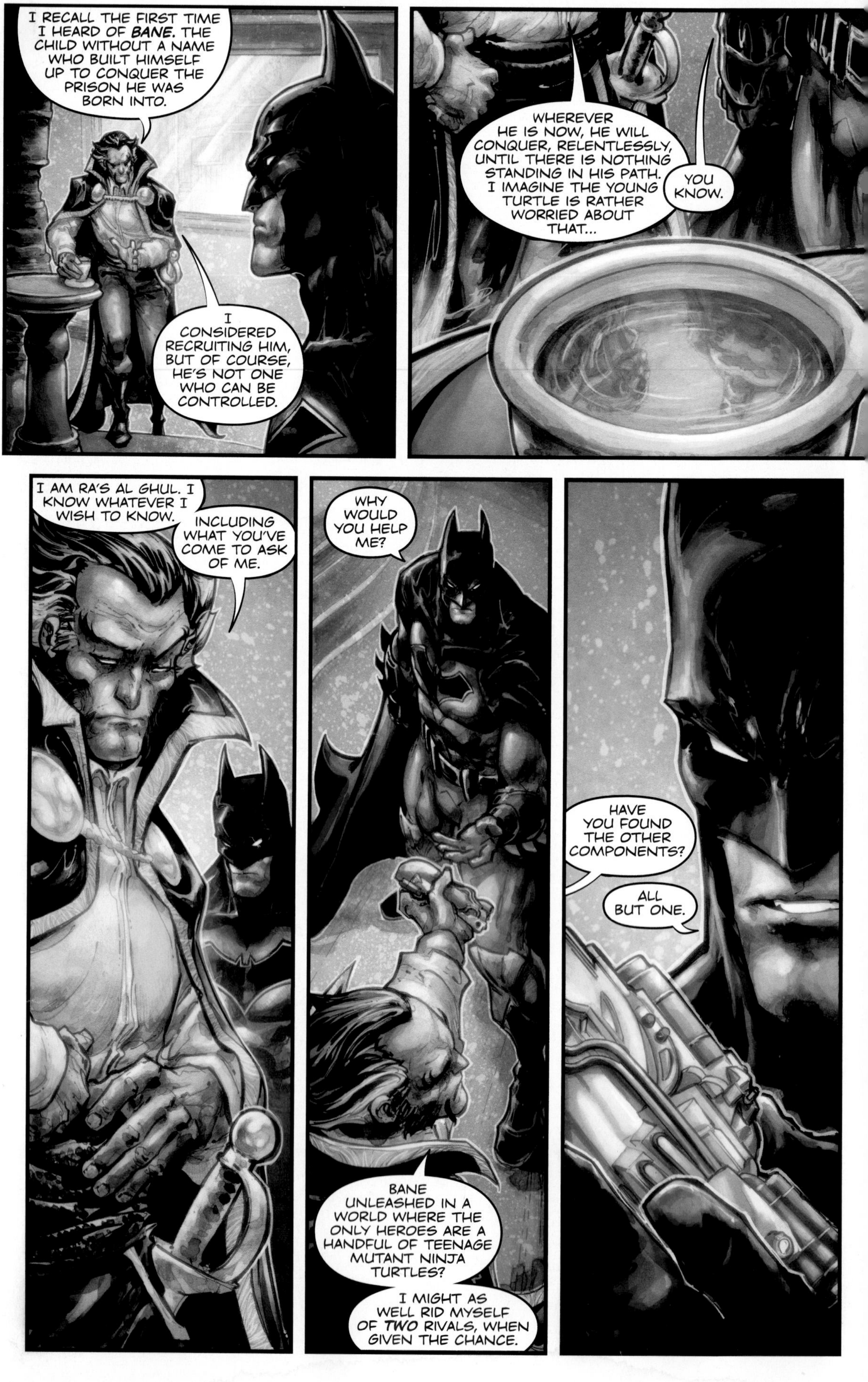
I RECALL THE FIRST TIME I HEARD OF ***BANE.*** THE CHILD WITHOUT A NAME WHO BUILT HIMSELF UP TO CONQUER THE PRISON HE WAS BORN INTO.
I CONSIDERED RECRUITING HIM, BUT OF COURSE, HE'S NOT ONE WHO CAN BE CONTROLLED.
WHEREVER HE IS NOW, HE WILL CONQUER, RELENTLESSLY, UNTIL THERE IS NOTHING STANDING IN HIS PATH. I IMAGINE THE YOUNG TURTLE IS RATHER WORRIED ABOUT THAT...
YOU KNOW.
I AM RA'S AL GHUL. I KNOW WHATEVER I WISH TO KNOW.
INCLUDING WHAT YOU'VE COME TO ASK OF ME.
WHY WOULD YOU HELP ME?
BANE UNLEASHED IN A WORLD WHERE THE ONLY HEROES ARE A HANDFUL OF TEENAGE MUTANT NINJA TURTLES?
I MIGHT AS WELL RID MYSELF OF ***TWO*** RIVALS, WHEN GIVEN THE CHANCE.
HAVE YOU FOUND THE OTHER COMPONENTS?
ALL BUT ONE.

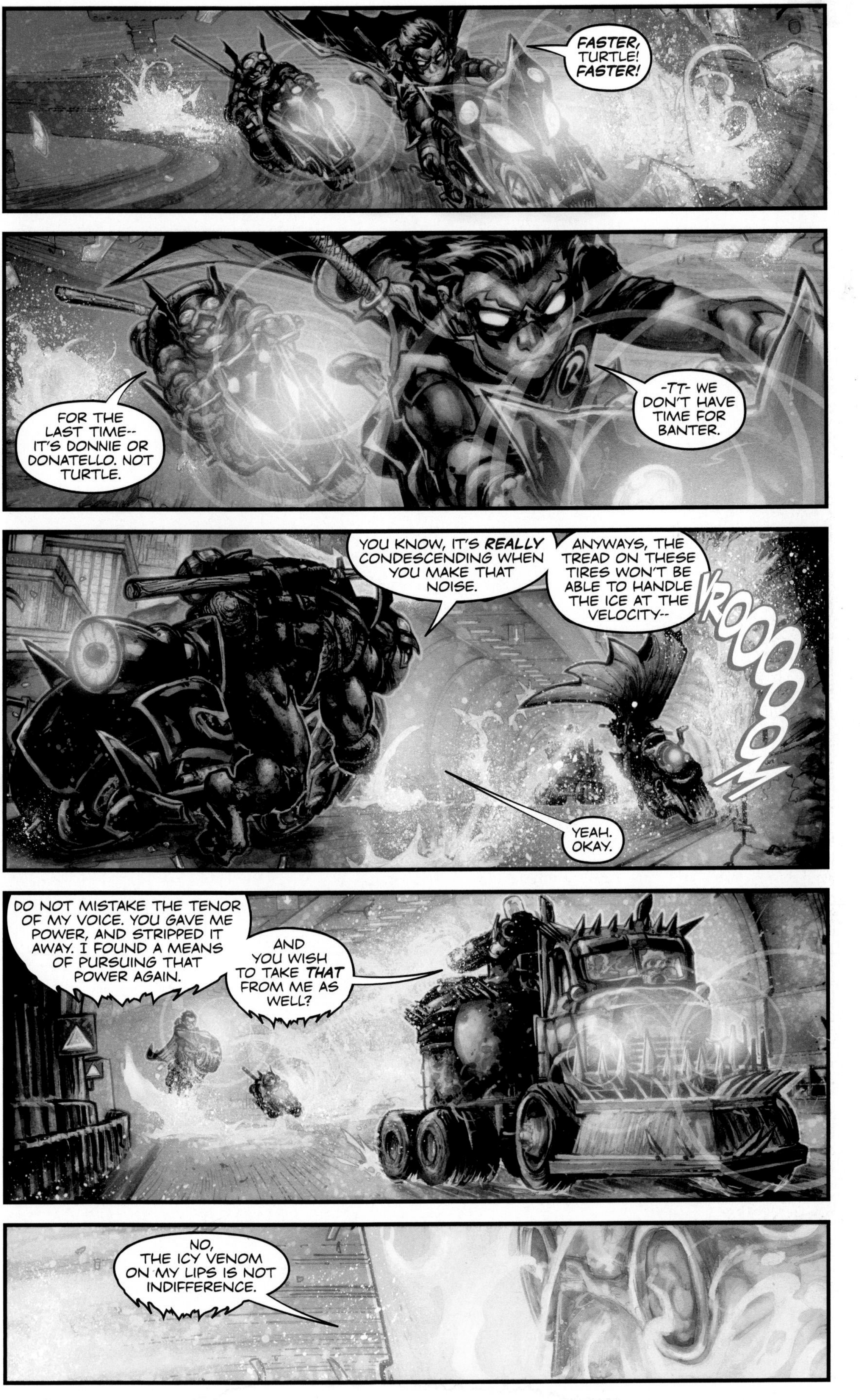
FASTER, TURTLE! FASTER!
FOR THE LAST TIME-- IT'S DONNIE OR DONATELLO. NOT TURTLE.
-TT- WE DON'T HAVE TIME FOR BANTER.
YOU KNOW, IT'S REALLY CONDESCENDING WHEN YOU MAKE THAT NOISE.
ANYWAYS, THE TREAD ON THESE TIRES WON'T BE ABLE TO HANDLE THE ICE AT THE VELOCITY--
VROOOOOOM
YEAH. OKAY.
DO NOT MISTAKE THE TENOR OF MY VOICE. YOU GAVE ME POWER, AND STRIPPED IT AWAY. I FOUND A MEANS OF PURSUING THAT POWER AGAIN.
AND YOU WISH TO TAKE THAT FROM ME AS WELL?
NO, THE ICY VENOM ON MY LIPS IS NOT INDIFFERENCE.

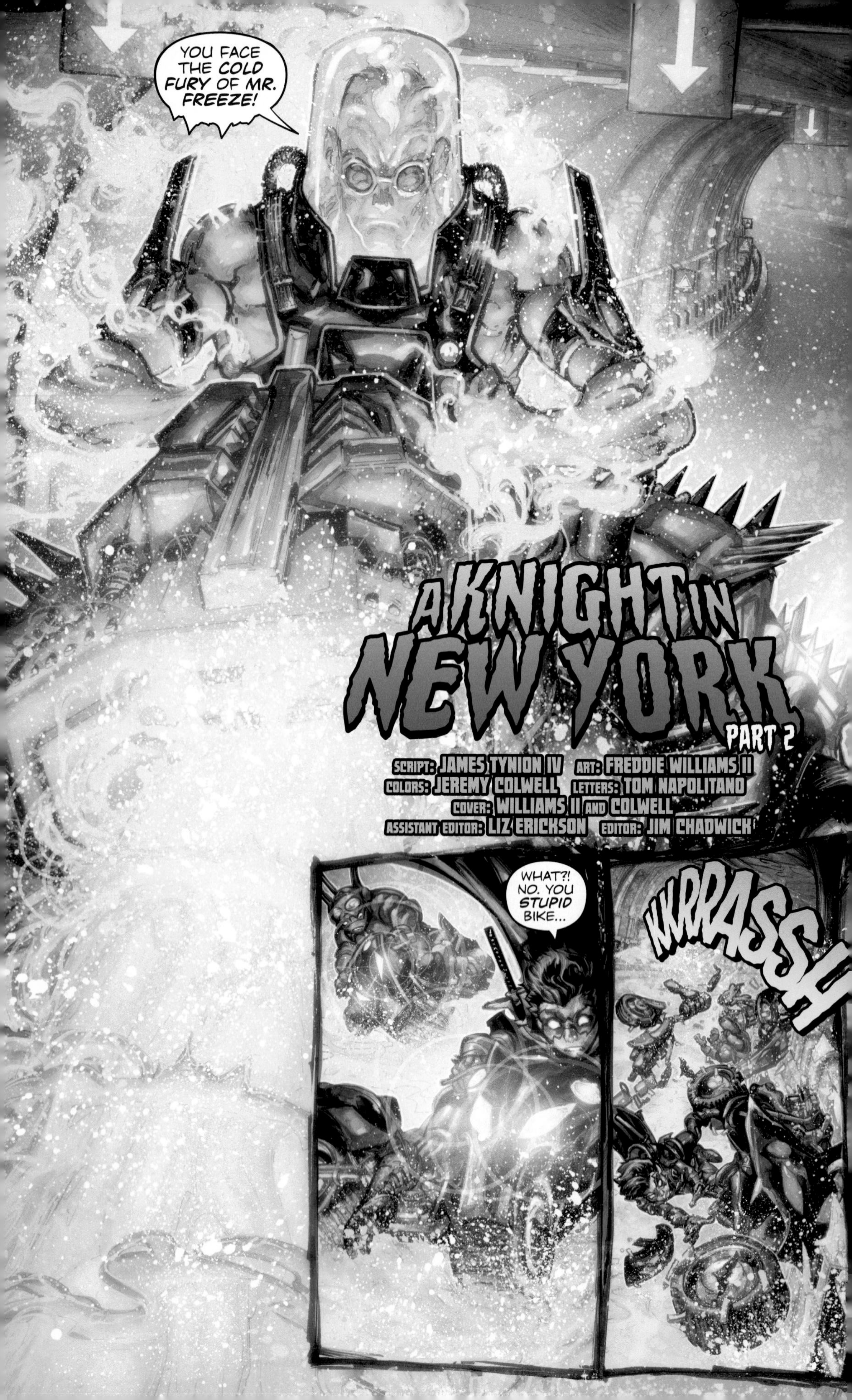
YOU FACE THE COLD FURY OF MR. FREEZE!
A KNIGHT IN NEW YORK
PART 2
SCRIPT: JAMES TYNION IV ART: FREDDIE WILLIAMS II
COLORS: JEREMY COLWELL LETTERS: TOM NAPOLITANO
COVER: WILLIAMS II AND COLWELL
ASSISTANT EDITOR: LIZ ERICKSON EDITOR: JIM CHADWICK
WHAT?! NO. YOU STUPID BIKE...
KKRRASSH

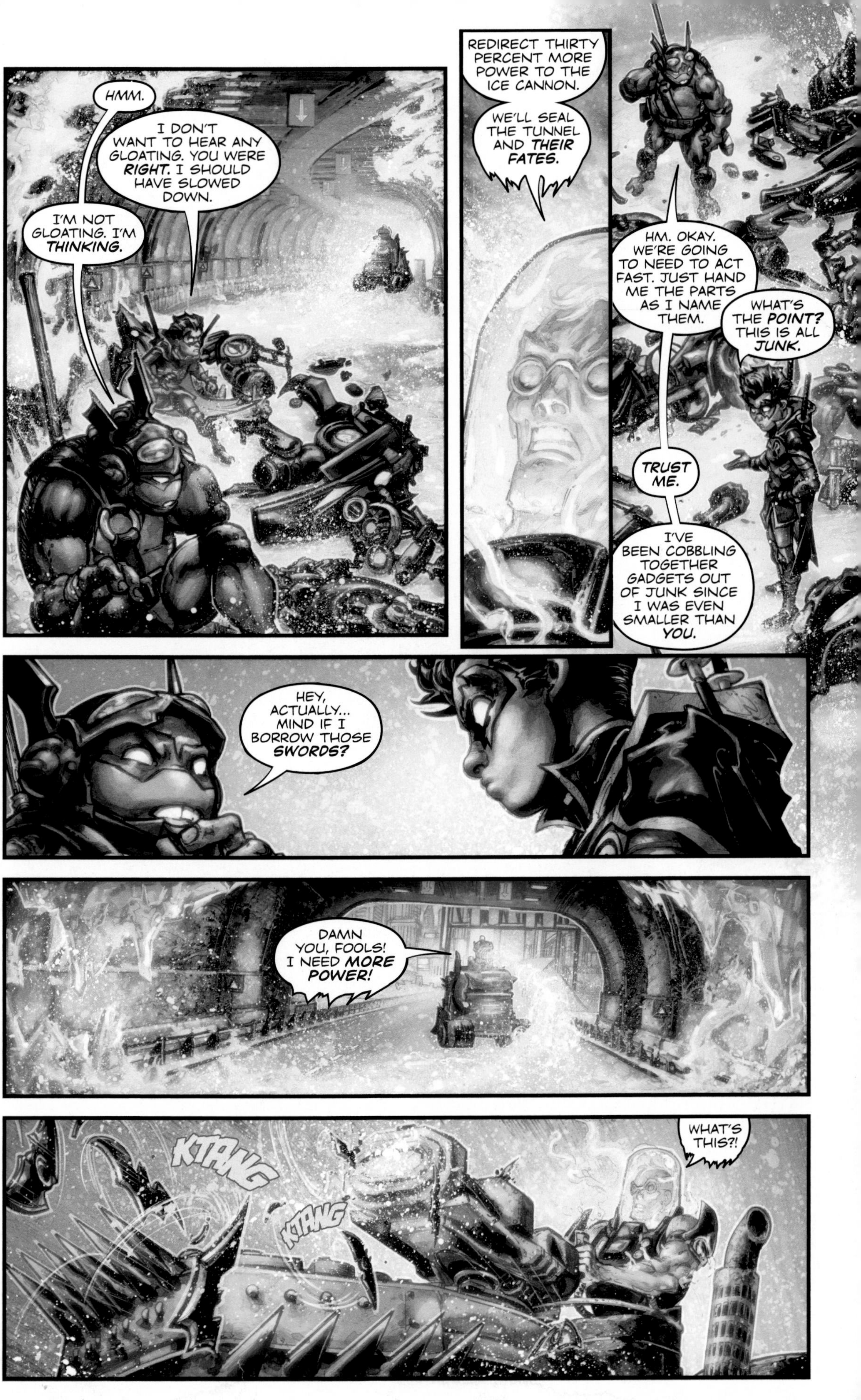
HMM.
I DON'T WANT TO HEAR ANY GLOATING. YOU WERE RIGHT. I SHOULD HAVE SLOWED DOWN.
I'M NOT GLOATING. I'M THINKING.
REDIRECT THIRTY PERCENT MORE POWER TO THE ICE CANNON.
WE'LL SEAL THE TUNNEL AND THEIR FATES.
HM. OKAY. WE'RE GOING TO NEED TO ACT FAST. JUST HAND ME THE PARTS AS I NAME THEM.
WHAT'S THE POINT? THIS IS ALL JUNK.
TRUST ME.
I'VE BEEN COBBLING TOGETHER GADGETS OUT OF JUNK SINCE I WAS EVEN SMALLER THAN YOU.
HEY, ACTUALLY... MIND IF I BORROW THOSE SWORDS?
DAMN YOU, FOOLS! I NEED MORE POWER!
KTANG
KTANG
WHAT'S THIS?!

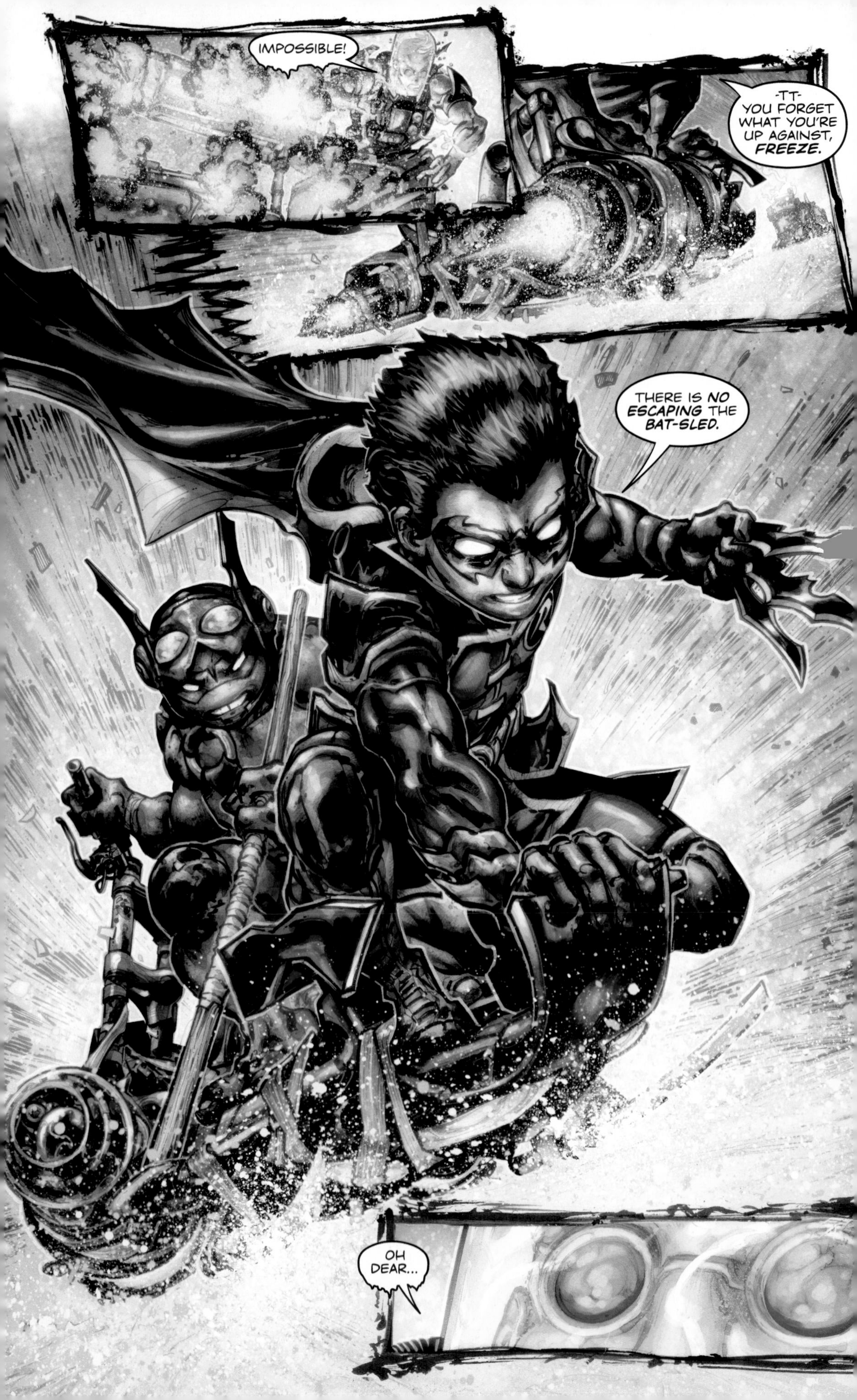
IMPOSSIBLE!
-TT- YOU FORGET WHAT YOU'RE UP AGAINST, FREEZE.
THERE IS NO ESCAPING THE BAT-SLED.
OH DEAR...

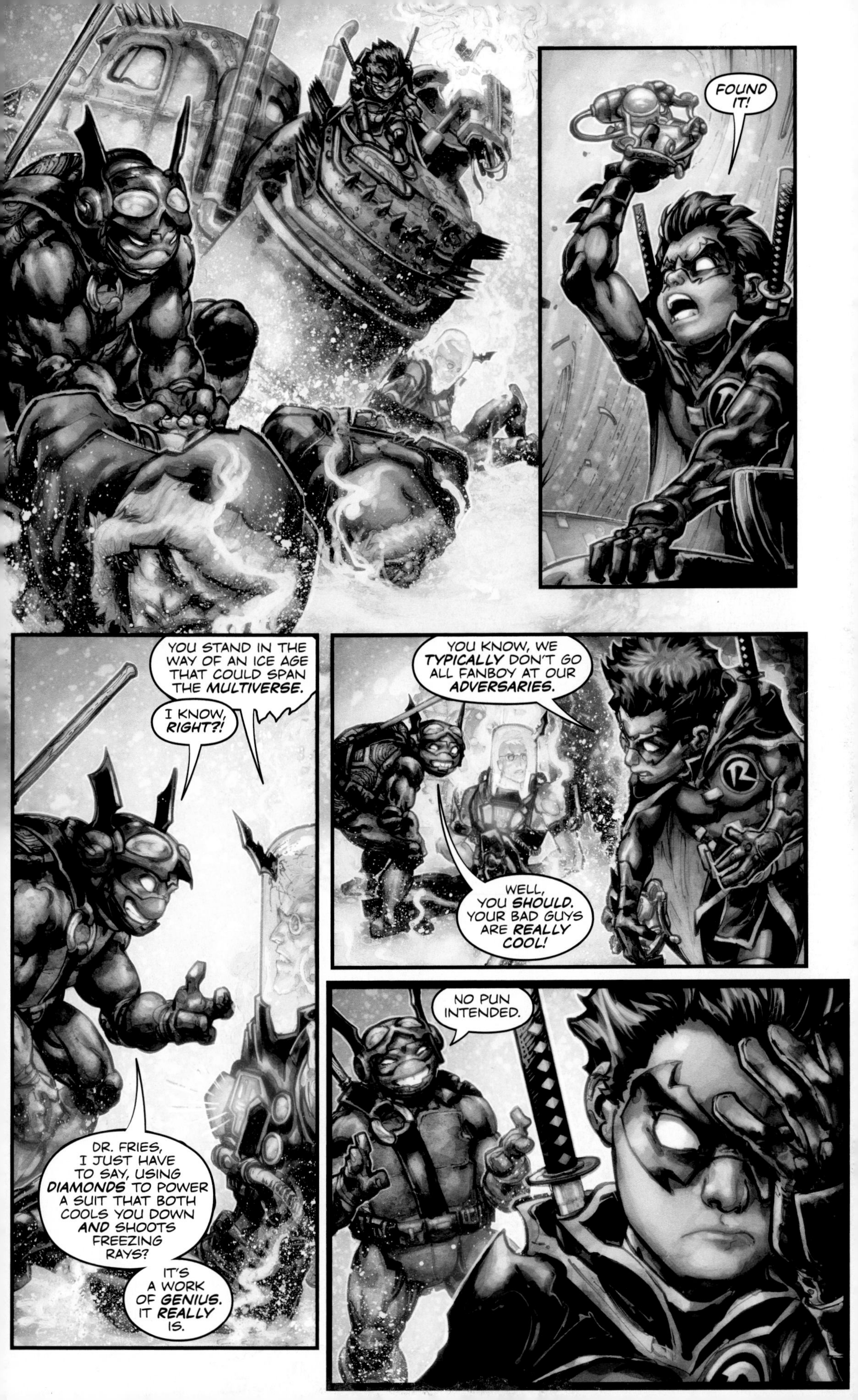
FOUND IT!
YOU STAND IN THE WAY OF AN ICE AGE THAT COULD SPAN THE MULTIVERSE.
I KNOW, RIGHT?!
DR. FRIES, I JUST HAVE TO SAY, USING DIAMONDS TO POWER A SUIT THAT BOTH COOLS YOU DOWN AND SHOOTS FREEZING RAYS?
IT'S A WORK OF GENIUS. IT REALLY IS.
YOU KNOW, WE TYPICALLY DON'T GO ALL FANBOY AT OUR ADVERSARIES.
WELL, YOU SHOULD. YOUR BAD GUYS ARE REALLY COOL!
NO PUN INTENDED.

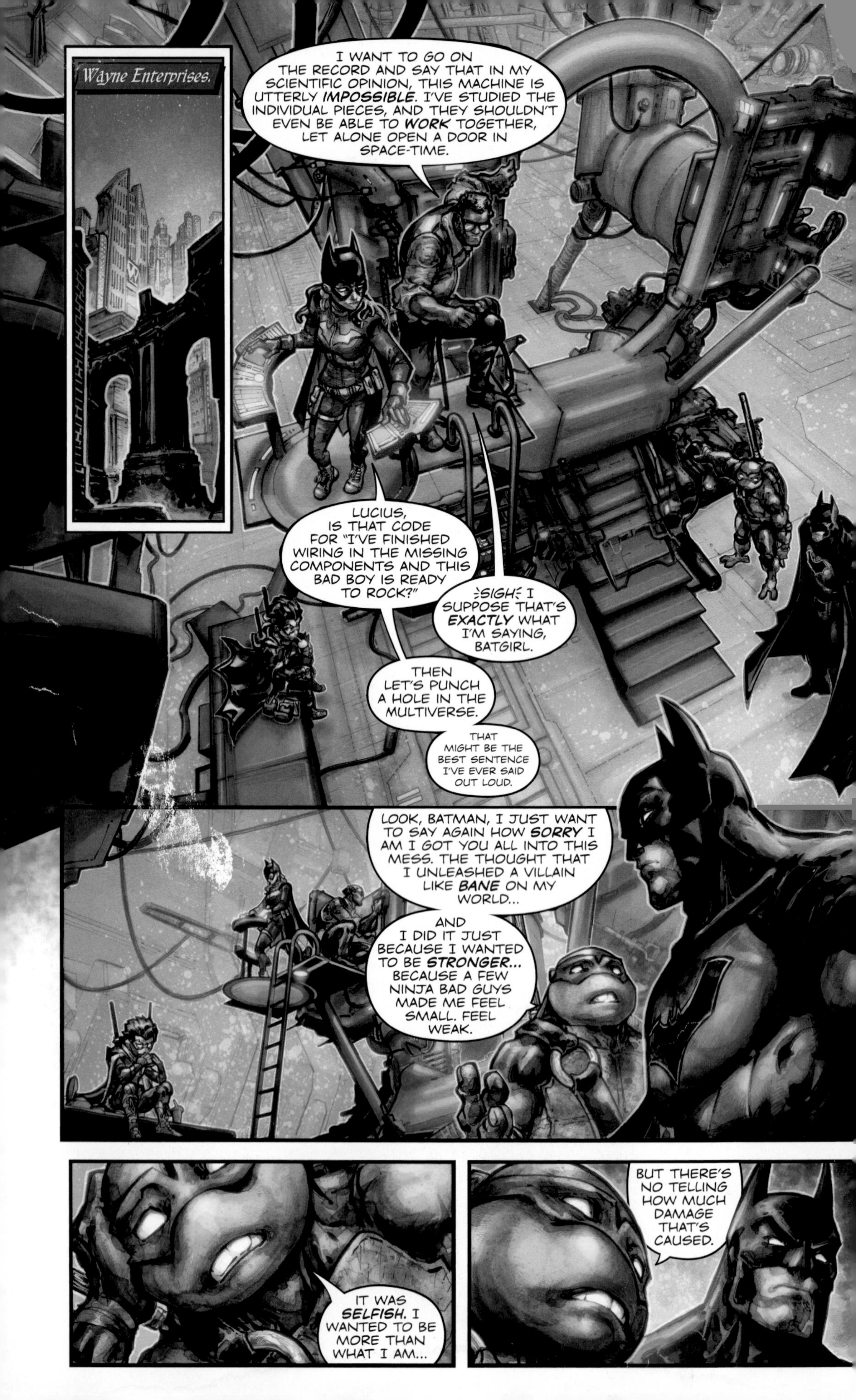
Wayne Enterprises.
I WANT TO GO ON THE RECORD AND SAY THAT IN MY SCIENTIFIC OPINION, THIS MACHINE IS UTTERLY *IMPOSSIBLE*. I'VE STUDIED THE INDIVIDUAL PIECES, AND THEY SHOULDN'T EVEN BE ABLE TO *WORK* TOGETHER, LET ALONE OPEN A DOOR IN SPACE-TIME.
LUCIUS, IS THAT CODE FOR "I'VE FINISHED WIRING IN THE MISSING COMPONENTS AND THIS BAD BOY IS READY TO ROCK?"
SIGH I SUPPOSE THAT'S *EXACTLY* WHAT I'M SAYING, BATGIRL.
THEN LET'S PUNCH A HOLE IN THE MULTIVERSE.
THAT MIGHT BE THE BEST SENTENCE I'VE EVER SAID OUT LOUD.
LOOK, BATMAN, I JUST WANT TO SAY AGAIN HOW *SORRY* I AM I GOT YOU ALL INTO THIS MESS. THE THOUGHT THAT I UNLEASHED A VILLAIN LIKE *BANE* ON MY WORLD...
AND I DID IT JUST BECAUSE I WANTED TO BE *STRONGER...* BECAUSE A FEW NINJA BAD GUYS MADE ME FEEL SMALL. FEEL WEAK.
IT WAS *SELFISH*. I WANTED TO BE MORE THAN WHAT I AM...
BUT THERE'S NO TELLING HOW MUCH DAMAGE THAT'S CAUSED.

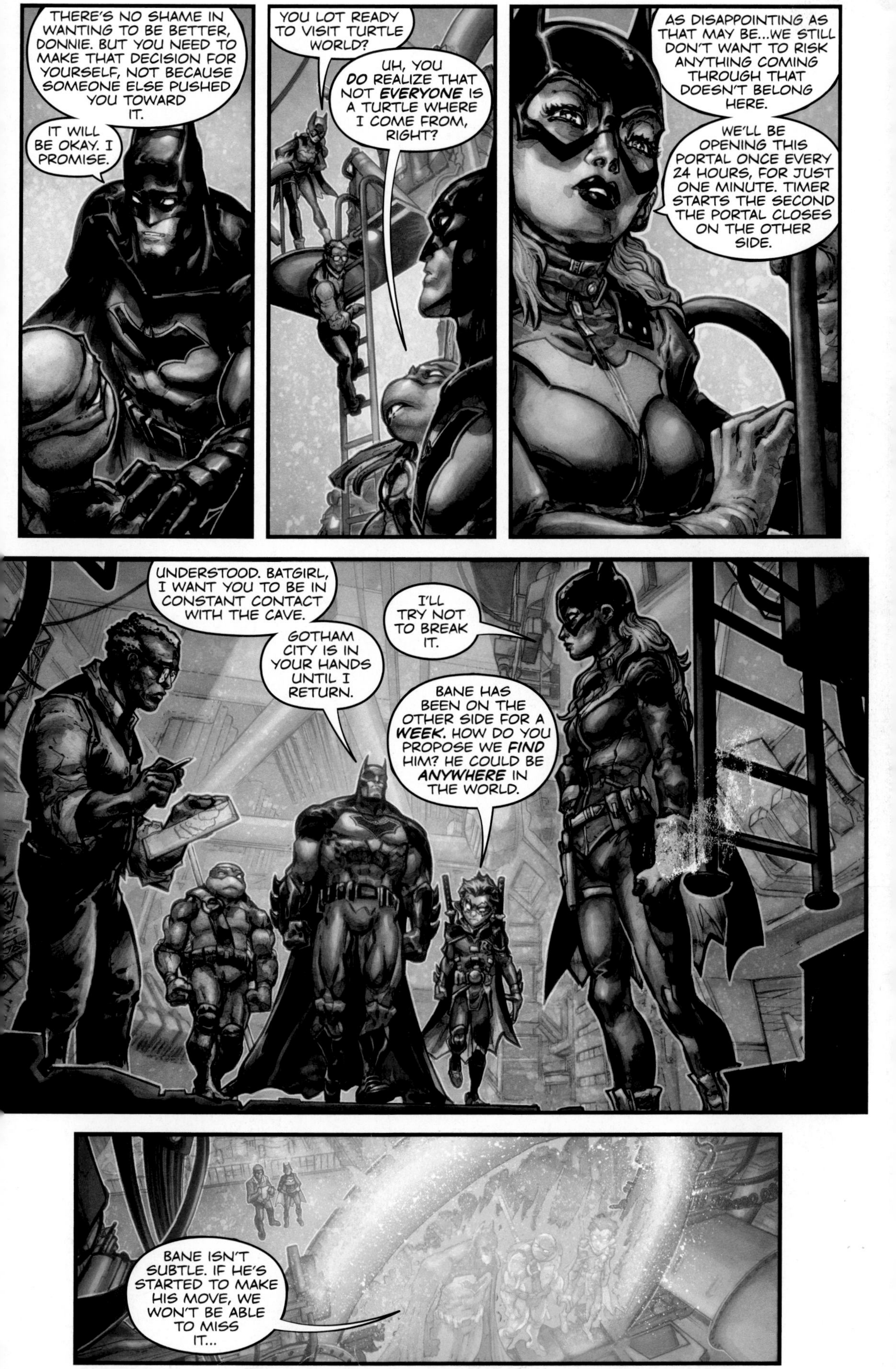

THERE'S NO SHAME IN WANTING TO BE BETTER, DONNIE. BUT YOU NEED TO MAKE THAT DECISION FOR YOURSELF, NOT BECAUSE SOMEONE ELSE PUSHED YOU TOWARD IT.
IT WILL BE OKAY. I PROMISE.
YOU LOT READY TO VISIT TURTLE WORLD?
UH, YOU **DO** REALIZE THAT NOT **EVERYONE** IS A TURTLE WHERE I COME FROM, RIGHT?
AS DISAPPOINTING AS THAT MAY BE...WE STILL DON'T WANT TO RISK ANYTHING COMING THROUGH THAT DOESN'T BELONG HERE.
WE'LL BE OPENING THIS PORTAL ONCE EVERY 24 HOURS, FOR JUST ONE MINUTE. TIMER STARTS THE SECOND THE PORTAL CLOSES ON THE OTHER SIDE.
UNDERSTOOD. BATGIRL, I WANT YOU TO BE IN CONSTANT CONTACT WITH THE CAVE.
GOTHAM CITY IS IN YOUR HANDS UNTIL I RETURN.
I'LL TRY NOT TO BREAK IT.
BANE HAS BEEN ON THE OTHER SIDE FOR A **WEEK**. HOW DO YOU PROPOSE WE **FIND** HIM? HE COULD BE **ANYWHERE** IN THE WORLD.
BANE ISN'T SUBTLE. IF HE'S STARTED TO MAKE HIS MOVE, WE WON'T BE ABLE TO MISS IT...

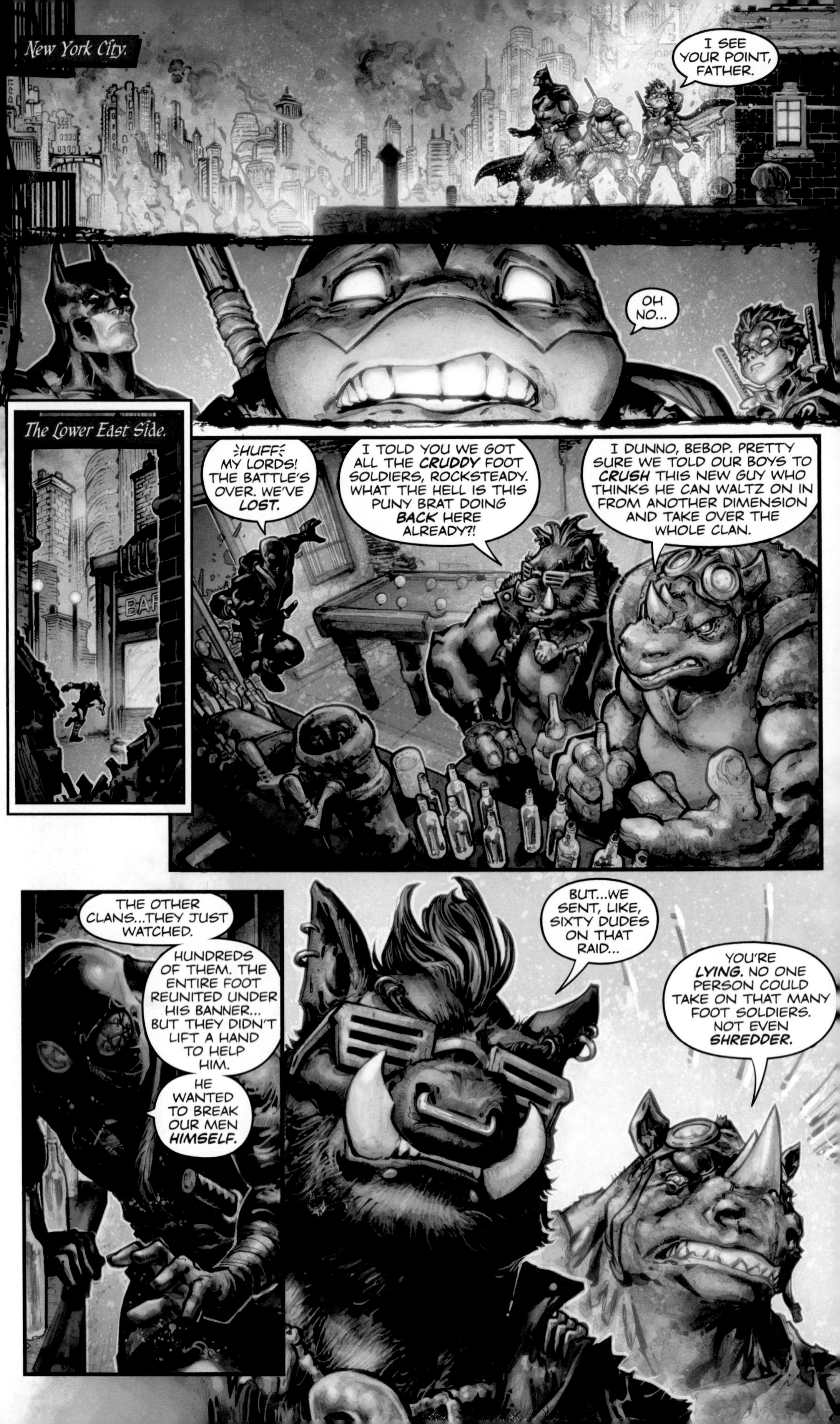
New York City.
I SEE YOUR POINT, FATHER.
OH NO...
The Lower East Side.
HUFF MY LORDS! THE BATTLE'S OVER. WE'VE LOST.
I TOLD YOU WE GOT ALL THE CRUDDY FOOT SOLDIERS, ROCKSTEADY. WHAT THE HELL IS THIS PUNY BRAT DOING BACK HERE ALREADY?!
I DUNNO, BEBOP. PRETTY SURE WE TOLD OUR BOYS TO CRUSH THIS NEW GUY WHO THINKS HE CAN WALTZ ON IN FROM ANOTHER DIMENSION AND TAKE OVER THE WHOLE CLAN.
BAR
THE OTHER CLANS...THEY JUST WATCHED.
HUNDREDS OF THEM. THE ENTIRE FOOT REUNITED UNDER HIS BANNER... BUT THEY DIDN'T LIFT A HAND TO HELP HIM.
HE WANTED TO BREAK OUR MEN HIMSELF.
BUT...WE SENT, LIKE, SIXTY DUDES ON THAT RAID...
YOU'RE LYING. NO ONE PERSON COULD TAKE ON THAT MANY FOOT SOLDIERS. NOT EVEN SHREDDER.

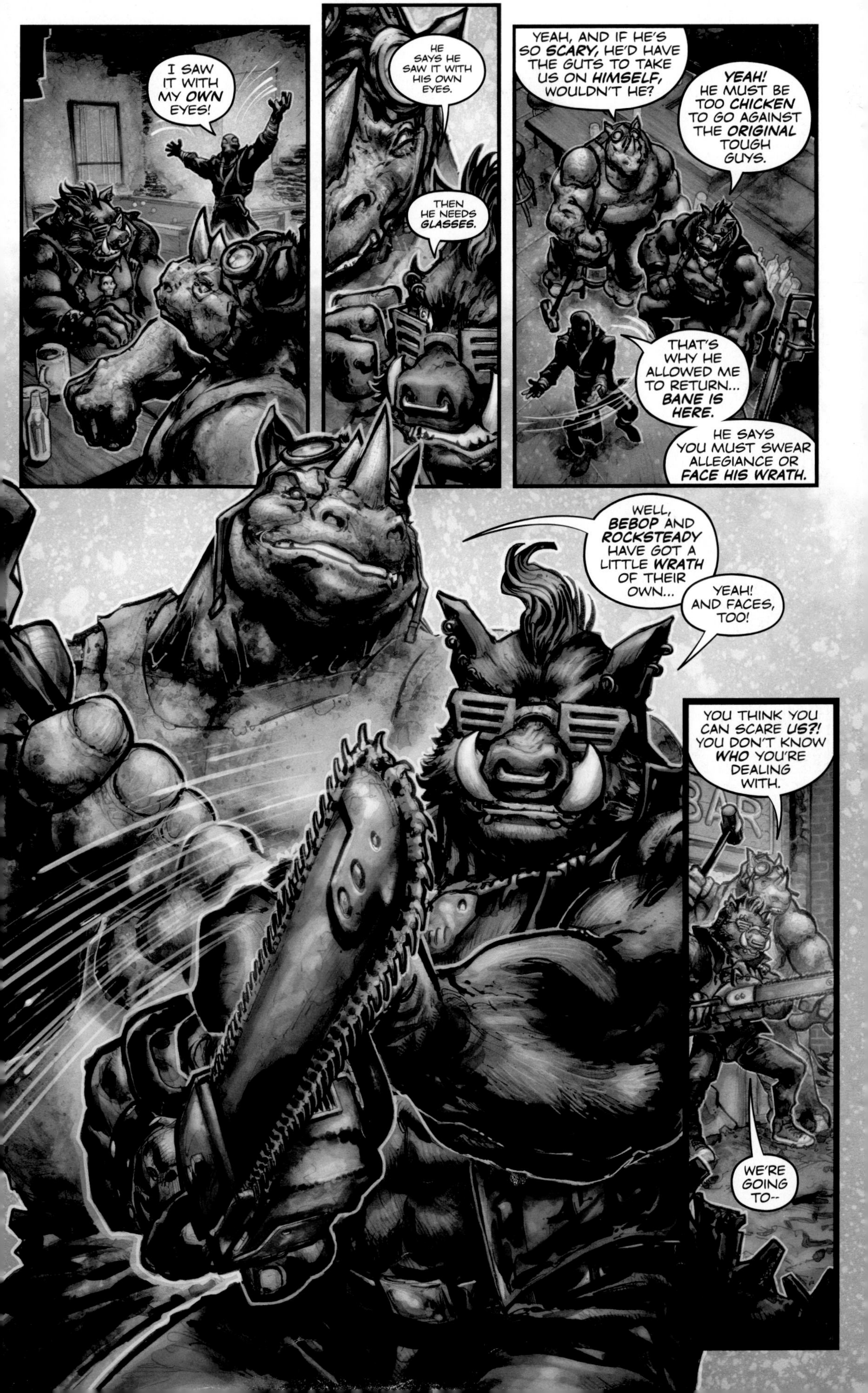
I SAW IT WITH MY OWN EYES!
HE SAYS HE SAW IT WITH HIS OWN EYES.
THEN HE NEEDS GLASSES.
YEAH, AND IF HE'S SO SCARY, HE'D HAVE THE GUTS TO TAKE US ON HIMSELF, WOULDN'T HE?
YEAH! HE MUST BE TOO CHICKEN TO GO AGAINST THE ORIGINAL TOUGH GUYS.
THAT'S WHY HE ALLOWED ME TO RETURN... BANE IS HERE.
HE SAYS YOU MUST SWEAR ALLEGIANCE OR FACE HIS WRATH.
WELL, BEBOP AND ROCKSTEADY HAVE GOT A LITTLE WRATH OF THEIR OWN...
YEAH! AND FACES, TOO!
YOU THINK YOU CAN SCARE US?! YOU DON'T KNOW WHO YOU'RE DEALING WITH.
BAR
WE'RE GOING TO--

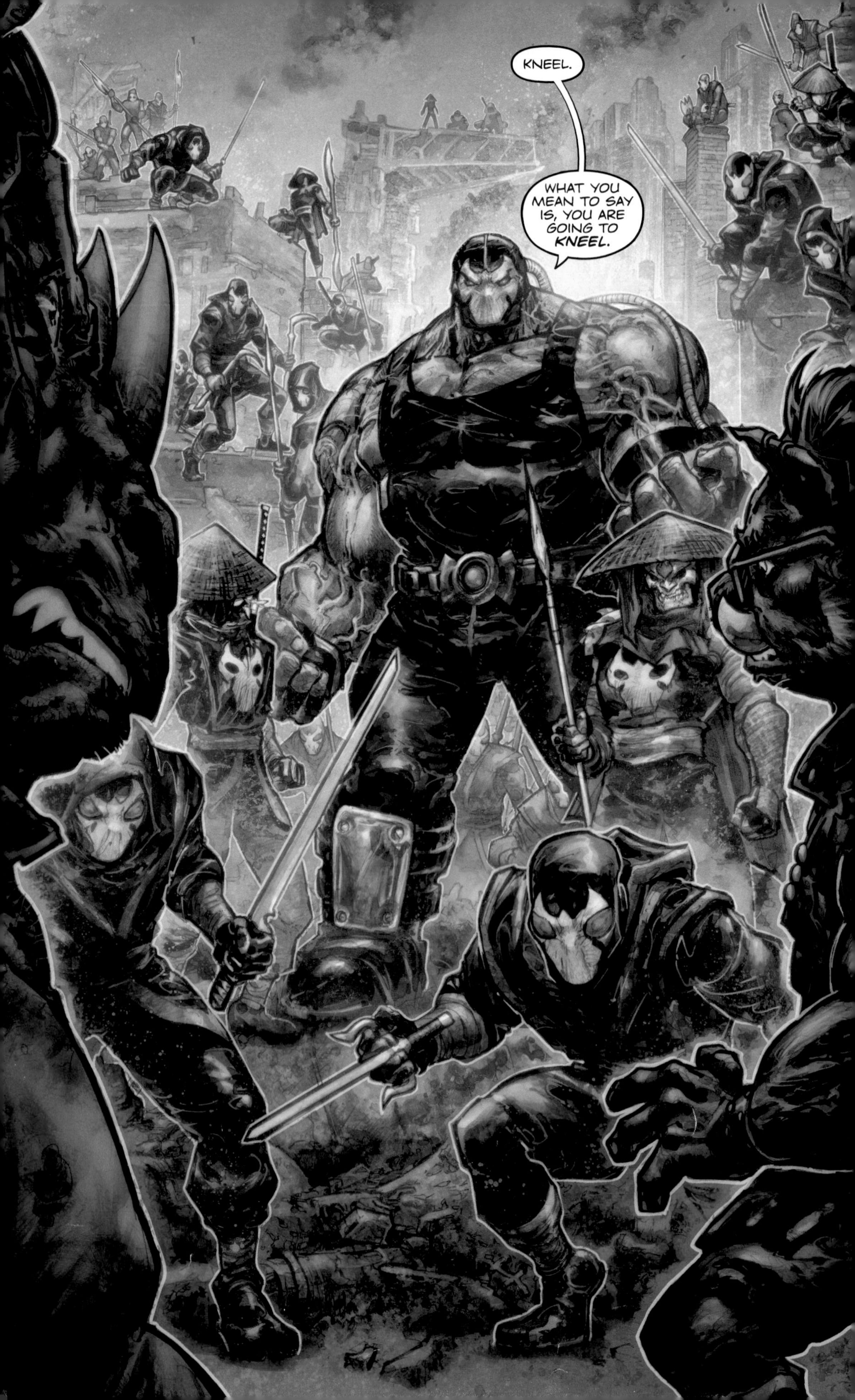
KNEEL.
WHAT YOU MEAN TO SAY IS, YOU ARE GOING TO KNEEL.

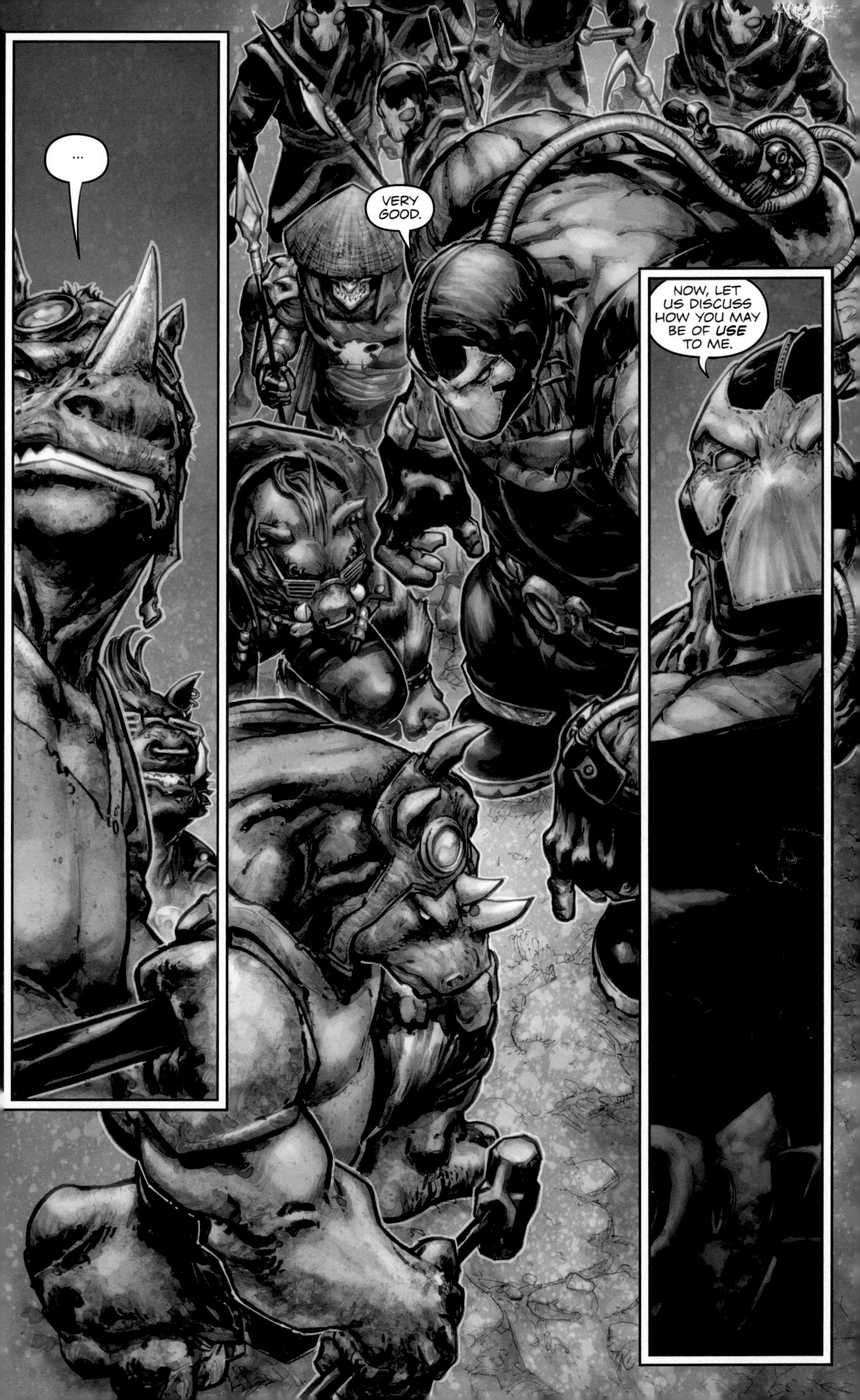
...
VERY GOOD.
NOW, LET US DISCUSS HOW YOU MAY BE OF USE TO ME.

I'M *DYING*, MAN! THE PAIN...THE PAIN IS *TOO* MUCH!

YOU SPRAINED YOUR FREAKING ANKLE. YOU'RE *FINE*.

NO, *DUDE!* IT'S MORE THAN THAT! I KNOW IT...

I SEE THE *LIGHT*, MAN. I SEE *ANGELS MADE OF PIZZA* DANCING BEFORE MY EYES!

THIS IS *IT*. THIS IS THE *END!*

IT WILL BE IF YOU DON'T *SHUT UP.*

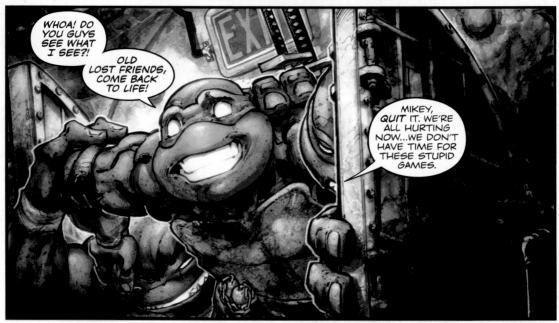

WHOA! DO YOU GUYS SEE WHAT I SEE?! *OLD LOST FRIENDS,* COME BACK TO LIFE!

MIKEY, *QUIT* IT. WE'RE ALL HURTING NOW...WE DON'T HAVE TIME FOR THESE STUPID GAMES.

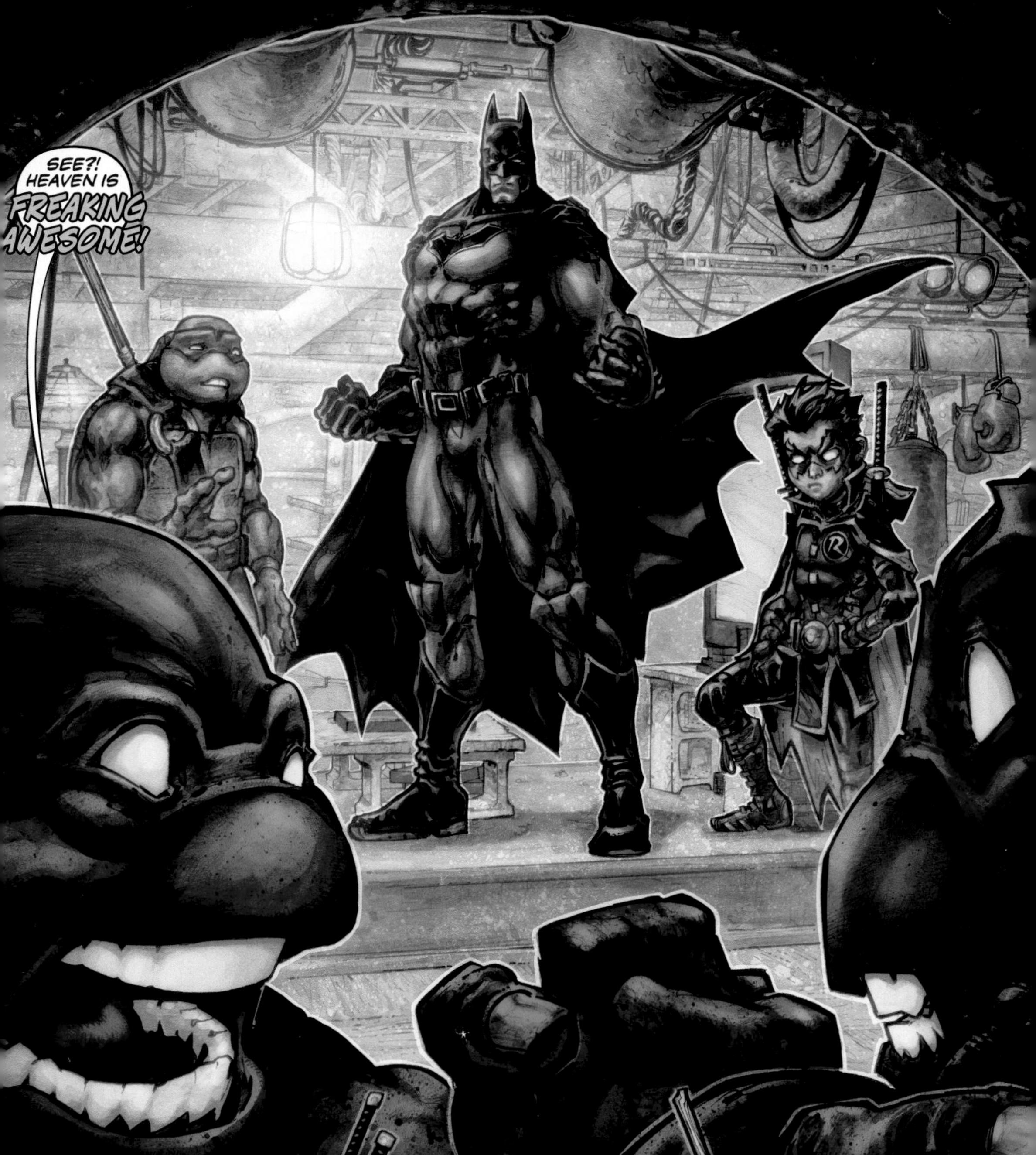
SEE?! HEAVEN IS FREAKING AWESOME!

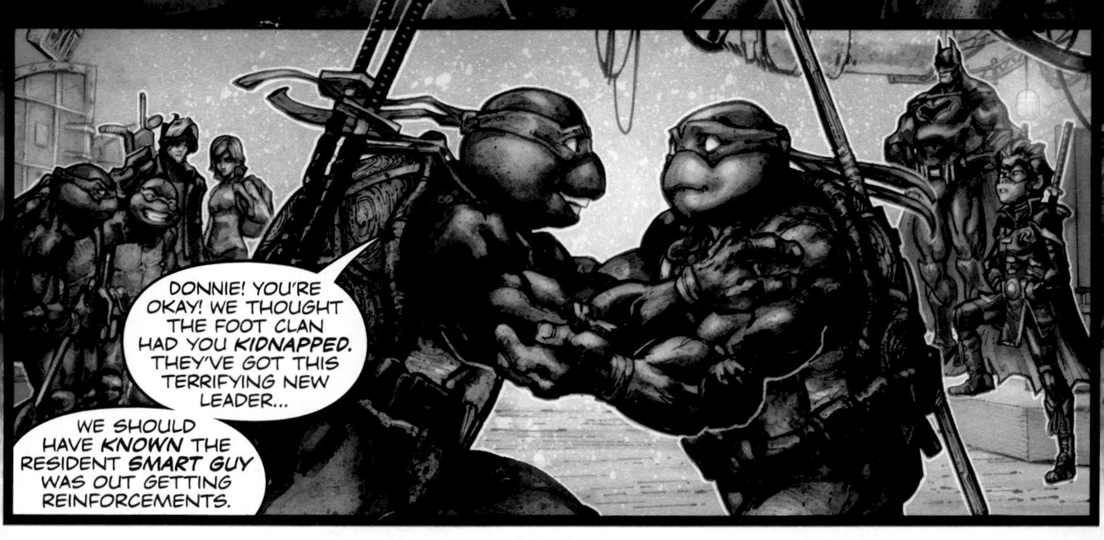
DONNIE! YOU'RE OKAY! WE THOUGHT THE FOOT CLAN HAD YOU KIDNAPPED. THEY'VE GOT THIS TERRIFYING NEW LEADER...
WE SHOULD HAVE KNOWN THE RESIDENT SMART GUY WAS OUT GETTING REINFORCEMENTS.

WELL... THAT'S NOT *EXACTLY* WHAT HAPPENED...

-TT- THE NEW LEADER, *BANE*, HE'S FROM *OUR* WORLD. YOUR BROTHER IS THE ONE WHO BROUGHT HIM HERE.

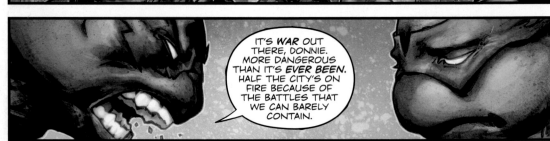

WHAT?!

DONNIE? IS THAT TRUE?

IT'S *WAR* OUT THERE, DONNIE. MORE DANGEROUS THAN IT'S *EVER BEEN*. HALF THE CITY'S ON FIRE BECAUSE OF THE BATTLES THAT WE CAN BARELY CONTAIN.

WE'VE BEEN *WORRIED SICK* ABOUT YOU, AND NOW WE FIND OUT THAT *YOU* ACTUALLY CAUSED ALL OF THIS?

RAPHAEL. I AM CERTAIN YOUR BROTHER FEELS TERRIBLE ENOUGH WITHOUT YOUR HELP.

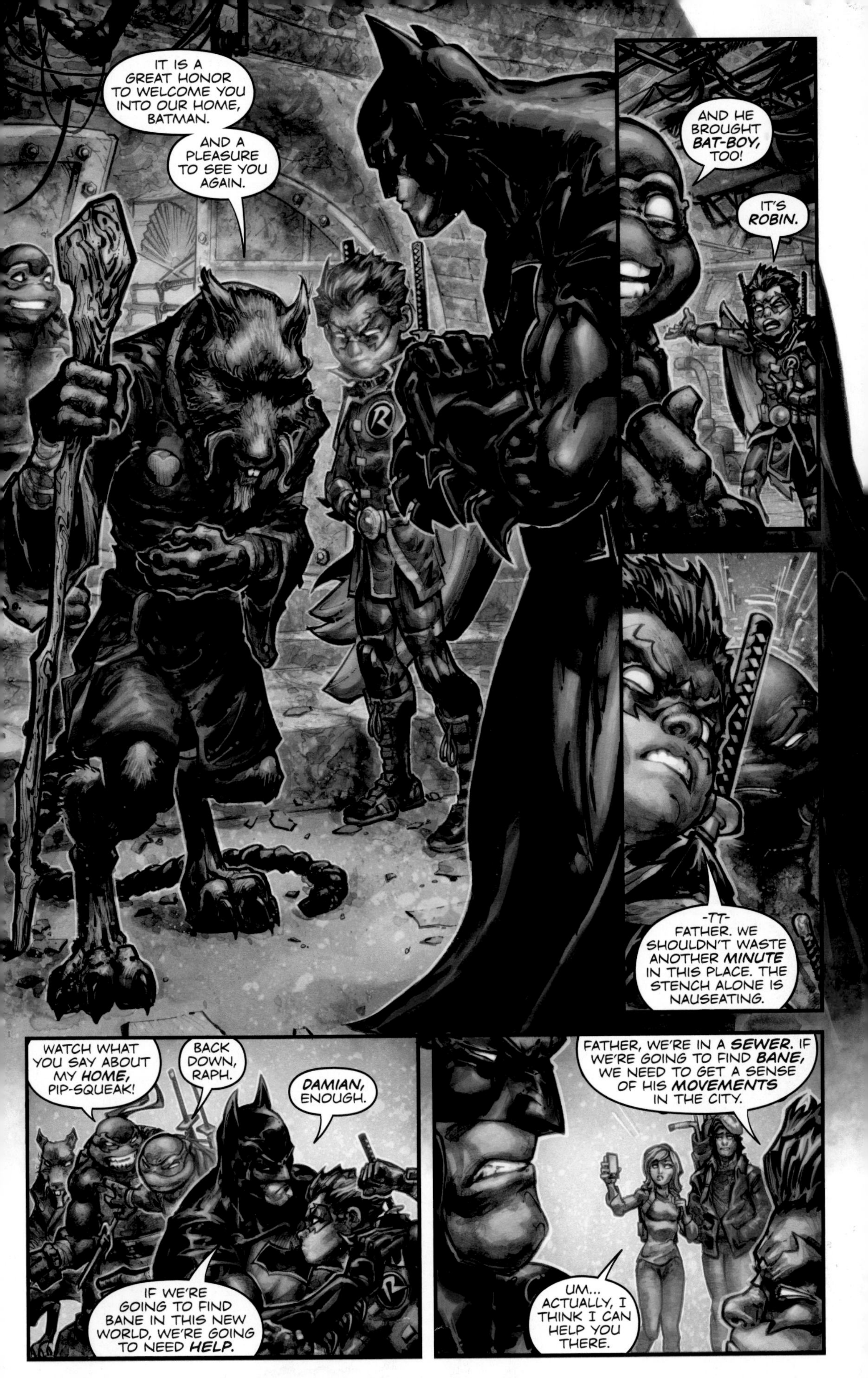
IT IS A GREAT HONOR TO WELCOME YOU INTO OUR HOME, BATMAN.
AND A PLEASURE TO SEE YOU AGAIN.
AND HE BROUGHT BAT-BOY, TOO!
IT'S ROBIN.
-TT- FATHER. WE SHOULDN'T WASTE ANOTHER MINUTE IN THIS PLACE. THE STENCH ALONE IS NAUSEATING.
WATCH WHAT YOU SAY ABOUT MY HOME, PIP-SQUEAK!
BACK DOWN, RAPH.
DAMIAN, ENOUGH.
IF WE'RE GOING TO FIND BANE IN THIS NEW WORLD, WE'RE GOING TO NEED HELP.
FATHER, WE'RE IN A SEWER. IF WE'RE GOING TO FIND BANE, WE NEED TO GET A SENSE OF HIS MOVEMENTS IN THE CITY.
UM... ACTUALLY, I THINK I CAN HELP YOU THERE.

I'VE BEEN SNEAKING AROUND GETTING ALL THE FOOTAGE I CAN ON MY PHONE... SEEING WHAT PATTERNS WE MIGHT BE ABLE TO FIND.

THIS IS *REALLY* IMPRESSIVE, APRIL...HOW DID YOU GET THAT CLOSE?

THIS NEW GUY, HE DOESN'T CARE AS MUCH ABOUT KEEPING QUIET. I GOT MAYBE TWELVE SHOTS OF SHREDDER IN THE ENTIRE LAST YEAR HE WAS IN POWER. BUT WITH BANE? I'VE GOT HUNDREDS.

DO YOU HAVE ANY MORE PICTURES WITH THE TANK ON BANE'S BACK? A CLOSER SHOT.

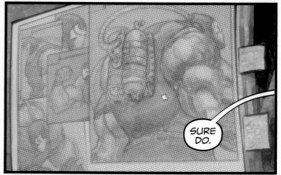

SURE DO.

BANE'S STRENGTH COMES FROM A DANGEROUS LIQUID STEROID UNIQUE TO MY WORLD. IT'S CALLED *VENOM*.

IT'S HIGHLY ADDICTIVE, AND THE MORE ENERGY HE EXERTS, THE MORE HE'S FORCED TO USE.

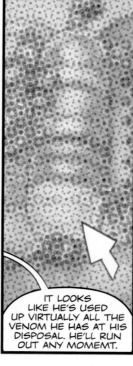

IT LOOKS LIKE HE'S USED UP VIRTUALLY ALL THE VENOM HE HAS AT HIS DISPOSAL. HE'LL RUN OUT ANY MOMEMT.

WE'LL STRIKE IN THE NEXT 24 HOURS. WHEN THE WITHDRAWAL SYMPTOMS ARE THE MOST DEBILITATING.

AND THEN YOUR CITY'S NIGHTMARE WILL FINALLY BE OVER.

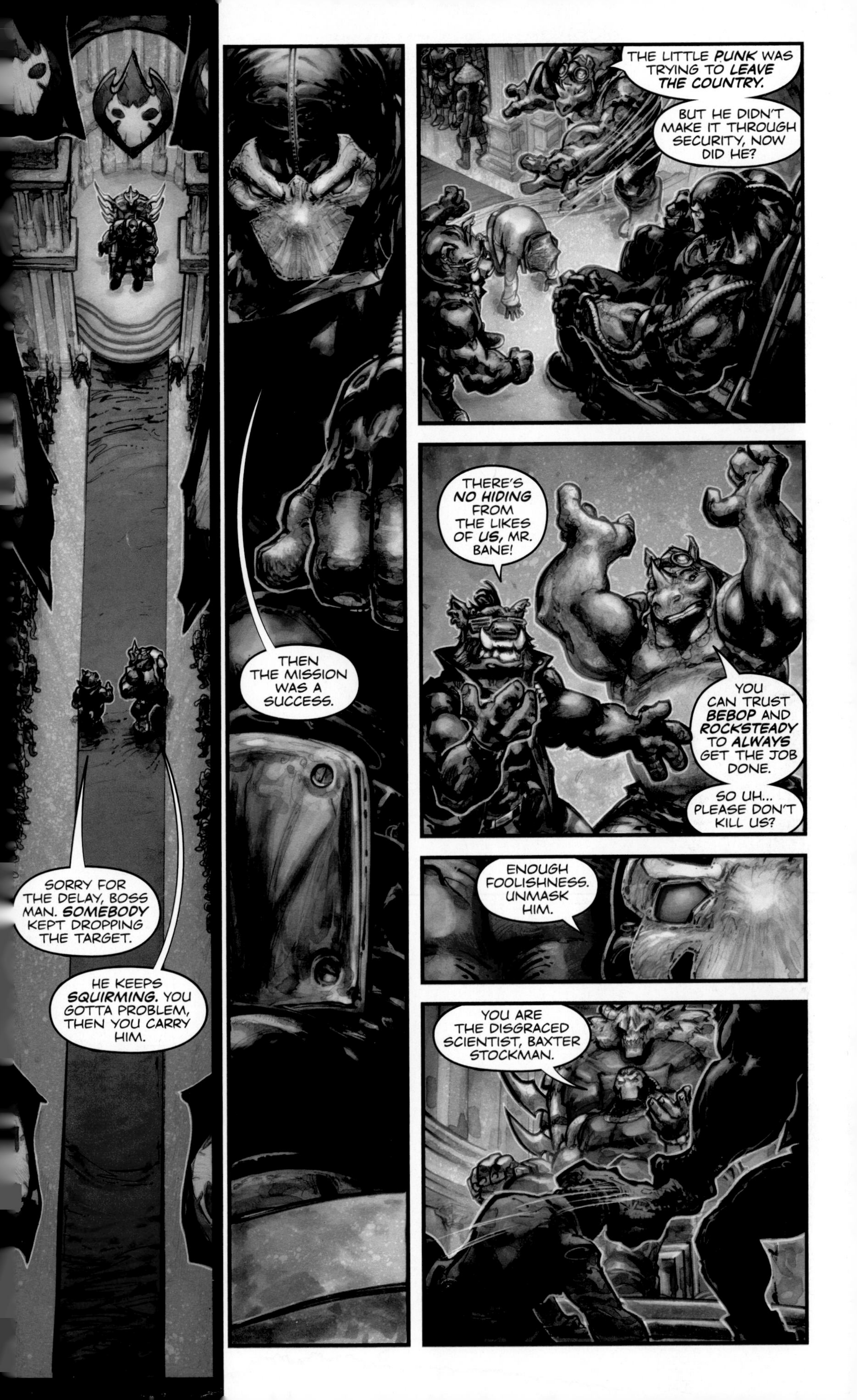
SORRY FOR THE DELAY, BOSS MAN. **SOMEBODY** KEPT DROPPING THE TARGET.
HE KEEPS **SQUIRMING.** YOU GOTTA PROBLEM, THEN YOU CARRY HIM.
THEN THE MISSION WAS A SUCCESS.
THE LITTLE **PUNK** WAS TRYING TO **LEAVE THE COUNTRY.**
BUT HE DIDN'T MAKE IT THROUGH SECURITY, NOW DID HE?
THERE'S **NO HIDING** FROM THE LIKES OF **US,** MR. BANE!
YOU CAN TRUST **BEBOP** AND **ROCKSTEADY** TO **ALWAYS** GET THE JOB DONE.
SO UH... PLEASE DON'T KILL US?
ENOUGH FOOLISHNESS. UNMASK HIM.
YOU ARE THE DISGRACED SCIENTIST, BAXTER STOCKMAN.

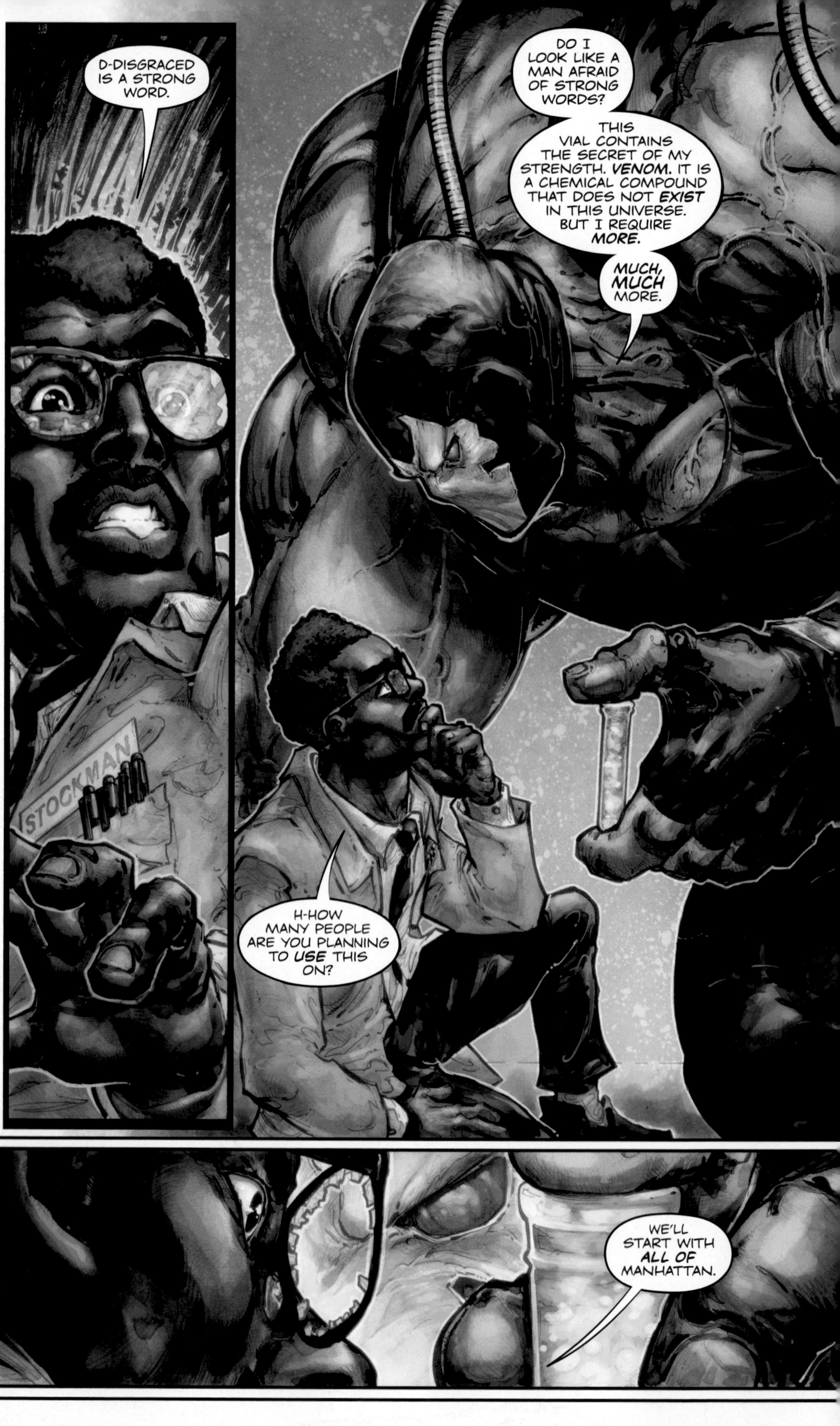

D-DISGRACED IS A STRONG WORD.
DO I LOOK LIKE A MAN AFRAID OF STRONG WORDS?
THIS VIAL CONTAINS THE SECRET OF MY STRENGTH. VENOM. IT IS A CHEMICAL COMPOUND THAT DOES NOT EXIST IN THIS UNIVERSE. BUT I REQUIRE MORE.
MUCH, MUCH MORE.
STOCKMAN
H-HOW MANY PEOPLE ARE YOU PLANNING TO USE THIS ON?
WE'LL START WITH ALL OF MANHATTAN.

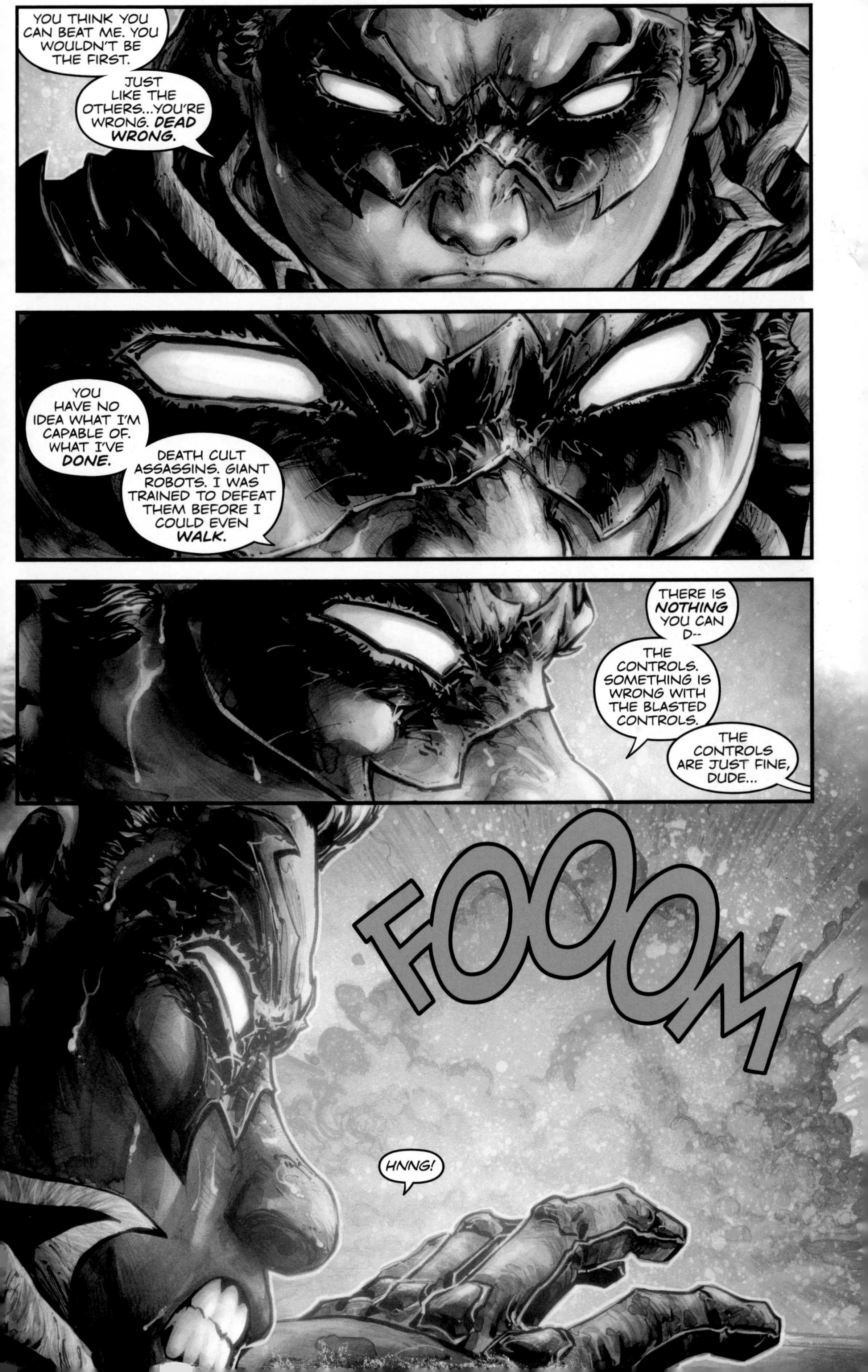
YOU THINK YOU CAN BEAT ME. YOU WOULDN'T BE THE FIRST.
JUST LIKE THE OTHERS...YOU'RE WRONG. **DEAD WRONG.**
YOU HAVE NO IDEA WHAT I'M CAPABLE OF. WHAT I'VE **DONE.**
DEATH CULT ASSASSINS. GIANT ROBOTS. I WAS TRAINED TO DEFEAT THEM BEFORE I COULD EVEN **WALK.**
THERE IS **NOTHING** YOU CAN D--
THE CONTROLS. SOMETHING IS WRONG WITH THE BLASTED CONTROLS.
THE CONTROLS ARE JUST FINE, DUDE...
FOOOM
HNNG!

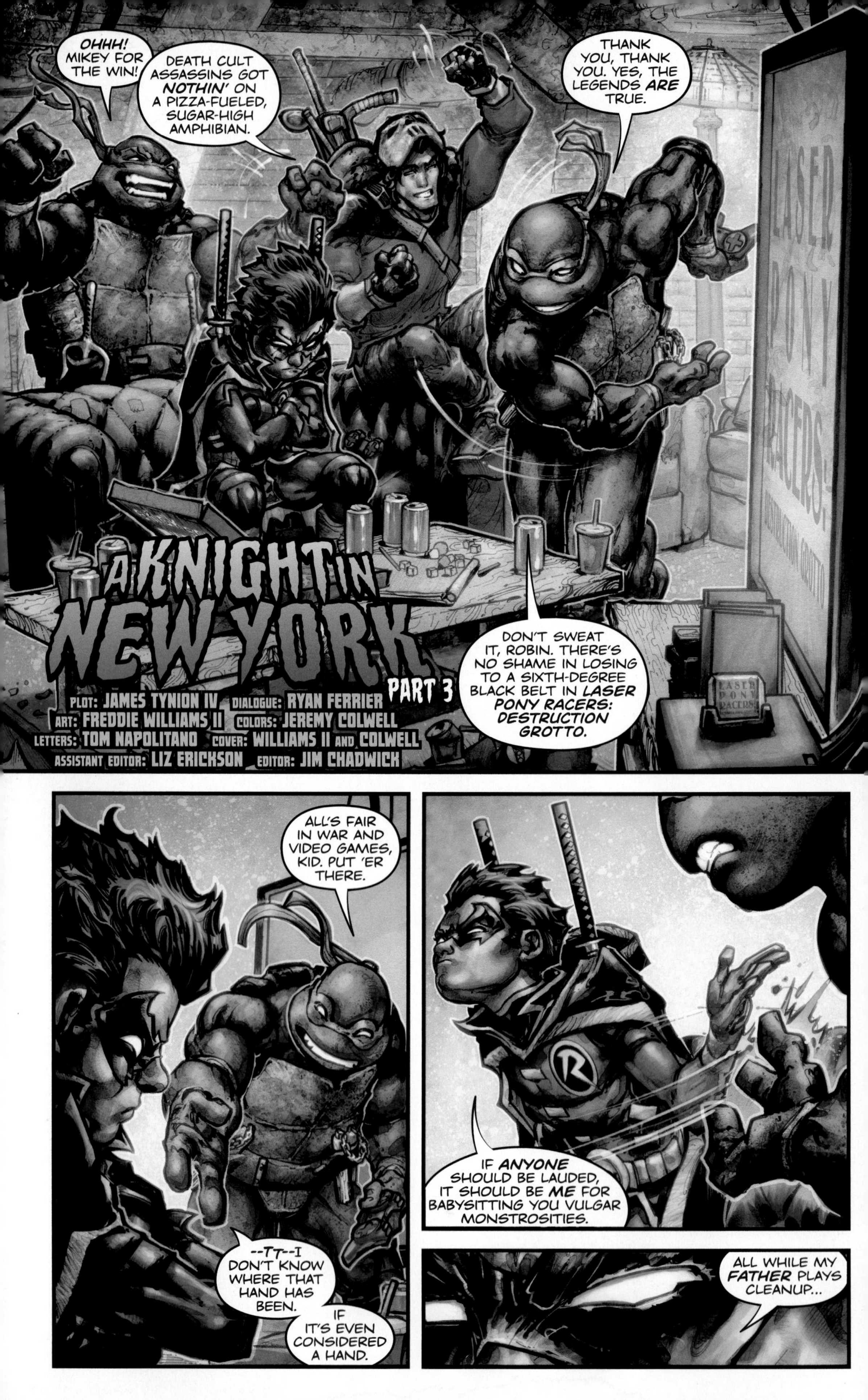
OHHH! MIKEY FOR THE WIN!
DEATH CULT ASSASSINS GOT NOTHIN' ON A PIZZA-FUELED, SUGAR-HIGH AMPHIBIAN.
THANK YOU, THANK YOU. YES, THE LEGENDS ARE TRUE.
LASER PONY RACERS: DESTRUCTION GROTTO
A KNIGHT IN NEW YORK PART 3
PLOT: JAMES TYNION IV DIALOGUE: RYAN FERRIER
ART: FREDDIE WILLIAMS II COLORS: JEREMY COLWELL
LETTERS: TOM NAPOLITANO COVER: WILLIAMS II AND COLWELL
ASSISTANT EDITOR: LIZ ERICKSON EDITOR: JIM CHADWICK
DON'T SWEAT IT, ROBIN. THERE'S NO SHAME IN LOSING TO A SIXTH-DEGREE BLACK BELT IN LASER PONY RACERS: DESTRUCTION GROTTO.
LASER PONY RACERS
ALL'S FAIR IN WAR AND VIDEO GAMES, KID. PUT 'ER THERE.
--TT--I DON'T KNOW WHERE THAT HAND HAS BEEN.
IF IT'S EVEN CONSIDERED A HAND.
IF ANYONE SHOULD BE LAUDED, IT SHOULD BE ME FOR BABYSITTING YOU VULGAR MONSTROSITIES.
ALL WHILE MY FATHER PLAYS CLEANUP...

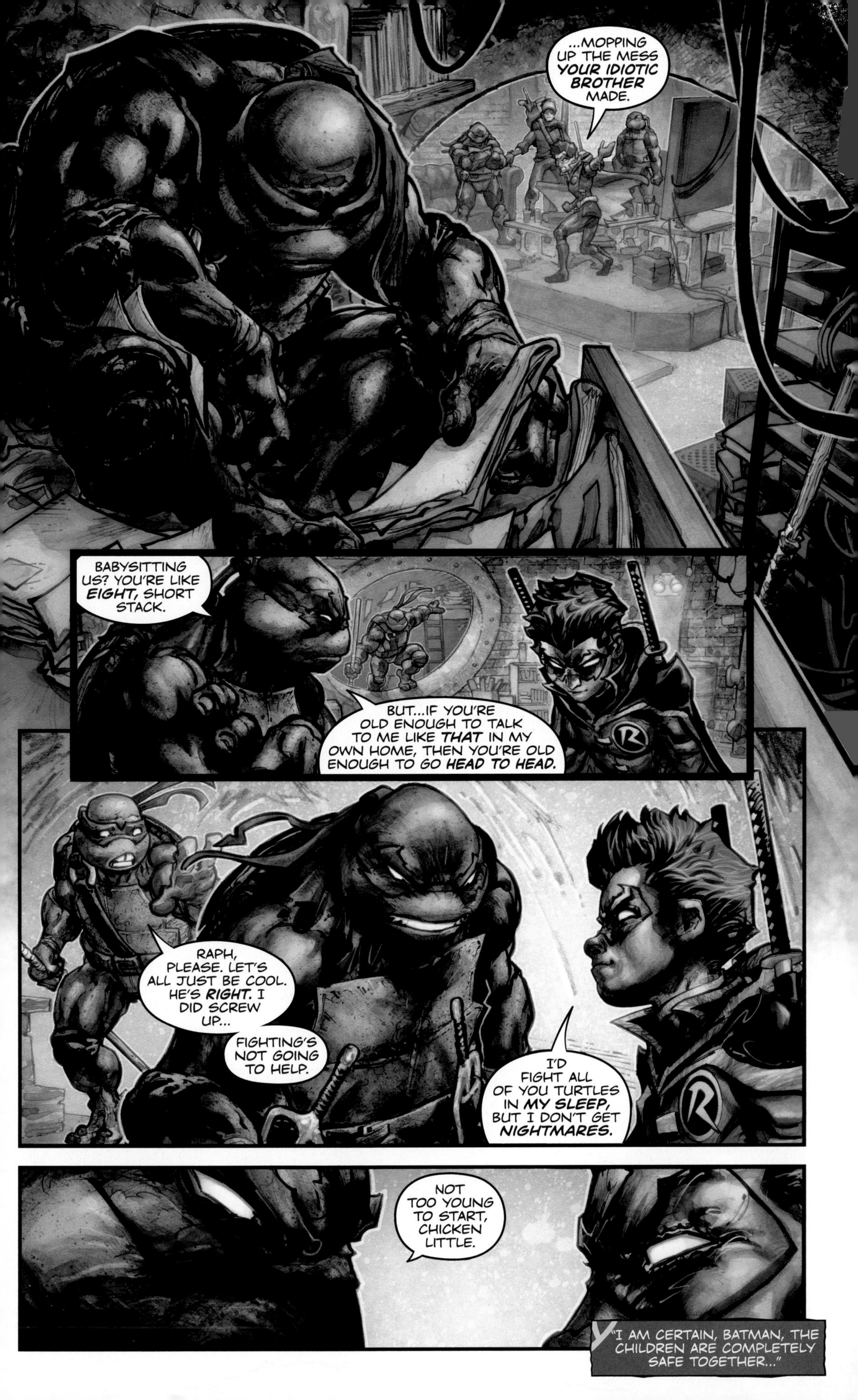
...MOPPING UP THE MESS YOUR IDIOTIC BROTHER MADE.
BABYSITTING US? YOU'RE LIKE EIGHT, SHORT STACK.
BUT...IF YOU'RE OLD ENOUGH TO TALK TO ME LIKE THAT IN MY OWN HOME, THEN YOU'RE OLD ENOUGH TO GO HEAD TO HEAD.
RAPH, PLEASE. LET'S ALL JUST BE COOL. HE'S RIGHT. I DID SCREW UP...
FIGHTING'S NOT GOING TO HELP.
I'D FIGHT ALL OF YOU TURTLES IN MY SLEEP, BUT I DON'T GET NIGHTMARES.
NOT TOO YOUNG TO START, CHICKEN LITTLE.
"I AM CERTAIN, BATMAN, THE CHILDREN ARE COMPLETELY SAFE TOGETHER..."

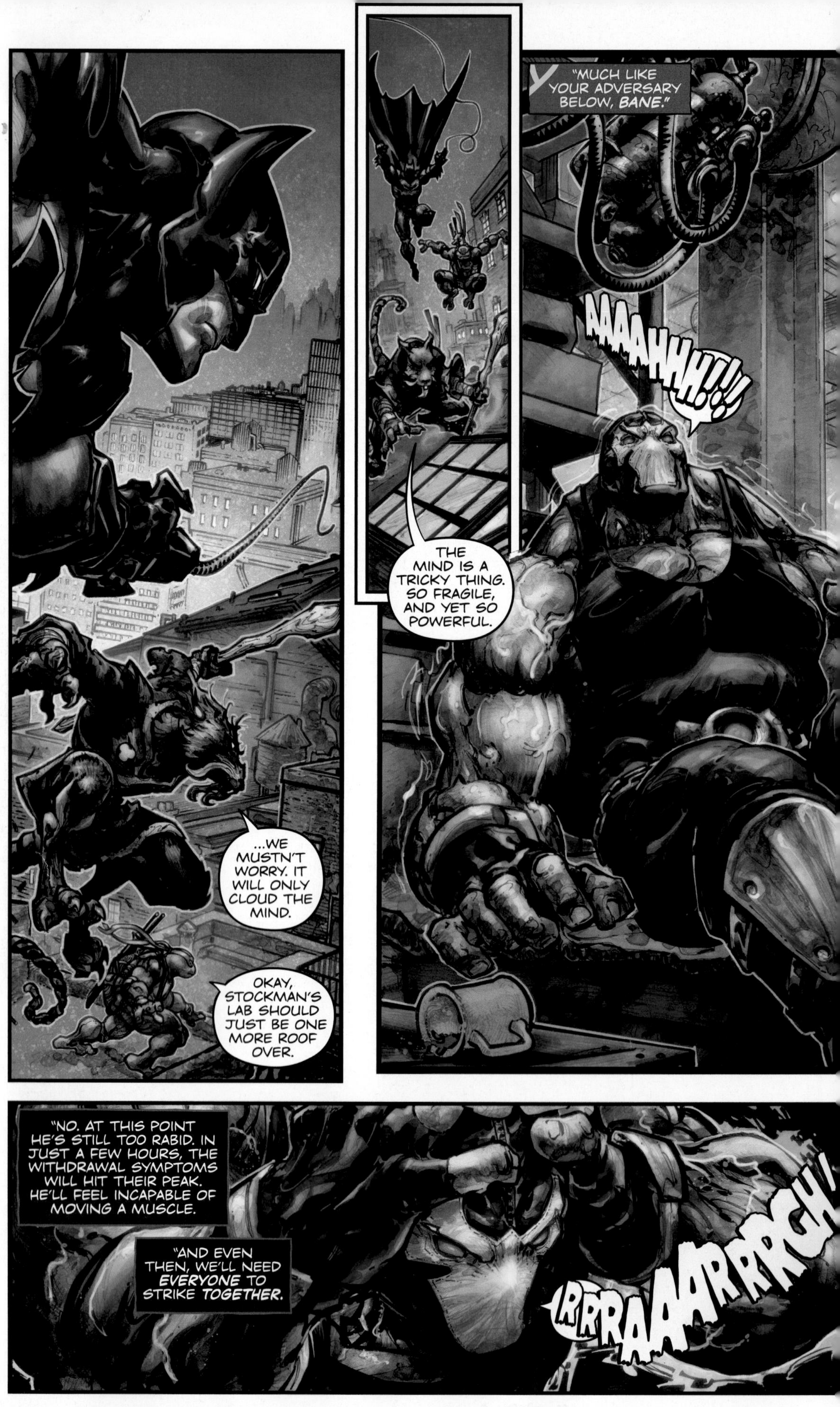
"MUCH LIKE YOUR ADVERSARY BELOW, BANE."
AAAAHHH!!!
THE MIND IS A TRICKY THING. SO FRAGILE, AND YET SO POWERFUL.
...WE MUSTN'T WORRY. IT WILL ONLY CLOUD THE MIND.
OKAY, STOCKMAN'S LAB SHOULD JUST BE ONE MORE ROOF OVER.
"NO. AT THIS POINT HE'S STILL TOO RABID. IN JUST A FEW HOURS, THE WITHDRAWAL SYMPTOMS WILL HIT THEIR PEAK. HE'LL FEEL INCAPABLE OF MOVING A MUSCLE.
"AND EVEN THEN, WE'LL NEED EVERYONE TO STRIKE TOGETHER.
RRRAAARRRGH!

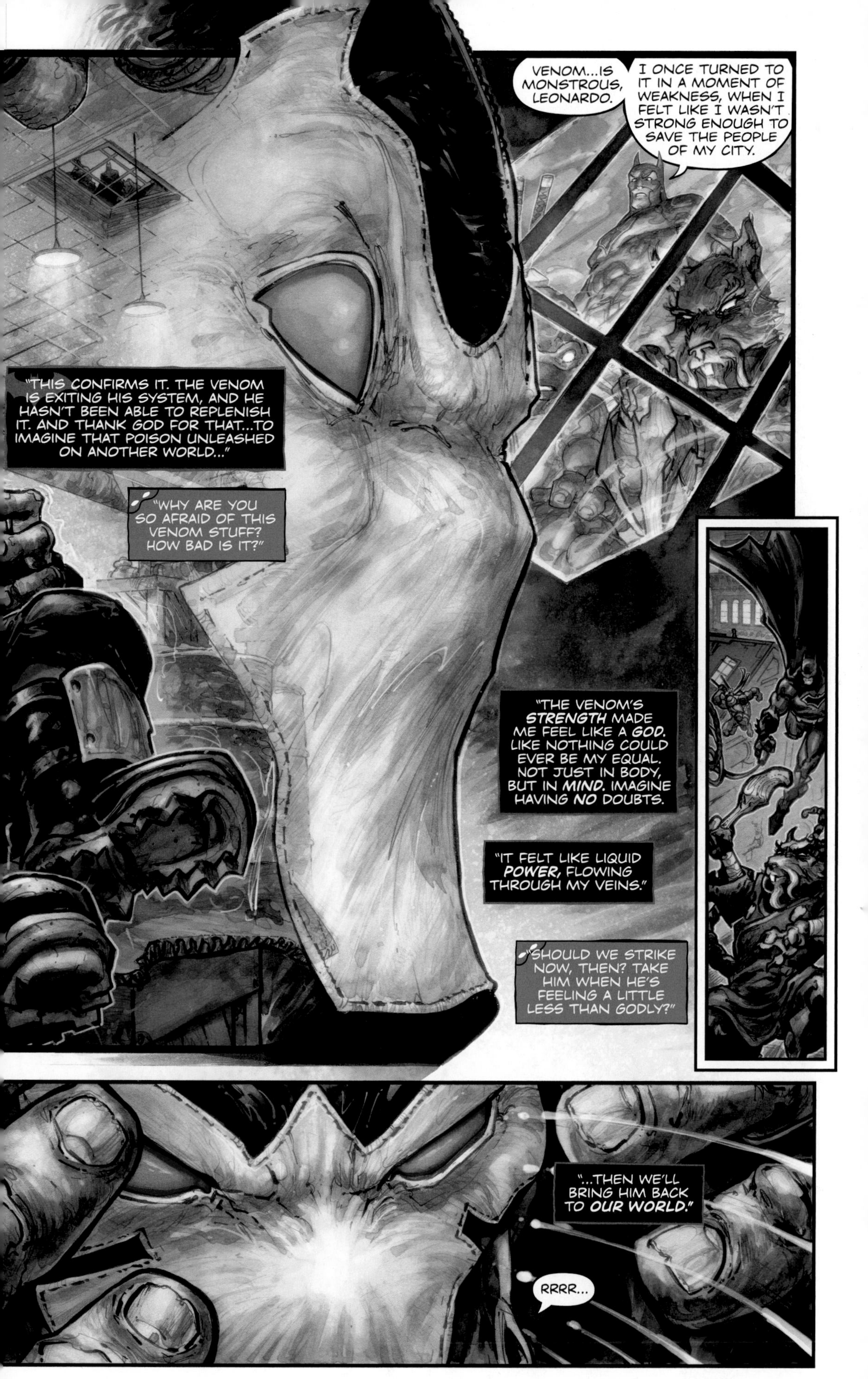
VENOM...IS MONSTROUS, LEONARDO.
I ONCE TURNED TO IT IN A MOMENT OF WEAKNESS, WHEN I FELT LIKE I WASN'T STRONG ENOUGH TO SAVE THE PEOPLE OF MY CITY.
"THIS CONFIRMS IT. THE VENOM IS EXITING HIS SYSTEM, AND HE HASN'T BEEN ABLE TO REPLENISH IT. AND THANK GOD FOR THAT...TO IMAGINE THAT POISON UNLEASHED ON ANOTHER WORLD..."
"WHY ARE YOU SO AFRAID OF THIS VENOM STUFF? HOW BAD IS IT?"
"THE VENOM'S STRENGTH MADE ME FEEL LIKE A GOD. LIKE NOTHING COULD EVER BE MY EQUAL. NOT JUST IN BODY, BUT IN MIND. IMAGINE HAVING NO DOUBTS.
"IT FELT LIKE LIQUID POWER, FLOWING THROUGH MY VEINS."
"SHOULD WE STRIKE NOW, THEN? TAKE HIM WHEN HE'S FEELING A LITTLE LESS THAN GODLY?"
"...THEN WE'LL BRING HIM BACK TO OUR WORLD."
RRRR...

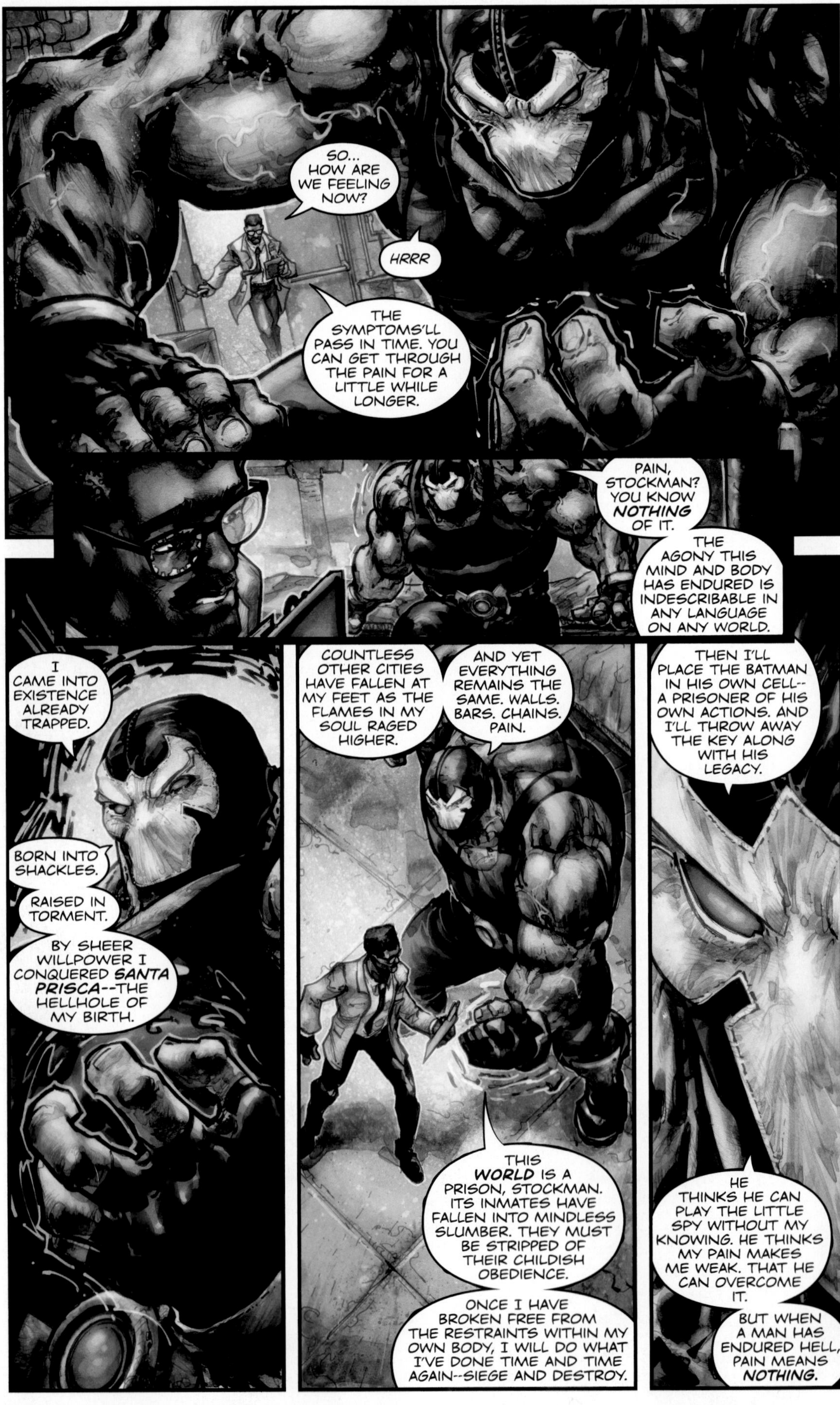
SO... HOW ARE WE FEELING NOW?
HRRR
THE SYMPTOMS'LL PASS IN TIME. YOU CAN GET THROUGH THE PAIN FOR A LITTLE WHILE LONGER.
PAIN, STOCKMAN? YOU KNOW **NOTHING** OF IT.
THE AGONY THIS MIND AND BODY HAS ENDURED IS INDESCRIBABLE IN ANY LANGUAGE ON ANY WORLD.
I CAME INTO EXISTENCE ALREADY TRAPPED.
BORN INTO SHACKLES.
RAISED IN TORMENT.
BY SHEER WILLPOWER I CONQUERED **SANTA PRISCA**--THE HELLHOLE OF MY BIRTH.
COUNTLESS OTHER CITIES HAVE FALLEN AT MY FEET AS THE FLAMES IN MY SOUL RAGED HIGHER.
AND YET EVERYTHING REMAINS THE SAME. WALLS. BARS. CHAINS. PAIN.
THIS **WORLD** IS A PRISON, STOCKMAN. ITS INMATES HAVE FALLEN INTO MINDLESS SLUMBER. THEY MUST BE STRIPPED OF THEIR CHILDISH OBEDIENCE.
ONCE I HAVE BROKEN FREE FROM THE RESTRAINTS WITHIN MY OWN BODY, I WILL DO WHAT I'VE DONE TIME AND TIME AGAIN--SIEGE AND DESTROY.
THEN I'LL PLACE THE BATMAN IN HIS OWN CELL-- A PRISONER OF HIS OWN ACTIONS. AND I'LL THROW AWAY THE KEY ALONG WITH HIS LEGACY.
HE THINKS HE CAN PLAY THE LITTLE SPY WITHOUT MY KNOWING. HE THINKS MY PAIN MAKES ME WEAK. THAT HE CAN OVERCOME IT.
BUT WHEN A MAN HAS ENDURED HELL, PAIN MEANS **NOTHING.**

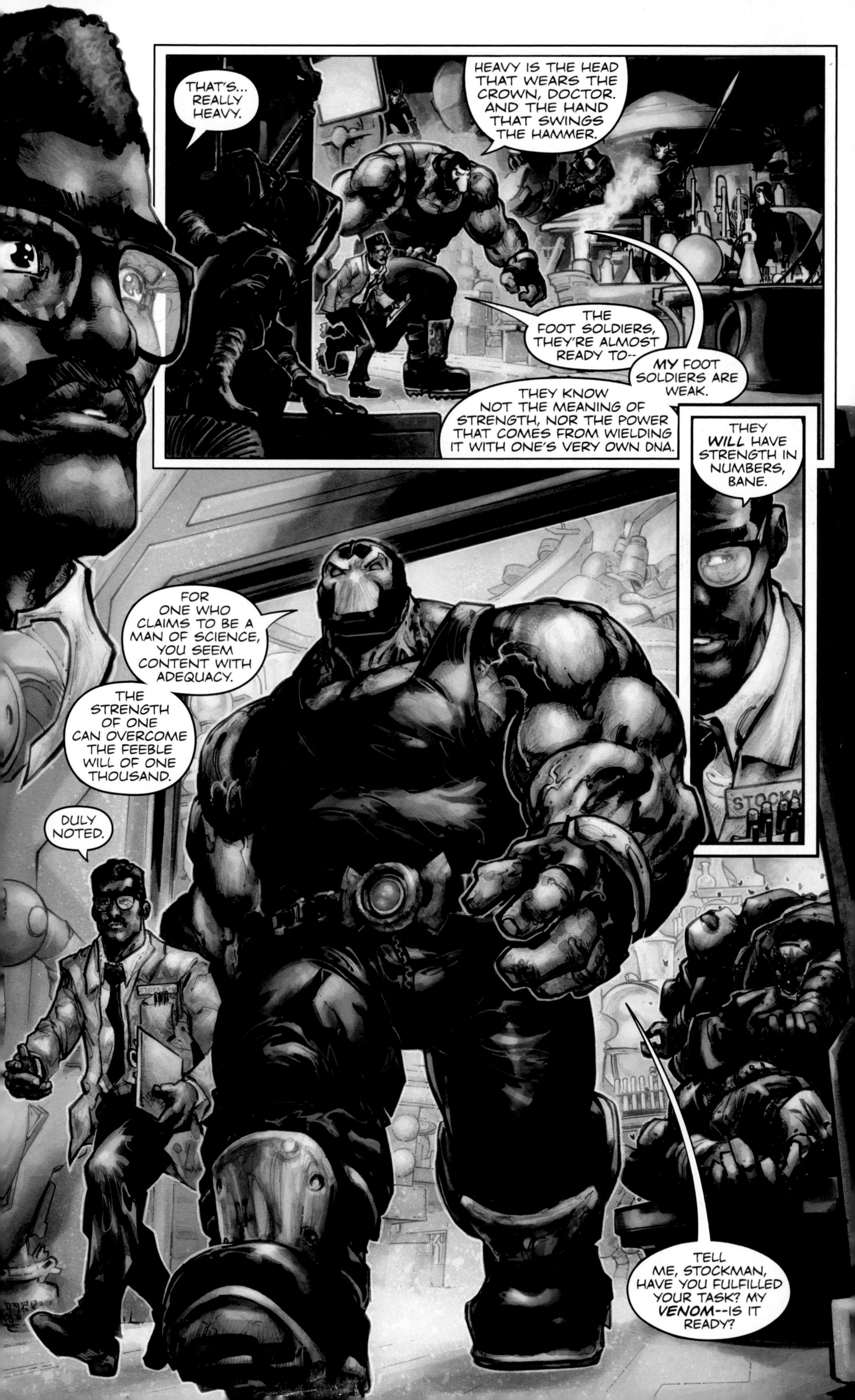
THAT'S... REALLY HEAVY.
HEAVY IS THE HEAD THAT WEARS THE CROWN, DOCTOR. AND THE HAND THAT SWINGS THE HAMMER.
THE FOOT SOLDIERS, THEY'RE ALMOST READY TO--
MY FOOT SOLDIERS ARE WEAK.
THEY KNOW NOT THE MEANING OF STRENGTH, NOR THE POWER THAT COMES FROM WIELDING IT WITH ONE'S VERY OWN DNA.
THEY WILL HAVE STRENGTH IN NUMBERS, BANE.
STOCKM
FOR ONE WHO CLAIMS TO BE A MAN OF SCIENCE, YOU SEEM CONTENT WITH ADEQUACY.
THE STRENGTH OF ONE CAN OVERCOME THE FEEBLE WILL OF ONE THOUSAND.
DULY NOTED.
TELL ME, STOCKMAN, HAVE YOU FULFILLED YOUR TASK? MY VENOM--IS IT READY?

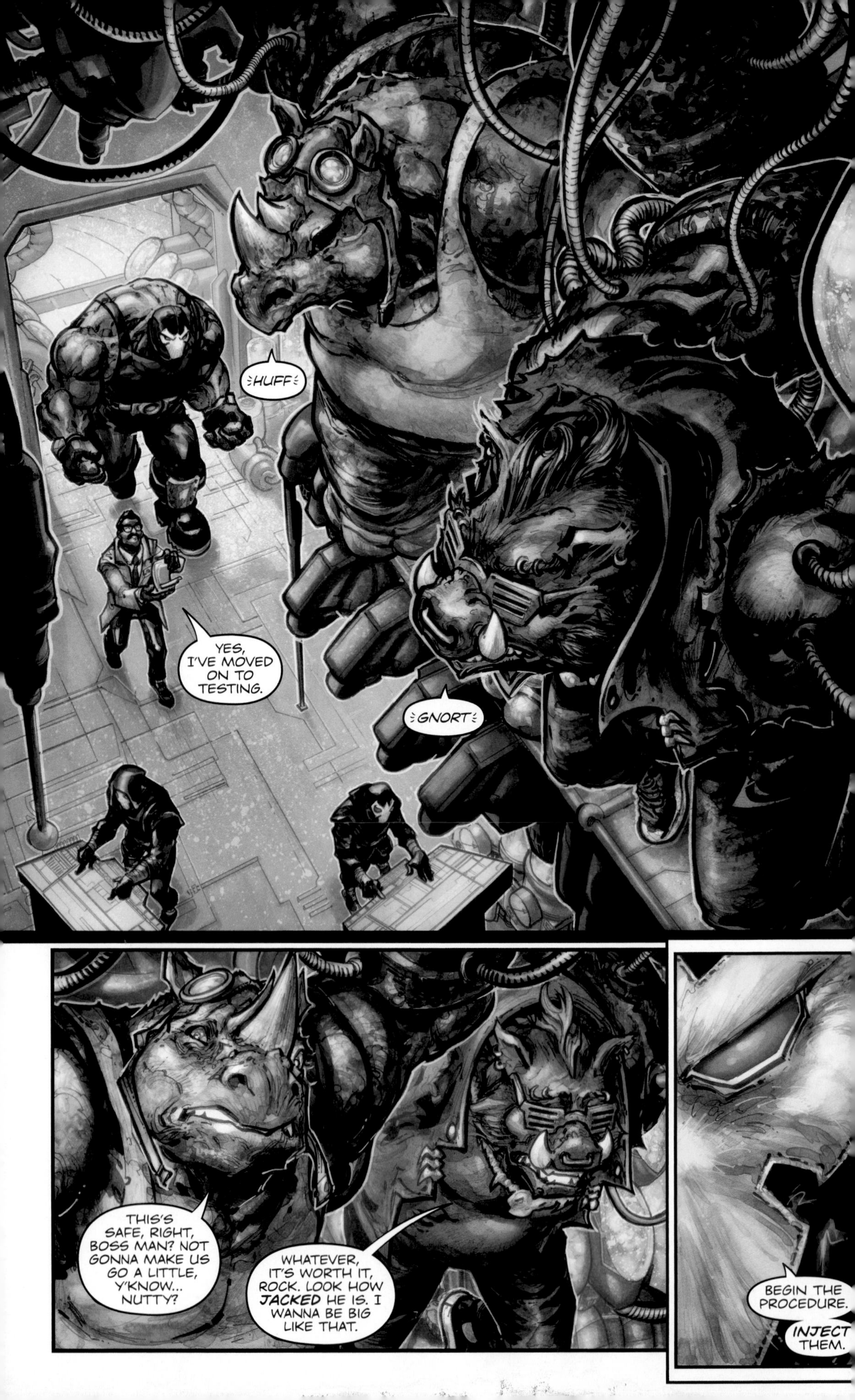
HUFF
YES, I'VE MOVED ON TO TESTING.
GNORT
THIS'S SAFE, RIGHT, BOSS MAN? NOT GONNA MAKE US GO A LITTLE, Y'KNOW... NUTTY?
WHATEVER, IT'S WORTH IT, ROCK. LOOK HOW JACKED HE IS. I WANNA BE BIG LIKE THAT.
BEGIN THE PROCEDURE.
INJECT THEM.

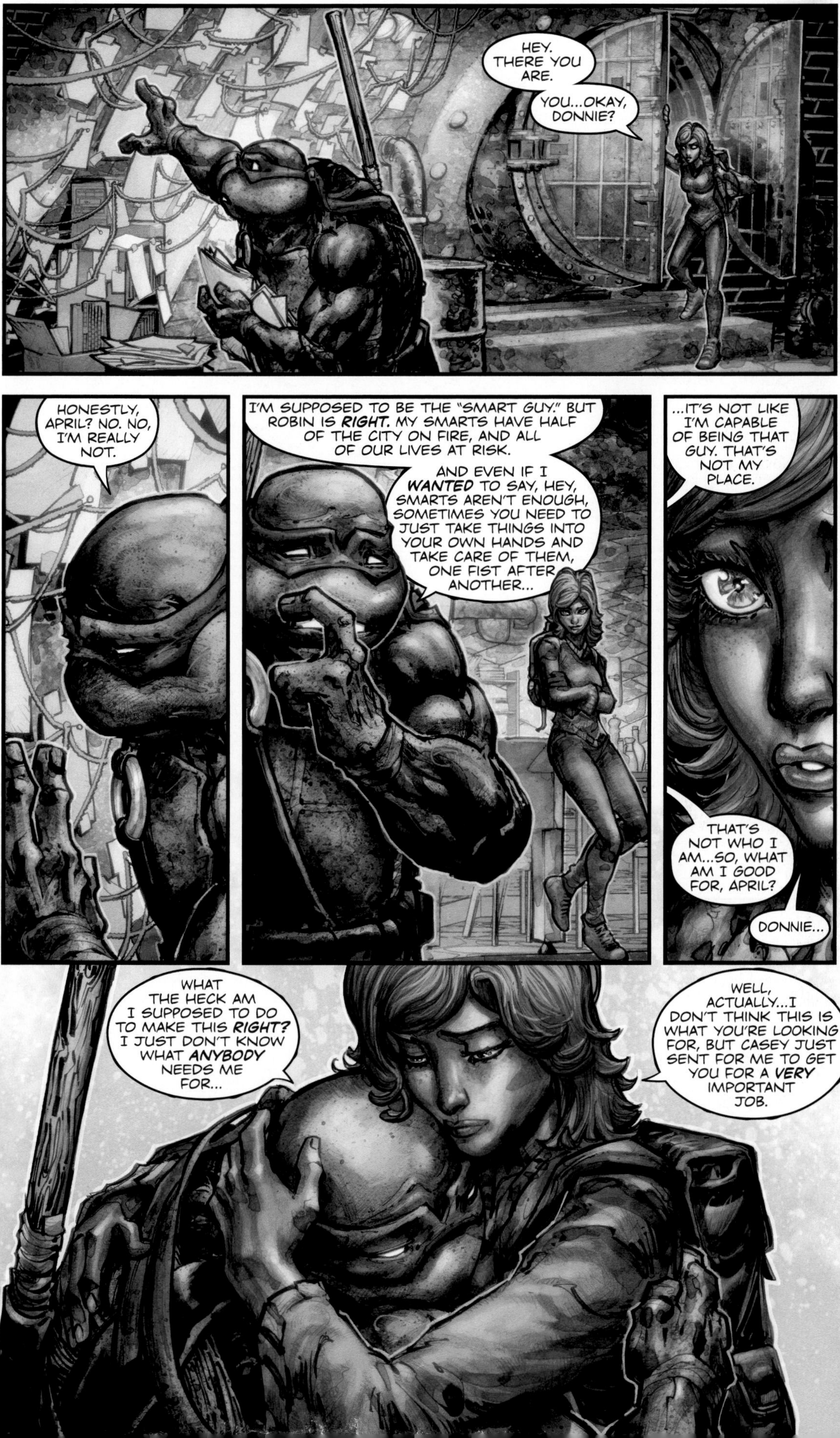
HEY. THERE YOU ARE.
YOU...OKAY, DONNIE?
HONESTLY, APRIL? NO. NO, I'M REALLY NOT.
I'M SUPPOSED TO BE THE "SMART GUY." BUT ROBIN IS **RIGHT.** MY SMARTS HAVE HALF OF THE CITY ON FIRE, AND ALL OF OUR LIVES AT RISK.
AND EVEN IF I **WANTED** TO SAY, HEY, SMARTS AREN'T ENOUGH, SOMETIMES YOU NEED TO JUST TAKE THINGS INTO YOUR OWN HANDS AND TAKE CARE OF THEM, ONE FIST AFTER ANOTHER...
...IT'S NOT LIKE I'M CAPABLE OF BEING THAT GUY. THAT'S NOT MY PLACE.
THAT'S NOT WHO I AM...SO, WHAT AM I GOOD FOR, APRIL?
DONNIE...
WHAT THE HECK AM I SUPPOSED TO DO TO MAKE THIS **RIGHT?** I JUST DON'T KNOW WHAT **ANYBODY** NEEDS ME FOR...
WELL, ACTUALLY...I DON'T THINK THIS IS WHAT YOU'RE LOOKING FOR, BUT CASEY JUST SENT FOR ME TO GET YOU FOR A **VERY** IMPORTANT JOB.

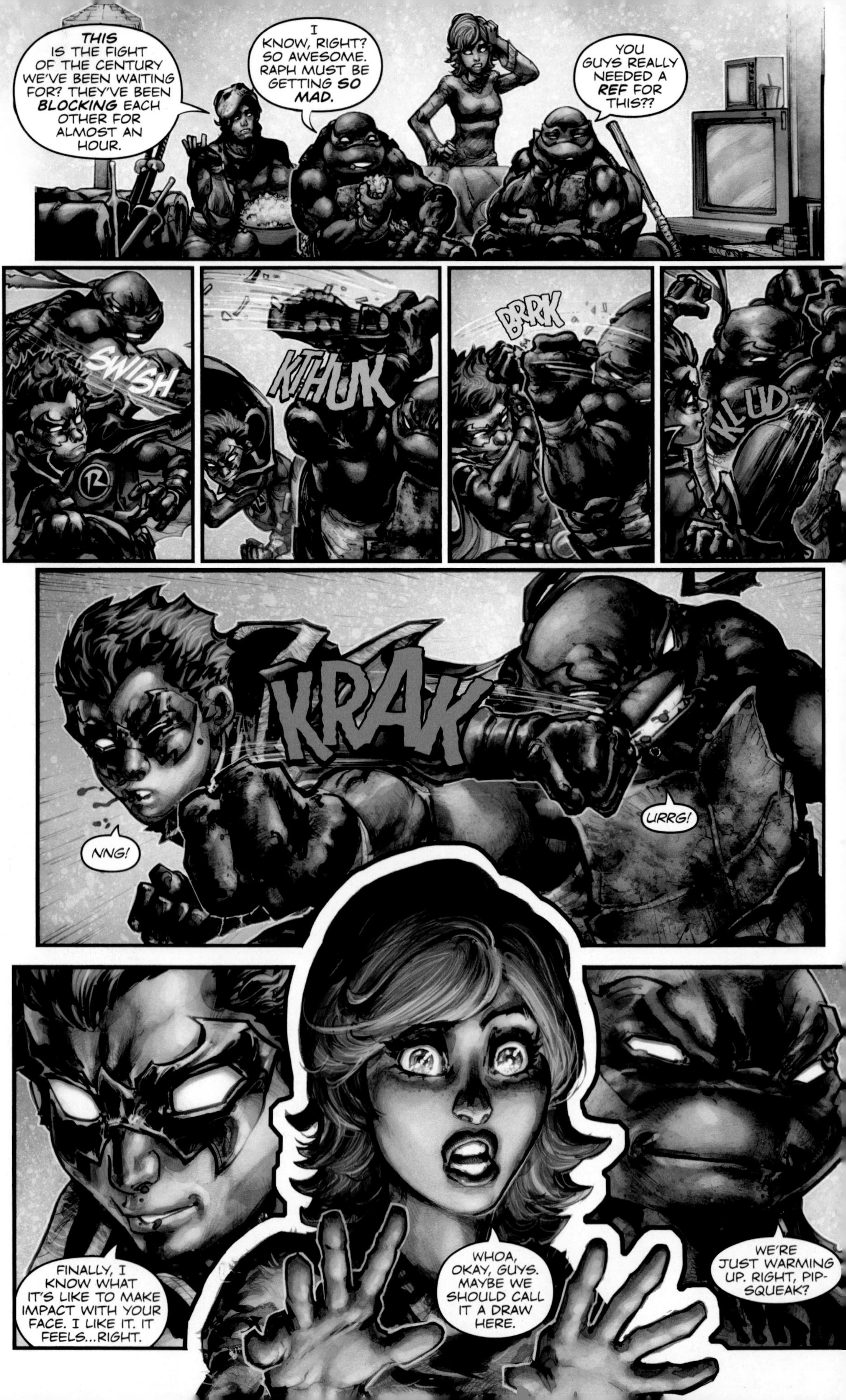

THIS IS THE FIGHT OF THE CENTURY WE'VE BEEN WAITING FOR? THEY'VE BEEN BLOCKING EACH OTHER FOR ALMOST AN HOUR.
I KNOW, RIGHT? SO AWESOME. RAPH MUST BE GETTING SO MAD.
YOU GUYS REALLY NEEDED A REF FOR THIS??
SWISH
KTHUK
BRRK
KLUD
KRAK
NNG!
URRG!
FINALLY, I KNOW WHAT IT'S LIKE TO MAKE IMPACT WITH YOUR FACE. I LIKE IT. IT FEELS...RIGHT.
WHOA, OKAY, GUYS. MAYBE WE SHOULD CALL IT A DRAW HERE.
WE'RE JUST WARMING UP. RIGHT, PIP-SQUEAK?

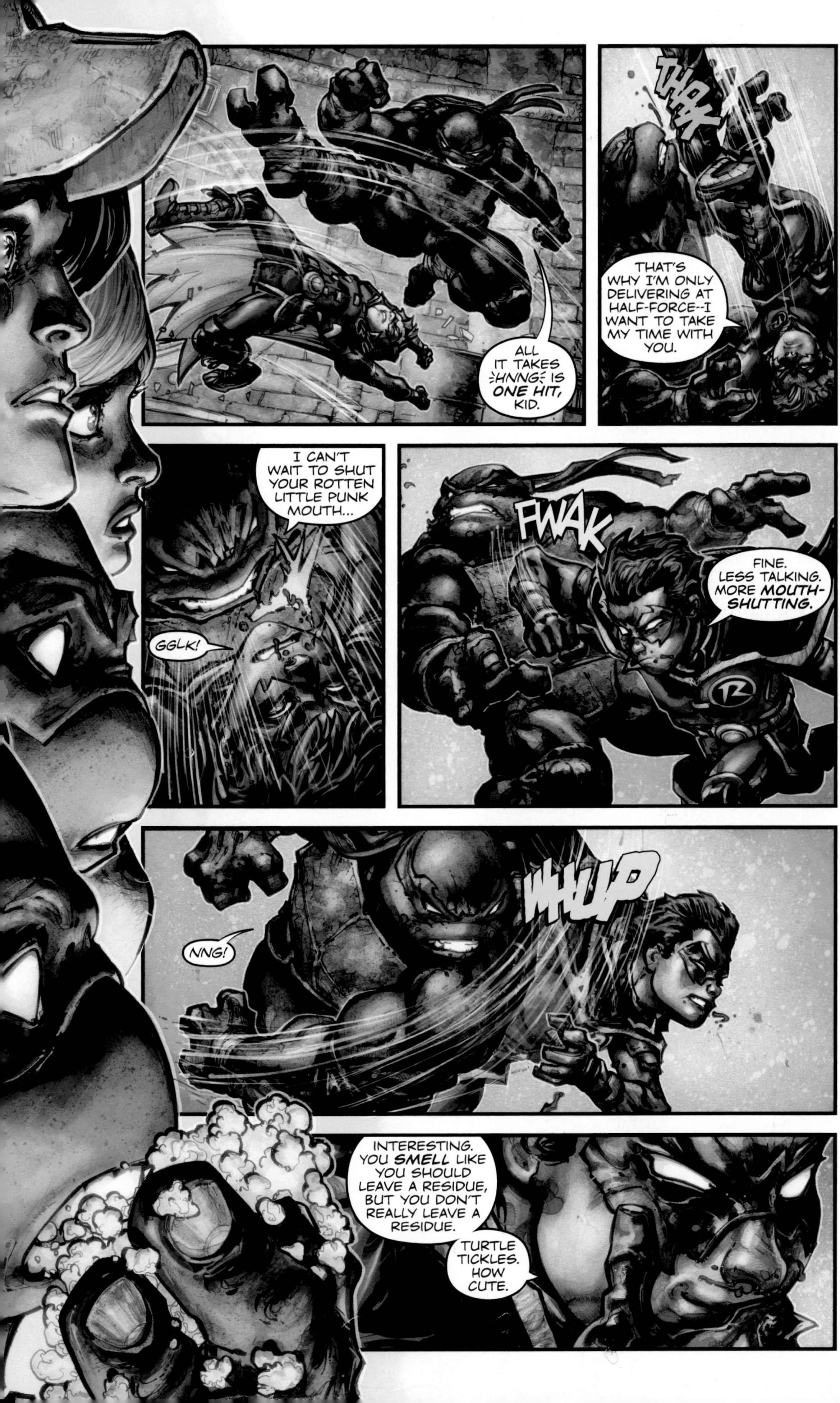
ALL IT TAKES -HNNG- IS ONE HIT, KID.
THAK
THAT'S WHY I'M ONLY DELIVERING AT HALF-FORCE--I WANT TO TAKE MY TIME WITH YOU.
I CAN'T WAIT TO SHUT YOUR ROTTEN LITTLE PUNK MOUTH...
GGLK!
FWAK
FINE. LESS TALKING. MORE MOUTH-SHUTTING.
WHUD
NNG!
INTERESTING. YOU SMELL LIKE YOU SHOULD LEAVE A RESIDUE, BUT YOU DON'T REALLY LEAVE A RESIDUE.
TURTLE TICKLES. HOW CUTE.

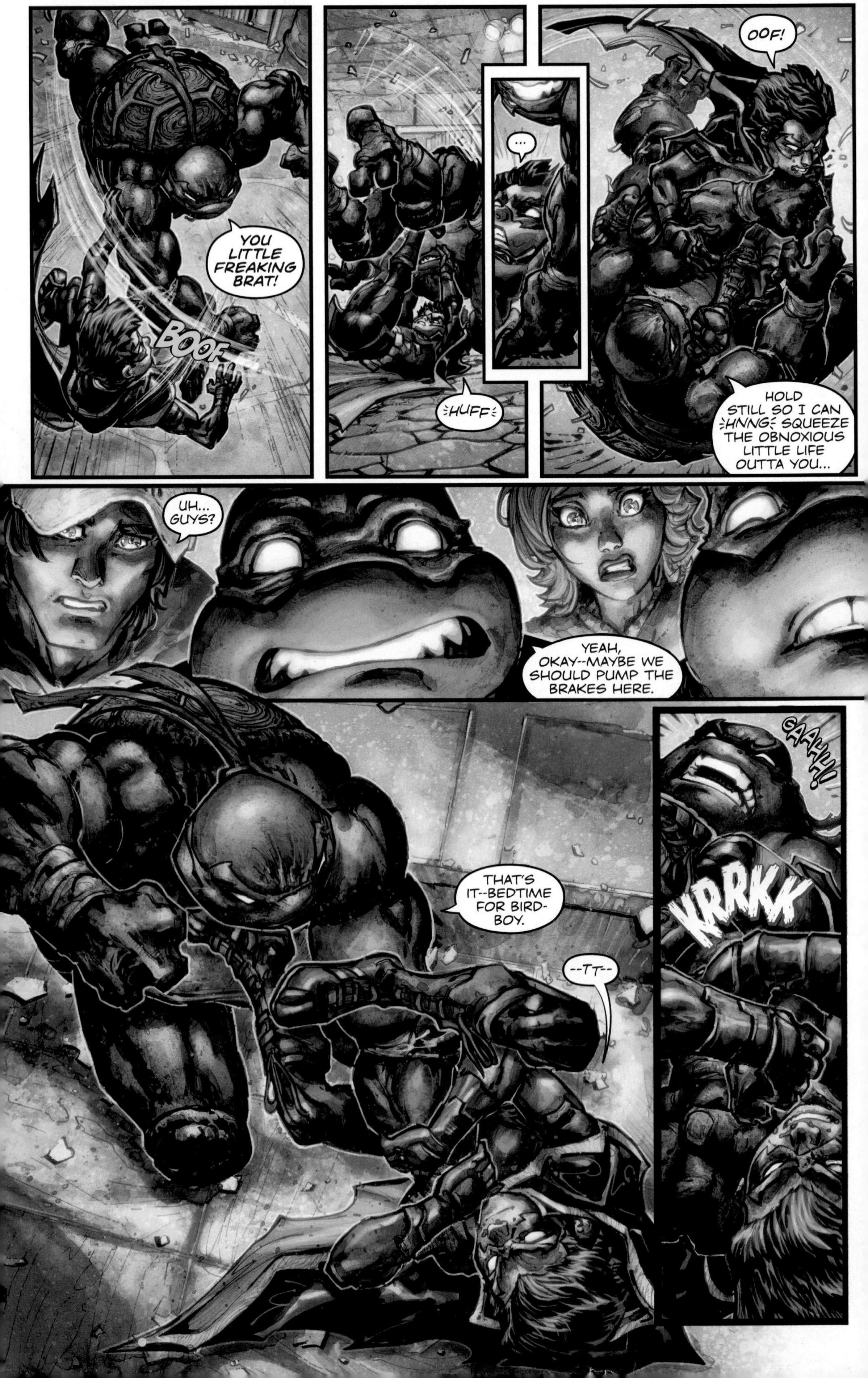
YOU LITTLE FREAKING BRAT!
BOOF
...
HUFF
OOF!
HOLD STILL SO I CAN HNNG SQUEEZE THE OBNOXIOUS LITTLE LIFE OUTTA YOU...
UH... GUYS?
YEAH, OKAY--MAYBE WE SHOULD PUMP THE BRAKES HERE.
THAT'S IT--BEDTIME FOR BIRD-BOY.
--TT--
GAAHH!
KRRKK

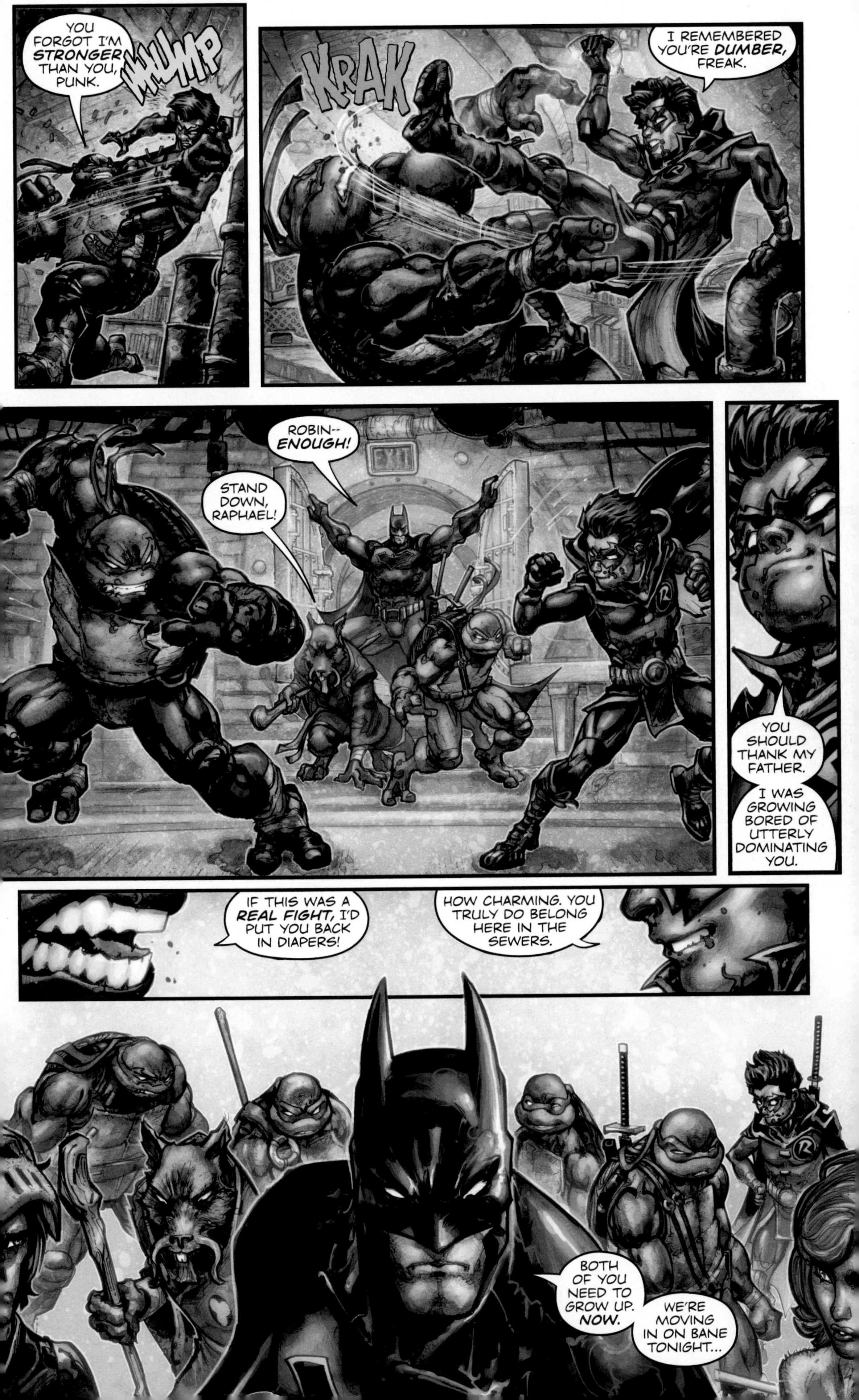
YOU FORGOT I'M STRONGER THAN YOU, PUNK.
WHUMP
KRAK
I REMEMBERED YOU'RE DUMBER, FREAK.
ROBIN-- ENOUGH!
STAND DOWN, RAPHAEL!
EXIT
YOU SHOULD THANK MY FATHER.
I WAS GROWING BORED OF UTTERLY DOMINATING YOU.
IF THIS WAS A REAL FIGHT, I'D PUT YOU BACK IN DIAPERS!
HOW CHARMING. YOU TRULY DO BELONG HERE IN THE SEWERS.
BOTH OF YOU NEED TO GROW UP. NOW.
WE'RE MOVING IN ON BANE TONIGHT...

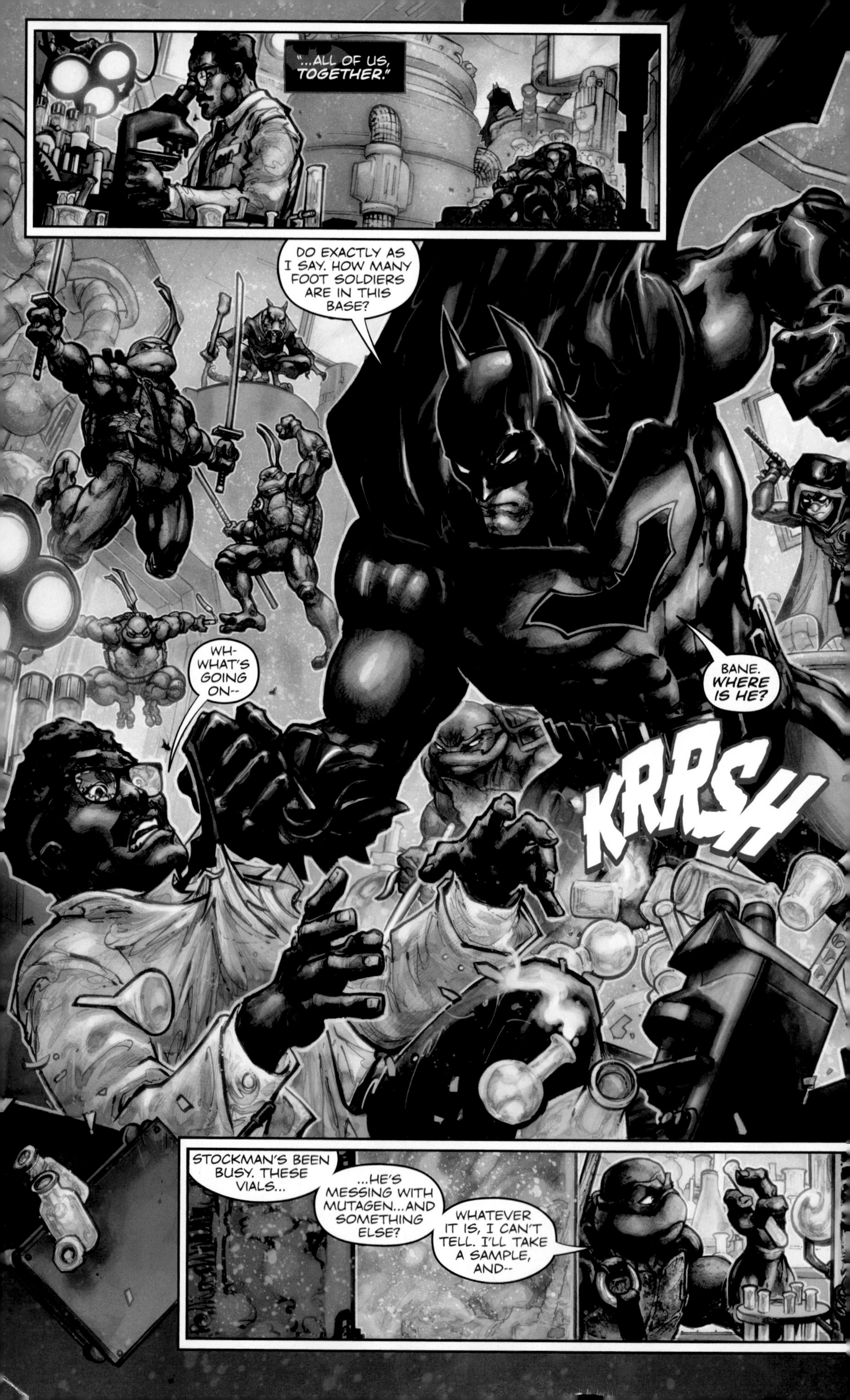
"...ALL OF US, TOGETHER."
DO EXACTLY AS I SAY. HOW MANY FOOT SOLDIERS ARE IN THIS BASE?
WH-WHAT'S GOING ON--
BANE. WHERE IS HE?
KRRSH
STOCKMAN'S BEEN BUSY. THESE VIALS...
...HE'S MESSING WITH MUTAGEN...AND SOMETHING ELSE?
WHATEVER IT IS, I CAN'T TELL. I'LL TAKE A SAMPLE, AND--

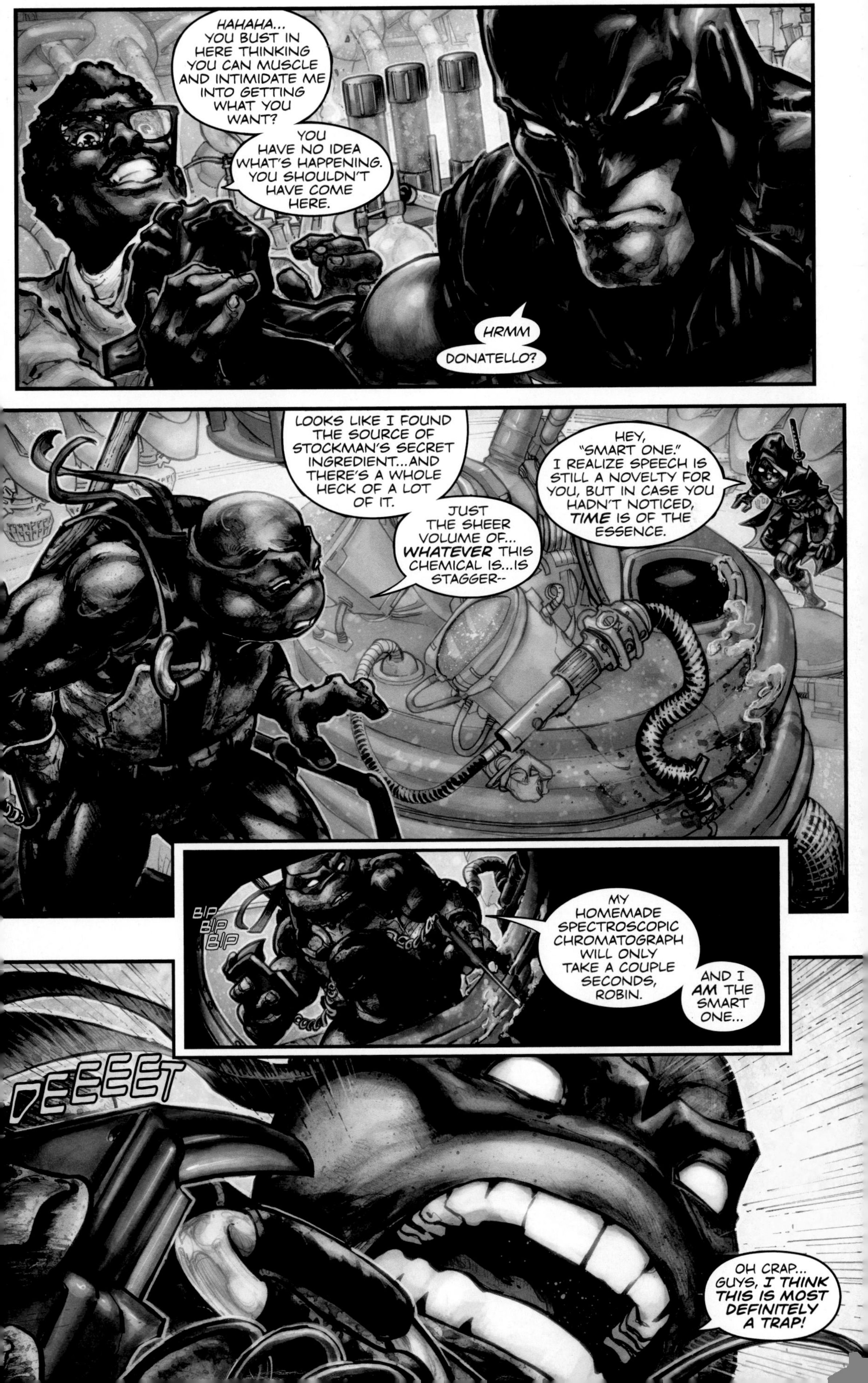

HAHAHA... YOU BUST IN HERE THINKING YOU CAN MUSCLE AND INTIMIDATE ME INTO GETTING WHAT YOU WANT?
YOU HAVE NO IDEA WHAT'S HAPPENING. YOU SHOULDN'T HAVE COME HERE.
HRMM
DONATELLO?
LOOKS LIKE I FOUND THE SOURCE OF STOCKMAN'S SECRET INGREDIENT...AND THERE'S A WHOLE HECK OF A LOT OF IT.
JUST THE SHEER VOLUME OF... WHATEVER THIS CHEMICAL IS...IS STAGGER--
HEY, "SMART ONE." I REALIZE SPEECH IS STILL A NOVELTY FOR YOU, BUT IN CASE YOU HADN'T NOTICED, TIME IS OF THE ESSENCE.
BIP BIP BIP
MY HOMEMADE SPECTROSCOPIC CHROMATOGRAPH WILL ONLY TAKE A COUPLE SECONDS, ROBIN.
AND I AM THE SMART ONE...
DEEEEET
OH CRAP... GUYS, I THINK THIS IS MOST DEFINITELY A TRAP!

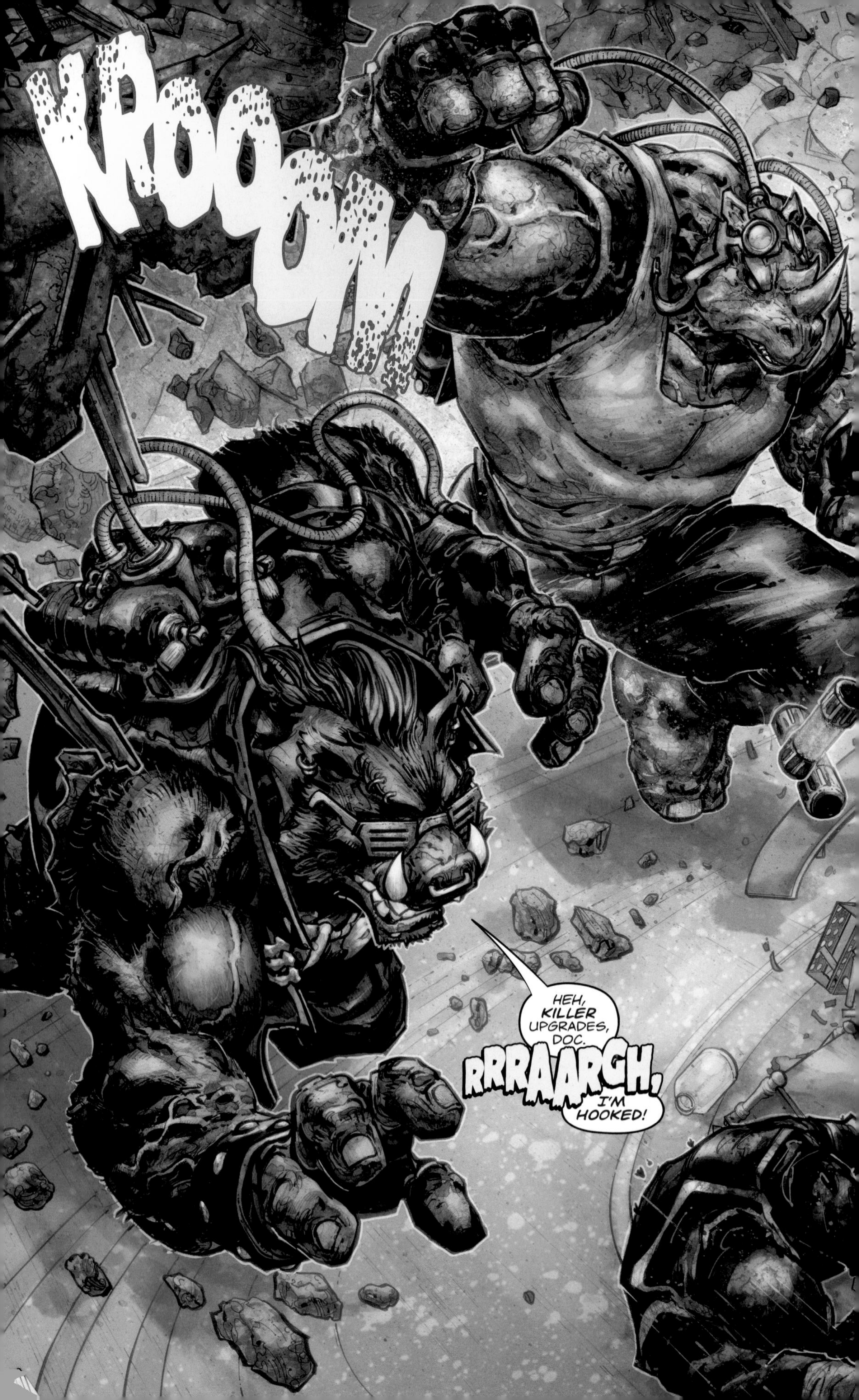
KROOOM
HEH, KILLER UPGRADES, DOC.
RRRAARGH, I'M HOOKED!

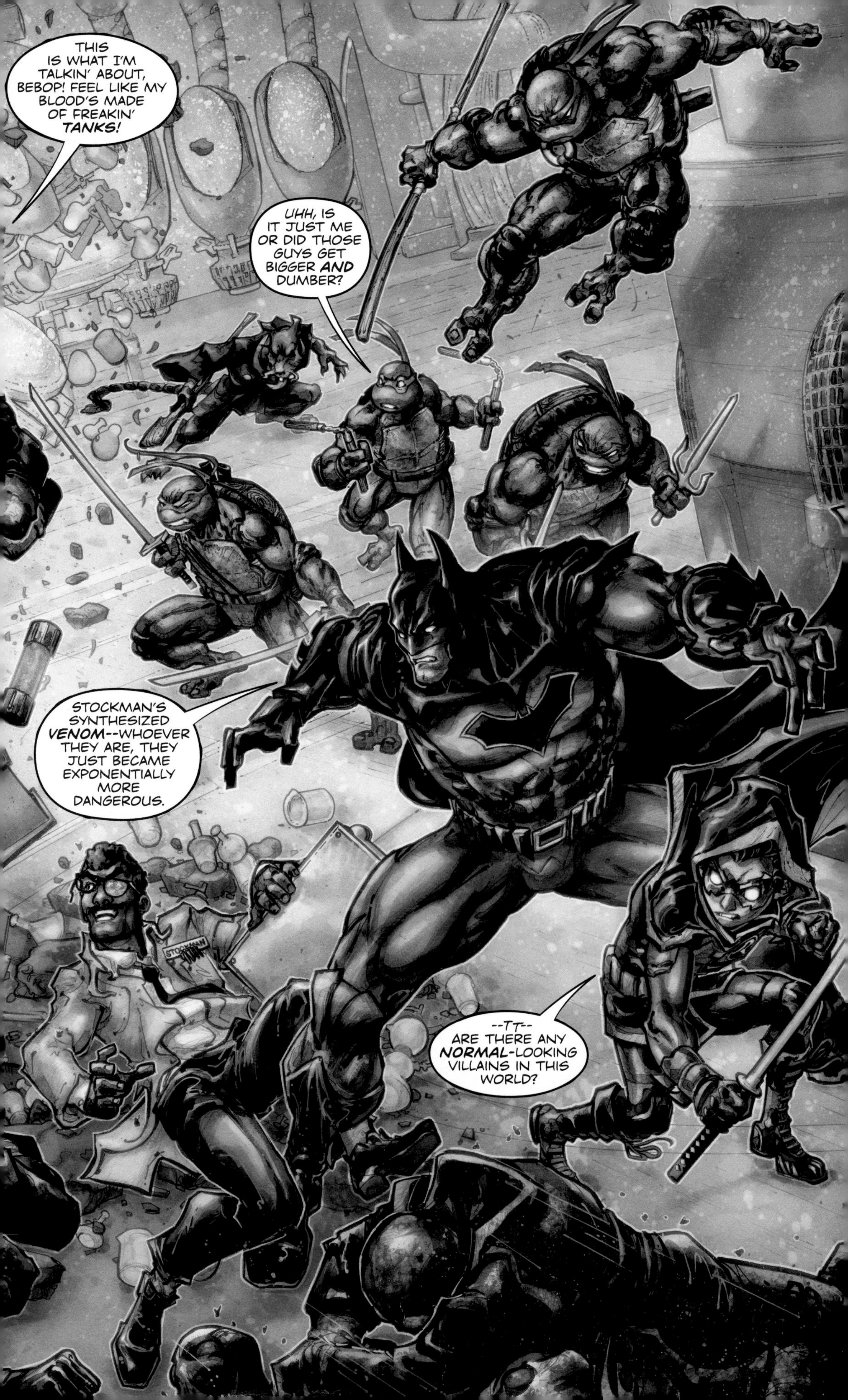
THIS IS WHAT I'M TALKIN' ABOUT, BEBOP! FEEL LIKE MY BLOOD'S MADE OF FREAKIN' **TANKS!**
UHH, IS IT JUST ME OR DID THOSE GUYS GET BIGGER **AND** DUMBER?
STOCKMAN'S SYNTHESIZED **VENOM**--WHOEVER THEY ARE, THEY JUST BECAME EXPONENTIALLY MORE DANGEROUS.
--TT-- ARE THERE ANY **NORMAL**-LOOKING VILLAINS IN THIS WORLD?

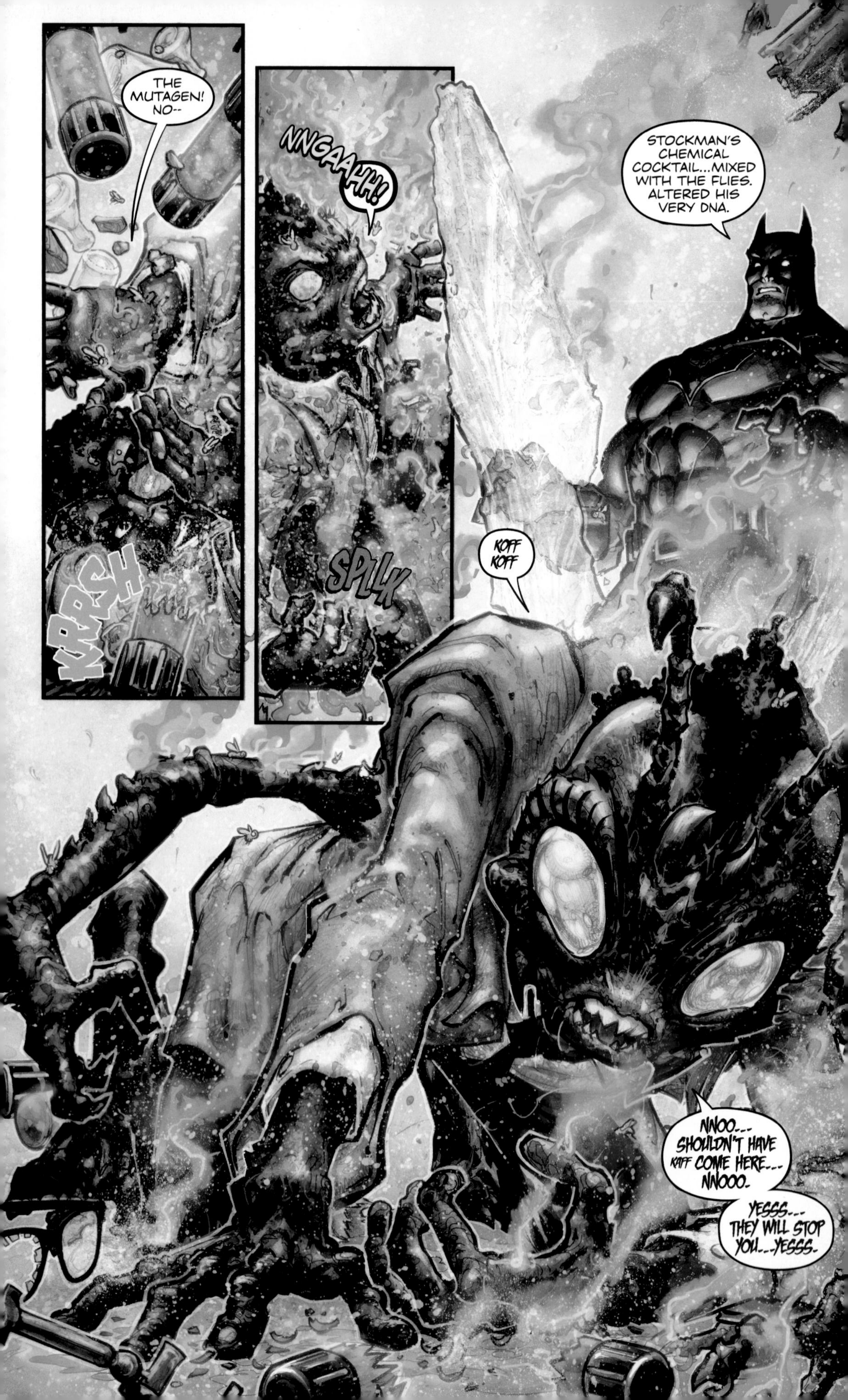
THE MUTAGEN! NO--
NNGAAHH!
KRRSH
SPLLK
STOCKMAN'S CHEMICAL COCKTAIL...MIXED WITH THE FLIES. ALTERED HIS VERY DNA.
KOFF KOFF
NNOO... SHOULDN'T HAVE KAFF COME HERE... NNOOO.
YESSS... THEY WILL STOP YOU...YESSS.

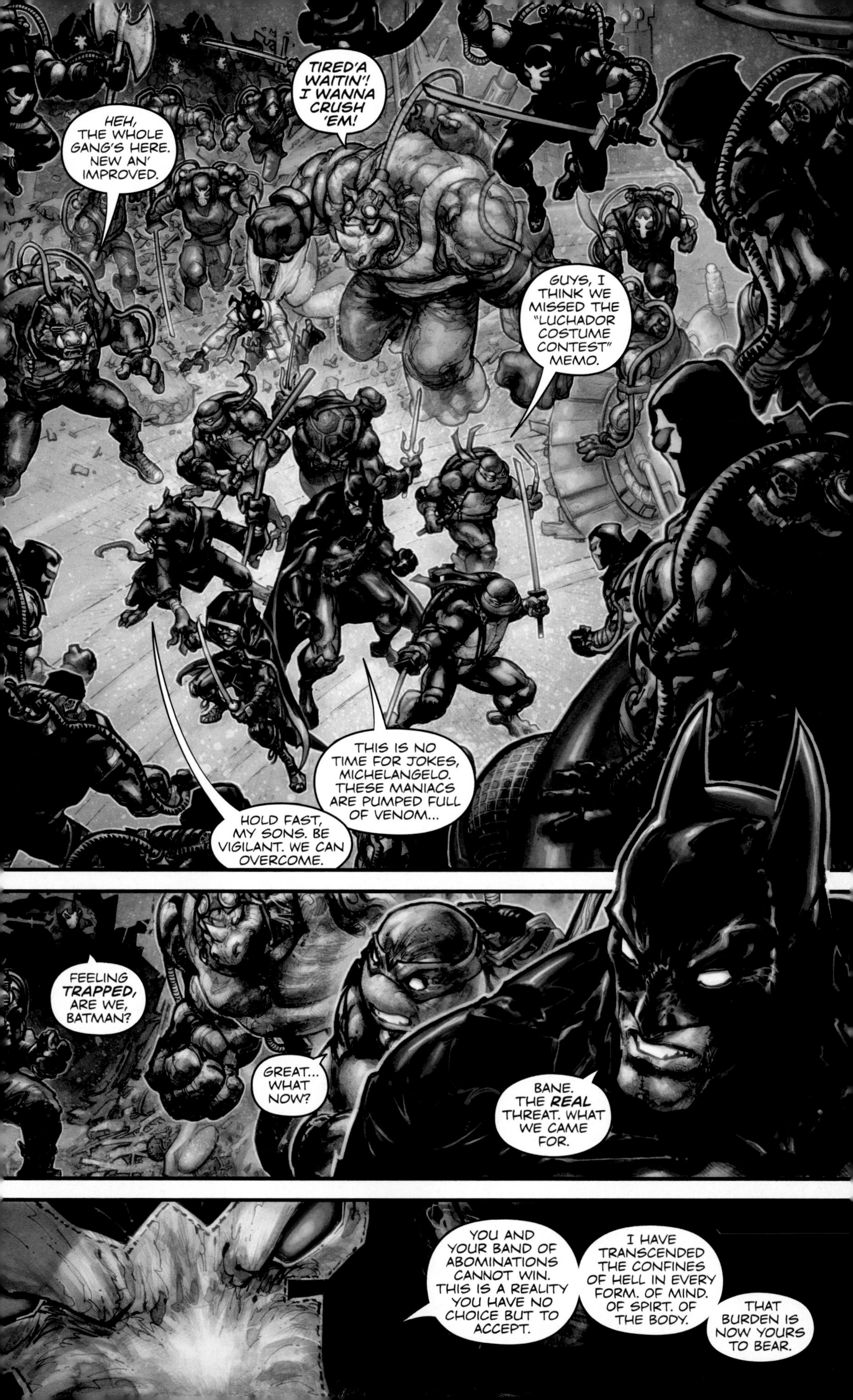
HEH, THE WHOLE GANG'S HERE. NEW AN' IMPROVED.
TIRED'A WAITIN'! I WANNA CRUSH 'EM!
GUYS, I THINK WE MISSED THE "LUCHADOR COSTUME CONTEST" MEMO.
THIS IS NO TIME FOR JOKES, MICHELANGELO. THESE MANIACS ARE PUMPED FULL OF VENOM...
HOLD FAST, MY SONS. BE VIGILANT. WE CAN OVERCOME.
FEELING TRAPPED, ARE WE, BATMAN?
GREAT... WHAT NOW?
BANE. THE REAL THREAT. WHAT WE CAME FOR.
YOU AND YOUR BAND OF ABOMINATIONS CANNOT WIN. THIS IS A REALITY YOU HAVE NO CHOICE BUT TO ACCEPT.
I HAVE TRANSCENDED THE CONFINES OF HELL IN EVERY FORM. OF MIND. OF SPIRT. OF THE BODY.
THAT BURDEN IS NOW YOURS TO BEAR.

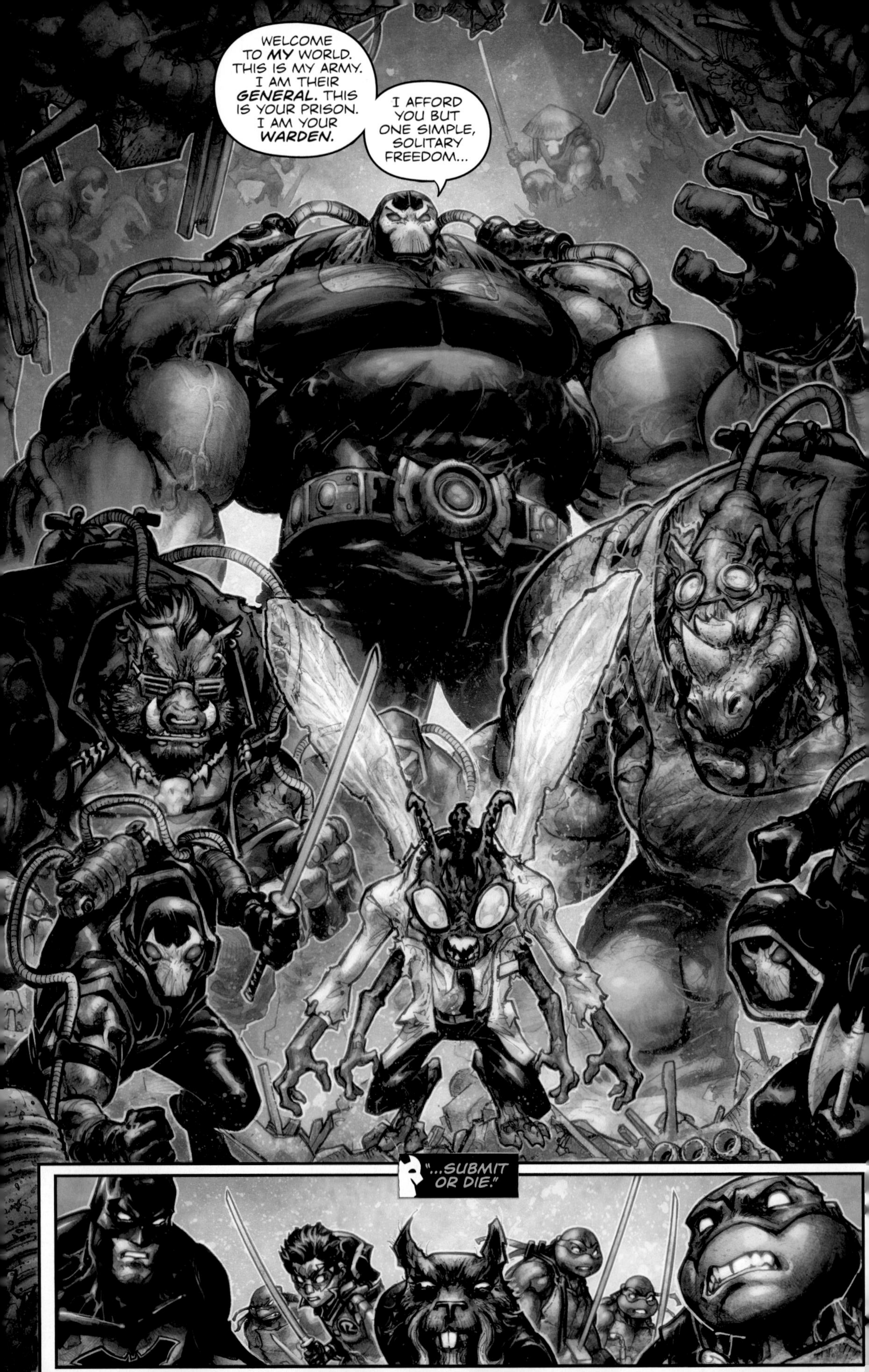
WELCOME TO MY WORLD. THIS IS MY ARMY. I AM THEIR GENERAL. THIS IS YOUR PRISON. I AM YOUR WARDEN.
I AFFORD YOU BUT ONE SIMPLE, SOLITARY FREEDOM...
"...SUBMIT OR DIE."

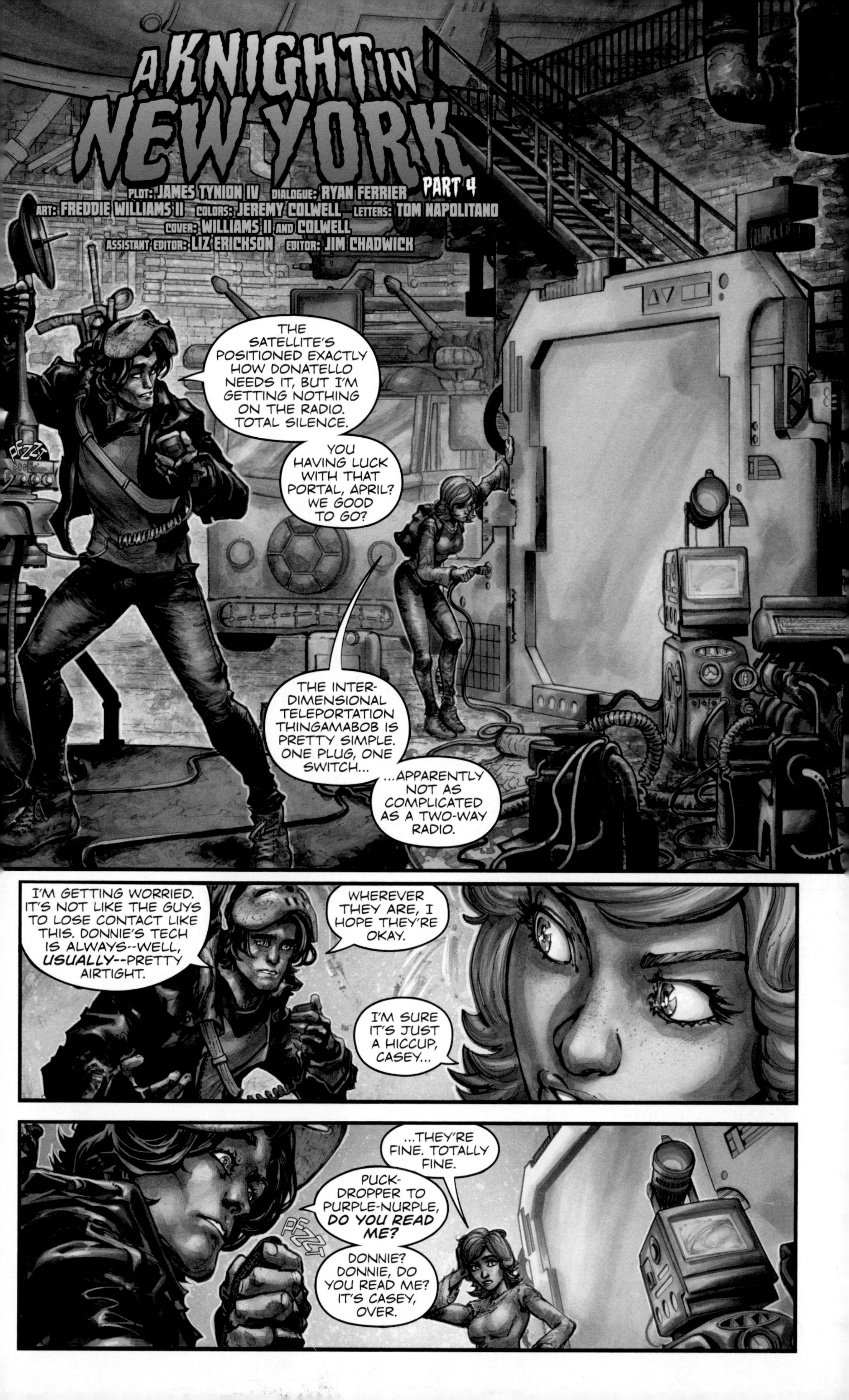
A KNIGHT IN NEW YORK
PART 4
PLOT: JAMES TYNION IV DIALOGUE: RYAN FERRIER
ART: FREDDIE WILLIAMS II COLORS: JEREMY COLWELL LETTERS: TOM NAPOLITANO
COVER: WILLIAMS II AND COLWELL
ASSISTANT EDITOR: LIZ ERICKSON EDITOR: JIM CHADWICK
THE SATELLITE'S POSITIONED EXACTLY HOW DONATELLO NEEDS IT, BUT I'M GETTING NOTHING ON THE RADIO. TOTAL SILENCE.
YOU HAVING LUCK WITH THAT PORTAL, APRIL? WE GOOD TO GO?
PFZZT
THE INTER-DIMENSIONAL TELEPORTATION THINGAMABOB IS PRETTY SIMPLE. ONE PLUG, ONE SWITCH...
...APPARENTLY NOT AS COMPLICATED AS A TWO-WAY RADIO.
I'M GETTING WORRIED. IT'S NOT LIKE THE GUYS TO LOSE CONTACT LIKE THIS. DONNIE'S TECH IS ALWAYS--WELL, USUALLY--PRETTY AIRTIGHT.
WHEREVER THEY ARE, I HOPE THEY'RE OKAY.
I'M SURE IT'S JUST A HICCUP, CASEY...
...THEY'RE FINE. TOTALLY FINE.
PUCK-DROPPER TO PURPLE-NURPLE, DO YOU READ ME?
PFZZT
DONNIE? DONNIE, DO YOU READ ME? IT'S CASEY, OVER.

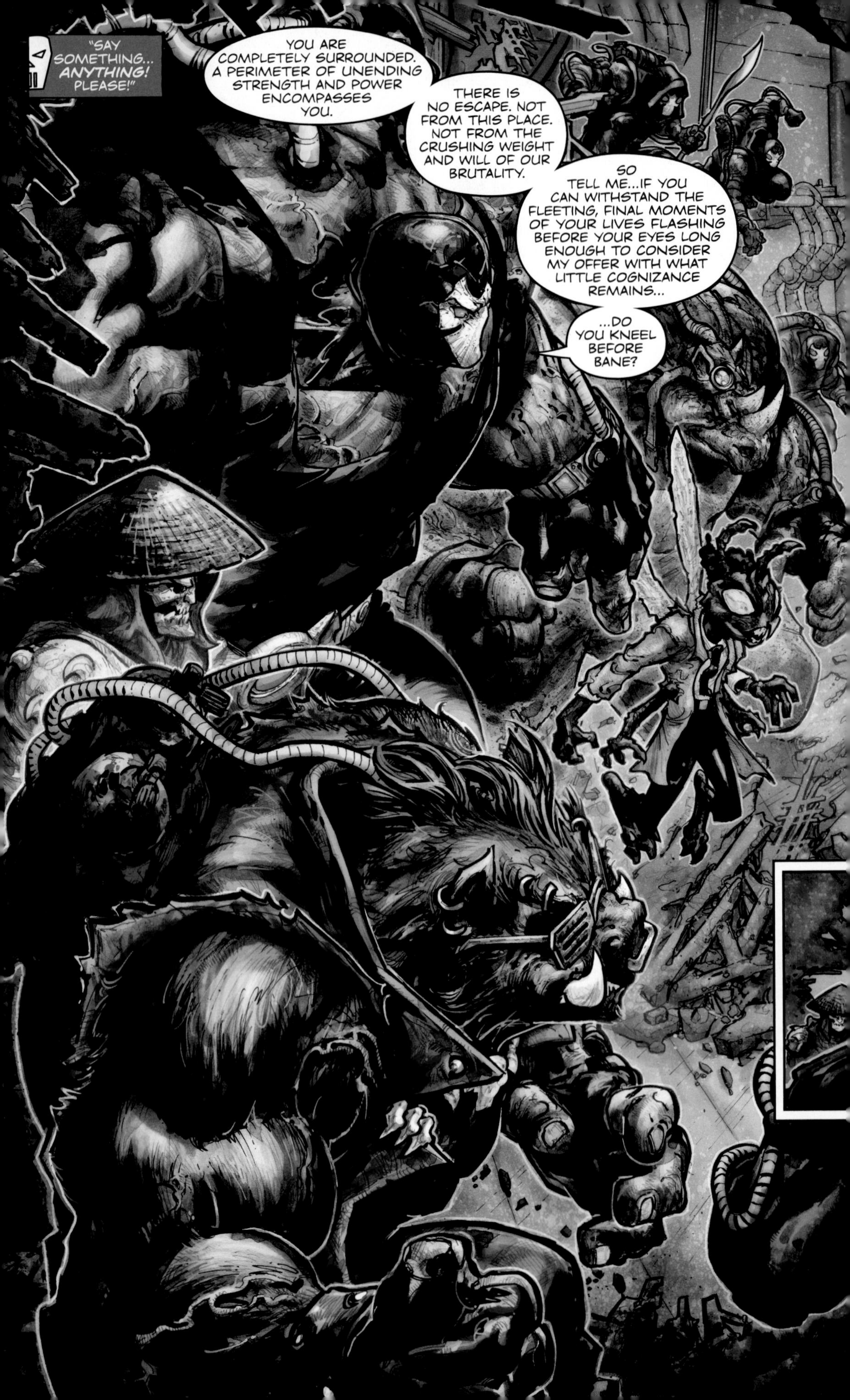
"SAY SOMETHING... ANYTHING! PLEASE!"
YOU ARE COMPLETELY SURROUNDED. A PERIMETER OF UNENDING STRENGTH AND POWER ENCOMPASSES YOU.
THERE IS NO ESCAPE. NOT FROM THIS PLACE. NOT FROM THE CRUSHING WEIGHT AND WILL OF OUR BRUTALITY.
SO TELL ME...IF YOU CAN WITHSTAND THE FLEETING, FINAL MOMENTS OF YOUR LIVES FLASHING BEFORE YOUR EYES LONG ENOUGH TO CONSIDER MY OFFER WITH WHAT LITTLE COGNIZANCE REMAINS...
...DO YOU KNEEL BEFORE BANE?

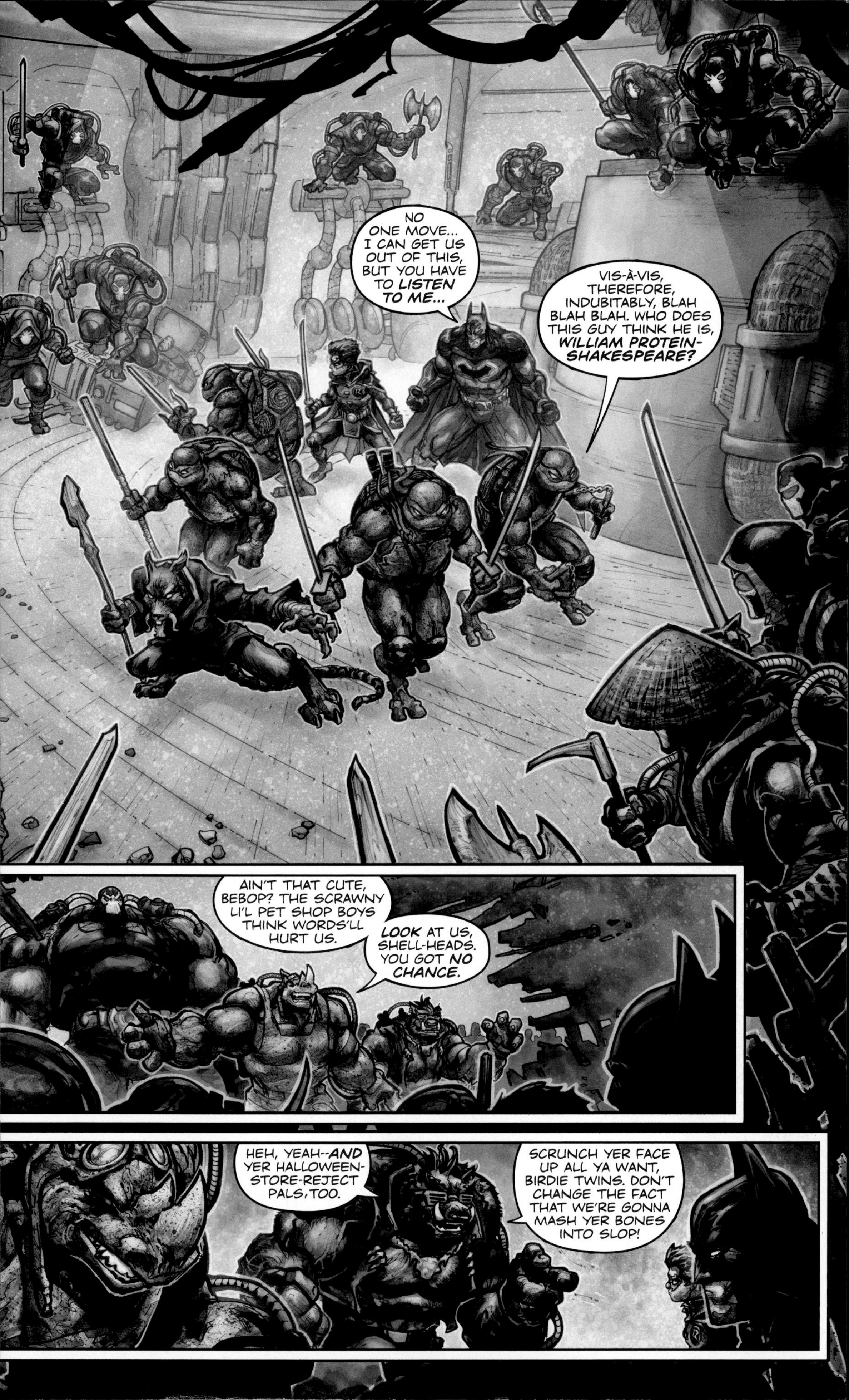
NO ONE MOVE... I CAN GET US OUT OF THIS, BUT YOU HAVE TO **LISTEN TO ME...**
VIS-À-VIS, THEREFORE, INDUBITABLY, BLAH BLAH BLAH. WHO DOES THIS GUY THINK HE IS, **WILLIAM PROTEIN-SHAKESPEARE?**
AIN'T THAT CUTE, BEBOP? THE SCRAWNY LI'L PET SHOP BOYS THINK WORDS'LL HURT US.
LOOK AT US, SHELL-HEADS. YOU GOT **NO CHANCE.**
HEH, YEAH--**AND** YER HALLOWEEN-STORE-REJECT PALS, TOO.
SCRUNCH YER FACE UP ALL YA WANT, BIRDIE TWINS. DON'T CHANGE THE FACT THAT WE'RE GONNA MASH YER BONES INTO SLOP!

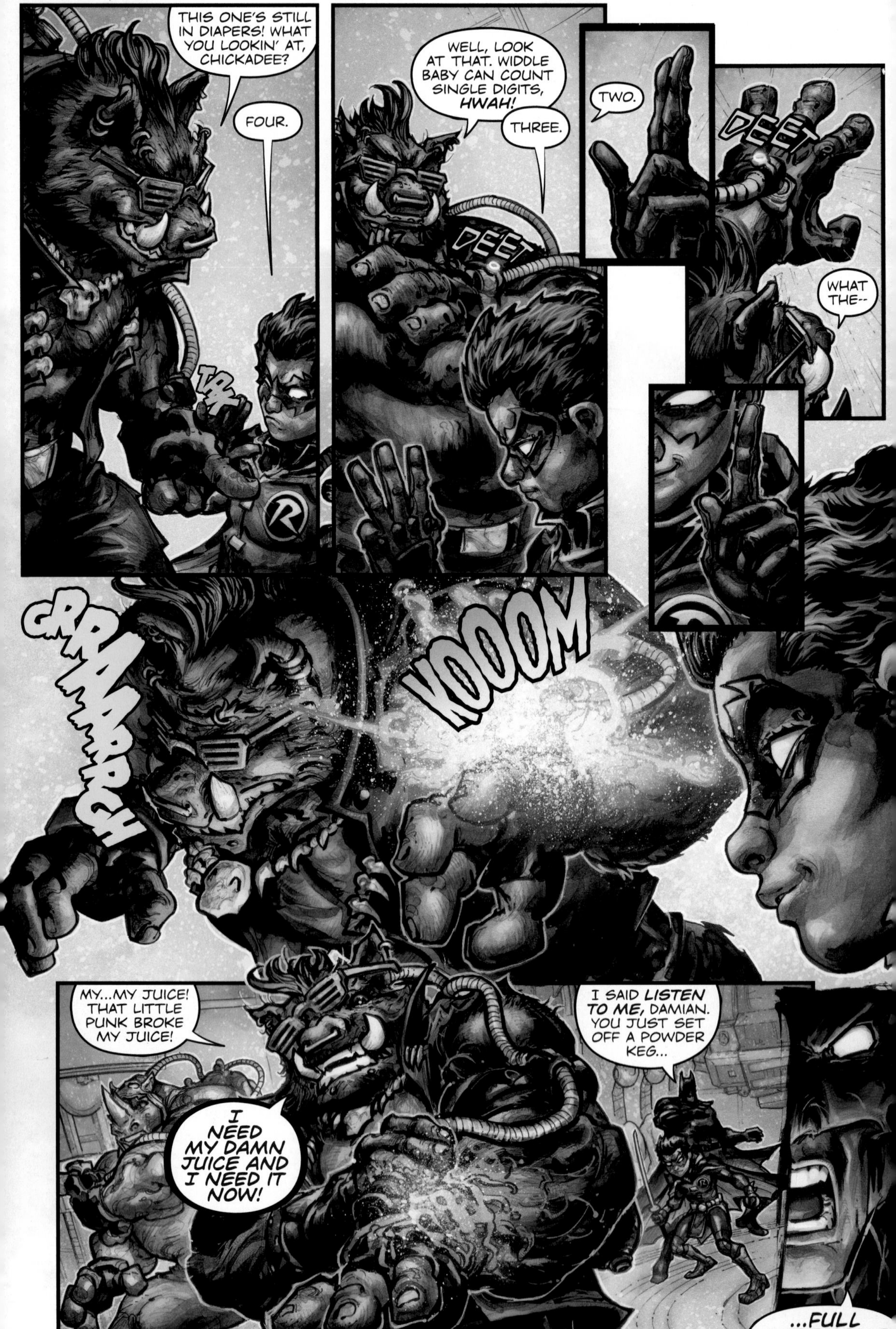

THIS ONE'S STILL IN DIAPERS! WHAT YOU LOOKIN' AT, CHICKADEE?
FOUR.
WELL, LOOK AT THAT. WIDDLE BABY CAN COUNT SINGLE DIGITS, HWAH!
THREE.
DEET
TWO.
DEET
WHAT THE--
GRRAAARRGH
VOOOM
MY...MY JUICE! THAT LITTLE PUNK BROKE MY JUICE!
I NEED MY DAMN JUICE AND I NEED IT NOW!
I SAID LISTEN TO ME, DAMIAN. YOU JUST SET OFF A POWDER KEG...
...FULL OFFENSIVE MANEUVERS NOW!

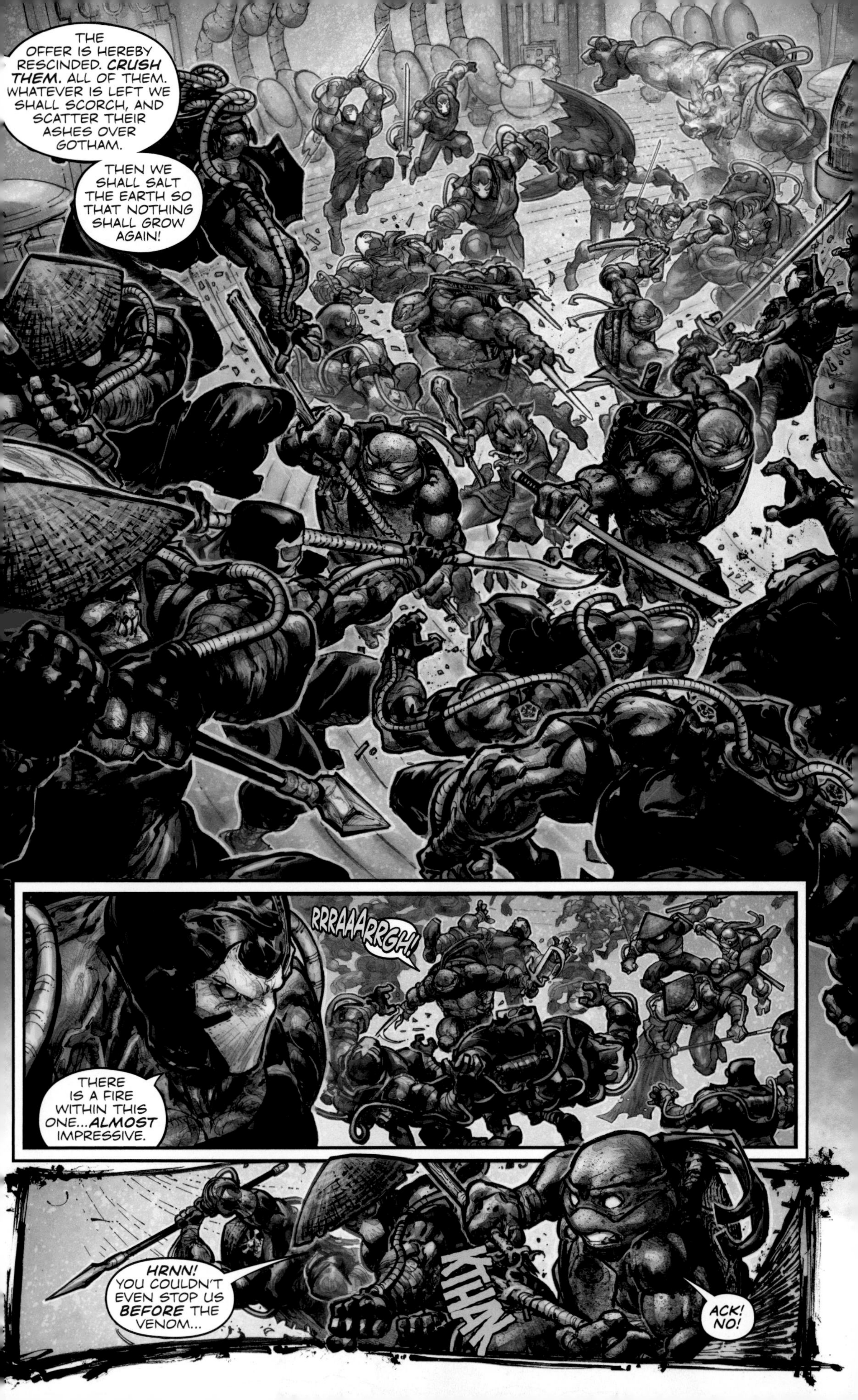
THE OFFER IS HEREBY RESCINDED. CRUSH THEM. ALL OF THEM. WHATEVER IS LEFT WE SHALL SCORCH, AND SCATTER THEIR ASHES OVER GOTHAM.
THEN WE SHALL SALT THE EARTH SO THAT NOTHING SHALL GROW AGAIN!
RRRAAARRGH!
THERE IS A FIRE WITHIN THIS ONE...ALMOST IMPRESSIVE.
HRNN! YOU COULDN'T EVEN STOP US BEFORE THE VENOM...
KTHAK
ACK! NO!

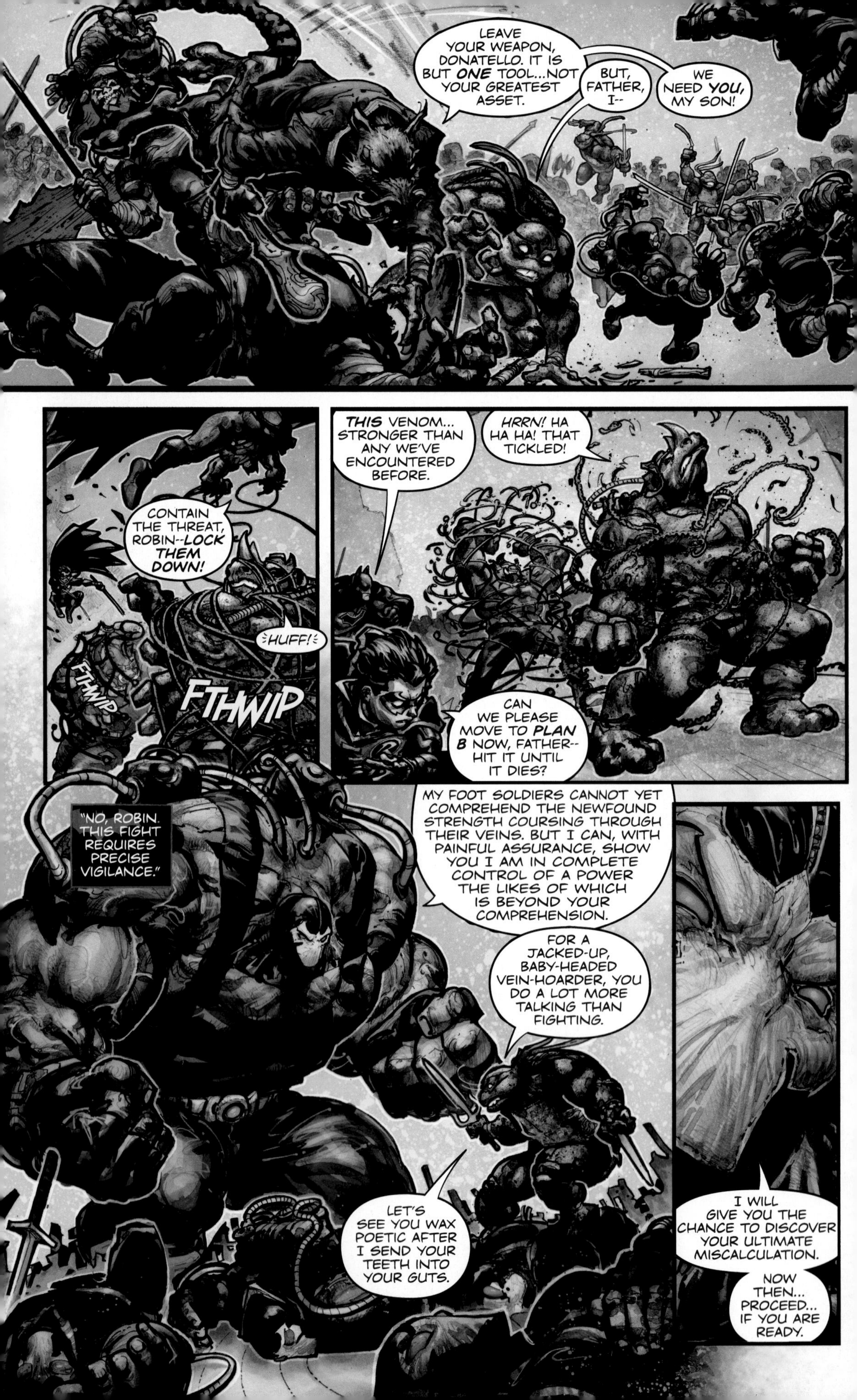
LEAVE YOUR WEAPON, DONATELLO. IT IS BUT ONE TOOL...NOT YOUR GREATEST ASSET.
BUT, FATHER, I--
WE NEED YOU, MY SON!
CONTAIN THE THREAT, ROBIN--LOCK THEM DOWN!
HUFF!
FTHWIP
FTHWIP
THIS VENOM... STRONGER THAN ANY WE'VE ENCOUNTERED BEFORE.
HRRN! HA HA HA! THAT TICKLED!
CAN WE PLEASE MOVE TO PLAN B NOW, FATHER-- HIT IT UNTIL IT DIES?
"NO, ROBIN. THIS FIGHT REQUIRES PRECISE VIGILANCE."
MY FOOT SOLDIERS CANNOT YET COMPREHEND THE NEWFOUND STRENGTH COURSING THROUGH THEIR VEINS. BUT I CAN, WITH PAINFUL ASSURANCE, SHOW YOU I AM IN COMPLETE CONTROL OF A POWER THE LIKES OF WHICH IS BEYOND YOUR COMPREHENSION.
FOR A JACKED-UP, BABY-HEADED VEIN-HOARDER, YOU DO A LOT MORE TALKING THAN FIGHTING.
LET'S SEE YOU WAX POETIC AFTER I SEND YOUR TEETH INTO YOUR GUTS.
I WILL GIVE YOU THE CHANCE TO DISCOVER YOUR ULTIMATE MISCALCULATION.
NOW THEN... PROCEED... IF YOU ARE READY.

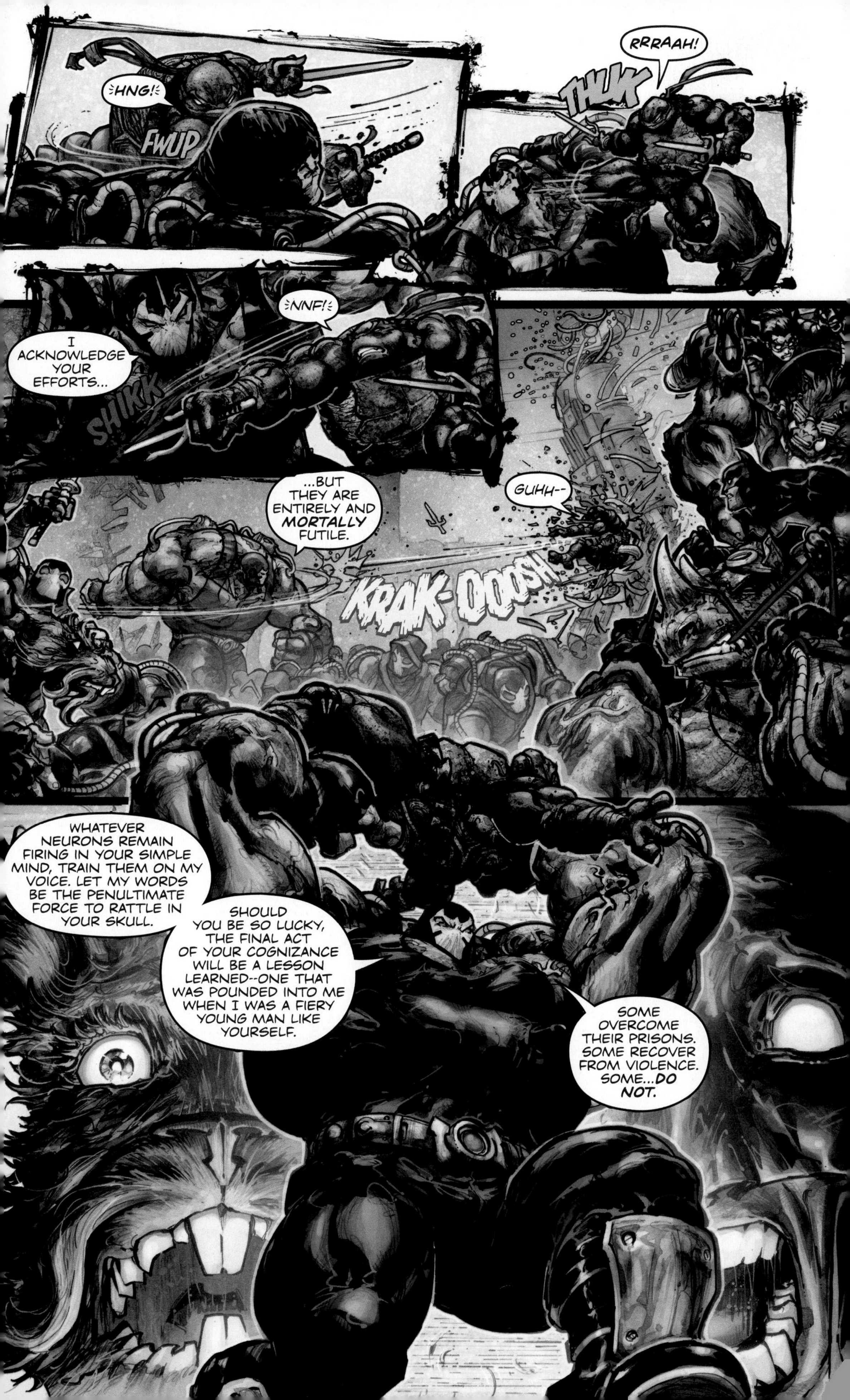
HNG!
FWUP
THUK
RRRAAH!
NNF!
I ACKNOWLEDGE YOUR EFFORTS...
SHIKK
...BUT THEY ARE ENTIRELY AND MORTALLY FUTILE.
GUHH--
KRAK-OOOSH
WHATEVER NEURONS REMAIN FIRING IN YOUR SIMPLE MIND, TRAIN THEM ON MY VOICE. LET MY WORDS BE THE PENULTIMATE FORCE TO RATTLE IN YOUR SKULL.
SHOULD YOU BE SO LUCKY, THE FINAL ACT OF YOUR COGNIZANCE WILL BE A LESSON LEARNED--ONE THAT WAS POUNDED INTO ME WHEN I WAS A FIERY YOUNG MAN LIKE YOURSELF.
SOME OVERCOME THEIR PRISONS. SOME RECOVER FROM VIOLENCE. SOME...DO NOT.

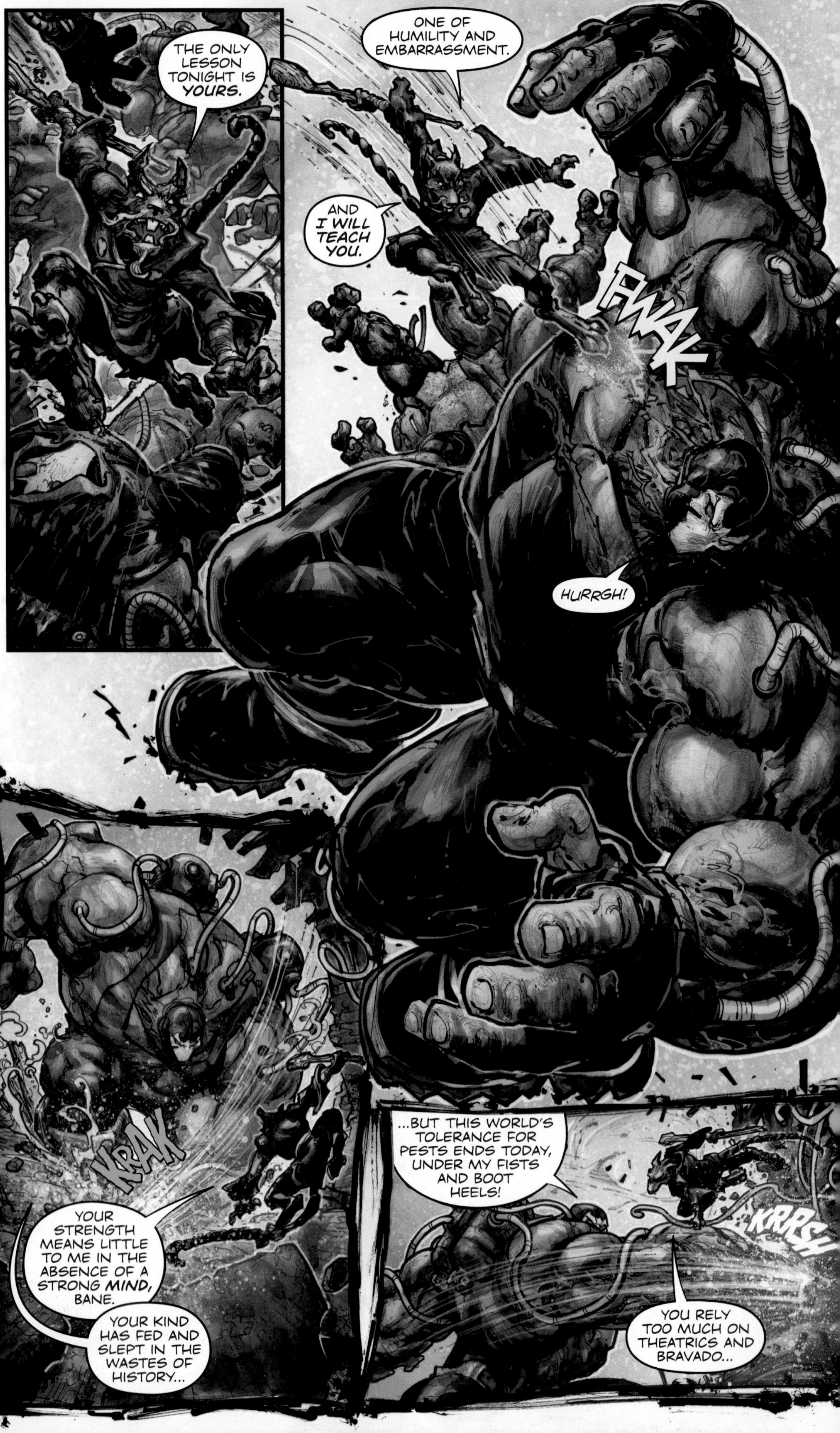
THE ONLY LESSON TONIGHT IS YOURS.
ONE OF HUMILITY AND EMBARRASSMENT.
AND I WILL TEACH YOU.
FWAK
HURRGH!
KRAK
YOUR STRENGTH MEANS LITTLE TO ME IN THE ABSENCE OF A STRONG MIND, BANE.
YOUR KIND HAS FED AND SLEPT IN THE WASTES OF HISTORY...
...BUT THIS WORLD'S TOLERANCE FOR PESTS ENDS TODAY, UNDER MY FISTS AND BOOT HEELS!
KRRSH
YOU RELY TOO MUCH ON THEATRICS AND BRAVADO...

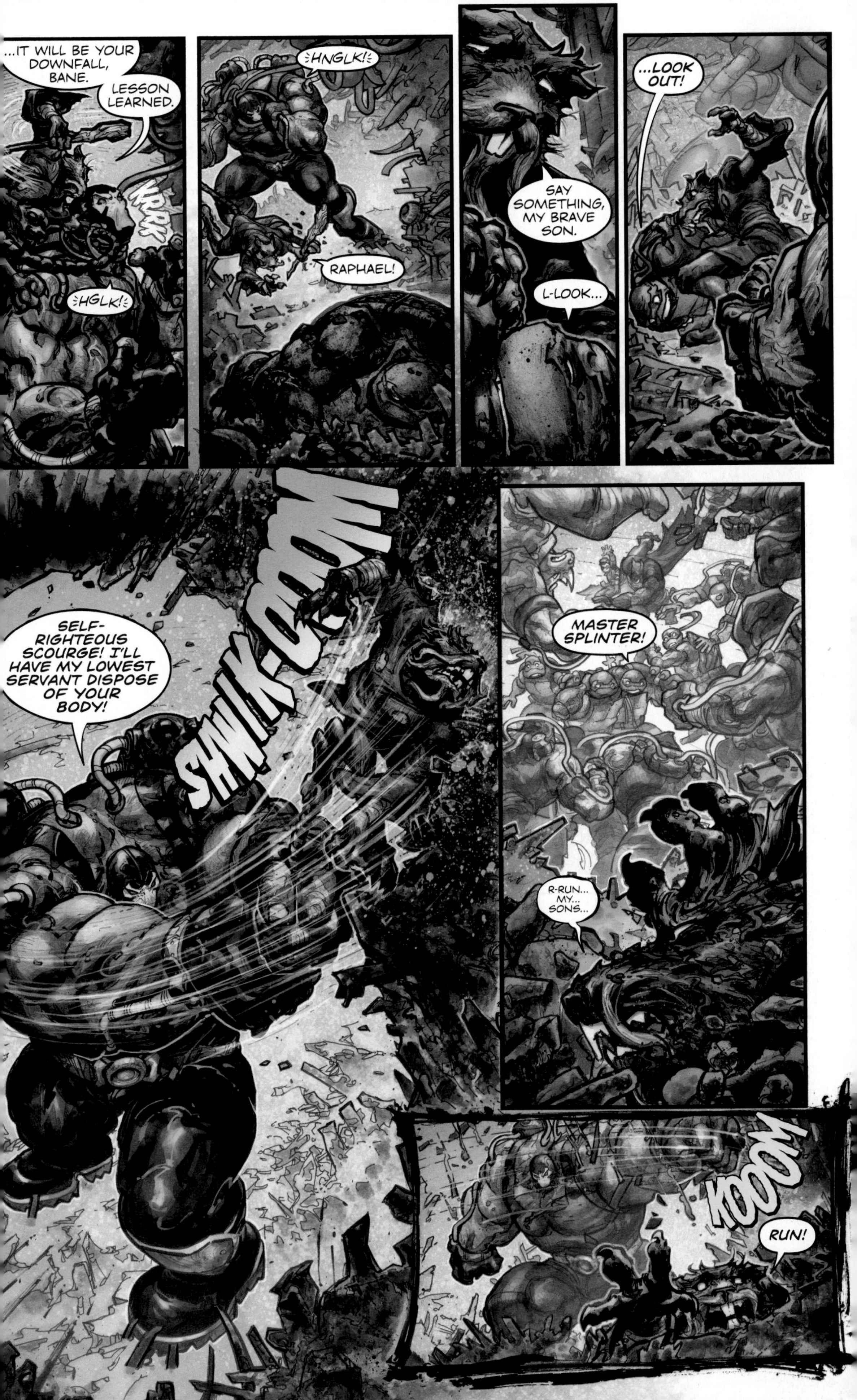

...IT WILL BE YOUR DOWNFALL, BANE.
LESSON LEARNED.
KRRK
HGLK!
HNGLK!
RAPHAEL!
SAY SOMETHING, MY BRAVE SON.
L-LOOK...
...LOOK OUT!
SELF-RIGHTEOUS SCOURGE! I'LL HAVE MY LOWEST SERVANT DISPOSE OF YOUR BODY!
SHWK-OOOM
MASTER SPLINTER!
R-RUN... MY... SONS...
KOOOM
RUN!

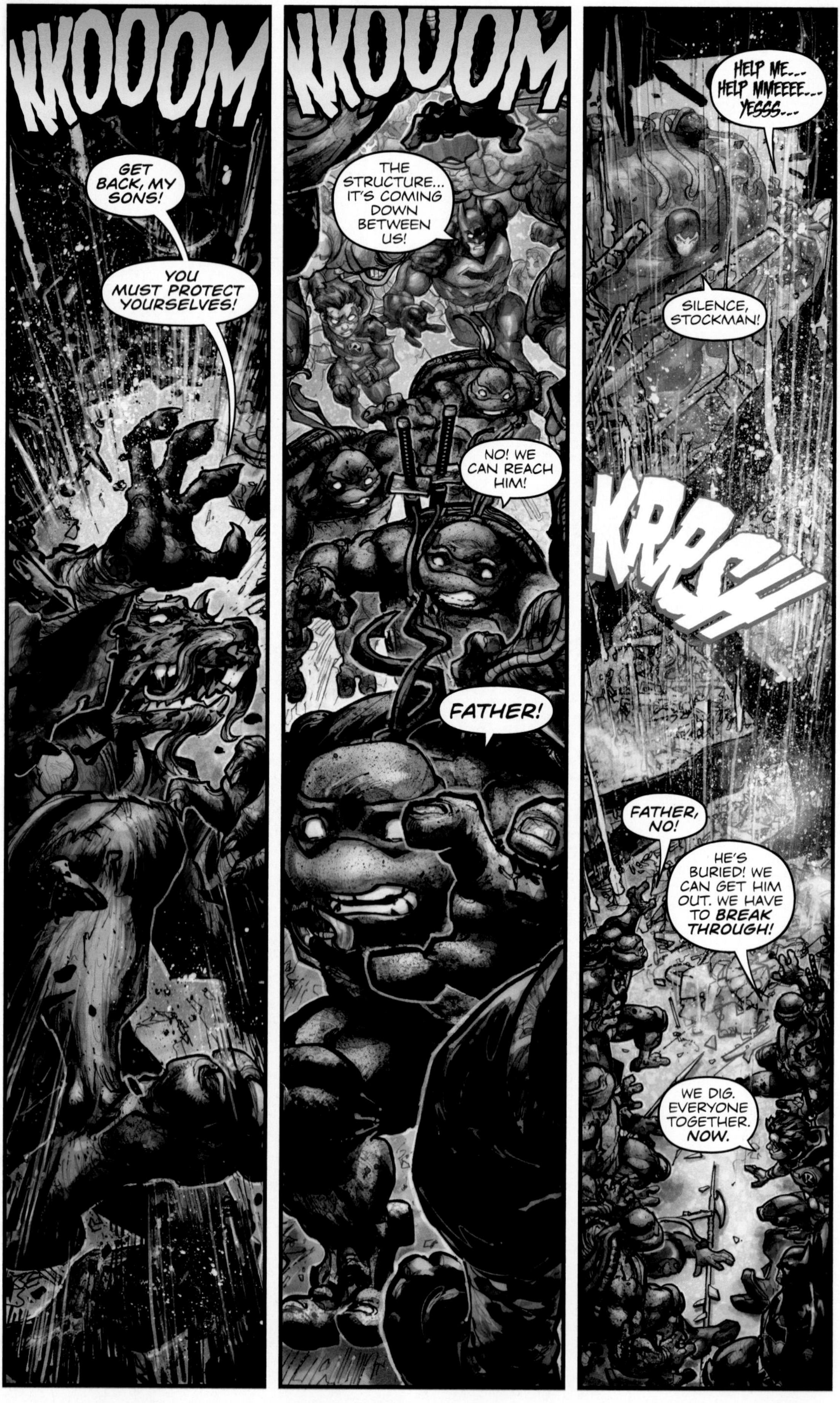
KKOOOM
GET BACK, MY SONS!
YOU MUST PROTECT YOURSELVES!
KKOOOM
THE STRUCTURE... IT'S COMING DOWN BETWEEN US!
NO! WE CAN REACH HIM!
FATHER!
HELP ME... HELP MMEEEE... YESSS...
SILENCE, STOCKMAN!
KRRSH
FATHER, NO!
HE'S BURIED! WE CAN GET HIM OUT. WE HAVE TO BREAK THROUGH!
WE DIG. EVERYONE TOGETHER. NOW.

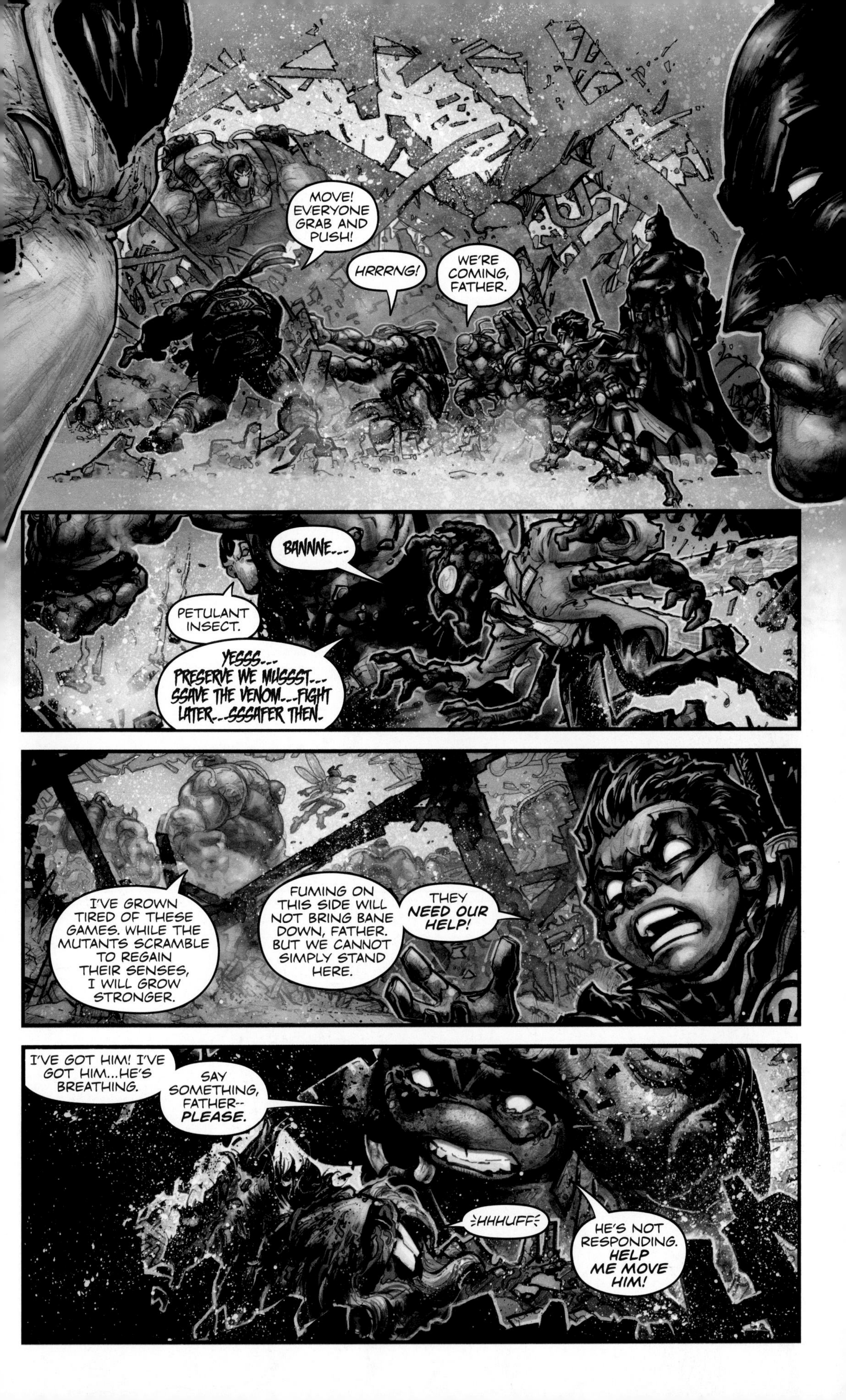

MOVE! EVERYONE GRAB AND PUSH!
HRRRNG!
WE'RE COMING, FATHER.
BANNNE...
PETULANT INSECT.
YESSS... PRESERVE WE MUSSST... SSAVE THE VENOM...FIGHT LATER...SSSAFER THEN.
I'VE GROWN TIRED OF THESE GAMES. WHILE THE MUTANTS SCRAMBLE TO REGAIN THEIR SENSES, I WILL GROW STRONGER.
FUMING ON THIS SIDE WILL NOT BRING BANE DOWN, FATHER. BUT WE CANNOT SIMPLY STAND HERE.
THEY NEED OUR HELP!
I'VE GOT HIM! I'VE GOT HIM...HE'S BREATHING.
SAY SOMETHING, FATHER--PLEASE.
HHHUFF
HE'S NOT RESPONDING. HELP ME MOVE HIM!

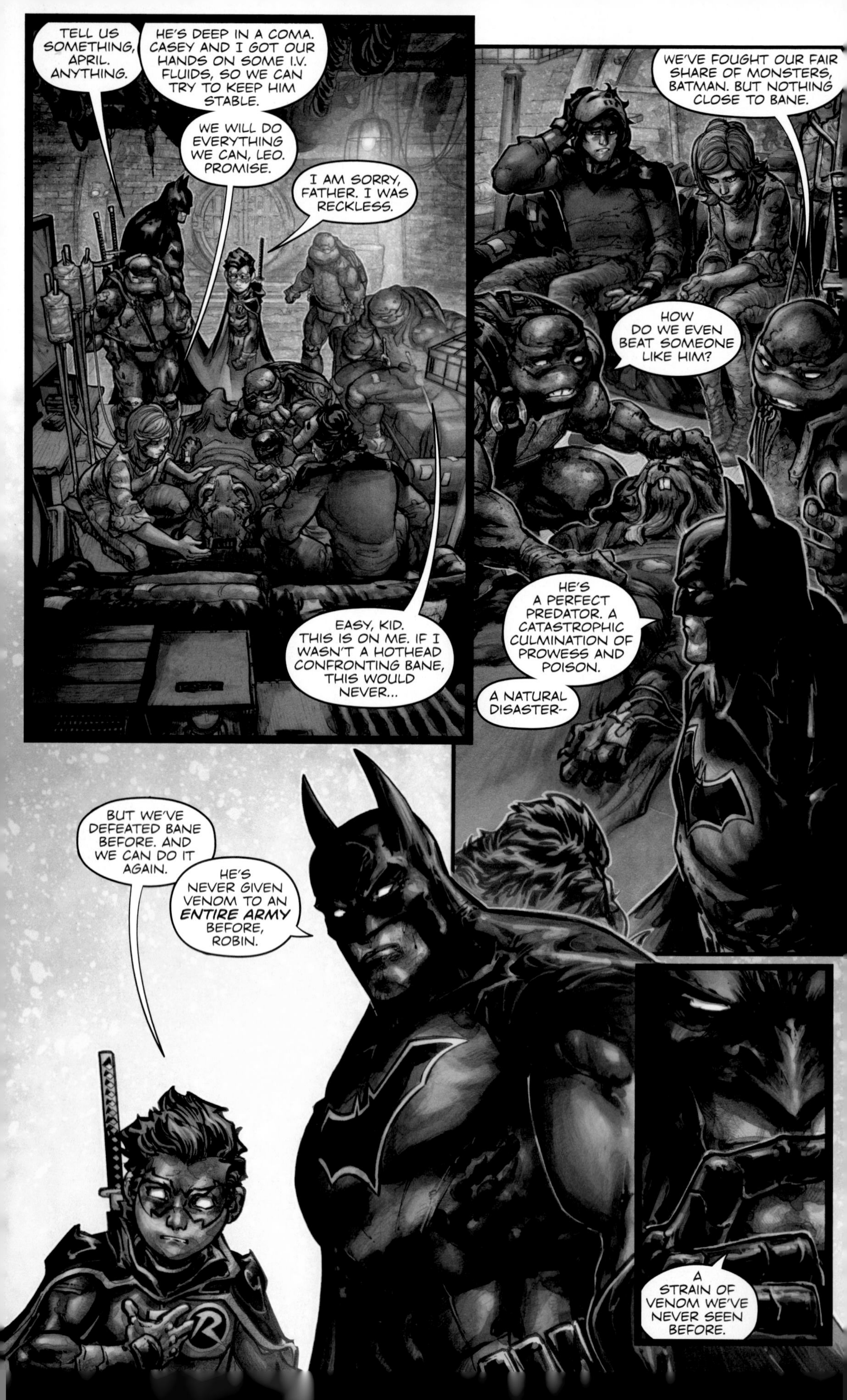
TELL US SOMETHING, APRIL. ANYTHING.
HE'S DEEP IN A COMA. CASEY AND I GOT OUR HANDS ON SOME I.V. FLUIDS, SO WE CAN TRY TO KEEP HIM STABLE.
WE WILL DO EVERYTHING WE CAN, LEO. PROMISE.
I AM SORRY, FATHER. I WAS RECKLESS.
EASY, KID. THIS IS ON ME. IF I WASN'T A HOTHEAD CONFRONTING BANE, THIS WOULD NEVER...
WE'VE FOUGHT OUR FAIR SHARE OF MONSTERS, BATMAN. BUT NOTHING CLOSE TO BANE.
HOW DO WE EVEN BEAT SOMEONE LIKE HIM?
HE'S A PERFECT PREDATOR. A CATASTROPHIC CULMINATION OF PROWESS AND POISON.
A NATURAL DISASTER--
BUT WE'VE DEFEATED BANE BEFORE. AND WE CAN DO IT AGAIN.
HE'S NEVER GIVEN VENOM TO AN ***ENTIRE ARMY*** BEFORE, ROBIN.
A STRAIN OF VENOM WE'VE NEVER SEEN BEFORE.

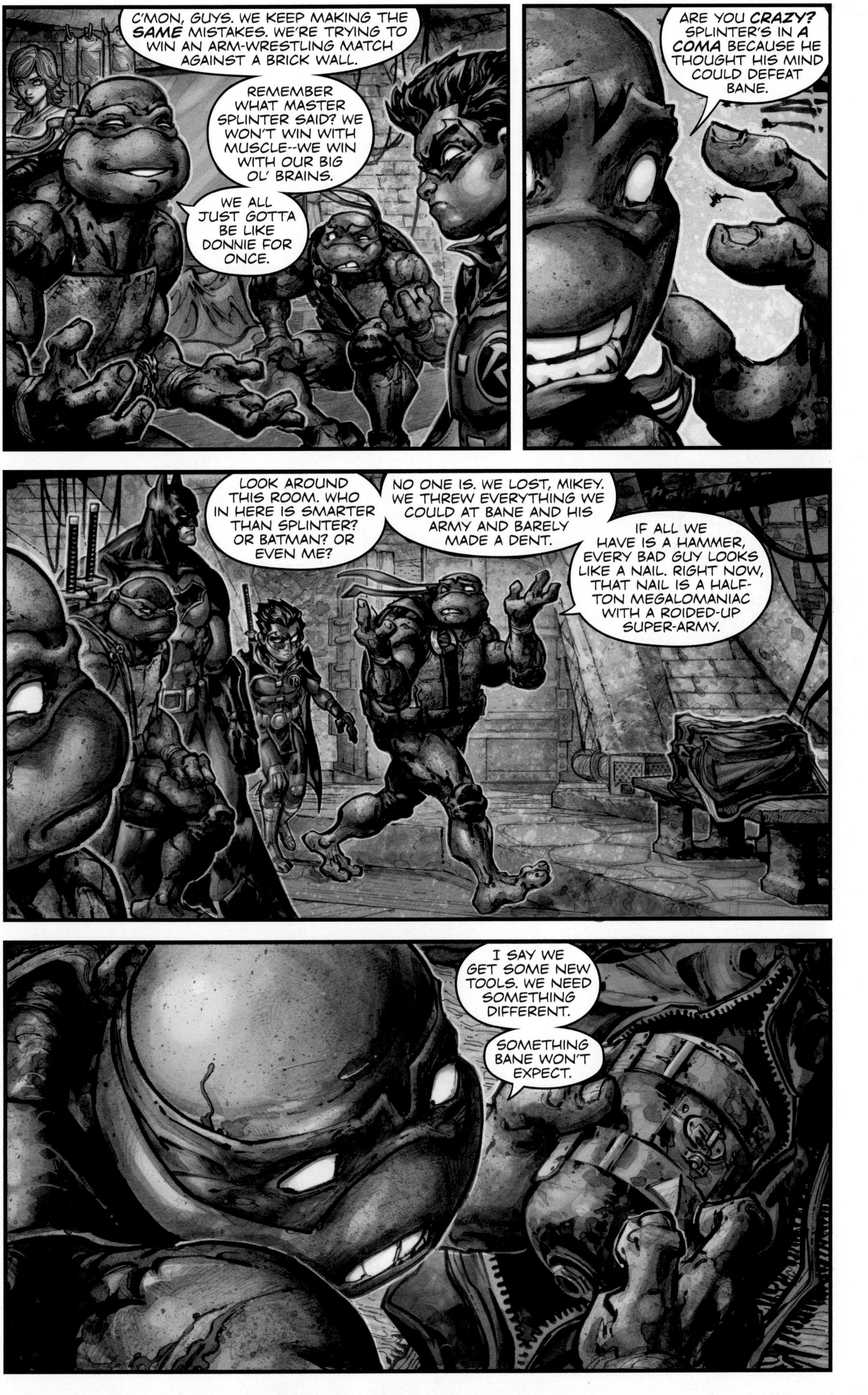
C'MON, GUYS. WE KEEP MAKING THE SAME MISTAKES. WE'RE TRYING TO WIN AN ARM-WRESTLING MATCH AGAINST A BRICK WALL.
REMEMBER WHAT MASTER SPLINTER SAID? WE WON'T WIN WITH MUSCLE--WE WIN WITH OUR BIG OL' BRAINS.
WE ALL JUST GOTTA BE LIKE DONNIE FOR ONCE.
ARE YOU CRAZY? SPLINTER'S IN A COMA BECAUSE HE THOUGHT HIS MIND COULD DEFEAT BANE.
LOOK AROUND THIS ROOM. WHO IN HERE IS SMARTER THAN SPLINTER? OR BATMAN? OR EVEN ME?
NO ONE IS. WE LOST, MIKEY. WE THREW EVERYTHING WE COULD AT BANE AND HIS ARMY AND BARELY MADE A DENT.
IF ALL WE HAVE IS A HAMMER, EVERY BAD GUY LOOKS LIKE A NAIL. RIGHT NOW, THAT NAIL IS A HALF-TON MEGALOMANIAC WITH A ROIDED-UP SUPER-ARMY.
I SAY WE GET SOME NEW TOOLS. WE NEED SOMETHING DIFFERENT.
SOMETHING BANE WON'T EXPECT.

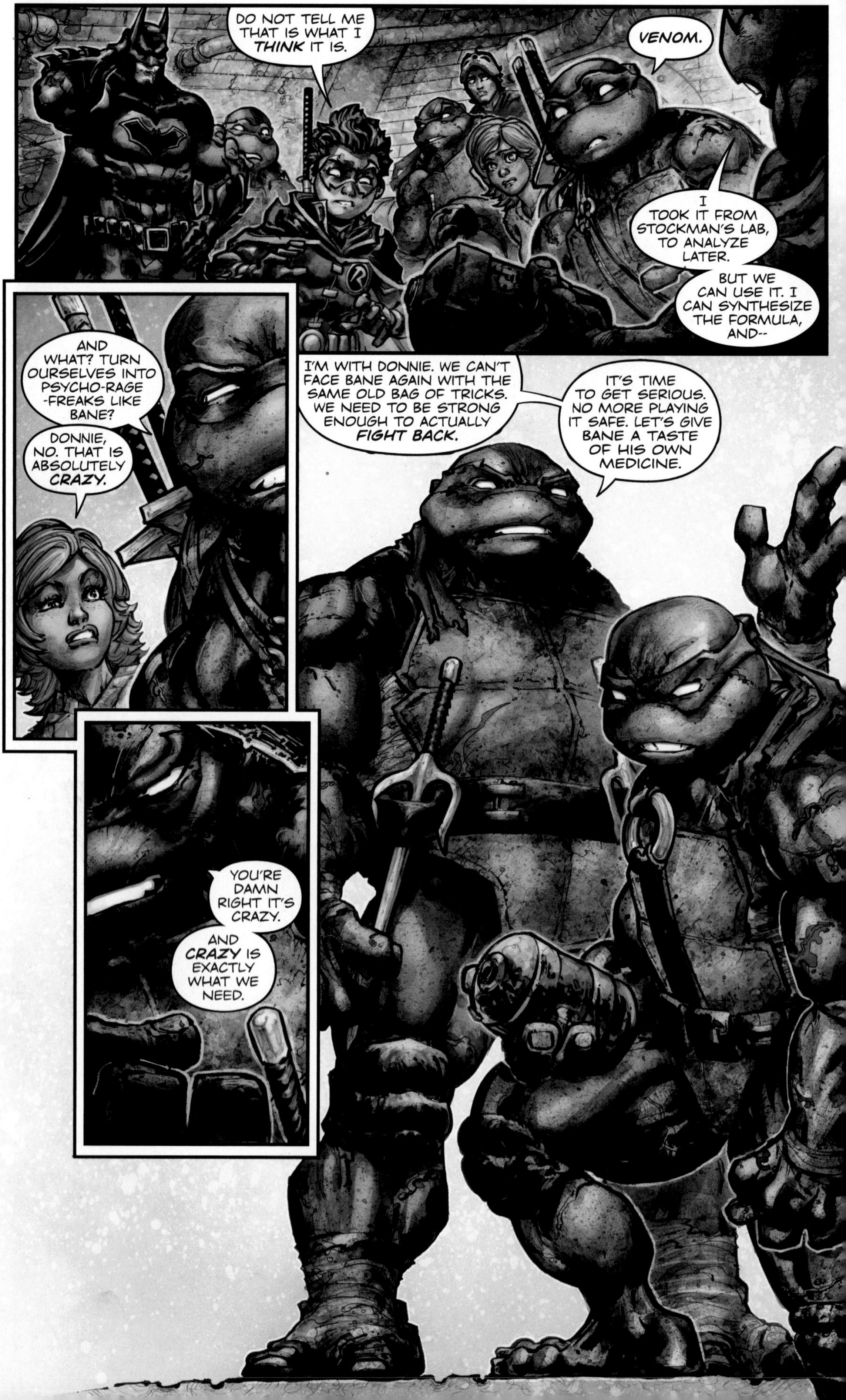
DO NOT TELL ME THAT IS WHAT I THINK IT IS.
VENOM.
I TOOK IT FROM STOCKMAN'S LAB, TO ANALYZE LATER.
BUT WE CAN USE IT. I CAN SYNTHESIZE THE FORMULA, AND--
AND WHAT? TURN OURSELVES INTO PSYCHO-RAGE -FREAKS LIKE BANE?
DONNIE, NO. THAT IS ABSOLUTELY CRAZY.
YOU'RE DAMN RIGHT IT'S CRAZY.
AND CRAZY IS EXACTLY WHAT WE NEED.
I'M WITH DONNIE. WE CAN'T FACE BANE AGAIN WITH THE SAME OLD BAG OF TRICKS. WE NEED TO BE STRONG ENOUGH TO ACTUALLY FIGHT BACK.
IT'S TIME TO GET SERIOUS. NO MORE PLAYING IT SAFE. LET'S GIVE BANE A TASTE OF HIS OWN MEDICINE.

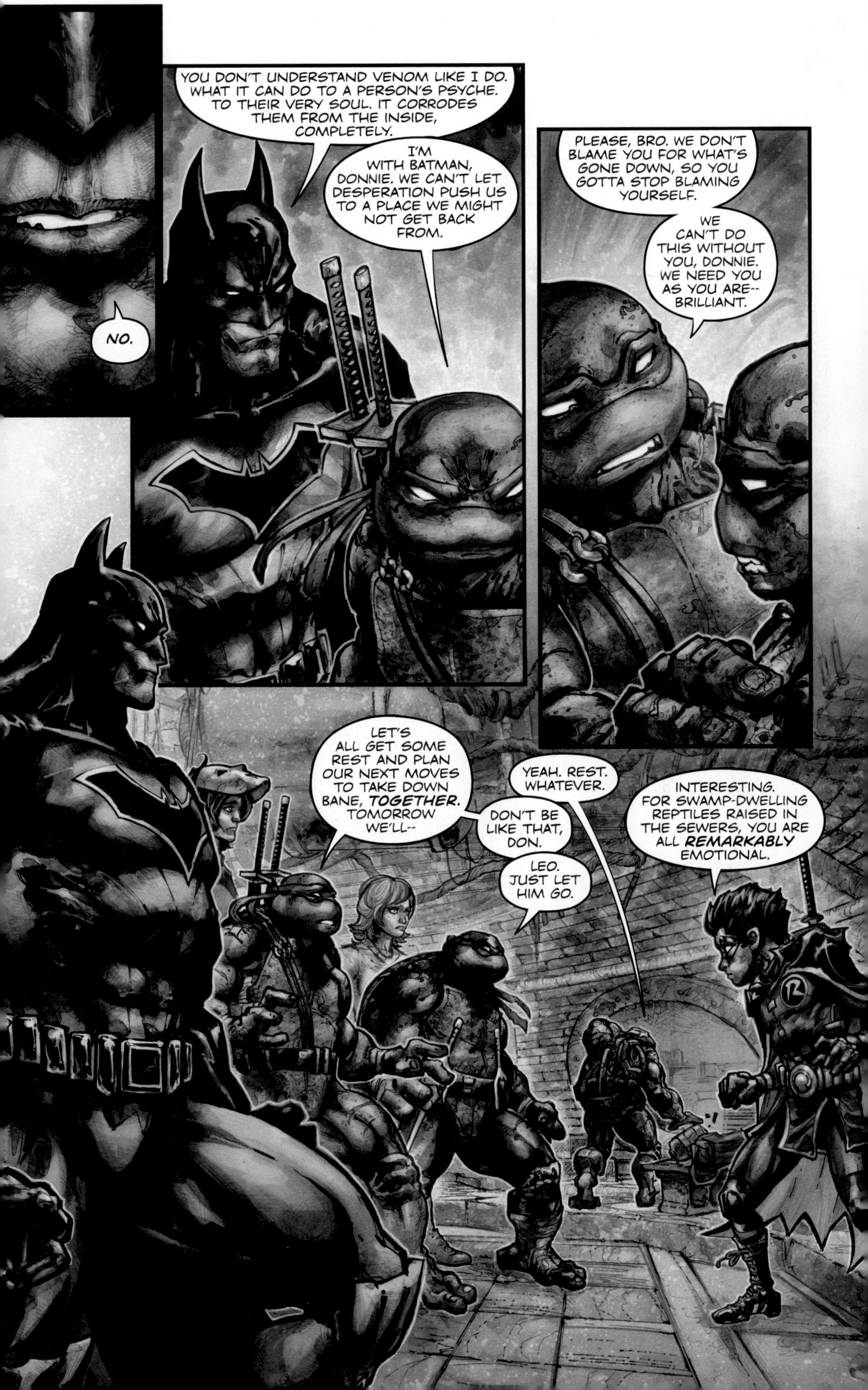

NO.
YOU DON'T UNDERSTAND VENOM LIKE I DO. WHAT IT CAN DO TO A PERSON'S PSYCHE. TO THEIR VERY SOUL. IT CORRODES THEM FROM THE INSIDE, COMPLETELY.
I'M WITH BATMAN, DONNIE. WE CAN'T LET DESPERATION PUSH US TO A PLACE WE MIGHT NOT GET BACK FROM.
PLEASE, BRO. WE DON'T BLAME YOU FOR WHAT'S GONE DOWN, SO YOU GOTTA STOP BLAMING YOURSELF.
WE CAN'T DO THIS WITHOUT YOU, DONNIE. WE NEED YOU AS YOU ARE-- BRILLIANT.
LET'S ALL GET SOME REST AND PLAN OUR NEXT MOVES TO TAKE DOWN BANE, *TOGETHER.* TOMORROW WE'LL--
YEAH. REST. WHATEVER.
DON'T BE LIKE THAT, DON.
LEO. JUST LET HIM GO.
INTERESTING. FOR SWAMP-DWELLING REPTILES RAISED IN THE SEWERS, YOU ARE ALL *REMARKABLY* EMOTIONAL.

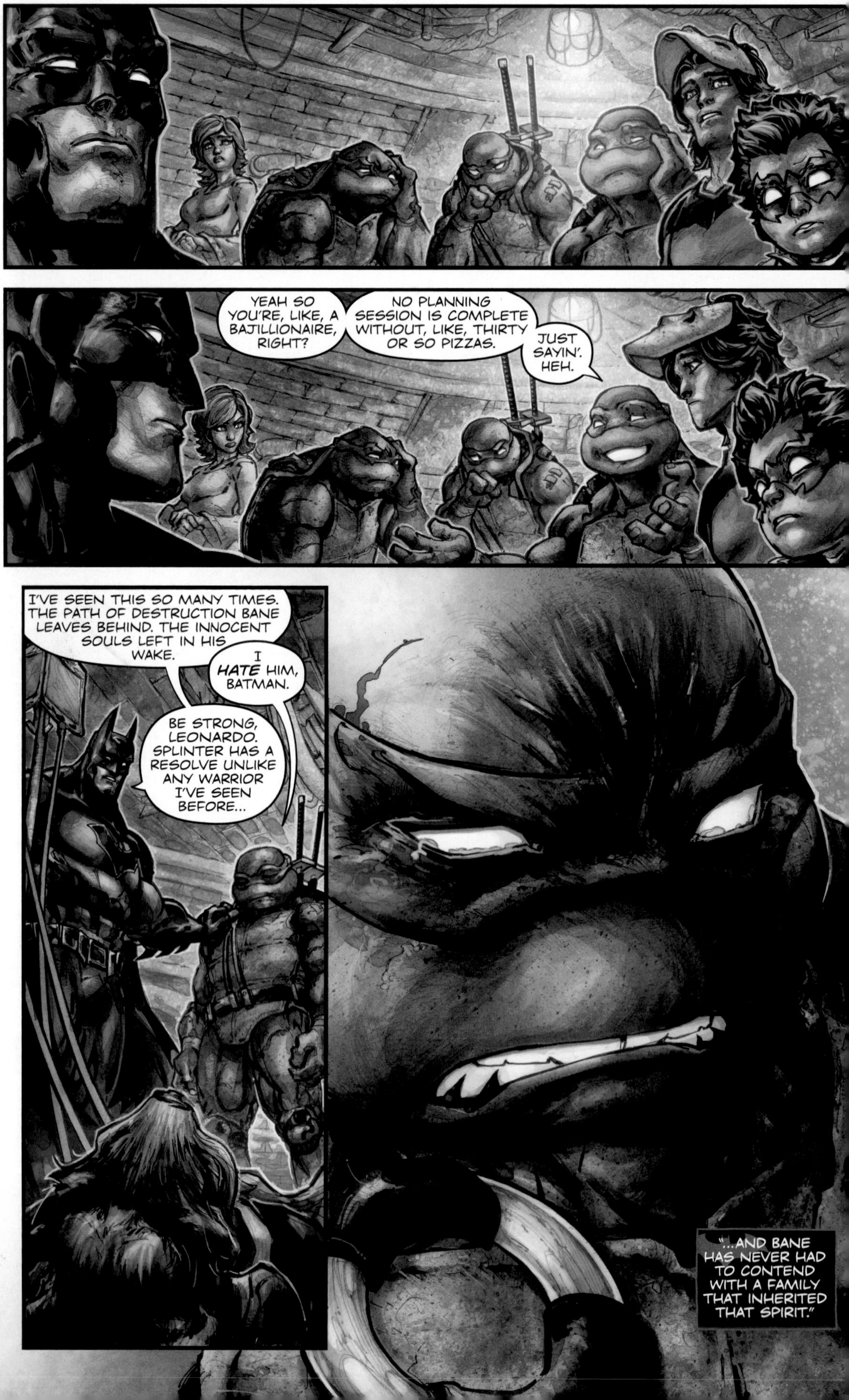
YEAH SO YOU'RE, LIKE, A BAJILLIONAIRE, RIGHT?
NO PLANNING SESSION IS COMPLETE WITHOUT, LIKE, THIRTY OR SO PIZZAS.
JUST SAYIN'. HEH.
I'VE SEEN THIS SO MANY TIMES. THE PATH OF DESTRUCTION BANE LEAVES BEHIND. THE INNOCENT SOULS LEFT IN HIS WAKE.
I HATE HIM, BATMAN.
BE STRONG, LEONARDO. SPLINTER HAS A RESOLVE UNLIKE ANY WARRIOR I'VE SEEN BEFORE...
"...AND BANE HAS NEVER HAD TO CONTEND WITH A FAMILY THAT INHERITED THAT SPIRIT."

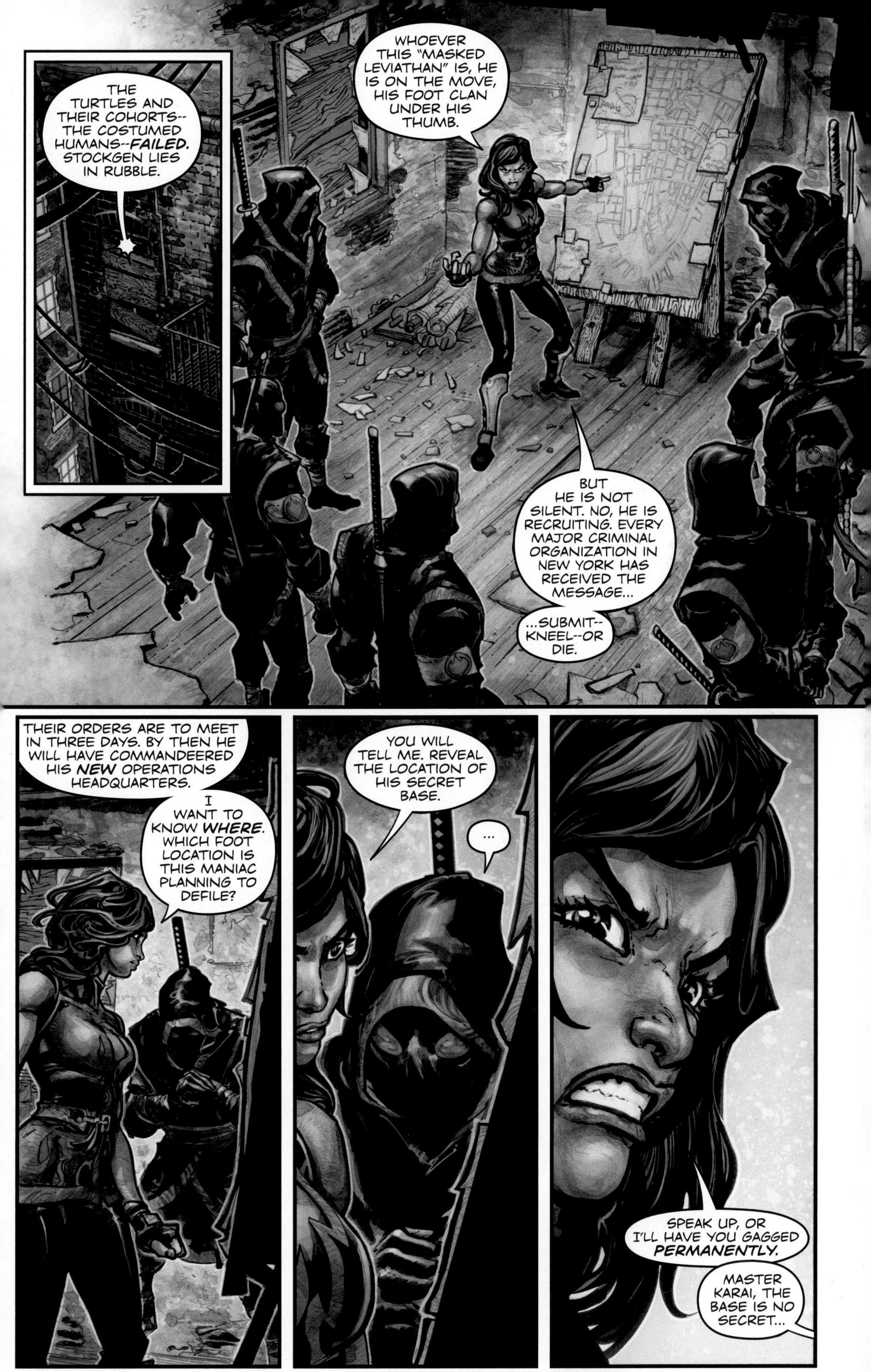
THE TURTLES AND THEIR COHORTS-- THE COSTUMED HUMANS--FAILED. STOCKGEN LIES IN RUBBLE.
WHOEVER THIS "MASKED LEVIATHAN" IS, HE IS ON THE MOVE, HIS FOOT CLAN UNDER HIS THUMB.
BUT HE IS NOT SILENT. NO, HE IS RECRUITING. EVERY MAJOR CRIMINAL ORGANIZATION IN NEW YORK HAS RECEIVED THE MESSAGE...
...SUBMIT-- KNEEL--OR DIE.
THEIR ORDERS ARE TO MEET IN THREE DAYS. BY THEN HE WILL HAVE COMMANDEERED HIS NEW OPERATIONS HEADQUARTERS.
I WANT TO KNOW WHERE. WHICH FOOT LOCATION IS THIS MANIAC PLANNING TO DEFILE?
YOU WILL TELL ME. REVEAL THE LOCATION OF HIS SECRET BASE.
...
SPEAK UP, OR I'LL HAVE YOU GAGGED PERMANENTLY.
MASTER KARAI, THE BASE IS NO SECRET...

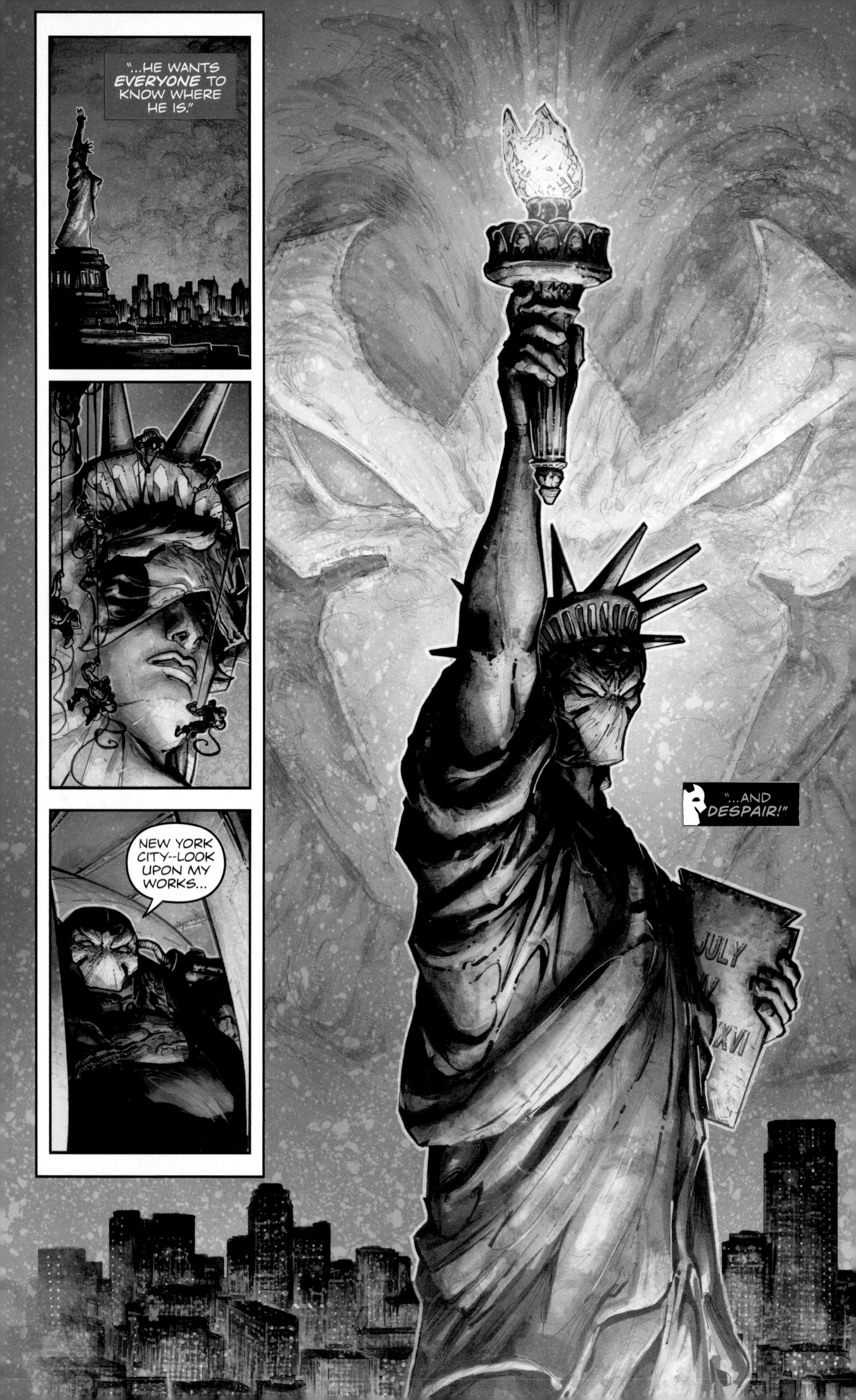
"...HE WANTS EVERYONE TO KNOW WHERE HE IS."
NEW YORK CITY--LOOK UPON MY WORKS...
"...AND DESPAIR!"
JULY
XVI

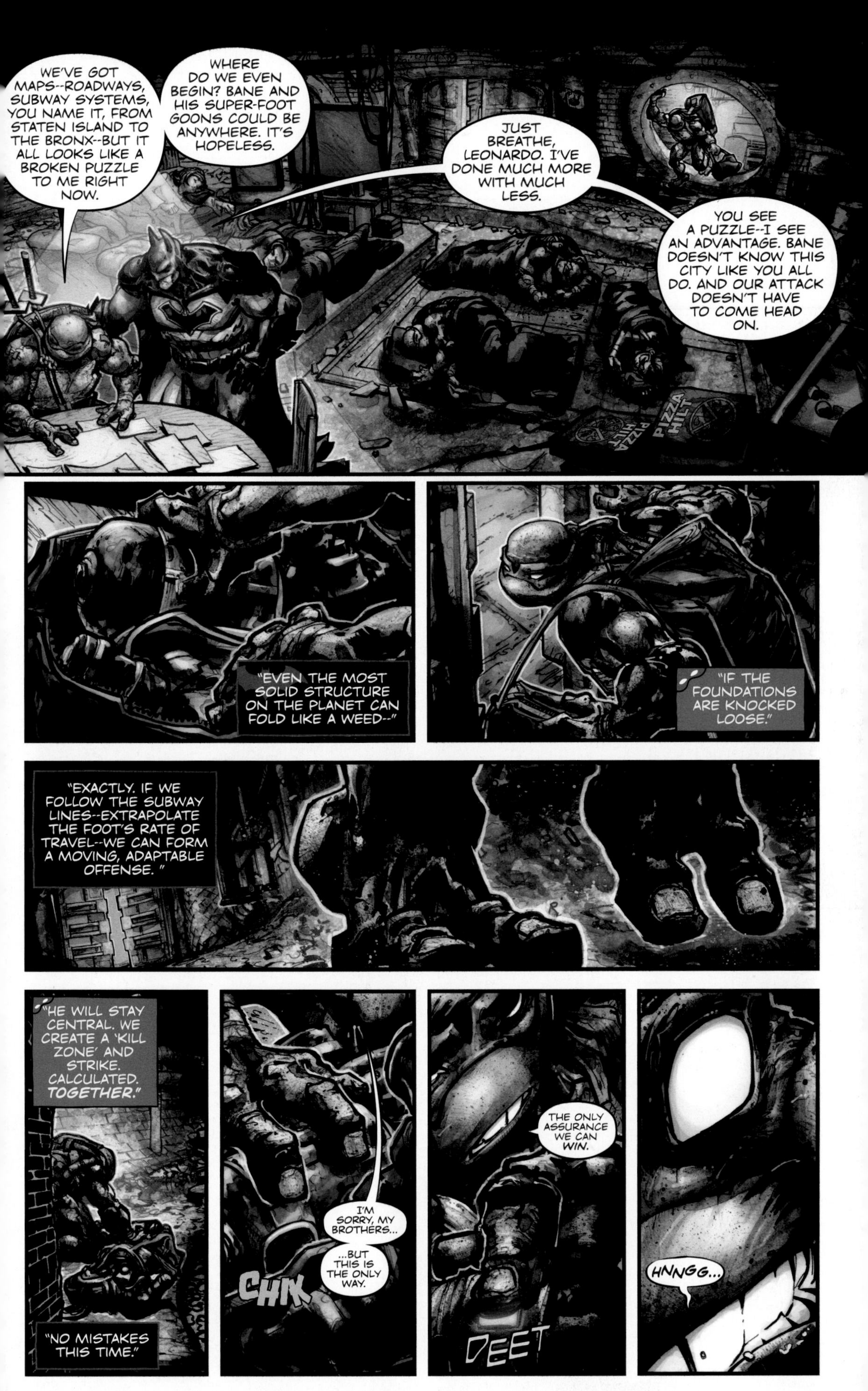
WE'VE GOT MAPS--ROADWAYS, SUBWAY SYSTEMS, YOU NAME IT, FROM STATEN ISLAND TO THE BRONX--BUT IT ALL LOOKS LIKE A BROKEN PUZZLE TO ME RIGHT NOW.
WHERE DO WE EVEN BEGIN? BANE AND HIS SUPER-FOOT GOONS COULD BE ANYWHERE. IT'S HOPELESS.
JUST BREATHE, LEONARDO. I'VE DONE MUCH MORE WITH MUCH LESS.
YOU SEE A PUZZLE--I SEE AN ADVANTAGE. BANE DOESN'T KNOW THIS CITY LIKE YOU ALL DO. AND OUR ATTACK DOESN'T HAVE TO COME HEAD ON.
PIZZA HILT
PIZZA HILT
"EVEN THE MOST SOLID STRUCTURE ON THE PLANET CAN FOLD LIKE A WEED--"
"IF THE FOUNDATIONS ARE KNOCKED LOOSE."
"EXACTLY. IF WE FOLLOW THE SUBWAY LINES--EXTRAPOLATE THE FOOT'S RATE OF TRAVEL--WE CAN FORM A MOVING, ADAPTABLE OFFENSE."
"HE WILL STAY CENTRAL. WE CREATE A 'KILL ZONE' AND STRIKE. CALCULATED. TOGETHER."
"NO MISTAKES THIS TIME."
I'M SORRY, MY BROTHERS...
...BUT THIS IS THE ONLY WAY.
CHIK
THE ONLY ASSURANCE WE CAN WIN.
DEET
HNNGG...

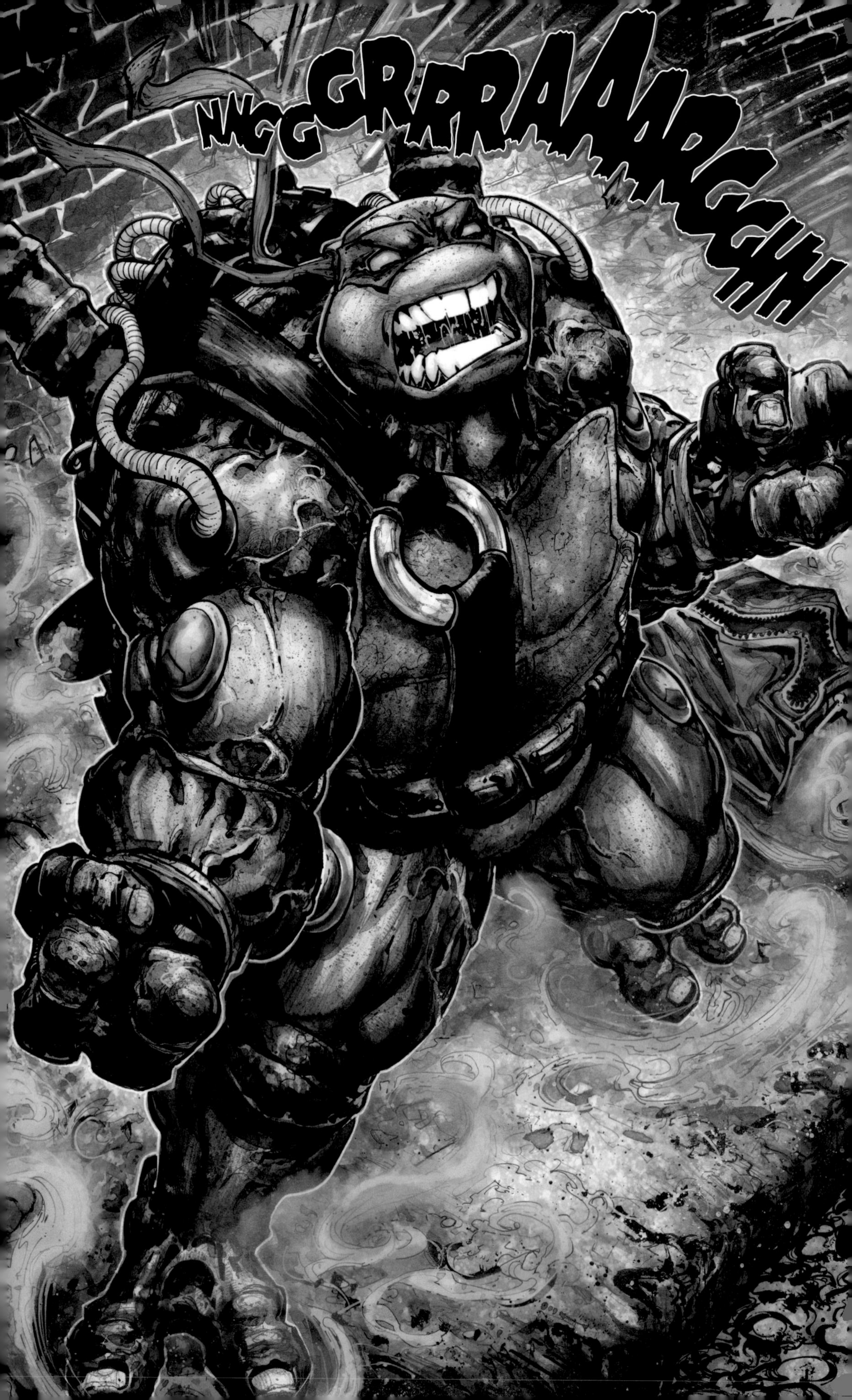
NNGGRRRAAARGGH

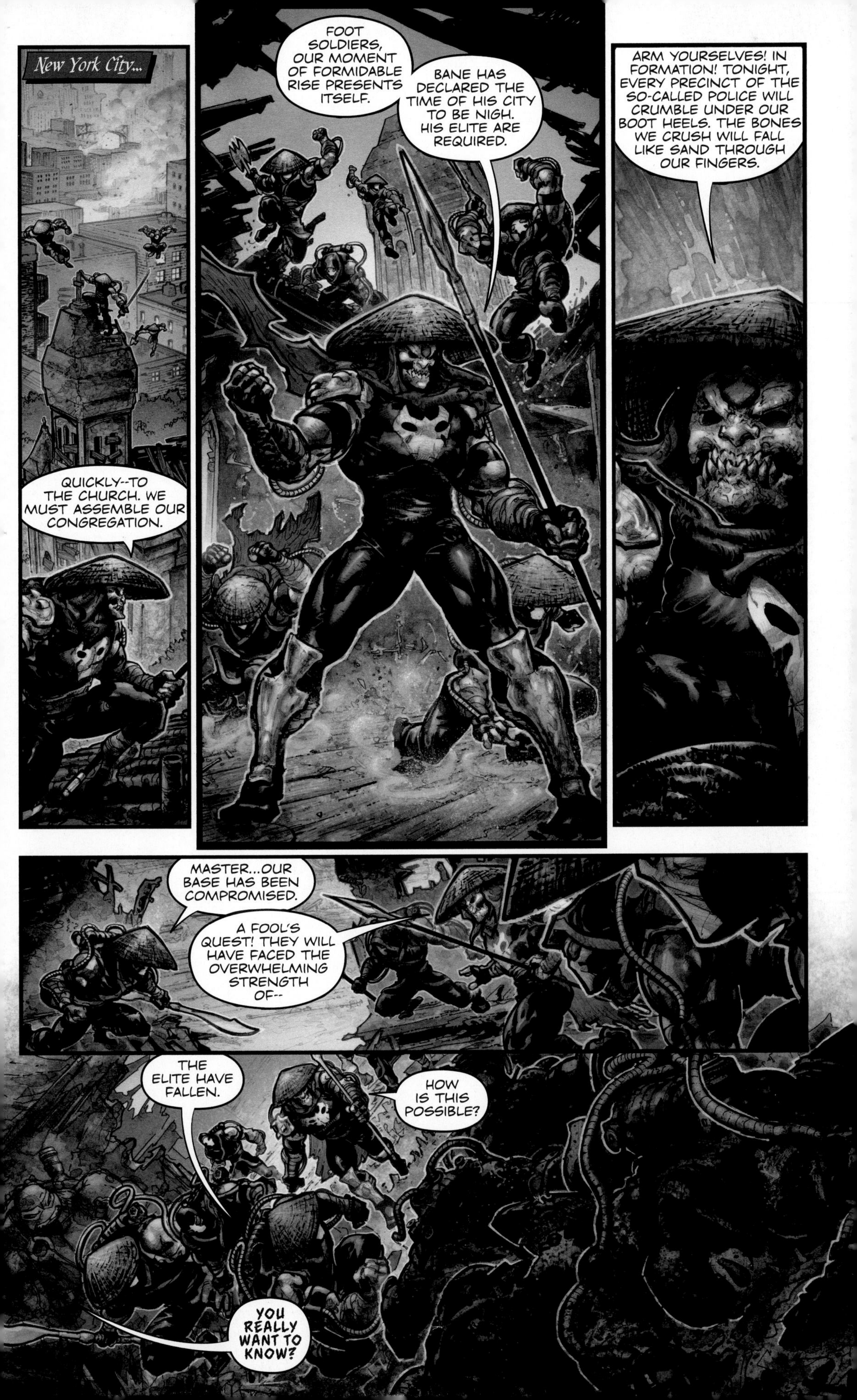
New York City...
QUICKLY--TO THE CHURCH. WE MUST ASSEMBLE OUR CONGREGATION.
FOOT SOLDIERS, OUR MOMENT OF FORMIDABLE RISE PRESENTS ITSELF.
BANE HAS DECLARED THE TIME OF HIS CITY TO BE NIGH. HIS ELITE ARE REQUIRED.
ARM YOURSELVES! IN FORMATION! TONIGHT, EVERY PRECINCT OF THE SO-CALLED POLICE WILL CRUMBLE UNDER OUR BOOT HEELS. THE BONES WE CRUSH WILL FALL LIKE SAND THROUGH OUR FINGERS.
MASTER...OUR BASE HAS BEEN COMPROMISED.
A FOOL'S QUEST! THEY WILL HAVE FACED THE OVERWHELMING STRENGTH OF--
THE ELITE HAVE FALLEN.
HOW IS THIS POSSIBLE?
YOU REALLY WANT TO KNOW?

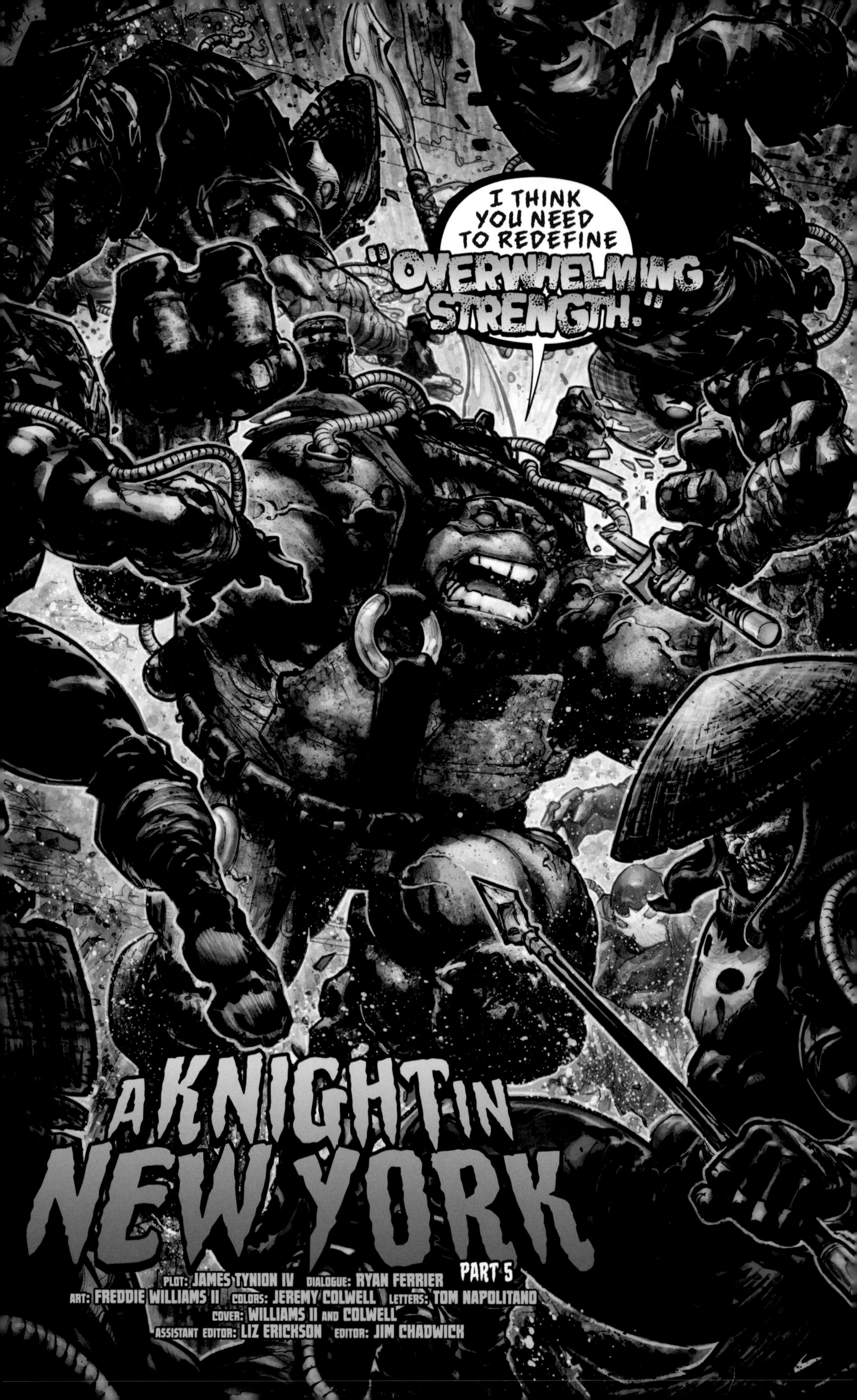
I THINK YOU NEED TO REDEFINE "OVERWHELMING STRENGTH."
A KNIGHT IN NEW YORK
PART 5
PLOT: JAMES TYNION IV DIALOGUE: RYAN FERRIER
ART: FREDDIE WILLIAMS II COLORS: JEREMY COLWELL LETTERS: TOM NAPOLITANO
COVER: WILLIAMS II AND COLWELL
ASSISTANT EDITOR: LIZ ERICKSON EDITOR: JIM CHADWICK

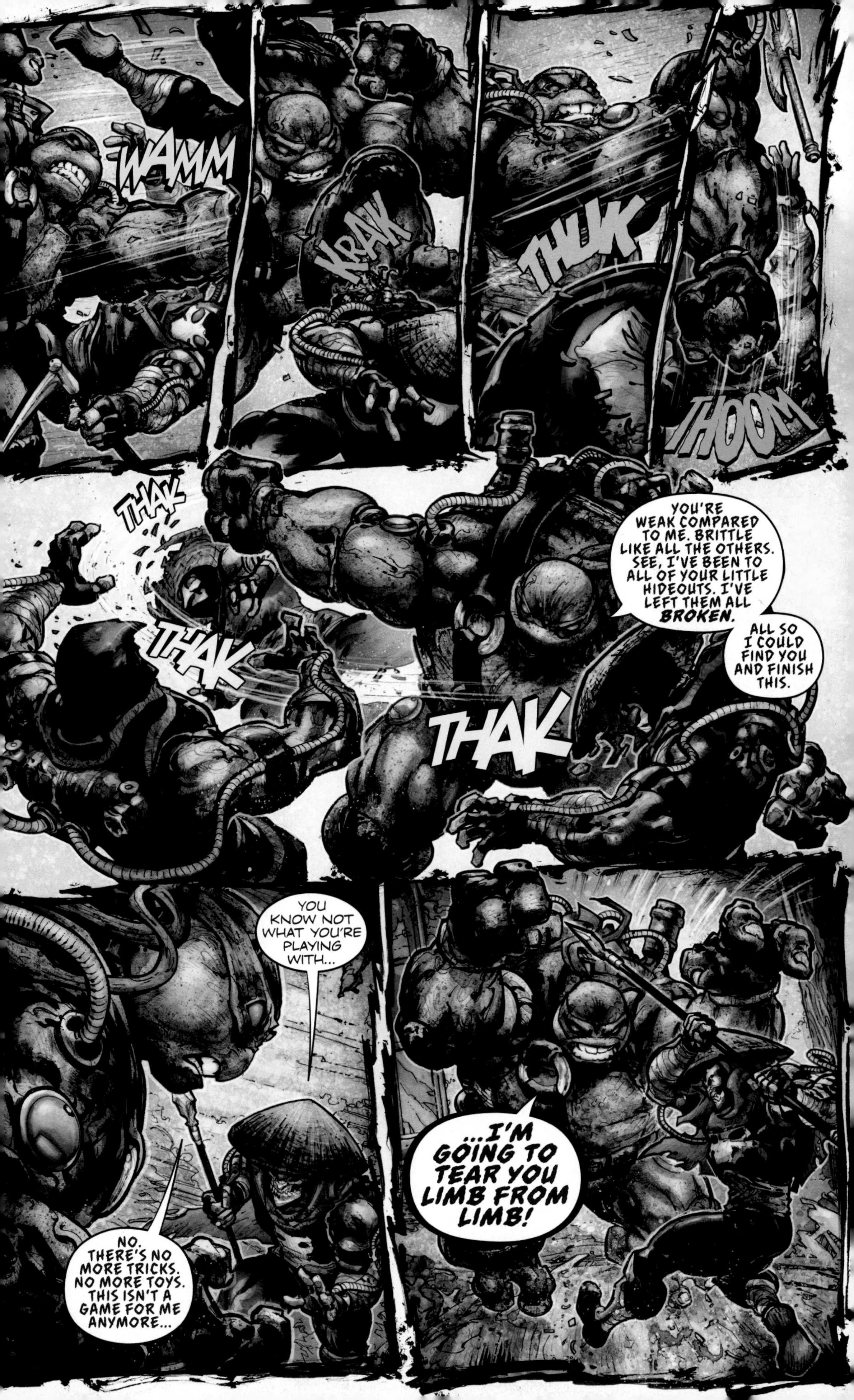
WAMM
KRAK
THUK
THOOM
THAK
THAK
YOU'RE WEAK COMPARED TO ME. BRITTLE LIKE ALL THE OTHERS. SEE, I'VE BEEN TO ALL OF YOUR LITTLE HIDEOUTS. I'VE LEFT THEM ALL BROKEN.
ALL SO I COULD FIND YOU AND FINISH THIS.
THAK
YOU KNOW NOT WHAT YOU'RE PLAYING WITH...
NO. THERE'S NO MORE TRICKS. NO MORE TOYS. THIS ISN'T A GAME FOR ME ANYMORE...
...I'M GOING TO TEAR YOU LIMB FROM LIMB!

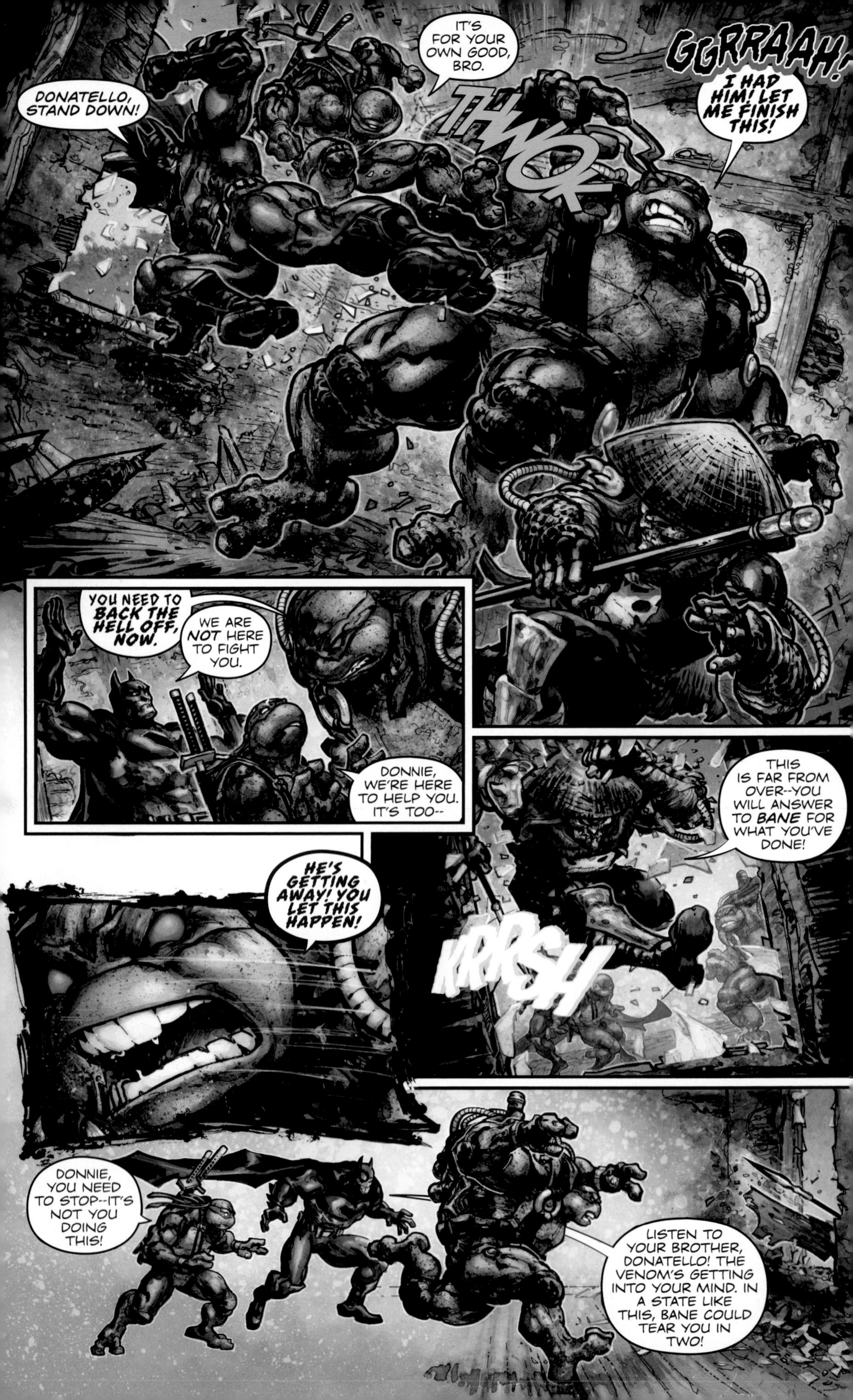
DONATELLO, STAND DOWN!
IT'S FOR YOUR OWN GOOD, BRO.
THWOK
GGRRAAH!
I HAD HIM! LET ME FINISH THIS!
YOU NEED TO BACK THE HELL OFF, NOW.
WE ARE NOT HERE TO FIGHT YOU.
DONNIE, WE'RE HERE TO HELP YOU. IT'S TOO--
THIS IS FAR FROM OVER--YOU WILL ANSWER TO BANE FOR WHAT YOU'VE DONE!
KRRSH
HE'S GETTING AWAY! YOU LET THIS HAPPEN!
DONNIE, YOU NEED TO STOP--IT'S NOT YOU DOING THIS!
LISTEN TO YOUR BROTHER, DONATELLO! THE VENOM'S GETTING INTO YOUR MIND. IN A STATE LIKE THIS, BANE COULD TEAR YOU IN TWO!

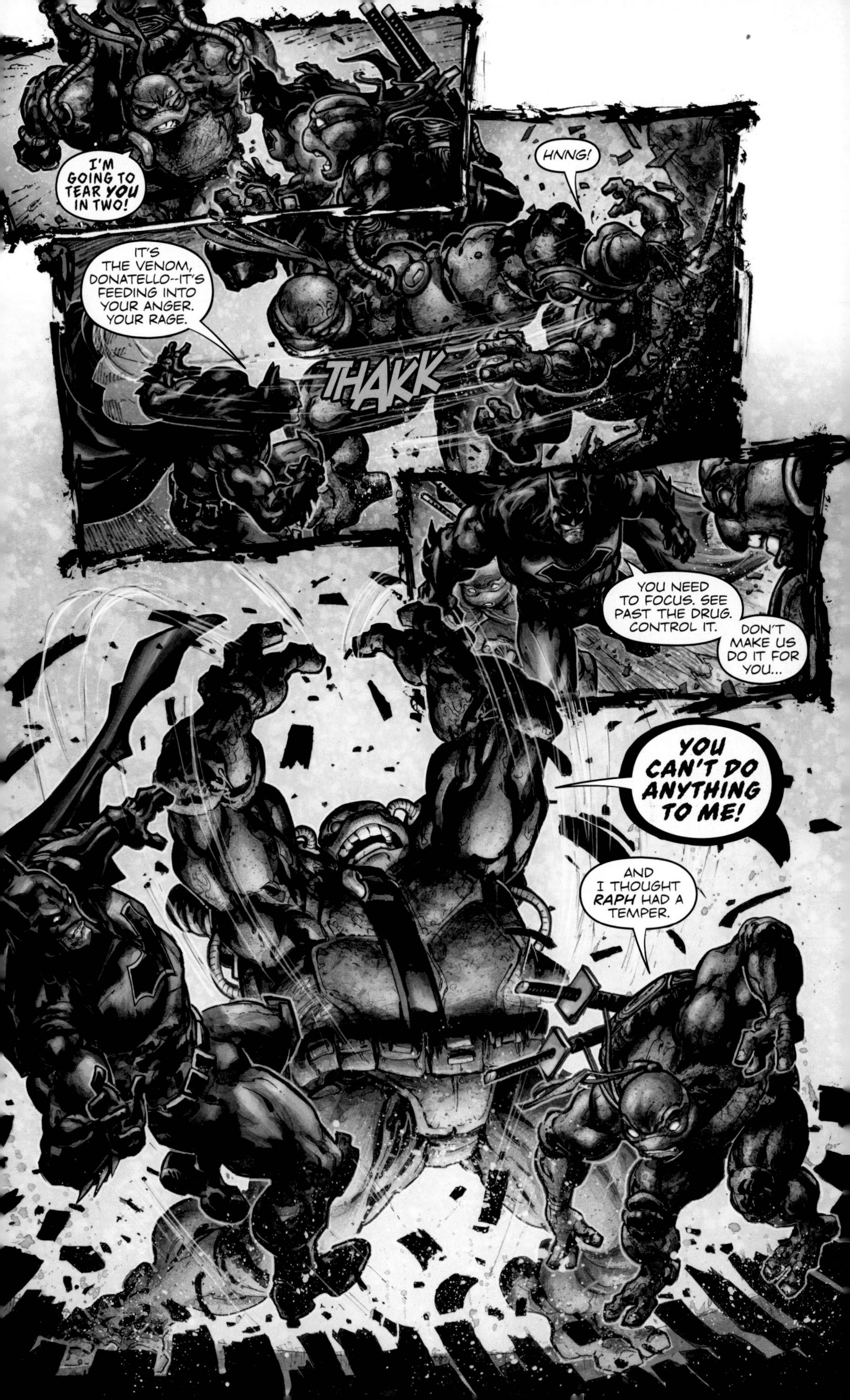
I'M GOING TO TEAR YOU IN TWO!
HNNG!
IT'S THE VENOM, DONATELLO--IT'S FEEDING INTO YOUR ANGER. YOUR RAGE.
THAKK
YOU NEED TO FOCUS. SEE PAST THE DRUG. CONTROL IT.
DON'T MAKE US DO IT FOR YOU...
YOU CAN'T DO ANYTHING TO ME!
AND I THOUGHT RAPH HAD A TEMPER.

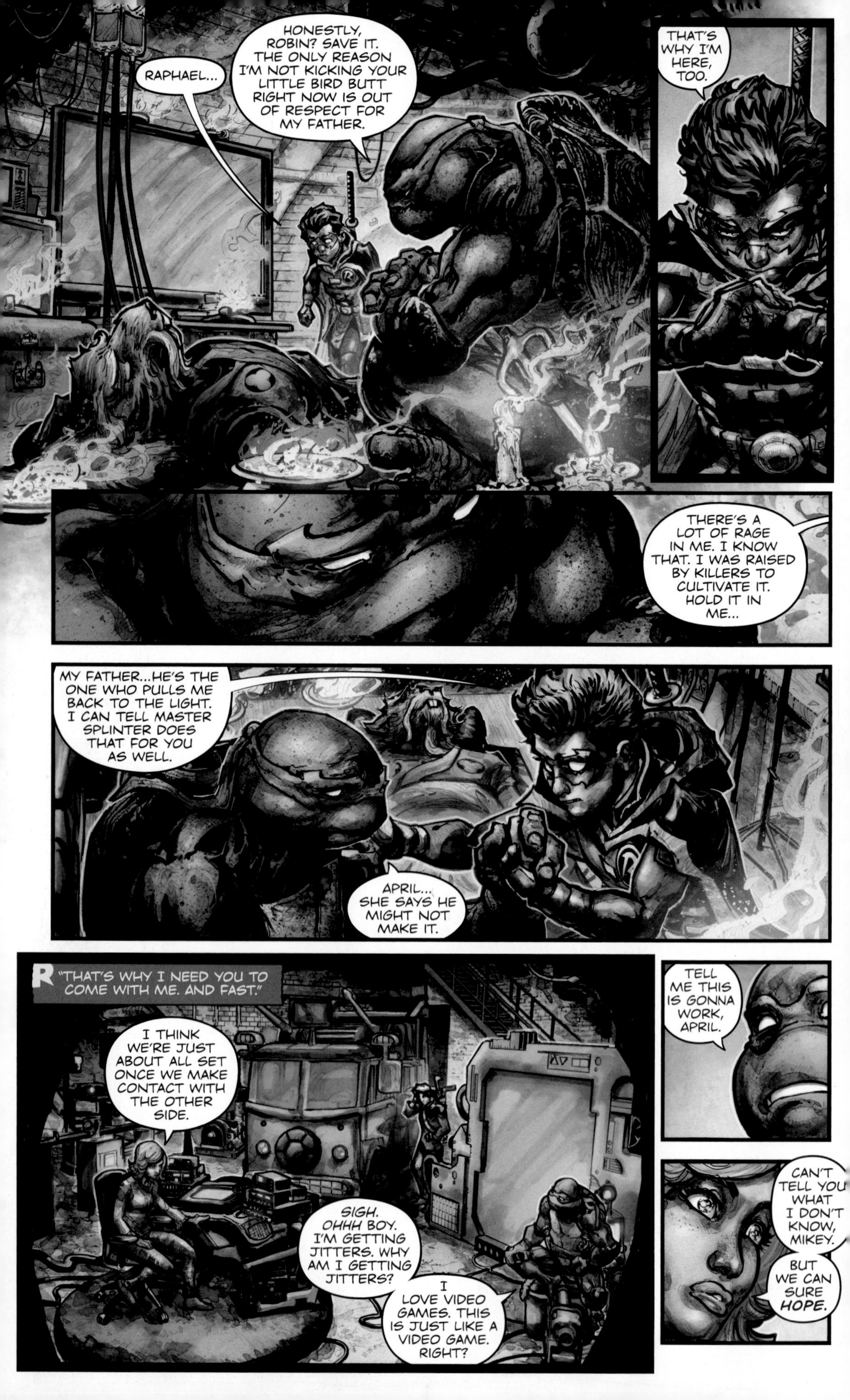

RAPHAEL...
HONESTLY, ROBIN? SAVE IT. THE ONLY REASON I'M NOT KICKING YOUR LITTLE BIRD BUTT RIGHT NOW IS OUT OF RESPECT FOR MY FATHER.
THAT'S WHY I'M HERE, TOO.
THERE'S A LOT OF RAGE IN ME. I KNOW THAT. I WAS RAISED BY KILLERS TO CULTIVATE IT. HOLD IT IN ME...
MY FATHER...HE'S THE ONE WHO PULLS ME BACK TO THE LIGHT. I CAN TELL MASTER SPLINTER DOES THAT FOR YOU AS WELL.
APRIL... SHE SAYS HE MIGHT NOT MAKE IT.
"THAT'S WHY I NEED YOU TO COME WITH ME. AND FAST."
I THINK WE'RE JUST ABOUT ALL SET ONCE WE MAKE CONTACT WITH THE OTHER SIDE.
SIGH. OHHH BOY. I'M GETTING JITTERS. WHY AM I GETTING JITTERS?
I LOVE VIDEO GAMES. THIS IS JUST LIKE A VIDEO GAME. RIGHT?
TELL ME THIS IS GONNA WORK, APRIL.
CAN'T TELL YOU WHAT I DON'T KNOW, MIKEY.
BUT WE CAN SURE HOPE.

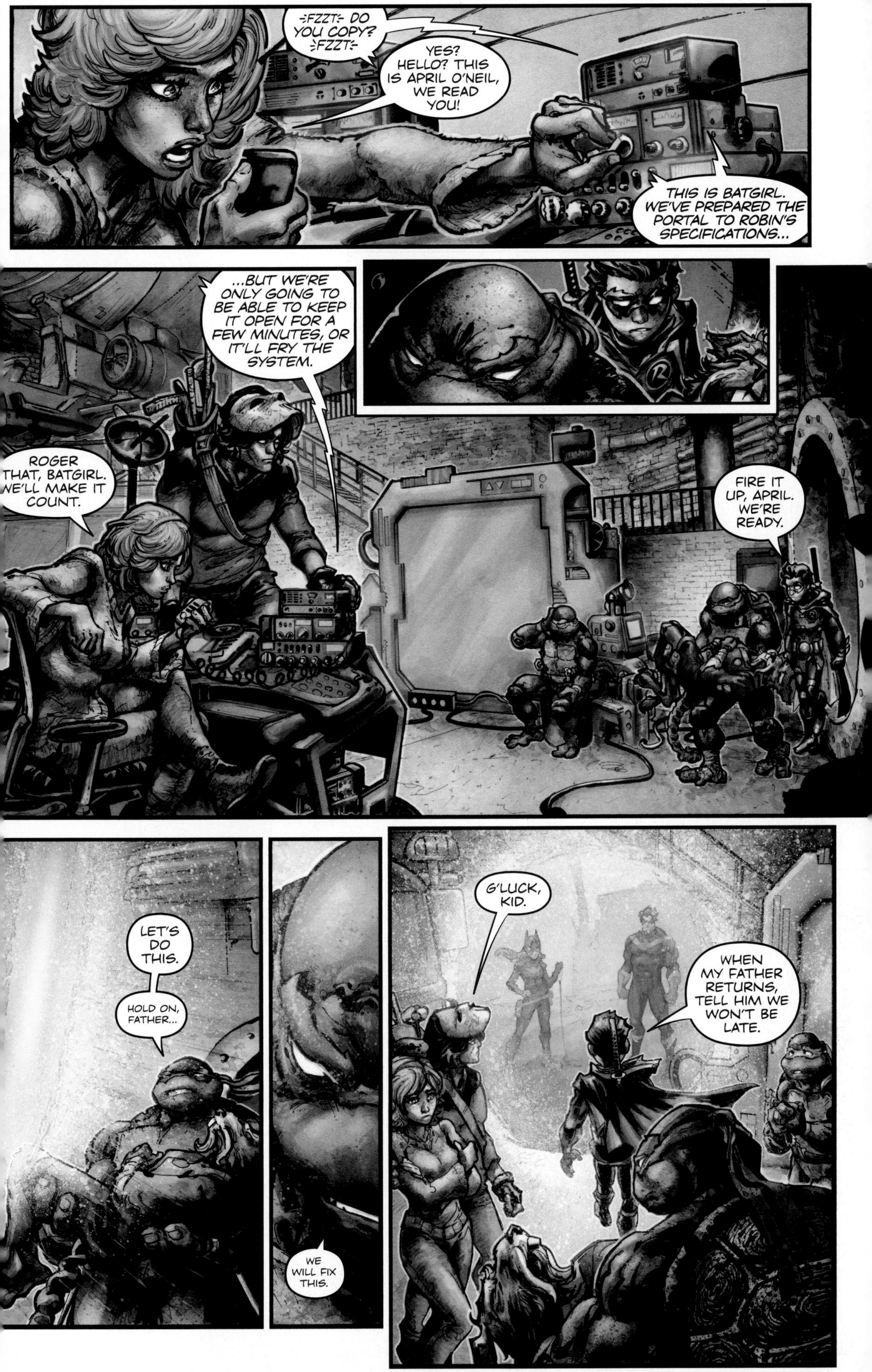

≡FZZT≡ DO YOU COPY? ≡FZZT≡
YES? HELLO? THIS IS APRIL O'NEIL, WE READ YOU!
THIS IS BATGIRL. WE'VE PREPARED THE PORTAL TO ROBIN'S SPECIFICATIONS...
...BUT WE'RE ONLY GOING TO BE ABLE TO KEEP IT OPEN FOR A FEW MINUTES, OR IT'LL FRY THE SYSTEM.
ROGER THAT, BATGIRL. WE'LL MAKE IT COUNT.
FIRE IT UP, APRIL. WE'RE READY.
LET'S DO THIS.
HOLD ON, FATHER...
WE WILL FIX THIS.
G'LUCK, KID.
WHEN MY FATHER RETURNS, TELL HIM WE WON'T BE LATE.

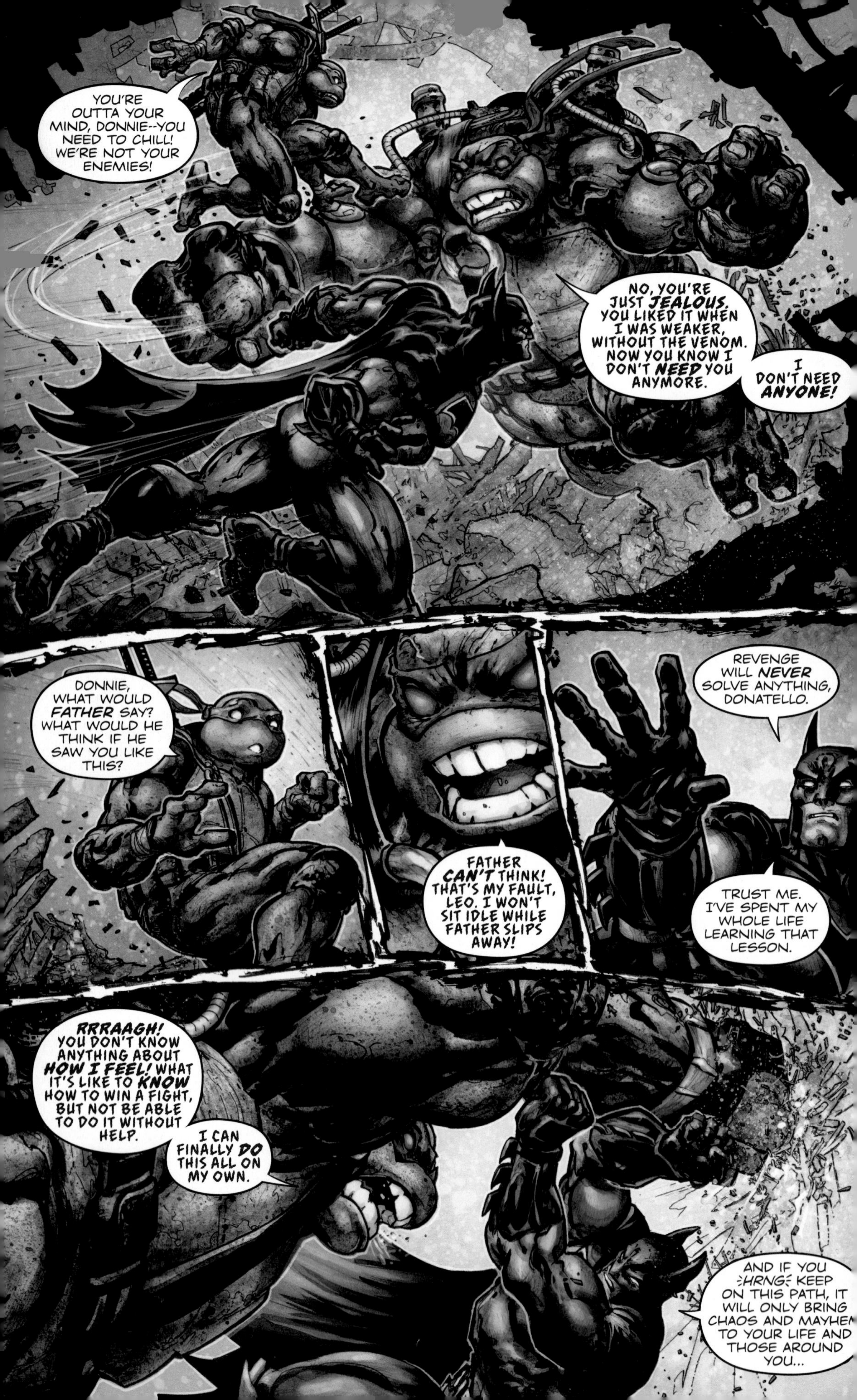
YOU'RE OUTTA YOUR MIND, DONNIE--YOU NEED TO CHILL! WE'RE NOT YOUR ENEMIES!
NO, YOU'RE JUST JEALOUS. YOU LIKED IT WHEN I WAS WEAKER, WITHOUT THE VENOM. NOW YOU KNOW I DON'T NEED YOU ANYMORE.
I DON'T NEED ANYONE!
DONNIE, WHAT WOULD FATHER SAY? WHAT WOULD HE THINK IF HE SAW YOU LIKE THIS?
FATHER CAN'T THINK! THAT'S MY FAULT, LEO. I WON'T SIT IDLE WHILE FATHER SLIPS AWAY!
REVENGE WILL NEVER SOLVE ANYTHING, DONATELLO.
TRUST ME. I'VE SPENT MY WHOLE LIFE LEARNING THAT LESSON.
RRRAAGH! YOU DON'T KNOW ANYTHING ABOUT HOW I FEEL! WHAT IT'S LIKE TO KNOW HOW TO WIN A FIGHT, BUT NOT BE ABLE TO DO IT WITHOUT HELP.
I CAN FINALLY DO THIS ALL ON MY OWN.
AND IF YOU HRNG KEEP ON THIS PATH, IT WILL ONLY BRING CHAOS AND MAYHEM TO YOUR LIFE AND THOSE AROUND YOU...

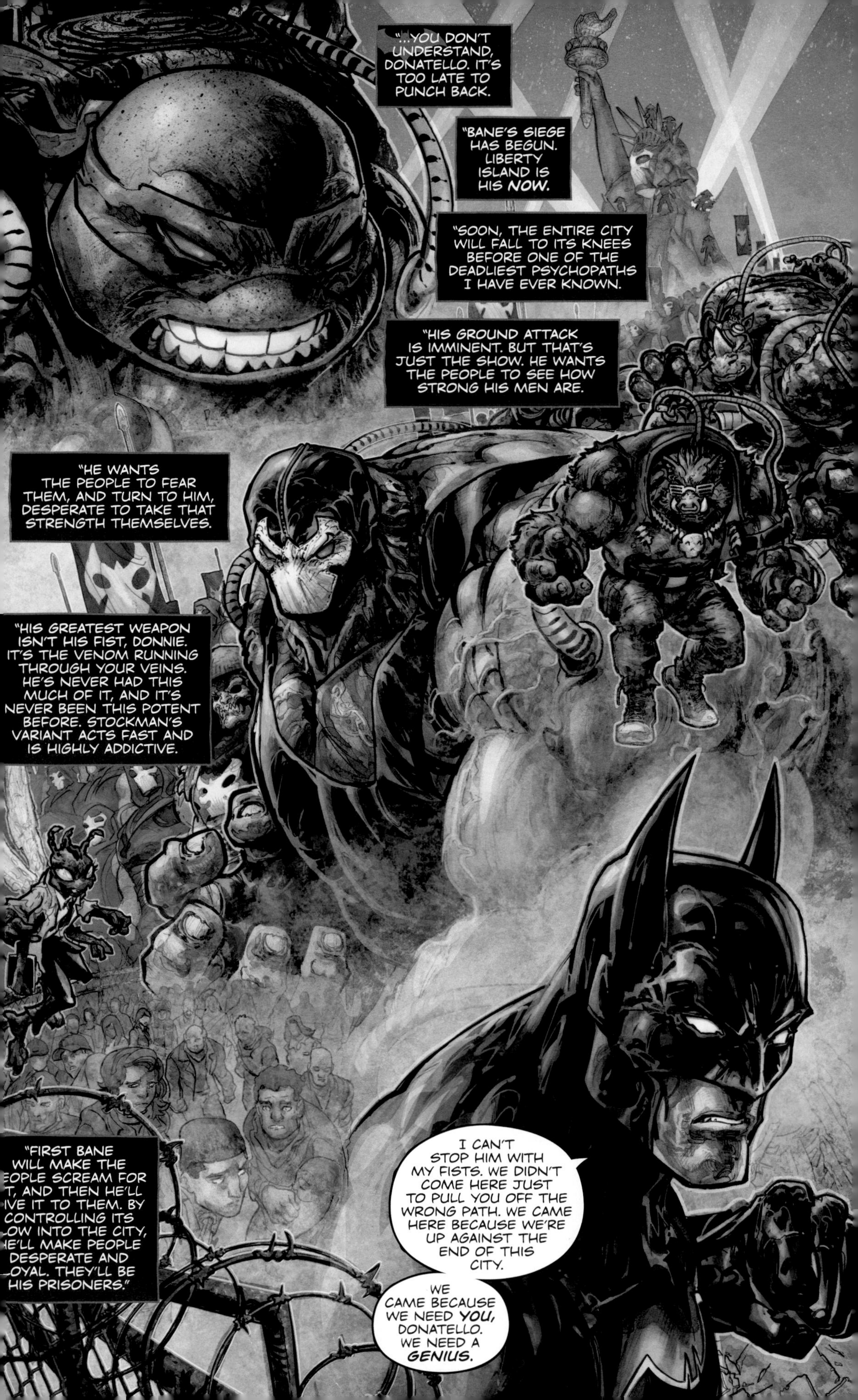
"...YOU DON'T UNDERSTAND, DONATELLO. IT'S TOO LATE TO PUNCH BACK.
"BANE'S SIEGE HAS BEGUN. LIBERTY ISLAND IS HIS NOW.
"SOON, THE ENTIRE CITY WILL FALL TO ITS KNEES BEFORE ONE OF THE DEADLIEST PSYCHOPATHS I HAVE EVER KNOWN.
"HIS GROUND ATTACK IS IMMINENT. BUT THAT'S JUST THE SHOW. HE WANTS THE PEOPLE TO SEE HOW STRONG HIS MEN ARE.
"HE WANTS THE PEOPLE TO FEAR THEM, AND TURN TO HIM, DESPERATE TO TAKE THAT STRENGTH THEMSELVES.
"HIS GREATEST WEAPON ISN'T HIS FIST, DONNIE. IT'S THE VENOM RUNNING THROUGH YOUR VEINS. HE'S NEVER HAD THIS MUCH OF IT, AND IT'S NEVER BEEN THIS POTENT BEFORE. STOCKMAN'S VARIANT ACTS FAST AND IS HIGHLY ADDICTIVE.
"FIRST BANE WILL MAKE THE EOPLE SCREAM FOR T, AND THEN HE'LL IVE IT TO THEM. BY CONTROLLING ITS OW INTO THE CITY, IE'LL MAKE PEOPLE DESPERATE AND OYAL. THEY'LL BE HIS PRISONERS."
I CAN'T STOP HIM WITH MY FISTS. WE DIDN'T COME HERE JUST TO PULL YOU OFF THE WRONG PATH. WE CAME HERE BECAUSE WE'RE UP AGAINST THE END OF THIS CITY.
WE CAME BECAUSE WE NEED YOU, DONATELLO. WE NEED A GENIUS.

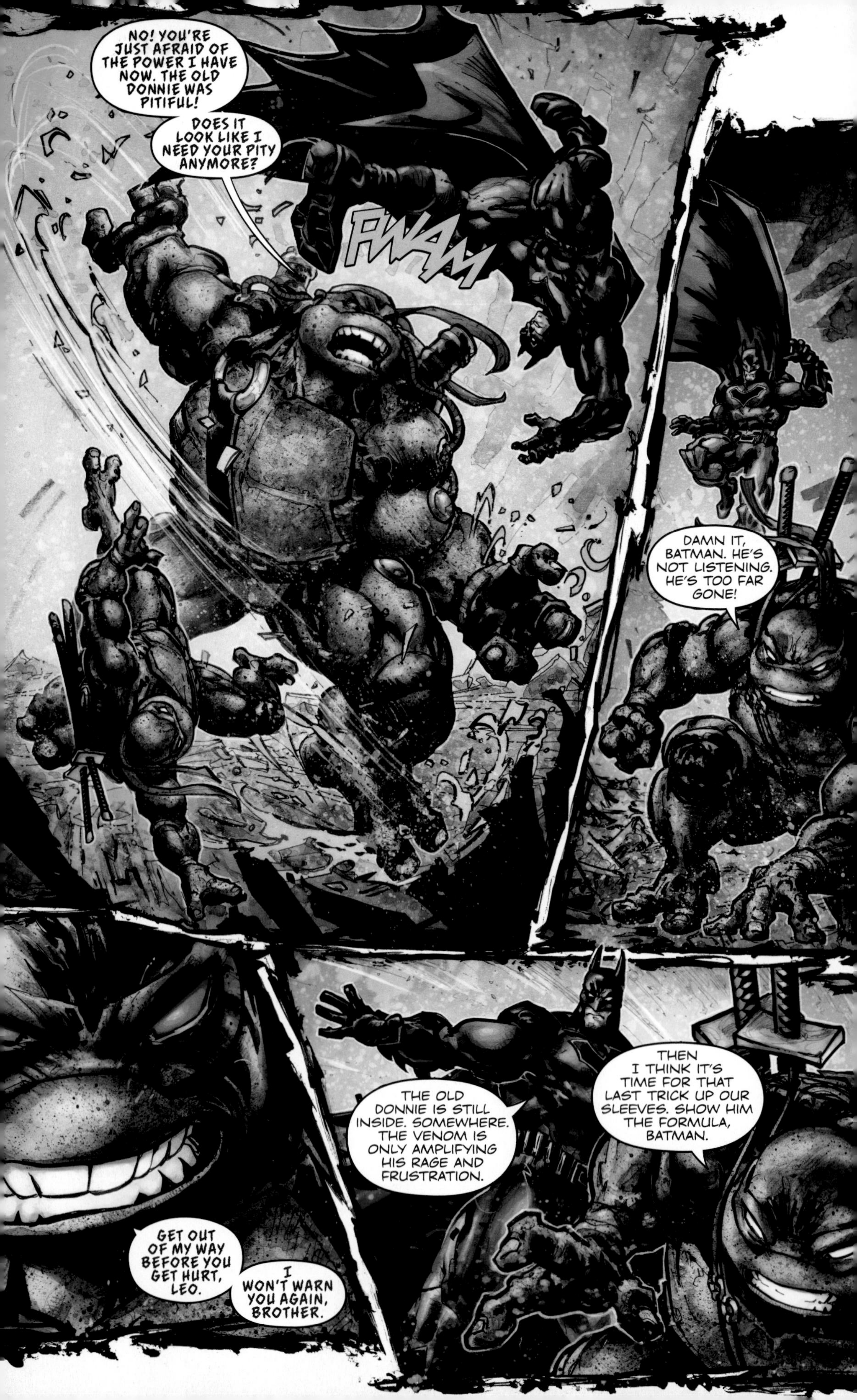
NO! YOU'RE JUST AFRAID OF THE POWER I HAVE NOW. THE OLD DONNIE WAS PITIFUL!
DOES IT LOOK LIKE I NEED YOUR PITY ANYMORE?
FWAM
DAMN IT, BATMAN. HE'S NOT LISTENING. HE'S TOO FAR GONE!
GET OUT OF MY WAY BEFORE YOU GET HURT, LEO.
I WON'T WARN YOU AGAIN, BROTHER.
THE OLD DONNIE IS STILL INSIDE. SOMEWHERE. THE VENOM IS ONLY AMPLIFYING HIS RAGE AND FRUSTRATION.
THEN I THINK IT'S TIME FOR THAT LAST TRICK UP OUR SLEEVES. SHOW HIM THE FORMULA, BATMAN.

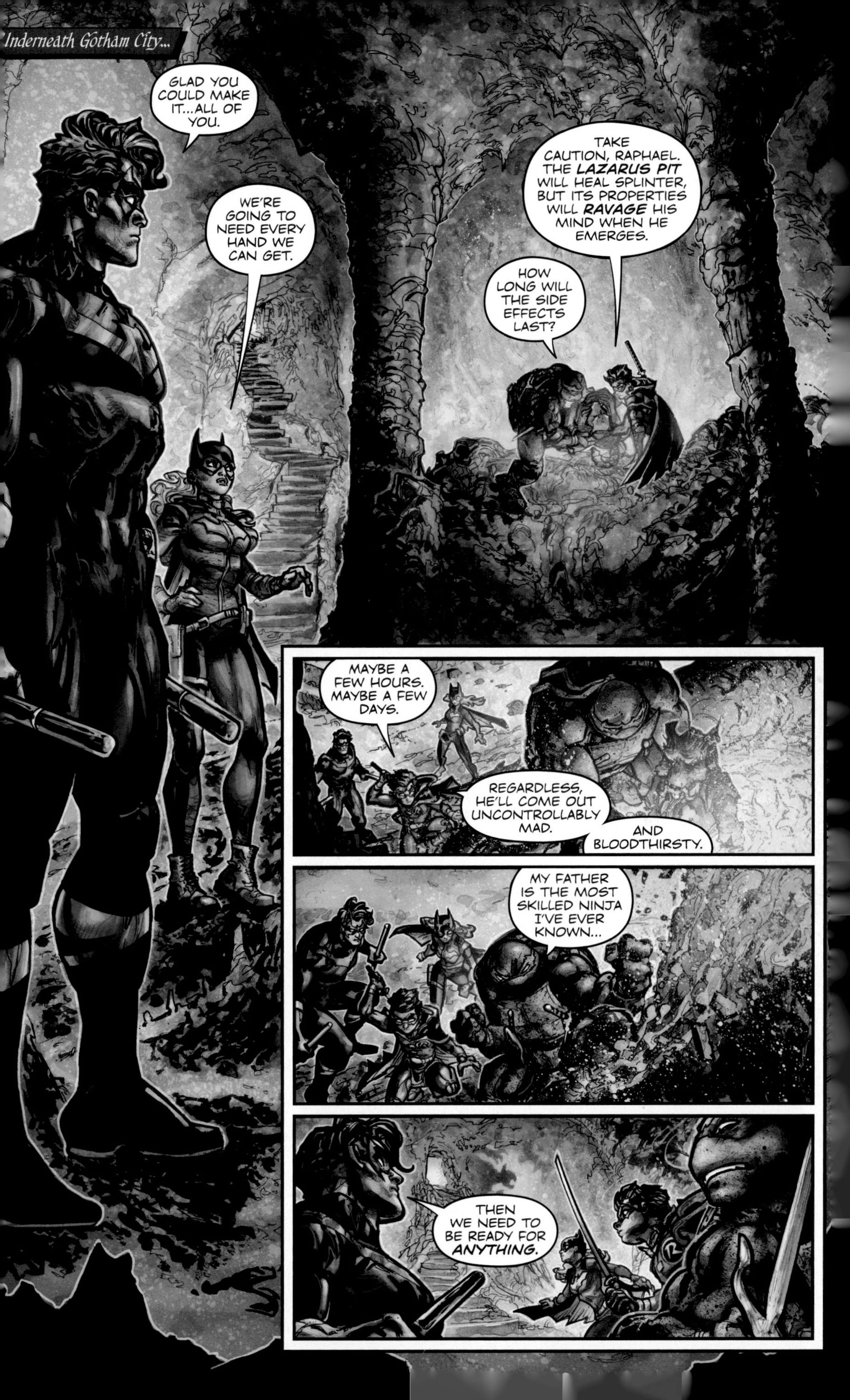
Underneath Gotham City...
GLAD YOU COULD MAKE IT...ALL OF YOU.
WE'RE GOING TO NEED EVERY HAND WE CAN GET.
TAKE CAUTION, RAPHAEL. THE LAZARUS PIT WILL HEAL SPLINTER, BUT ITS PROPERTIES WILL RAVAGE HIS MIND WHEN HE EMERGES.
HOW LONG WILL THE SIDE EFFECTS LAST?
MAYBE A FEW HOURS. MAYBE A FEW DAYS.
REGARDLESS, HE'LL COME OUT UNCONTROLLABLY MAD.
AND BLOODTHIRSTY.
MY FATHER IS THE MOST SKILLED NINJA I'VE EVER KNOWN...
THEN WE NEED TO BE READY FOR ANYTHING.

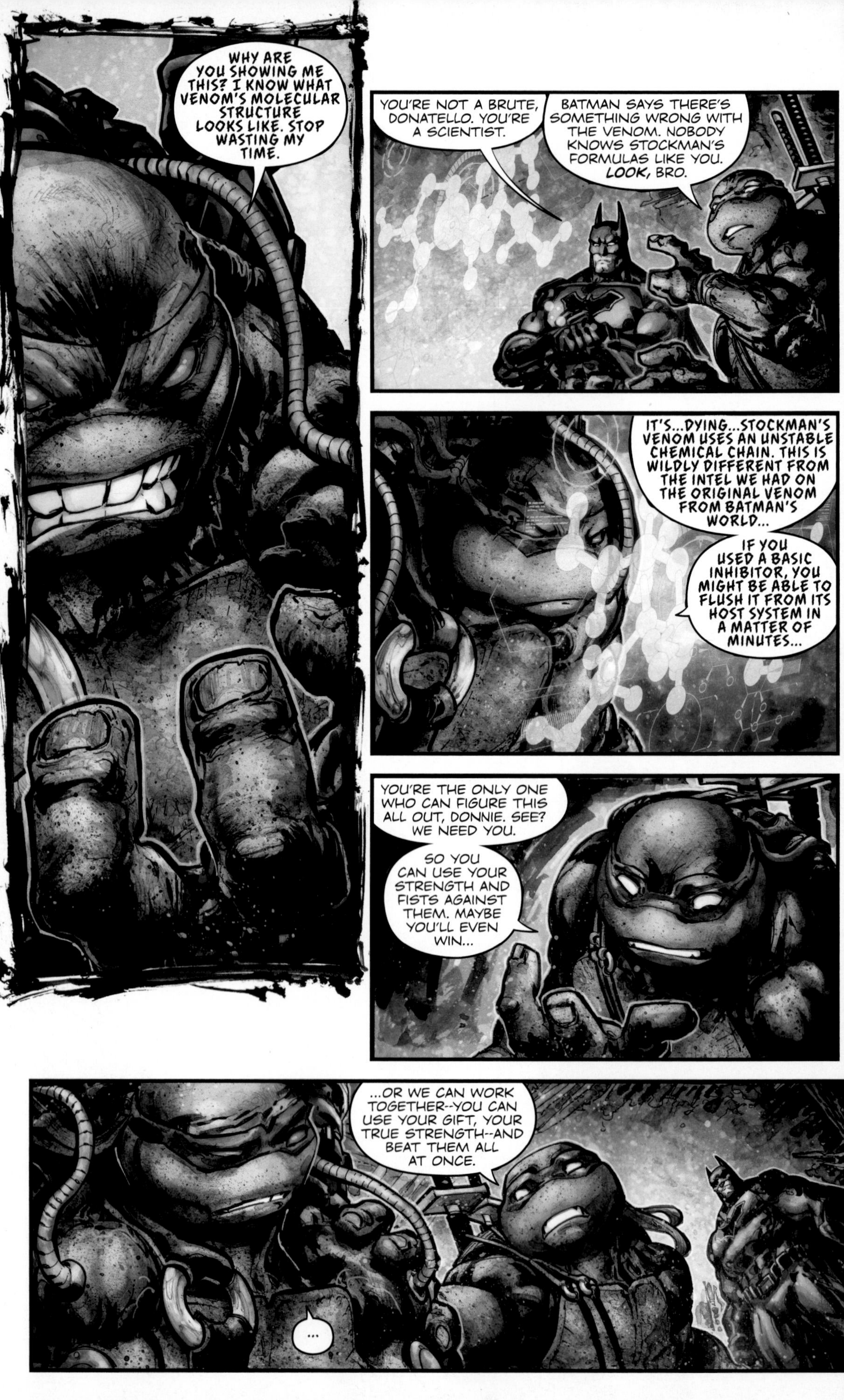
WHY ARE YOU SHOWING ME THIS? I KNOW WHAT VENOM'S MOLECULAR STRUCTURE LOOKS LIKE. STOP WASTING MY TIME.
YOU'RE NOT A BRUTE, DONATELLO. YOU'RE A SCIENTIST.
BATMAN SAYS THERE'S SOMETHING WRONG WITH THE VENOM. NOBODY KNOWS STOCKMAN'S FORMULAS LIKE YOU. LOOK, BRO.
IT'S...DYING...STOCKMAN'S VENOM USES AN UNSTABLE CHEMICAL CHAIN. THIS IS WILDLY DIFFERENT FROM THE INTEL WE HAD ON THE ORIGINAL VENOM FROM BATMAN'S WORLD...
IF YOU USED A BASIC INHIBITOR, YOU MIGHT BE ABLE TO FLUSH IT FROM ITS HOST SYSTEM IN A MATTER OF MINUTES...
YOU'RE THE ONLY ONE WHO CAN FIGURE THIS ALL OUT, DONNIE. SEE? WE NEED YOU.
SO YOU CAN USE YOUR STRENGTH AND FISTS AGAINST THEM. MAYBE YOU'LL EVEN WIN...
...OR WE CAN WORK TOGETHER--YOU CAN USE YOUR GIFT, YOUR TRUE STRENGTH--AND BEAT THEM ALL AT ONCE.
...

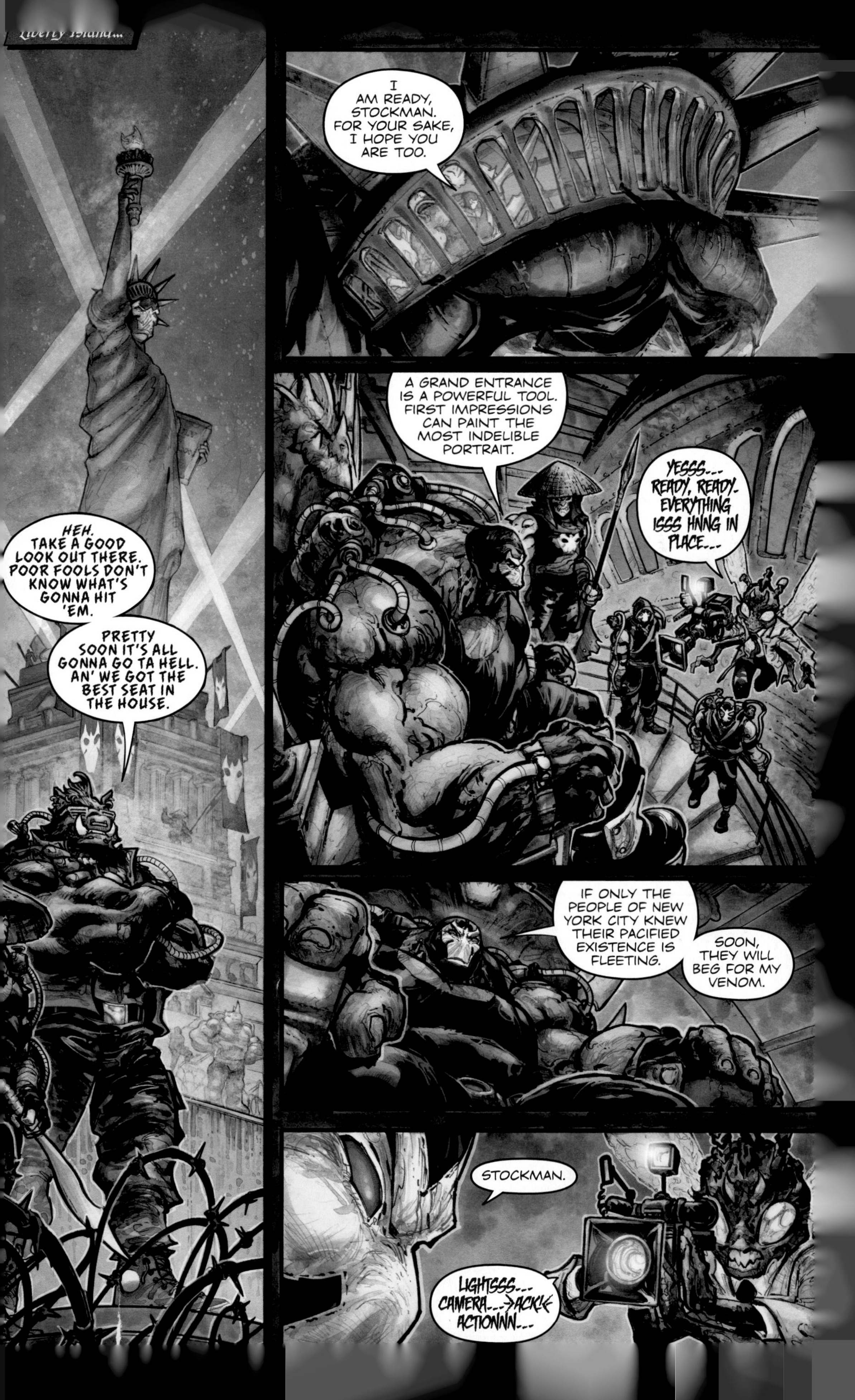
HEH. TAKE A GOOD LOOK OUT THERE. POOR FOOLS DON'T KNOW WHAT'S GONNA HIT 'EM.
PRETTY SOON IT'S ALL GONNA GO TA HELL. AN' WE GOT THE BEST SEAT IN THE HOUSE.
I AM READY, STOCKMAN. FOR YOUR SAKE, I HOPE YOU ARE TOO.
A GRAND ENTRANCE IS A POWERFUL TOOL. FIRST IMPRESSIONS CAN PAINT THE MOST INDELIBLE PORTRAIT.
YESSS... READY, READY. EVERYTHING ISSS HNNG IN PLACE...
IF ONLY THE PEOPLE OF NEW YORK CITY KNEW THEIR PACIFIED EXISTENCE IS FLEETING.
SOON, THEY WILL BEG FOR MY VENOM.
STOCKMAN.
LIGHTSSS... CAMERA...>ACK!< ACTIONNN...

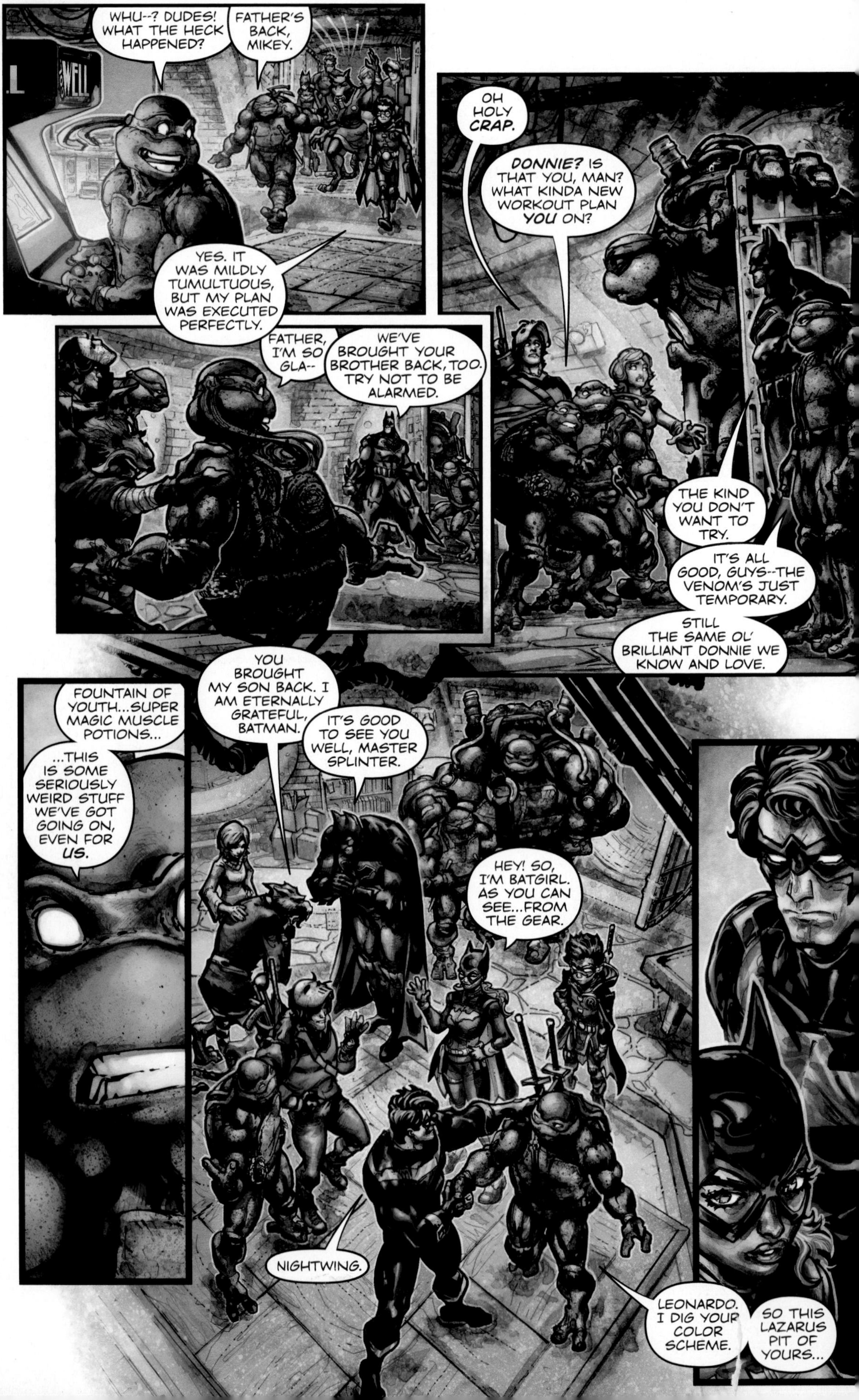

WHU--? DUDES! WHAT THE HECK HAPPENED?
FATHER'S BACK, MIKEY.
YES. IT WAS MILDLY TUMULTUOUS, BUT MY PLAN WAS EXECUTED PERFECTLY.
FATHER, I'M SO GLA--
WE'VE BROUGHT YOUR BROTHER BACK, TOO. TRY NOT TO BE ALARMED.
OH HOLY CRAP.
DONNIE? IS THAT YOU, MAN? WHAT KINDA NEW WORKOUT PLAN YOU ON?
THE KIND YOU DON'T WANT TO TRY.
IT'S ALL GOOD, GUYS--THE VENOM'S JUST TEMPORARY.
STILL THE SAME OL' BRILLIANT DONNIE WE KNOW AND LOVE.
FOUNTAIN OF YOUTH...SUPER MAGIC MUSCLE POTIONS...
...THIS IS SOME SERIOUSLY WEIRD STUFF WE'VE GOT GOING ON, EVEN FOR US.
YOU BROUGHT MY SON BACK. I AM ETERNALLY GRATEFUL, BATMAN.
IT'S GOOD TO SEE YOU WELL, MASTER SPLINTER.
HEY! SO, I'M BATGIRL. AS YOU CAN SEE...FROM THE GEAR.
NIGHTWING.
LEONARDO. I DIG YOUR COLOR SCHEME.
SO THIS LAZARUS PIT OF YOURS...

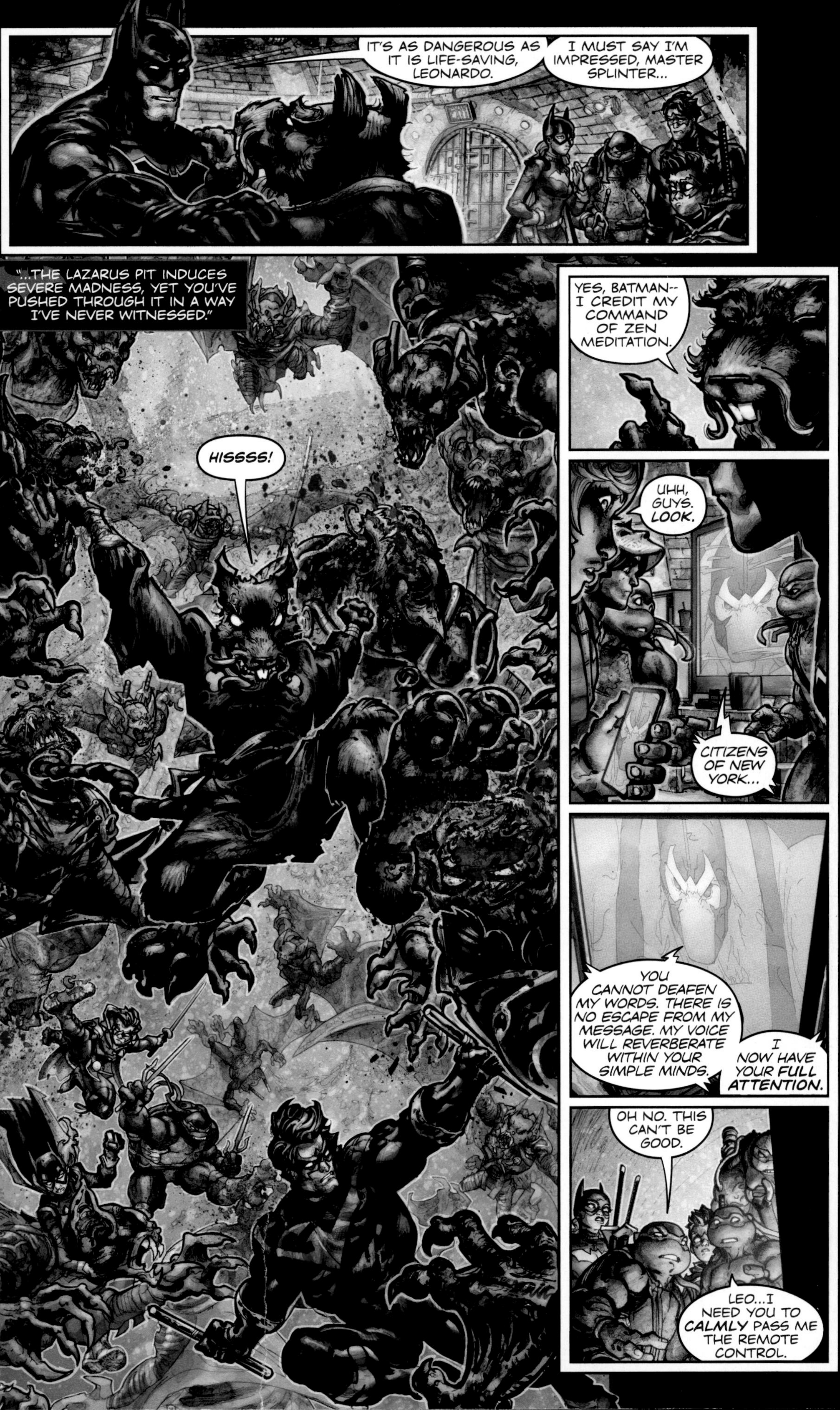
IT'S AS DANGEROUS AS IT IS LIFE-SAVING, LEONARDO.
I MUST SAY I'M IMPRESSED, MASTER SPLINTER...
"...THE LAZARUS PIT INDUCES SEVERE MADNESS, YET YOU'VE PUSHED THROUGH IT IN A WAY I'VE NEVER WITNESSED."
HISSSS!
YES, BATMAN-- I CREDIT MY COMMAND OF ZEN MEDITATION.
UHH, GUYS. **LOOK.**
CITIZENS OF NEW YORK...
YOU CANNOT DEAFEN MY WORDS. THERE IS NO ESCAPE FROM MY MESSAGE. MY VOICE WILL REVERBERATE WITHIN YOUR SIMPLE MINDS.
I NOW HAVE YOUR **FULL ATTENTION.**
OH NO. THIS CAN'T BE GOOD.
LEO...I NEED YOU TO **CALMLY** PASS ME THE REMOTE CONTROL.

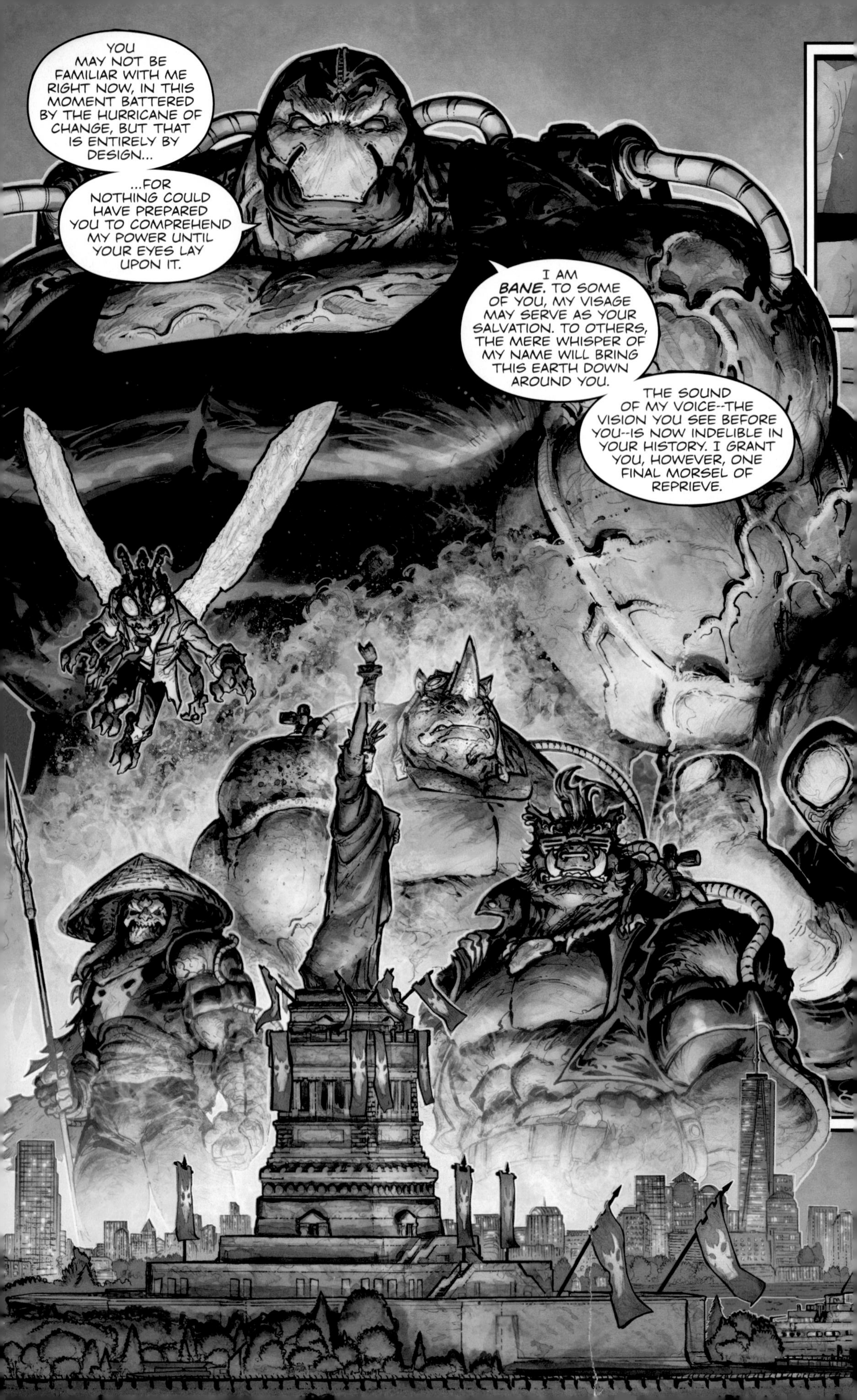
YOU MAY NOT BE FAMILIAR WITH ME RIGHT NOW, IN THIS MOMENT BATTERED BY THE HURRICANE OF CHANGE, BUT THAT IS ENTIRELY BY DESIGN...
...FOR NOTHING COULD HAVE PREPARED YOU TO COMPREHEND MY POWER UNTIL YOUR EYES LAY UPON IT.
I AM **BANE.** TO SOME OF YOU, MY VISAGE MAY SERVE AS YOUR SALVATION. TO OTHERS, THE MERE WHISPER OF MY NAME WILL BRING THIS EARTH DOWN AROUND YOU.
THE SOUND OF MY VOICE--THE VISION YOU SEE BEFORE YOU--IS NOW INDELIBLE IN YOUR HISTORY. I GRANT YOU, HOWEVER, ONE FINAL MORSEL OF REPRIEVE.

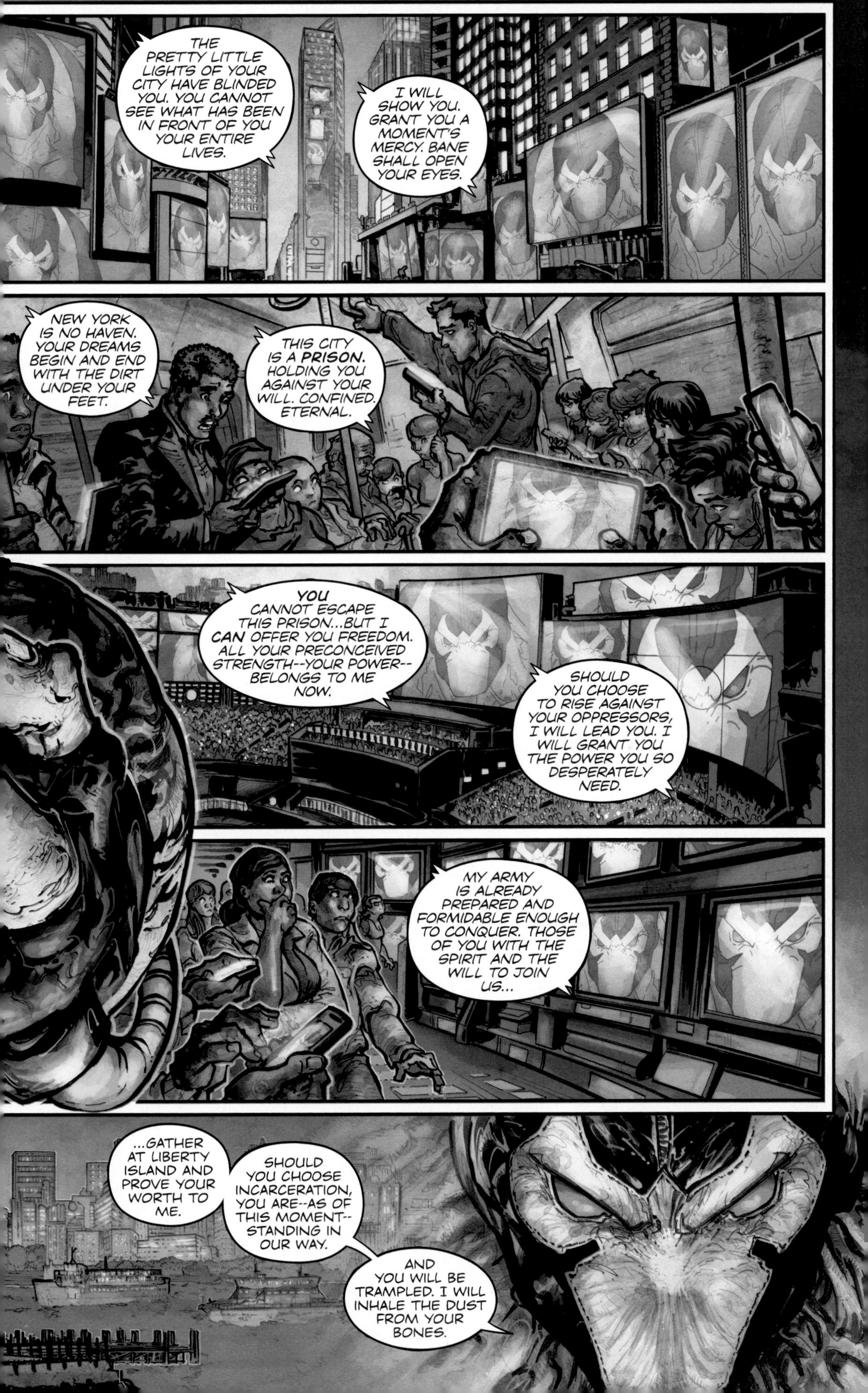
THE PRETTY LITTLE LIGHTS OF YOUR CITY HAVE BLINDED YOU. YOU CANNOT SEE WHAT HAS BEEN IN FRONT OF YOU YOUR ENTIRE LIVES.
I WILL SHOW YOU. GRANT YOU A MOMENT'S MERCY. BANE SHALL OPEN YOUR EYES.
NEW YORK IS NO HAVEN. YOUR DREAMS BEGIN AND END WITH THE DIRT UNDER YOUR FEET.
THIS CITY IS A PRISON. HOLDING YOU AGAINST YOUR WILL. CONFINED. ETERNAL.
YOU CANNOT ESCAPE THIS PRISON...BUT I CAN OFFER YOU FREEDOM. ALL YOUR PRECONCEIVED STRENGTH--YOUR POWER--BELONGS TO ME NOW.
SHOULD YOU CHOOSE TO RISE AGAINST YOUR OPPRESSORS, I WILL LEAD YOU. I WILL GRANT YOU THE POWER YOU SO DESPERATELY NEED.
MY ARMY IS ALREADY PREPARED AND FORMIDABLE ENOUGH TO CONQUER. THOSE OF YOU WITH THE SPIRIT AND THE WILL TO JOIN US...
...GATHER AT LIBERTY ISLAND AND PROVE YOUR WORTH TO ME.
SHOULD YOU CHOOSE INCARCERATION, YOU ARE--AS OF THIS MOMENT--STANDING IN OUR WAY.
AND YOU WILL BE TRAMPLED. I WILL INHALE THE DUST FROM YOUR BONES.

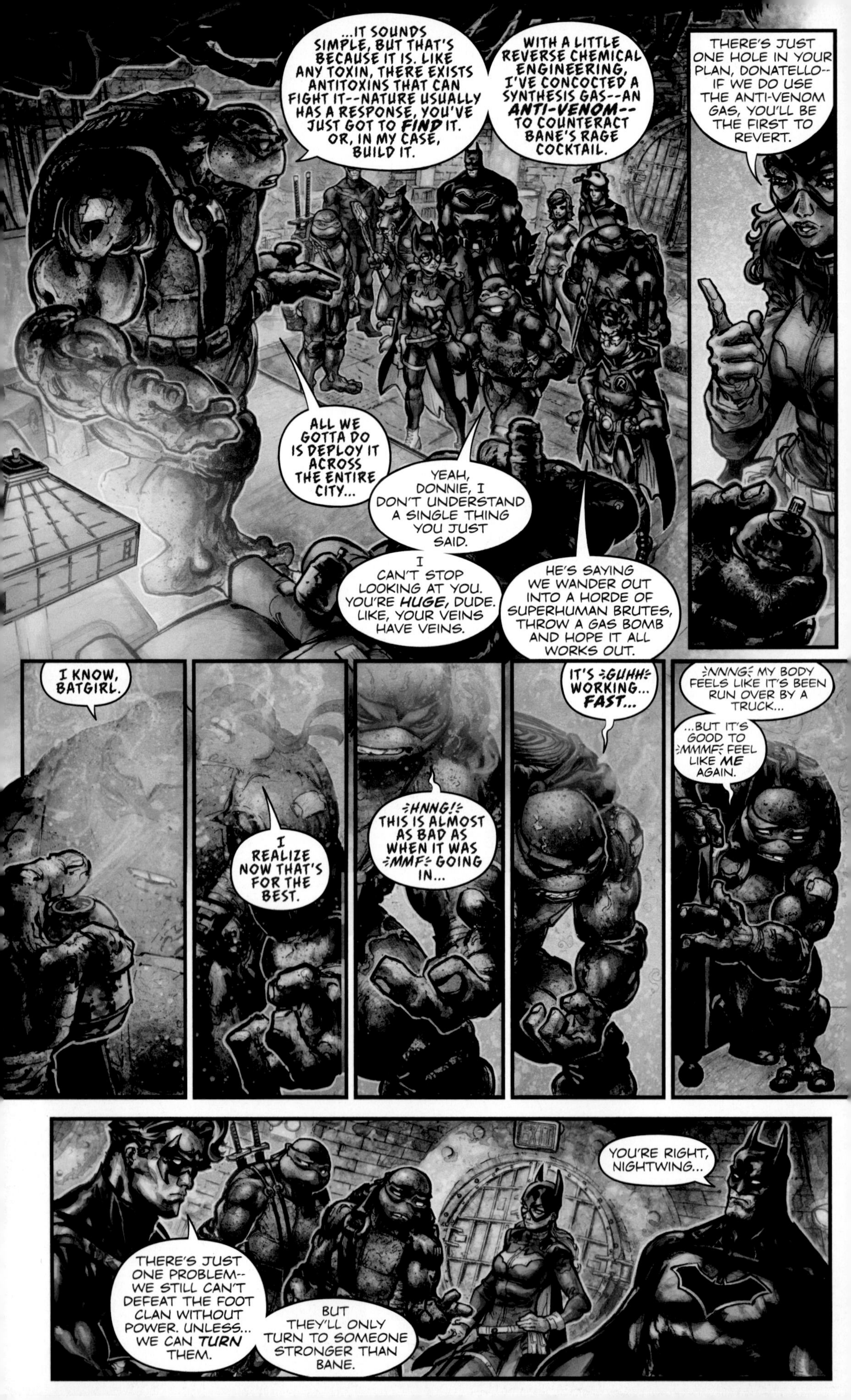
...IT SOUNDS SIMPLE, BUT THAT'S BECAUSE IT IS. LIKE ANY TOXIN, THERE EXISTS ANTITOXINS THAT CAN FIGHT IT--NATURE USUALLY HAS A RESPONSE, YOU'VE JUST GOT TO FIND IT. OR, IN MY CASE, BUILD IT.
WITH A LITTLE REVERSE CHEMICAL ENGINEERING, I'VE CONCOCTED A SYNTHESIS GAS--AN ANTI-VENOM--TO COUNTERACT BANE'S RAGE COCKTAIL.
ALL WE GOTTA DO IS DEPLOY IT ACROSS THE ENTIRE CITY...
YEAH, DONNIE, I DON'T UNDERSTAND A SINGLE THING YOU JUST SAID.
I CAN'T STOP LOOKING AT YOU. YOU'RE HUGE, DUDE. LIKE, YOUR VEINS HAVE VEINS.
HE'S SAYING WE WANDER OUT INTO A HORDE OF SUPERHUMAN BRUTES, THROW A GAS BOMB AND HOPE IT ALL WORKS OUT.
THERE'S JUST ONE HOLE IN YOUR PLAN, DONATELLO--IF WE DO USE THE ANTI-VENOM GAS, YOU'LL BE THE FIRST TO REVERT.
I KNOW, BATGIRL.
I REALIZE NOW THAT'S FOR THE BEST.
HNNG! THIS IS ALMOST AS BAD AS WHEN IT WAS MMF GOING IN...
IT'S GUHH WORKING... FAST...
NNNG MY BODY FEELS LIKE IT'S BEEN RUN OVER BY A TRUCK...
...BUT IT'S GOOD TO MMMF FEEL LIKE ME AGAIN.
EXIT
THERE'S JUST ONE PROBLEM--WE STILL CAN'T DEFEAT THE FOOT CLAN WITHOUT POWER. UNLESS... WE CAN TURN THEM.
BUT THEY'LL ONLY TURN TO SOMEONE STRONGER THAN BANE.
YOU'RE RIGHT, NIGHTWING...

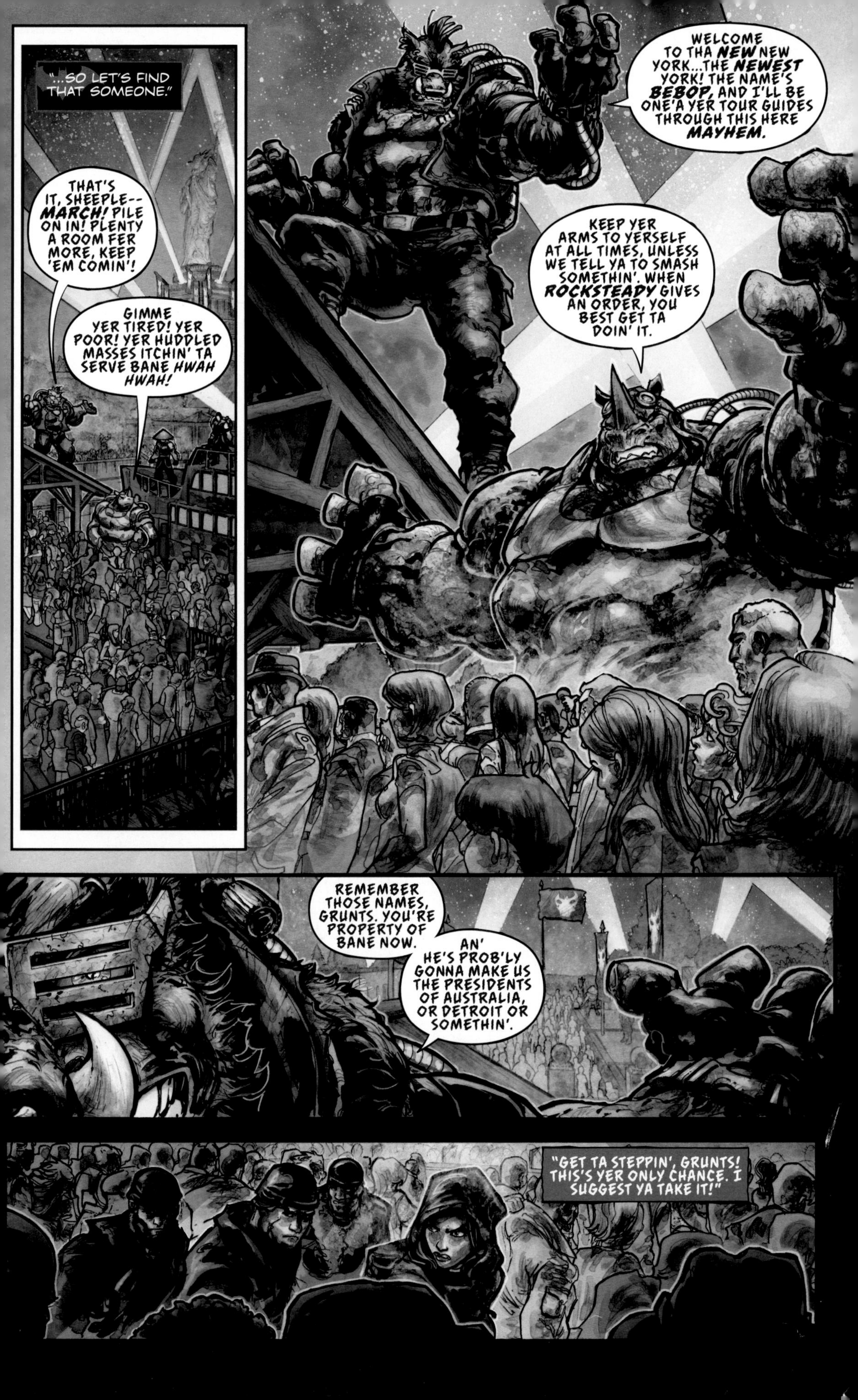
"...SO LET'S FIND THAT SOMEONE."
WELCOME TO THA NEW NEW YORK...THE NEWEST YORK! THE NAME'S BEBOP, AND I'LL BE ONE'A YER TOUR GUIDES THROUGH THIS HERE MAYHEM.
THAT'S IT, SHEEPLE--MARCH! PILE ON IN! PLENTY A ROOM FER MORE, KEEP 'EM COMIN'!
GIMME YER TIRED! YER POOR! YER HUDDLED MASSES ITCHIN' TA SERVE BANE HWAH HWAH!
KEEP YER ARMS TO YERSELF AT ALL TIMES, UNLESS WE TELL YA TO SMASH SOMETHIN'. WHEN ROCKSTEADY GIVES AN ORDER, YOU BEST GET TA DOIN' IT.
REMEMBER THOSE NAMES, GRUNTS. YOU'RE PROPERTY OF BANE NOW.
AN' HE'S PROB'LY GONNA MAKE US THE PRESIDENTS OF AUSTRALIA, OR DETROIT OR SOMETHIN'.
"GET TA STEPPIN', GRUNTS! THIS'S YER ONLY CHANCE. I SUGGEST YA TAKE IT!"

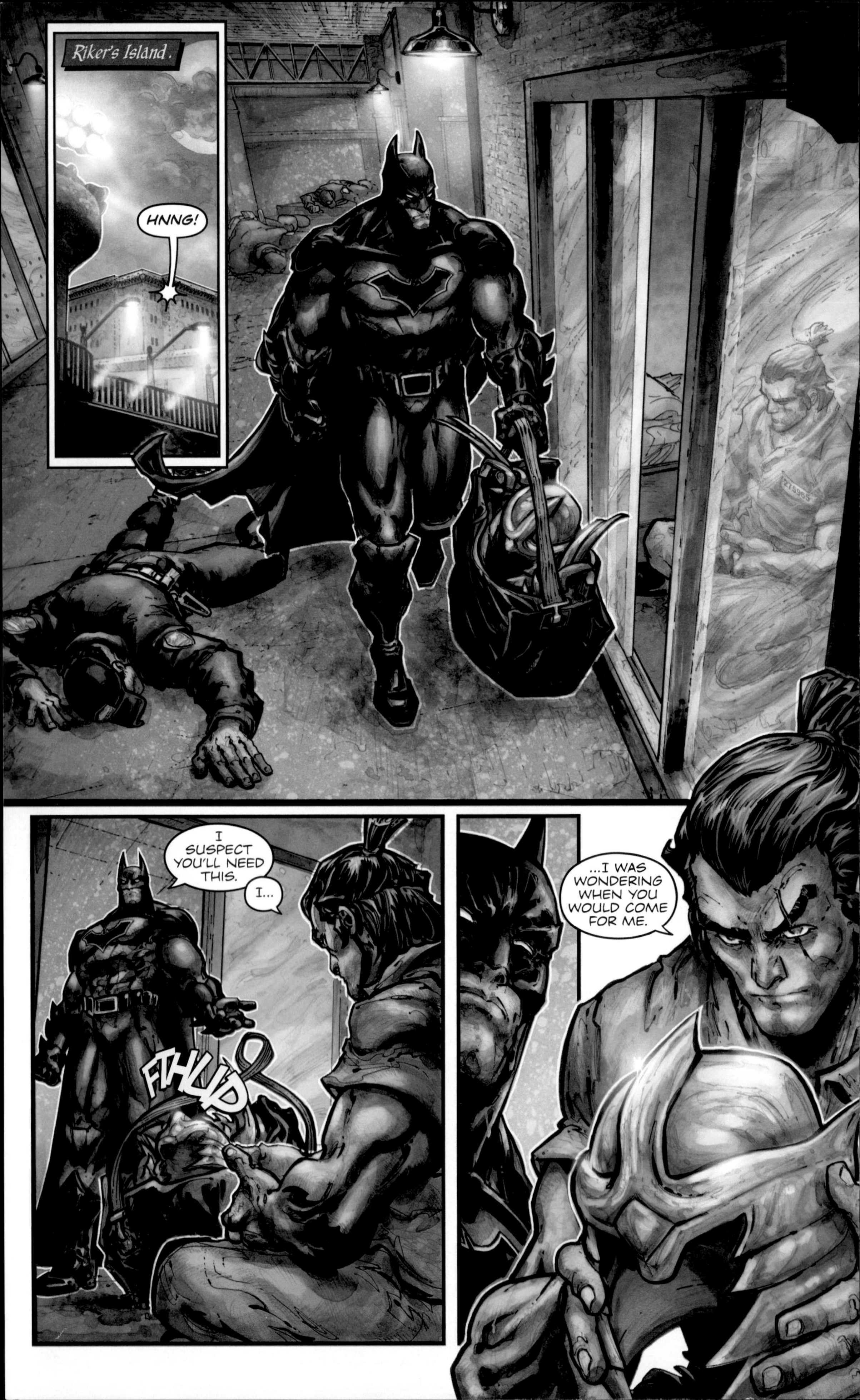
Riker's Island.
HNNG!
I SUSPECT YOU'LL NEED THIS.
I...
FTHUD
...I WAS WONDERING WHEN YOU WOULD COME FOR ME.

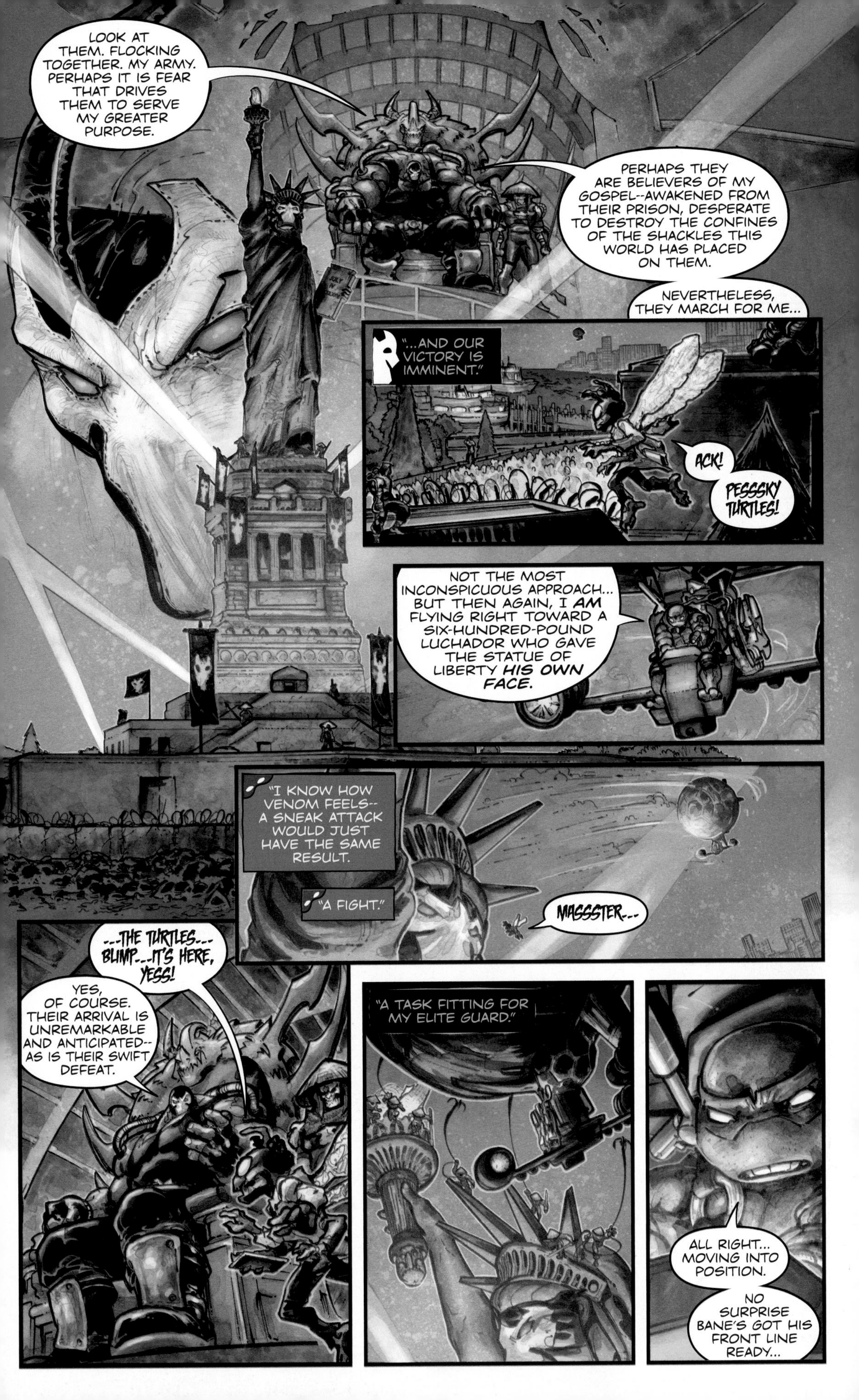

LOOK AT THEM. FLOCKING TOGETHER. MY ARMY. PERHAPS IT IS FEAR THAT DRIVES THEM TO SERVE MY GREATER PURPOSE.
PERHAPS THEY ARE BELIEVERS OF MY GOSPEL--AWAKENED FROM THEIR PRISON, DESPERATE TO DESTROY THE CONFINES OF THE SHACKLES THIS WORLD HAS PLACED ON THEM.
NEVERTHELESS, THEY MARCH FOR ME...
"...AND OUR VICTORY IS IMMINENT."
ACK!
PESSSKY TURTLES!
NOT THE MOST INCONSPICUOUS APPROACH... BUT THEN AGAIN, I AM FLYING RIGHT TOWARD A SIX-HUNDRED-POUND LUCHADOR WHO GAVE THE STATUE OF LIBERTY HIS OWN FACE.
"I KNOW HOW VENOM FEELS-- A SNEAK ATTACK WOULD JUST HAVE THE SAME RESULT.
"A FIGHT."
MASSSTER...
...THE TURTLES... BLIMP...IT'S HERE, YESS!
YES, OF COURSE. THEIR ARRIVAL IS UNREMARKABLE AND ANTICIPATED-- AS IS THEIR SWIFT DEFEAT.
"A TASK FITTING FOR MY ELITE GUARD."
ALL RIGHT... MOVING INTO POSITION.
NO SURPRISE BANE'S GOT HIS FRONT LINE READY...

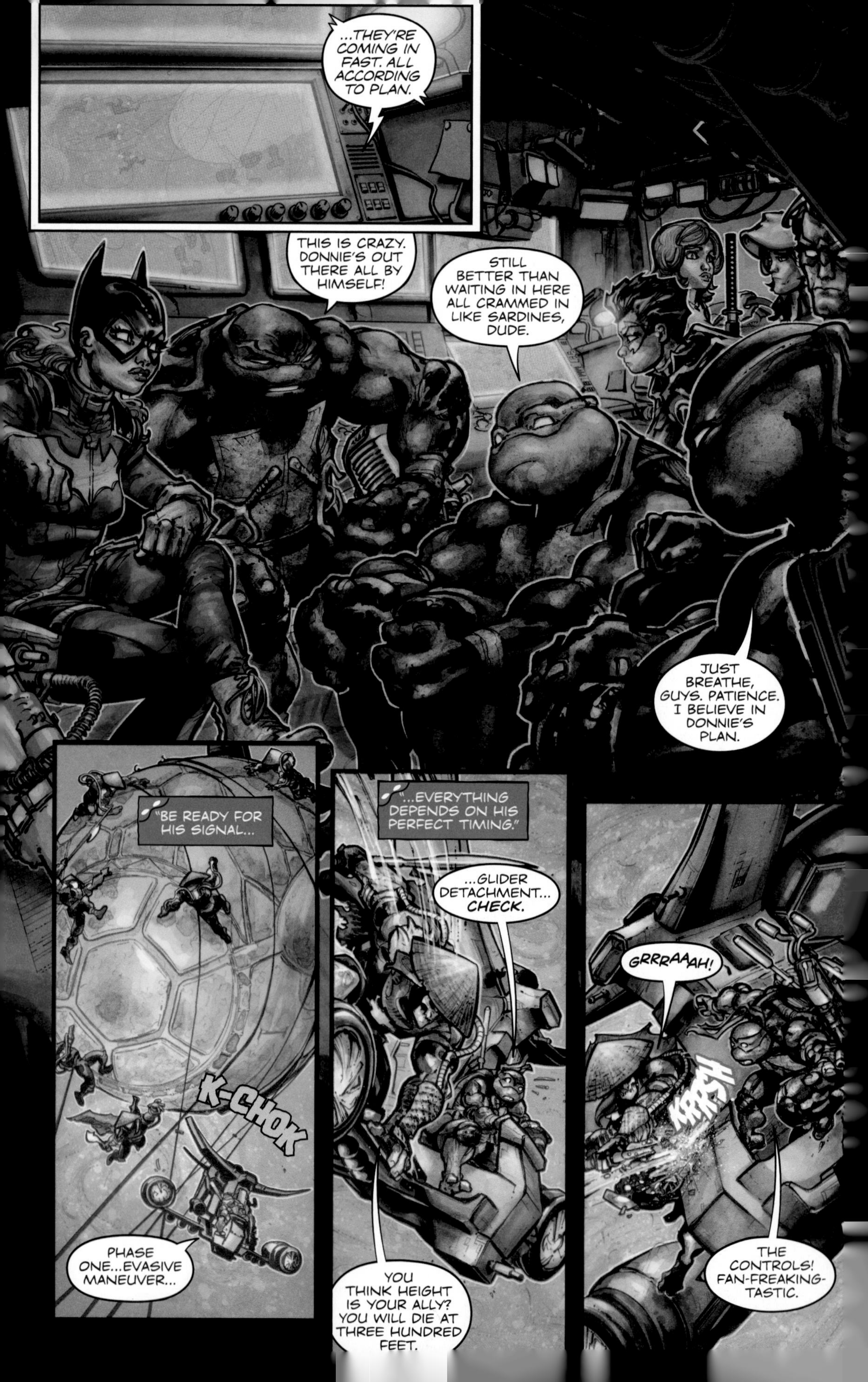
...THEY'RE COMING IN FAST. ALL ACCORDING TO PLAN.
THIS IS CRAZY. DONNIE'S OUT THERE ALL BY HIMSELF!
STILL BETTER THAN WAITING IN HERE ALL CRAMMED IN LIKE SARDINES, DUDE.
JUST BREATHE, GUYS. PATIENCE. I BELIEVE IN DONNIE'S PLAN.
"BE READY FOR HIS SIGNAL...
K-CHOK
PHASE ONE...EVASIVE MANEUVER...
"...EVERYTHING DEPENDS ON HIS PERFECT TIMING."
...GLIDER DETACHMENT... CHECK.
YOU THINK HEIGHT IS YOUR ALLY? YOU WILL DIE AT THREE HUNDRED FEET.
GRRRAAAAH!
KRRSH
THE CONTROLS! FAN-FREAKING-TASTIC.

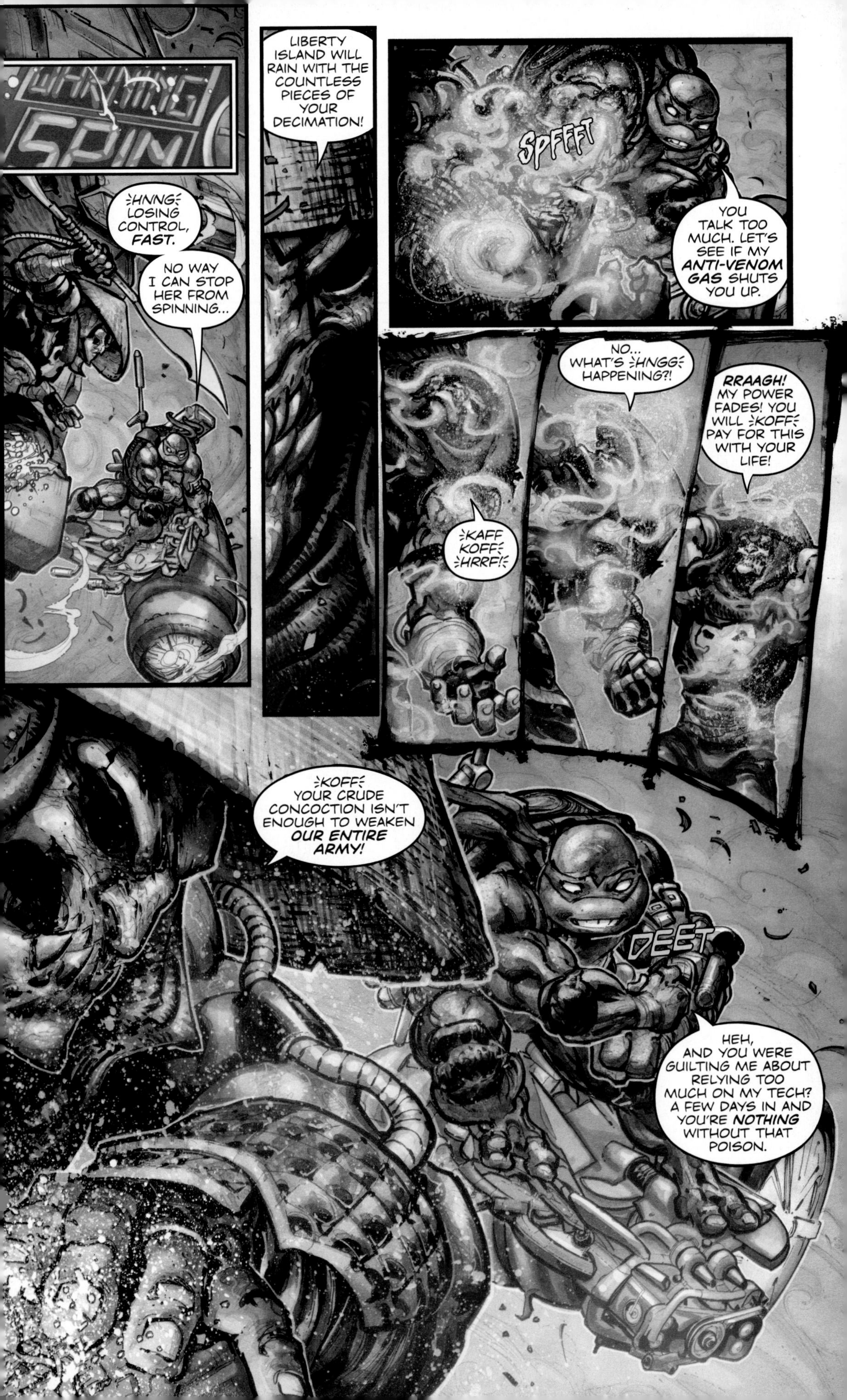
WHIRLING SPIN
LIBERTY ISLAND WILL RAIN WITH THE COUNTLESS PIECES OF YOUR DECIMATION!
SPFFFT
YOU TALK TOO MUCH. LET'S SEE IF MY ANTI-VENOM GAS SHUTS YOU UP.
HNNG LOSING CONTROL, FAST.
NO WAY I CAN STOP HER FROM SPINNING...
KAFF KOFF HRRF!
NO... WHAT'S HNGG HAPPENING?!
RRAAGH! MY POWER FADES! YOU WILL KOFF PAY FOR THIS WITH YOUR LIFE!
KOFF YOUR CRUDE CONCOCTION ISN'T ENOUGH TO WEAKEN OUR ENTIRE ARMY!
DEET
HEH, AND YOU WERE GUILTING ME ABOUT RELYING TOO MUCH ON MY TECH? A FEW DAYS IN AND YOU'RE NOTHING WITHOUT THAT POISON.

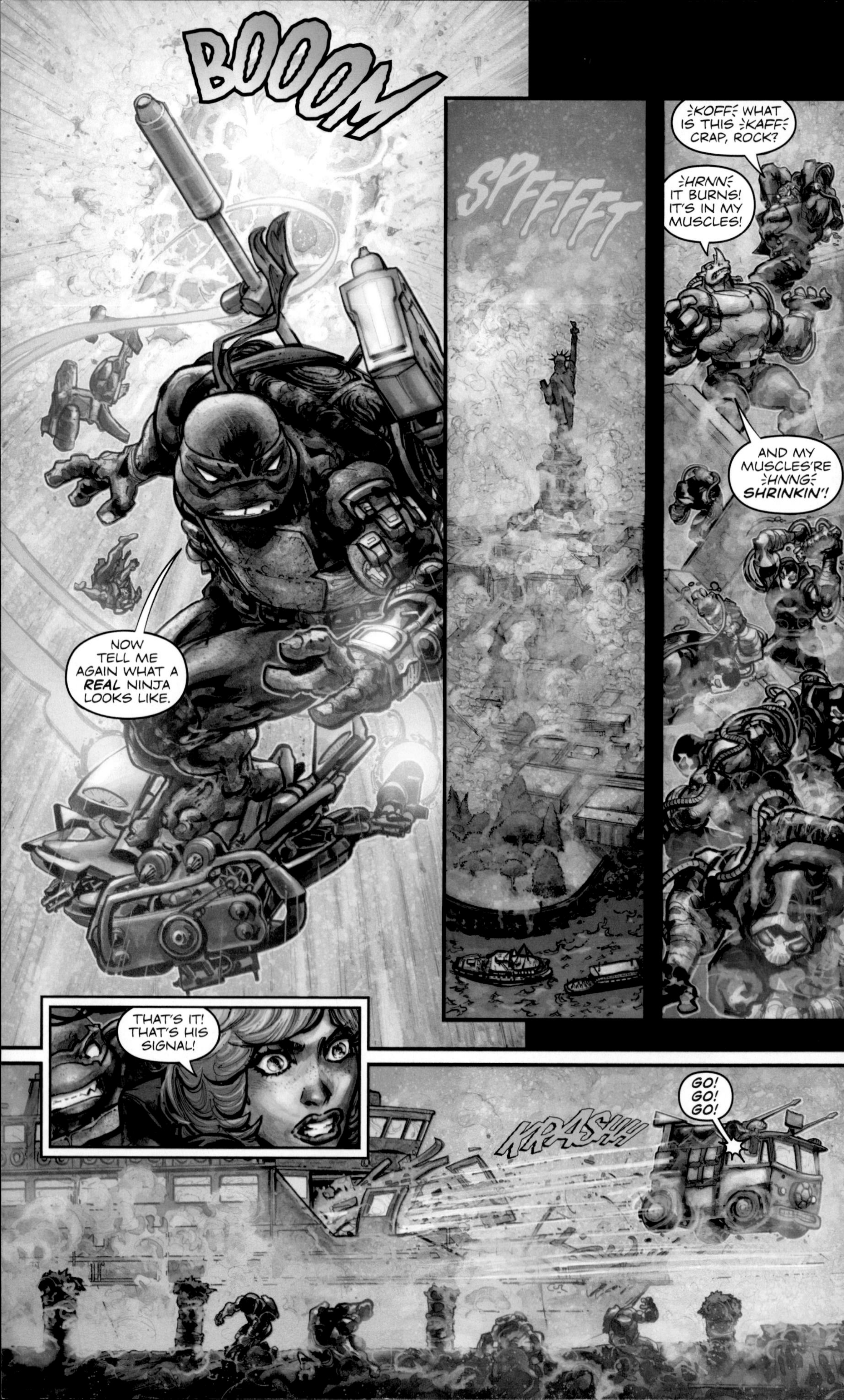
BOOOM
NOW TELL ME AGAIN WHAT A **REAL** NINJA LOOKS LIKE.
SPFFFFT
KOFF WHAT IS THIS KAFF CRAP, ROCK?
HRNN IT BURNS! IT'S IN MY MUSCLES!
AND MY MUSCLES'RE HNNG **SHRINKIN'!**
THAT'S IT! THAT'S HIS SIGNAL!
KRASHH
GO! GO! GO!

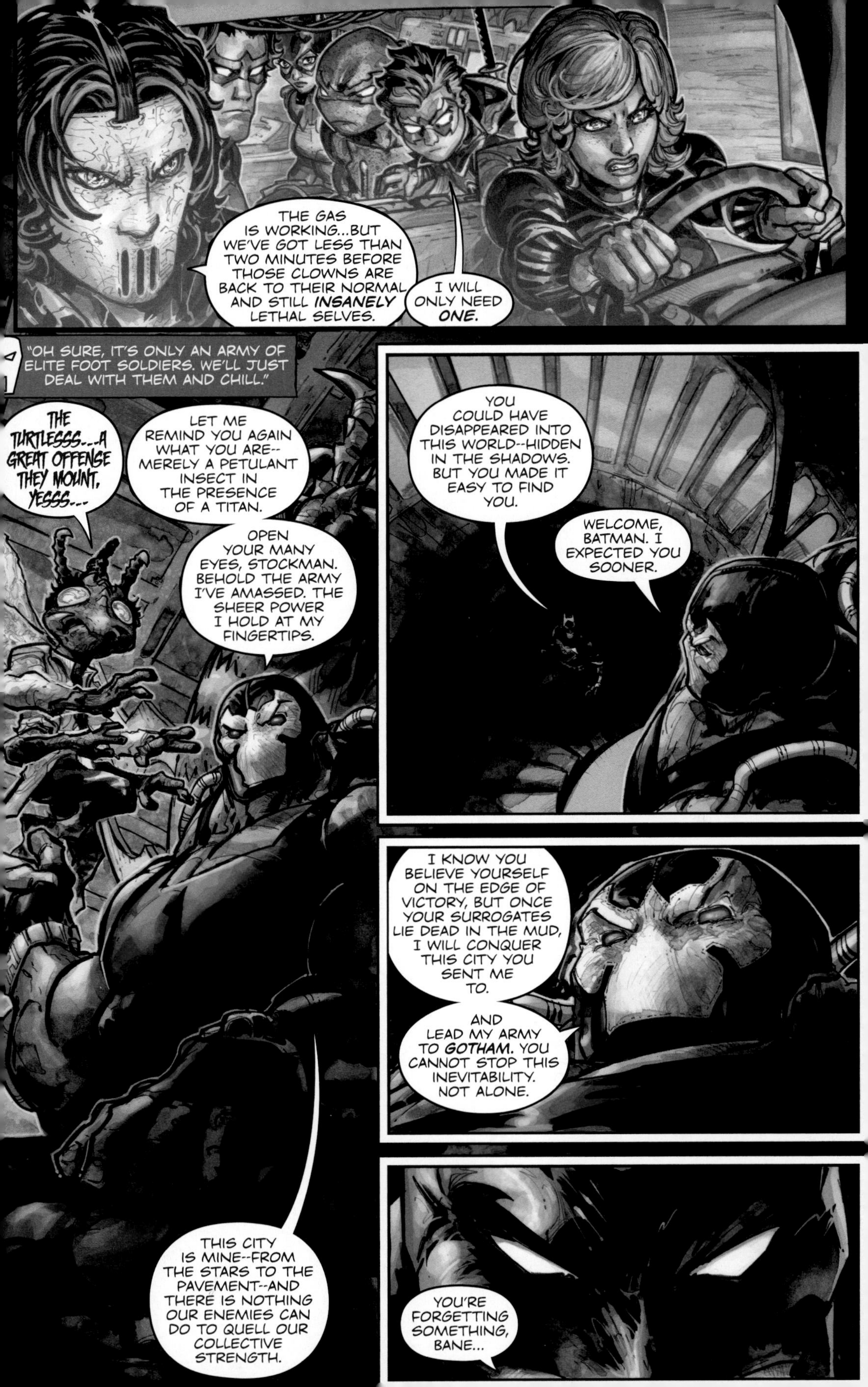
THE GAS IS WORKING...BUT WE'VE GOT LESS THAN TWO MINUTES BEFORE THOSE CLOWNS ARE BACK TO THEIR NORMAL AND STILL INSANELY LETHAL SELVES.
I WILL ONLY NEED ONE.
"OH SURE, IT'S ONLY AN ARMY OF ELITE FOOT SOLDIERS. WE'LL JUST DEAL WITH THEM AND CHILL."
THE TURTLESSS...A GREAT OFFENSE THEY MOUNT, YESSS...
LET ME REMIND YOU AGAIN WHAT YOU ARE--MERELY A PETULANT INSECT IN THE PRESENCE OF A TITAN.
OPEN YOUR MANY EYES, STOCKMAN. BEHOLD THE ARMY I'VE AMASSED. THE SHEER POWER I HOLD AT MY FINGERTIPS.
THIS CITY IS MINE--FROM THE STARS TO THE PAVEMENT--AND THERE IS NOTHING OUR ENEMIES CAN DO TO QUELL OUR COLLECTIVE STRENGTH.
YOU COULD HAVE DISAPPEARED INTO THIS WORLD--HIDDEN IN THE SHADOWS. BUT YOU MADE IT EASY TO FIND YOU.
WELCOME, BATMAN. I EXPECTED YOU SOONER.
I KNOW YOU BELIEVE YOURSELF ON THE EDGE OF VICTORY, BUT ONCE YOUR SURROGATES LIE DEAD IN THE MUD, I WILL CONQUER THIS CITY YOU SENT ME TO.
AND LEAD MY ARMY TO GOTHAM. YOU CANNOT STOP THIS INEVITABILITY. NOT ALONE.
YOU'RE FORGETTING SOMETHING, BANE...

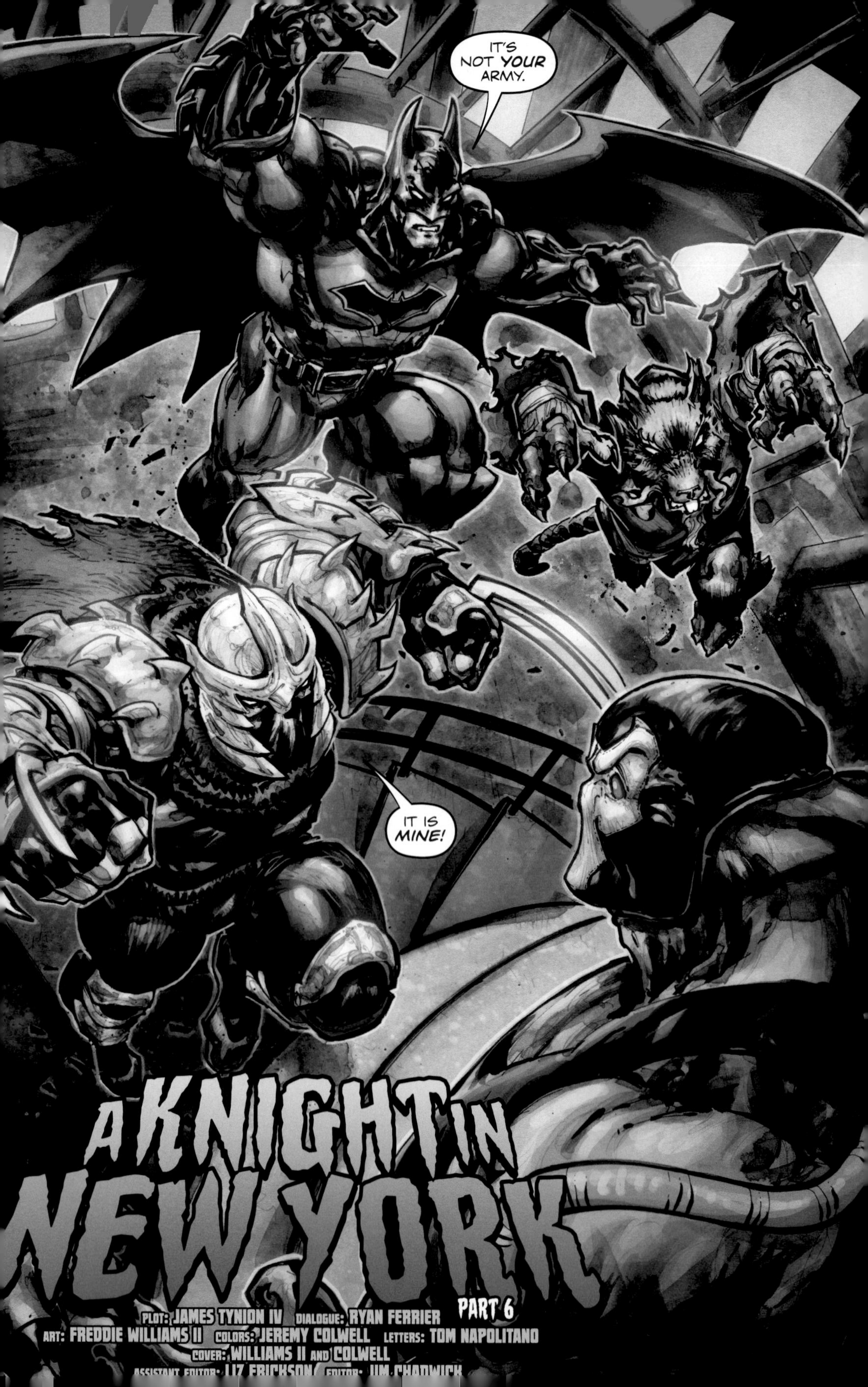
IT'S NOT YOUR ARMY.
IT IS MINE!
A KNIGHT IN NEW YORK
PART 6
PLOT: JAMES TYNION IV DIALOGUE: RYAN FERRIER
ART: FREDDIE WILLIAMS II COLORS: JEREMY COLWELL LETTERS: TOM NAPOLITANO
COVER: WILLIAMS II AND COLWELL
ASSISTANT EDITOR: LIZ ERICKSON EDITOR: JIM CHADWICK

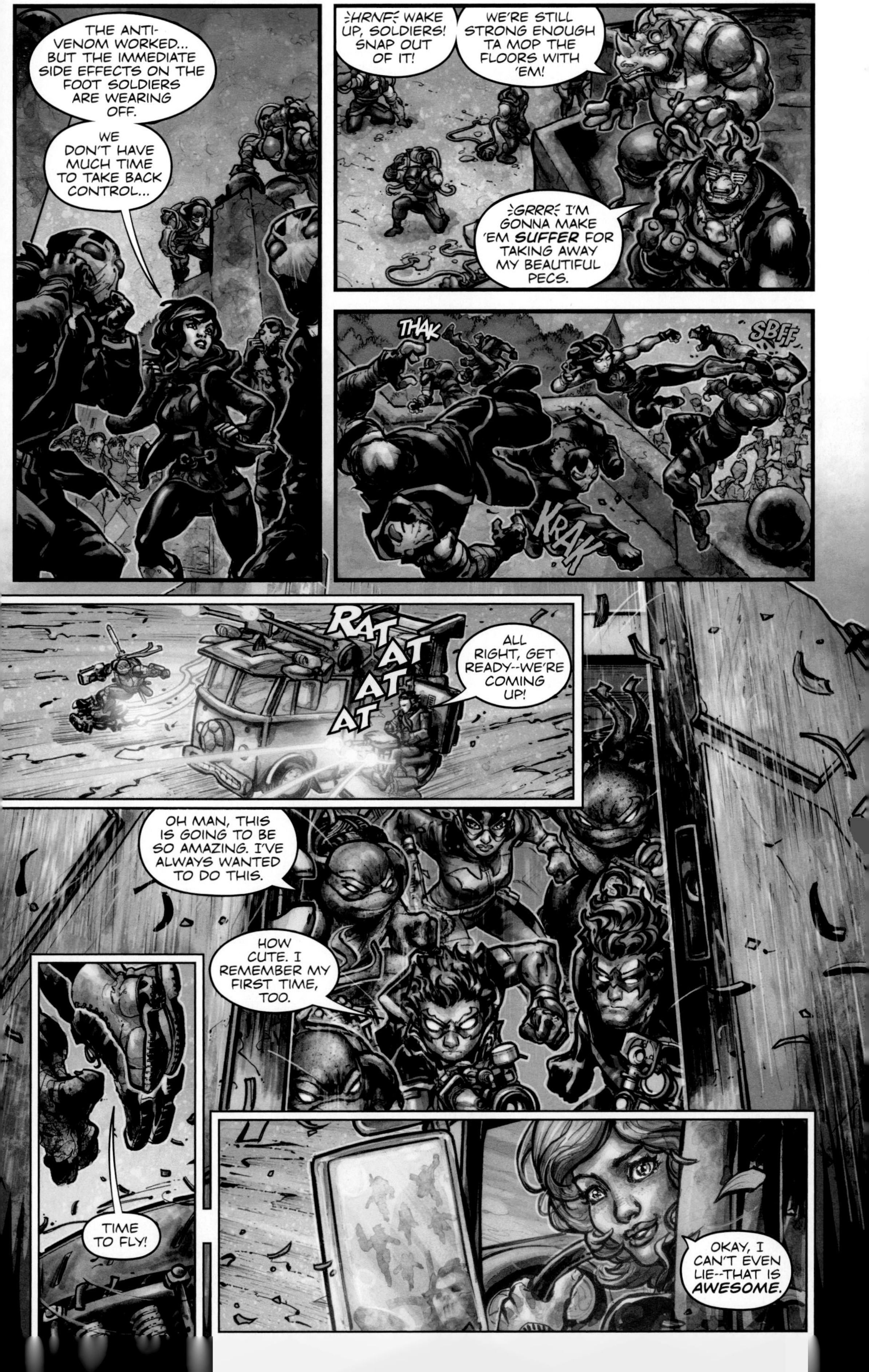
THE ANTI-VENOM WORKED... BUT THE IMMEDIATE SIDE EFFECTS ON THE FOOT SOLDIERS ARE WEARING OFF.
WE DON'T HAVE MUCH TIME TO TAKE BACK CONTROL...
HRNF WAKE UP, SOLDIERS! SNAP OUT OF IT!
WE'RE STILL STRONG ENOUGH TA MOP THE FLOORS WITH 'EM!
GRRR I'M GONNA MAKE 'EM SUFFER FOR TAKING AWAY MY BEAUTIFUL PECS.
THAK
SBFF
KRAK
RAT AT AT AT
ALL RIGHT, GET READY--WE'RE COMING UP!
OH MAN, THIS IS GOING TO BE SO AMAZING. I'VE ALWAYS WANTED TO DO THIS.
HOW CUTE. I REMEMBER MY FIRST TIME, TOO.
TIME TO FLY!
OKAY, I CAN'T EVEN LIE--THAT IS AWESOME.

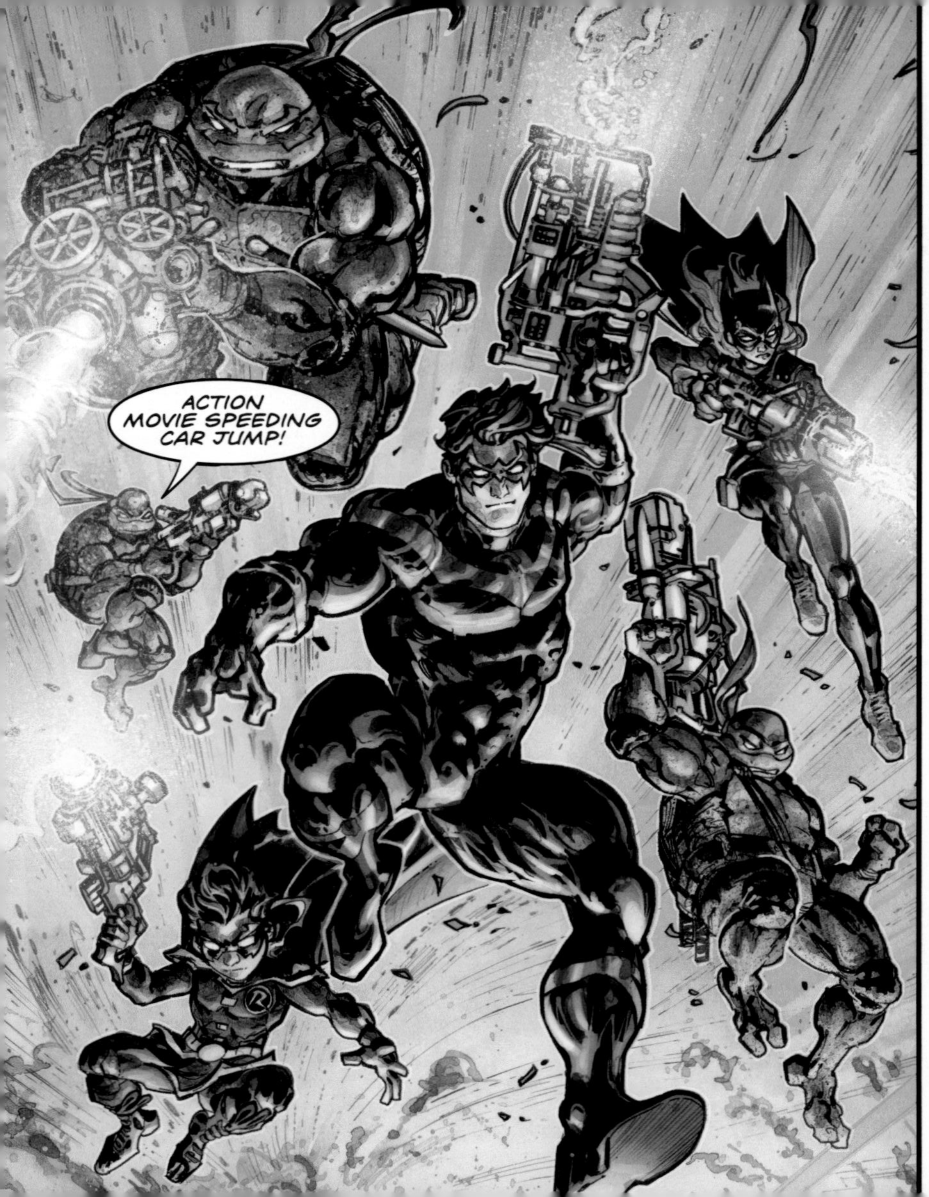
ACTION MOVIE SPEEDING CAR JUMP!

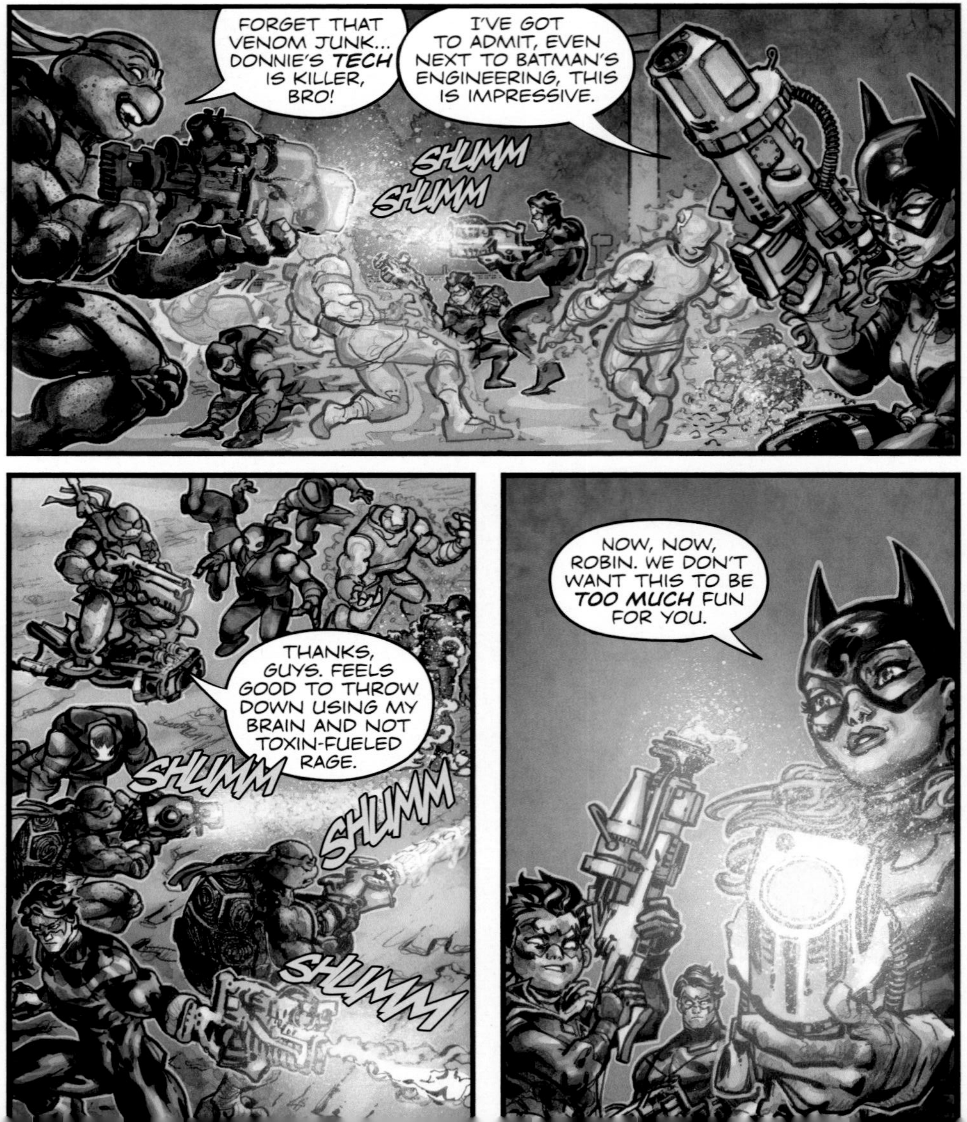
FORGET THAT VENOM JUNK... DONNIE'S **TECH** IS KILLER, BRO!
I'VE GOT TO ADMIT, EVEN NEXT TO BATMAN'S ENGINEERING, THIS IS IMPRESSIVE.
SHUMM
SHUMM
THANKS, GUYS. FEELS GOOD TO THROW DOWN USING MY BRAIN AND NOT TOXIN-FUELED RAGE.
SHUMM
SHUMM
SHUMM
NOW, NOW, ROBIN. WE DON'T WANT THIS TO BE ***TOO MUCH*** FUN FOR YOU.

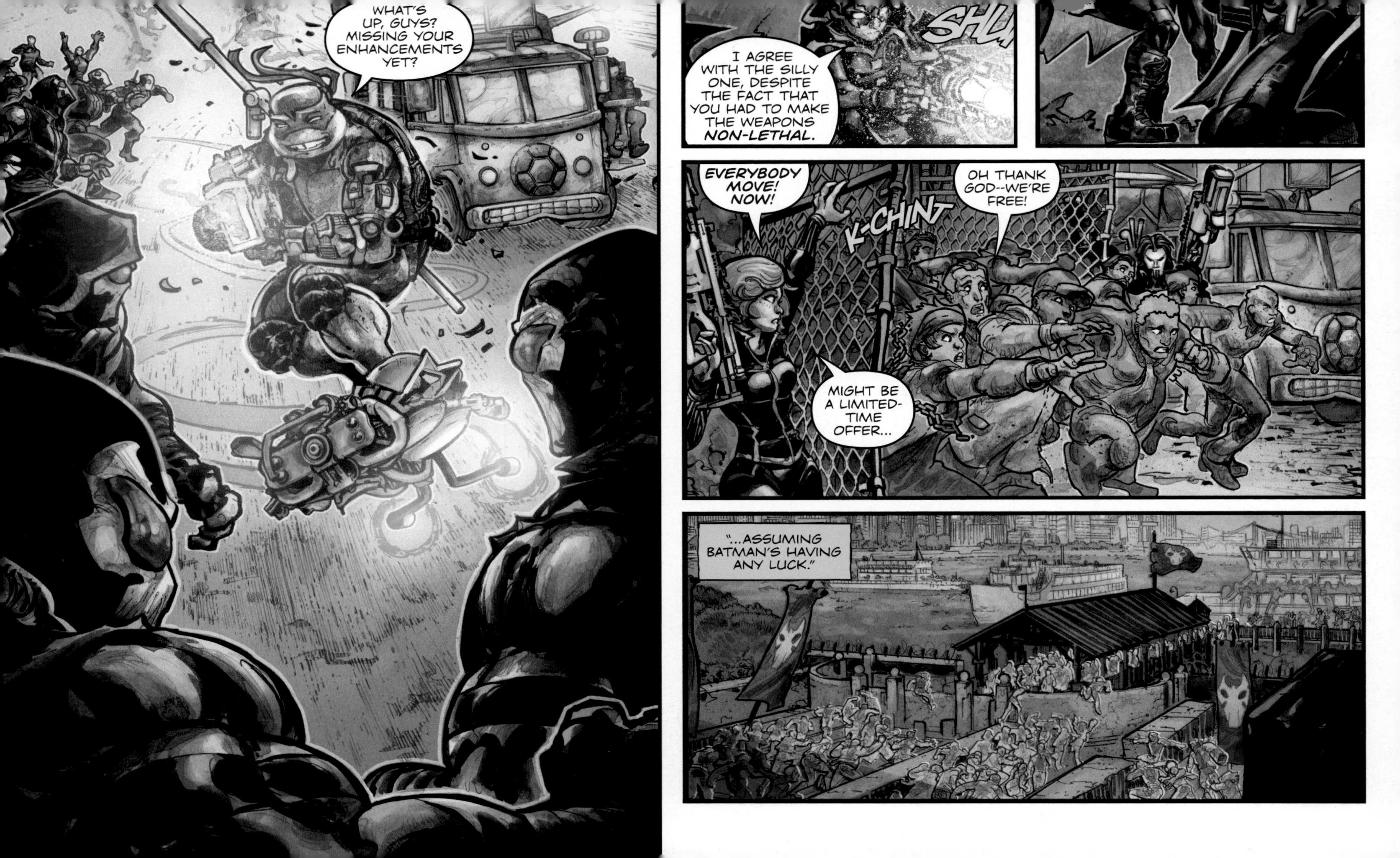
WHAT'S UP, GUYS? MISSING YOUR ENHANCEMENTS YET?
SHU
I AGREE WITH THE SILLY ONE, DESPITE THE FACT THAT YOU HAD TO MAKE THE WEAPONS NON-LETHAL.
EVERYBODY MOVE! NOW!
K-CHINT
OH THANK GOD--WE'RE FREE!
MIGHT BE A LIMITED-TIME OFFER...
"...ASSUMING BATMAN'S HAVING ANY LUCK."

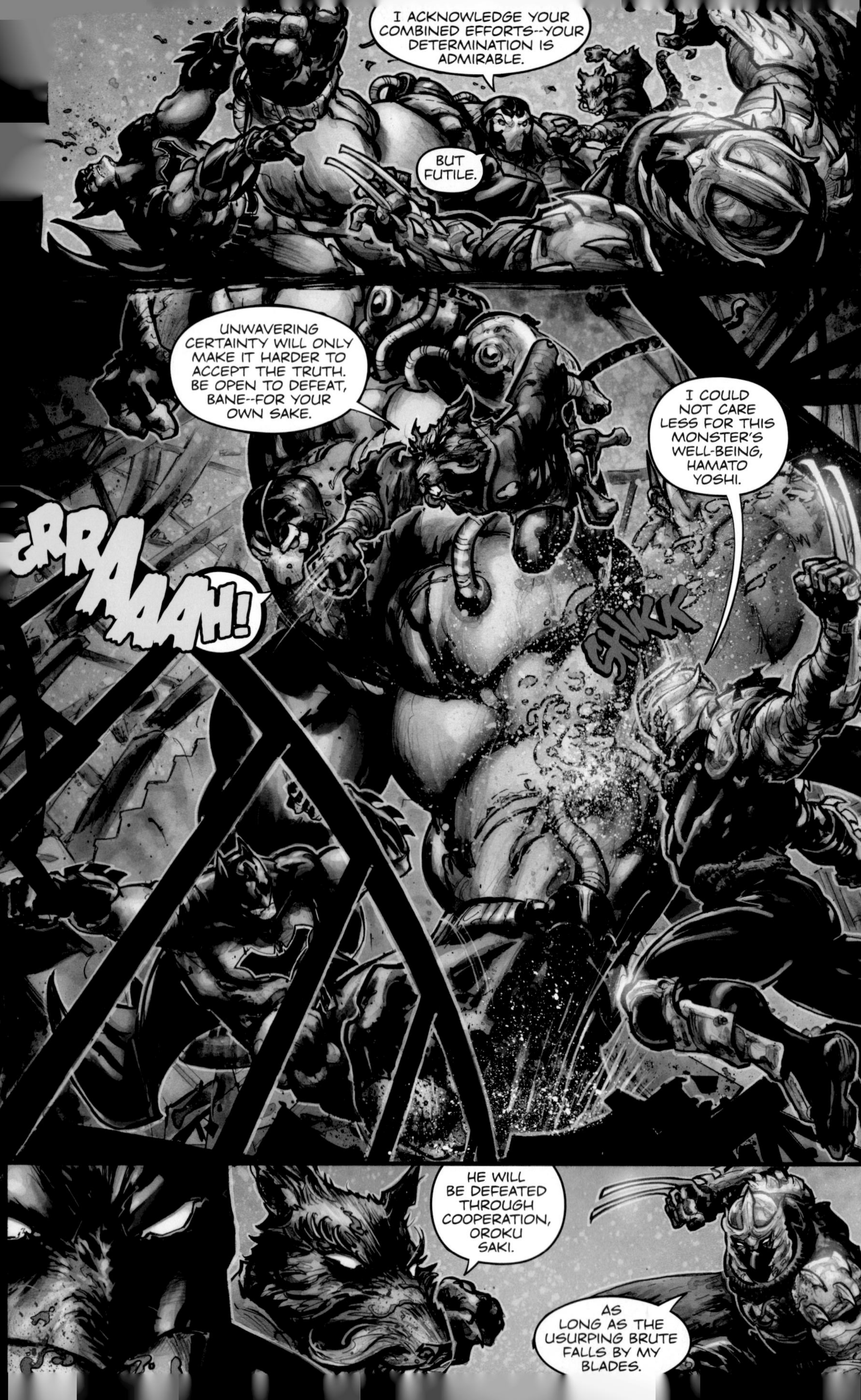
I ACKNOWLEDGE YOUR COMBINED EFFORTS--YOUR DETERMINATION IS ADMIRABLE.
BUT FUTILE.
UNWAVERING CERTAINTY WILL ONLY MAKE IT HARDER TO ACCEPT THE TRUTH. BE OPEN TO DEFEAT, BANE--FOR YOUR OWN SAKE.
I COULD NOT CARE LESS FOR THIS MONSTER'S WELL-BEING, HAMATO YOSHI.
GRRAAAAH!
SHKK
HE WILL BE DEFEATED THROUGH COOPERATION, OROKU SAKI.
AS LONG AS THE USURPING BRUTE FALLS BY MY BLADES.

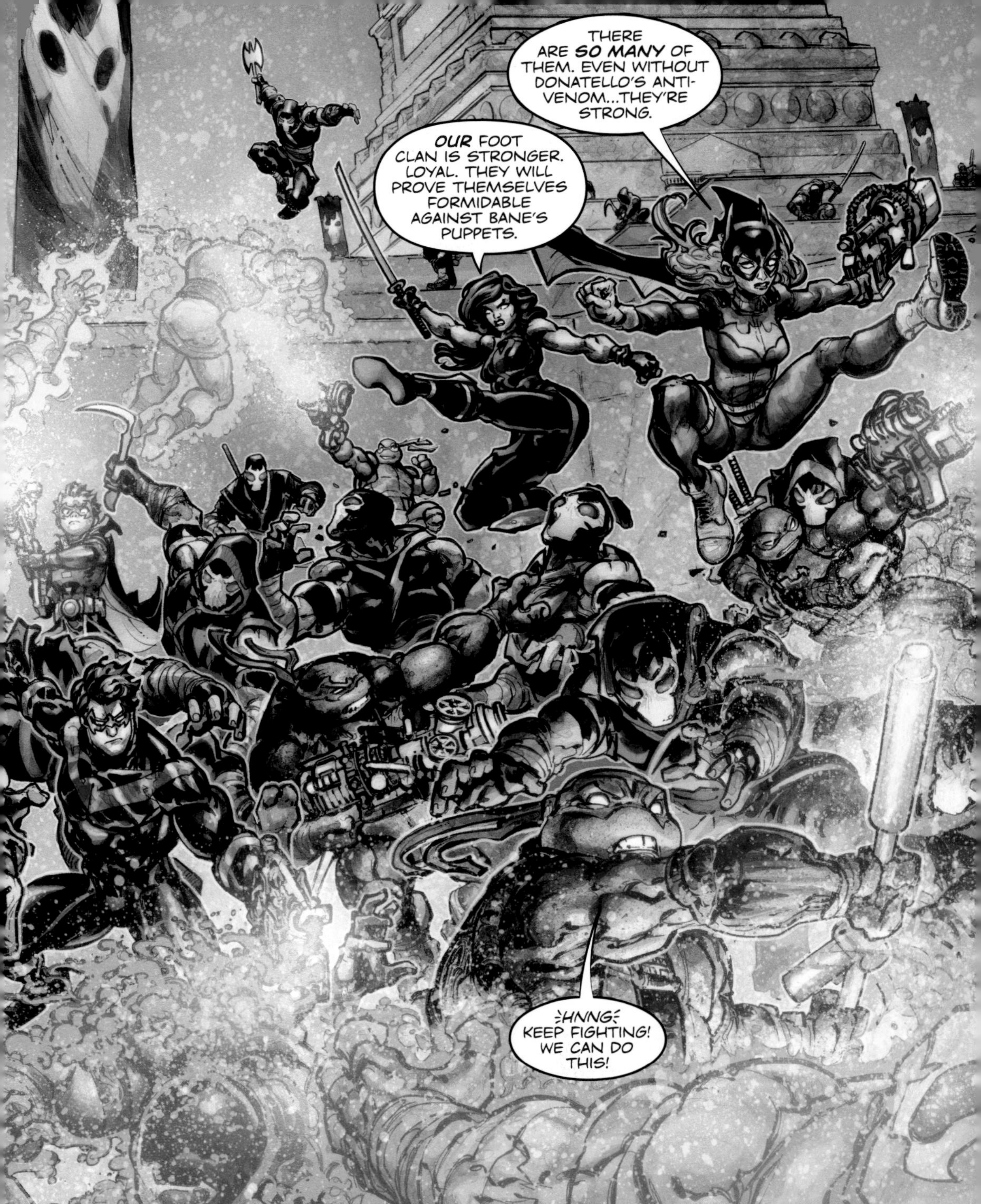
THERE ARE SO MANY OF THEM. EVEN WITHOUT DONATELLO'S ANTI-VENOM...THEY'RE STRONG.
OUR FOOT CLAN IS STRONGER. LOYAL. THEY WILL PROVE THEMSELVES FORMIDABLE AGAINST BANE'S PUPPETS.
HNNG KEEP FIGHTING! WE CAN DO THIS!

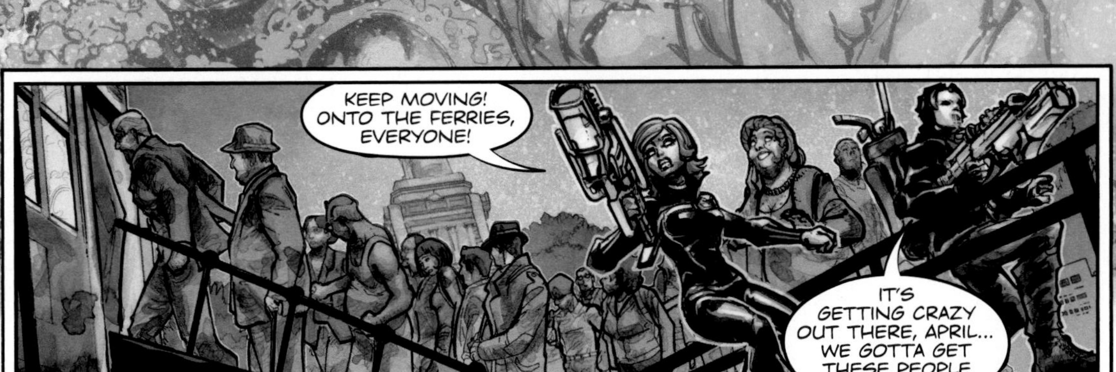
KEEP MOVING! ONTO THE FERRIES, EVERYONE!
IT'S GETTING CRAZY OUT THERE, APRIL... WE GOTTA GET THESE PEOPLE SAFE.

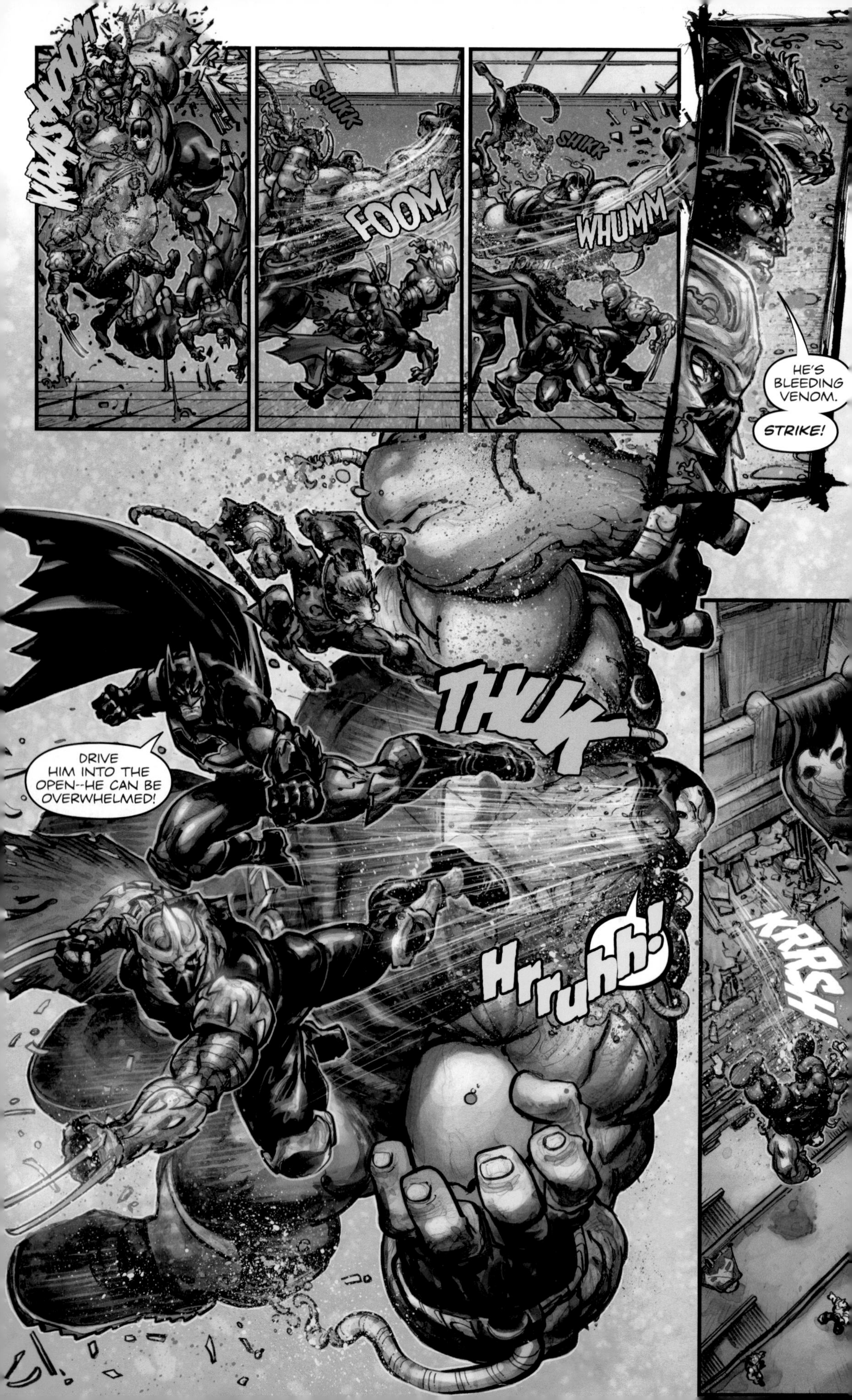
KRASHOOM
SHIKK
FOOM
SHIKK
WHUMM
HE'S BLEEDING VENOM.
STRIKE!
THUK
DRIVE HIM INTO THE OPEN--HE CAN BE OVERWHELMED!
Hrruhh!
KRRSH

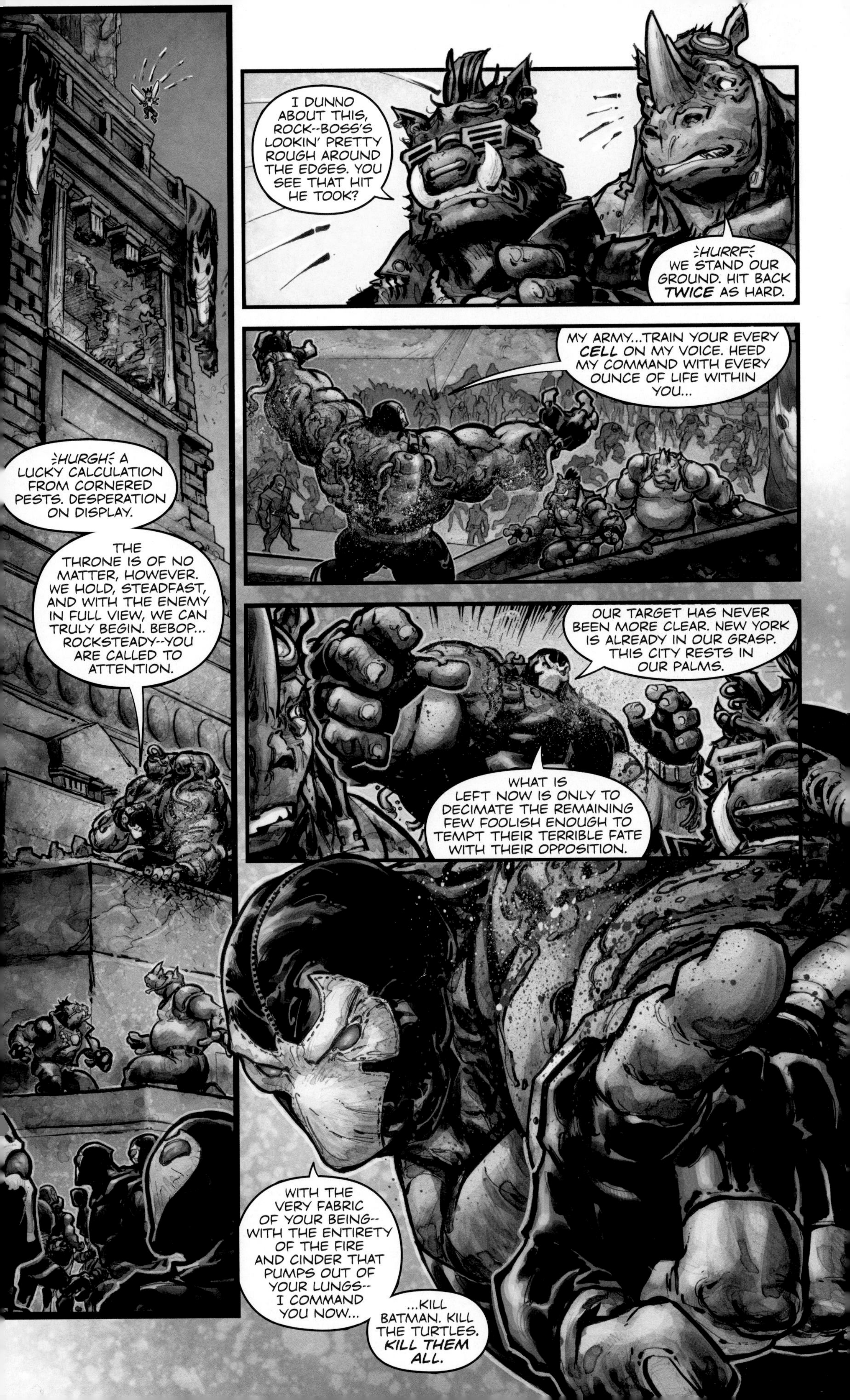
I DUNNO ABOUT THIS, ROCK--BOSS'S LOOKIN' PRETTY ROUGH AROUND THE EDGES. YOU SEE THAT HIT HE TOOK?
HURRF WE STAND OUR GROUND. HIT BACK TWICE AS HARD.
HURGH A LUCKY CALCULATION FROM CORNERED PESTS. DESPERATION ON DISPLAY.
THE THRONE IS OF NO MATTER, HOWEVER. WE HOLD, STEADFAST, AND WITH THE ENEMY IN FULL VIEW, WE CAN TRULY BEGIN. BEBOP... ROCKSTEADY--YOU ARE CALLED TO ATTENTION.
MY ARMY...TRAIN YOUR EVERY CELL ON MY VOICE. HEED MY COMMAND WITH EVERY OUNCE OF LIFE WITHIN YOU...
OUR TARGET HAS NEVER BEEN MORE CLEAR. NEW YORK IS ALREADY IN OUR GRASP. THIS CITY RESTS IN OUR PALMS.
WHAT IS LEFT NOW IS ONLY TO DECIMATE THE REMAINING FEW FOOLISH ENOUGH TO TEMPT THEIR TERRIBLE FATE WITH THEIR OPPOSITION.
WITH THE VERY FABRIC OF YOUR BEING--WITH THE ENTIRETY OF THE FIRE AND CINDER THAT PUMPS OUT OF YOUR LUNGS--I COMMAND YOU NOW...
...KILL BATMAN. KILL THE TURTLES. KILL THEM ALL.

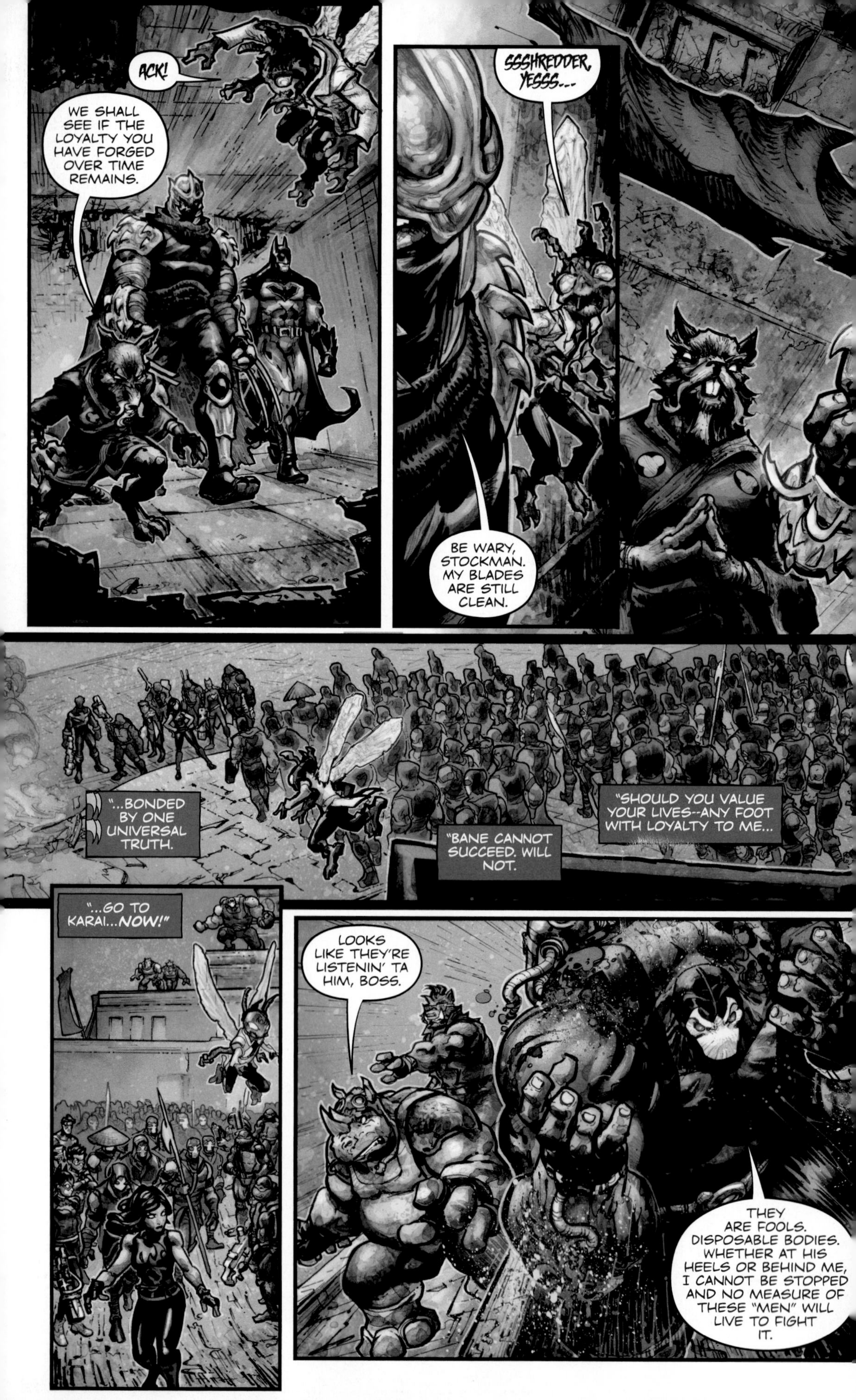
ACK!
WE SHALL SEE IF THE LOYALTY YOU HAVE FORGED OVER TIME REMAINS.
SSSHREDDER, YESSS...
BE WARY, STOCKMAN. MY BLADES ARE STILL CLEAN.
"...BONDED BY ONE UNIVERSAL TRUTH.
"BANE CANNOT SUCCEED. WILL NOT.
"SHOULD YOU VALUE YOUR LIVES--ANY FOOT WITH LOYALTY TO ME...
"...GO TO KARAI...NOW!"
LOOKS LIKE THEY'RE LISTENIN' TA HIM, BOSS.
THEY ARE FOOLS. DISPOSABLE BODIES. WHETHER AT HIS HEELS OR BEHIND ME, I CANNOT BE STOPPED AND NO MEASURE OF THESE "MEN" WILL LIVE TO FIGHT IT.

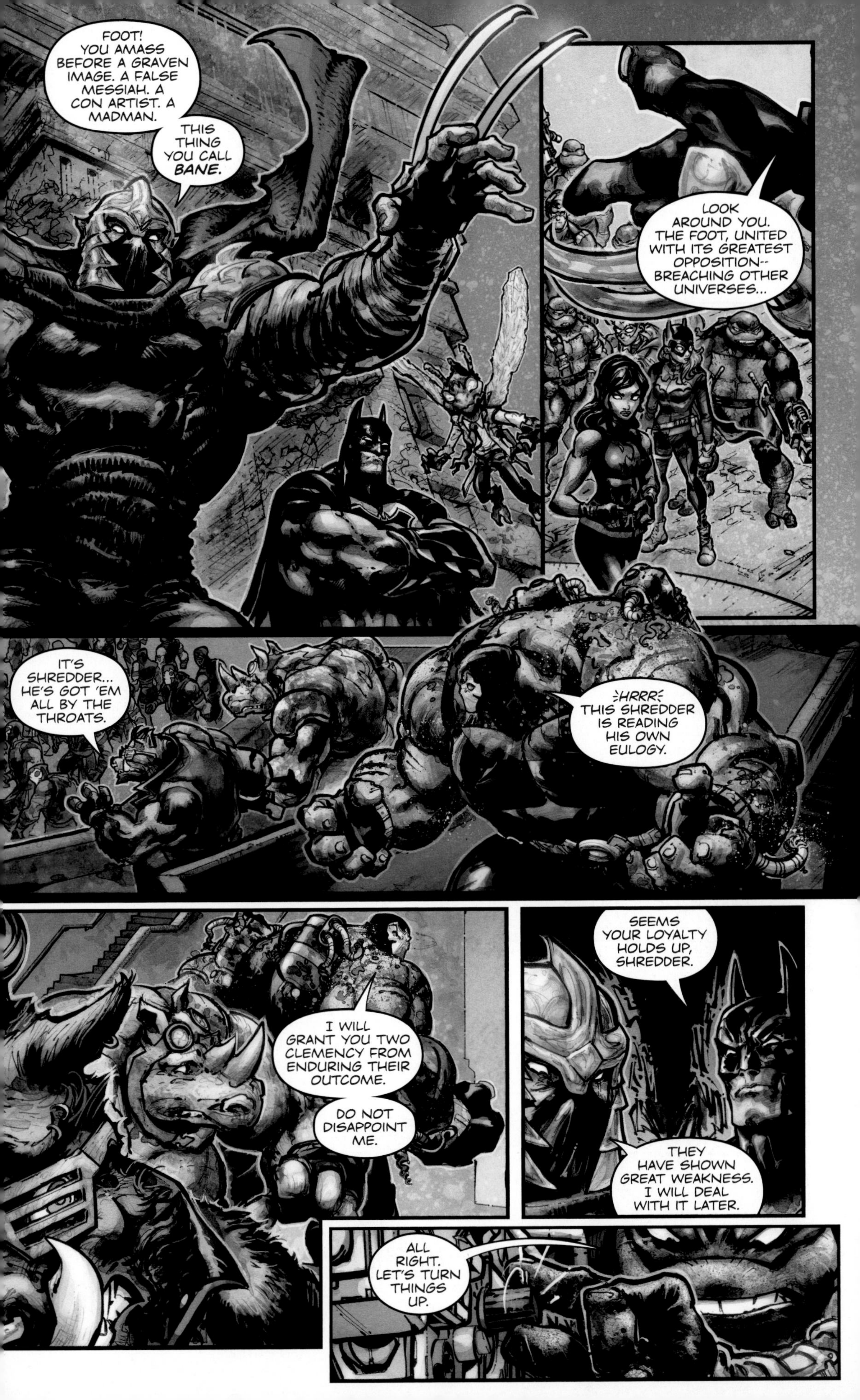

FOOT! YOU AMASS BEFORE A GRAVEN IMAGE. A FALSE MESSIAH. A CON ARTIST. A MADMAN.
THIS THING YOU CALL *BANE*.
LOOK AROUND YOU. THE FOOT, UNITED WITH ITS GREATEST OPPOSITION-- BREACHING OTHER UNIVERSES...
IT'S SHREDDER... HE'S GOT 'EM ALL BY THE THROATS.
HRRR. THIS SHREDDER IS READING HIS OWN EULOGY.
I WILL GRANT YOU TWO CLEMENCY FROM ENDURING THEIR OUTCOME.
DO NOT DISAPPOINT ME.
SEEMS YOUR LOYALTY HOLDS UP, SHREDDER.
THEY HAVE SHOWN GREAT WEAKNESS. I WILL DEAL WITH IT LATER.
ALL RIGHT. LET'S TURN THINGS UP.

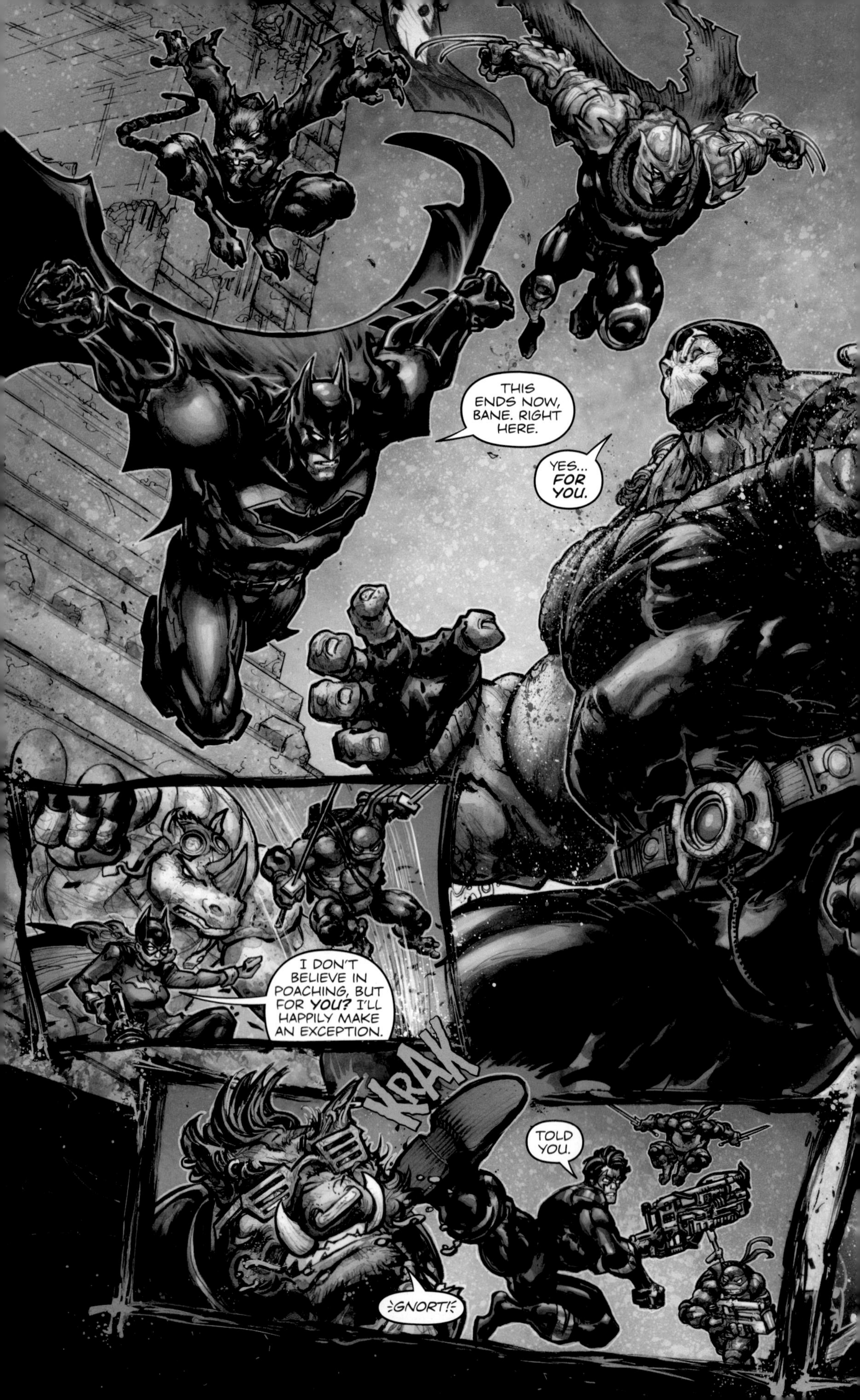
THIS ENDS NOW, BANE. RIGHT HERE.
YES... FOR YOU.
I DON'T BELIEVE IN POACHING, BUT FOR YOU? I'LL HAPPILY MAKE AN EXCEPTION.
KRAK
TOLD YOU.
GNORT!

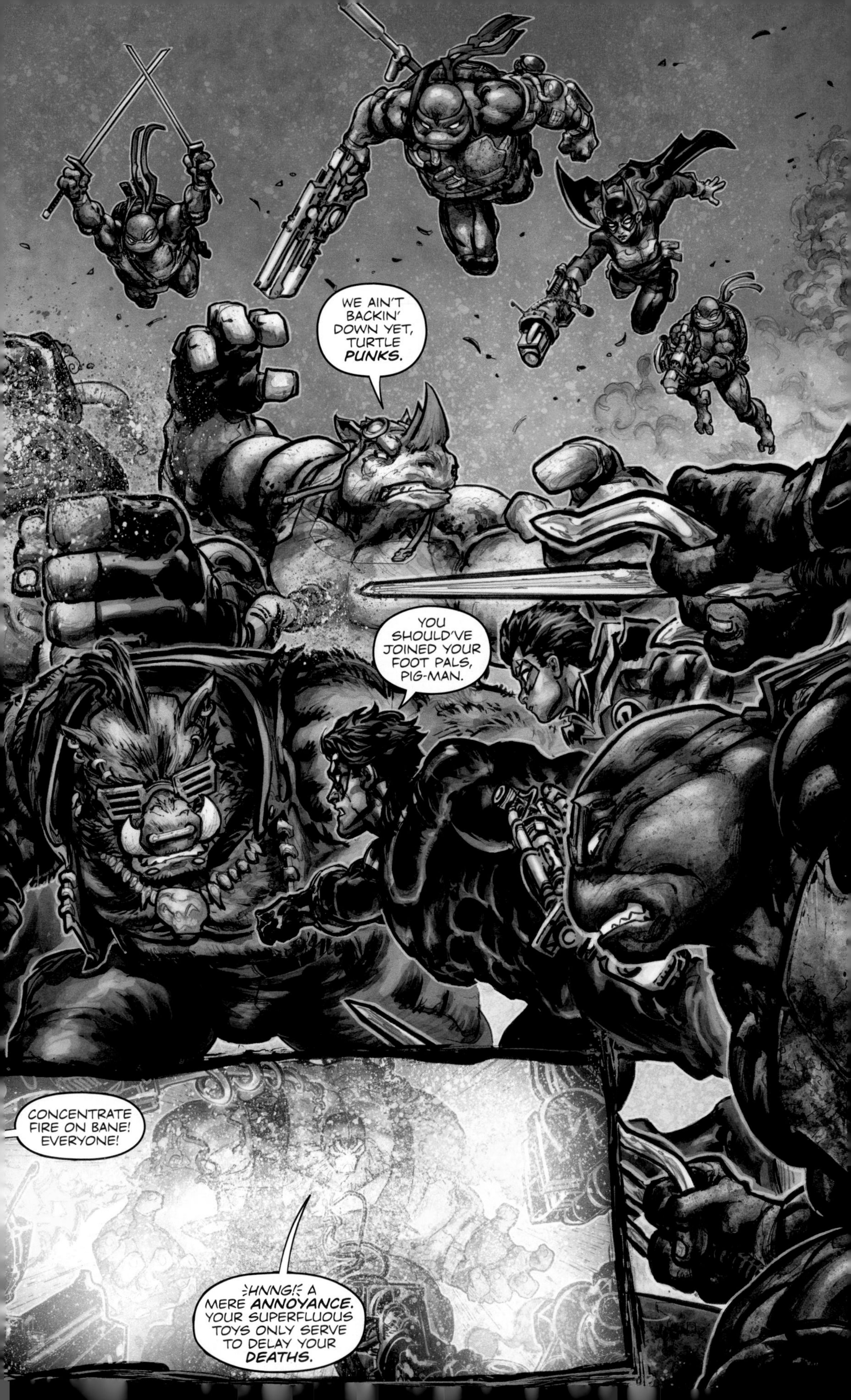
WE AIN'T BACKIN' DOWN YET, TURTLE **PUNKS.**
YOU SHOULD'VE JOINED YOUR FOOT PALS, PIG-MAN.
CONCENTRATE FIRE ON BANE! EVERYONE!
HNNG! A MERE **ANNOYANCE.** YOUR SUPERFLUOUS TOYS ONLY SERVE TO DELAY YOUR **DEATHS.**

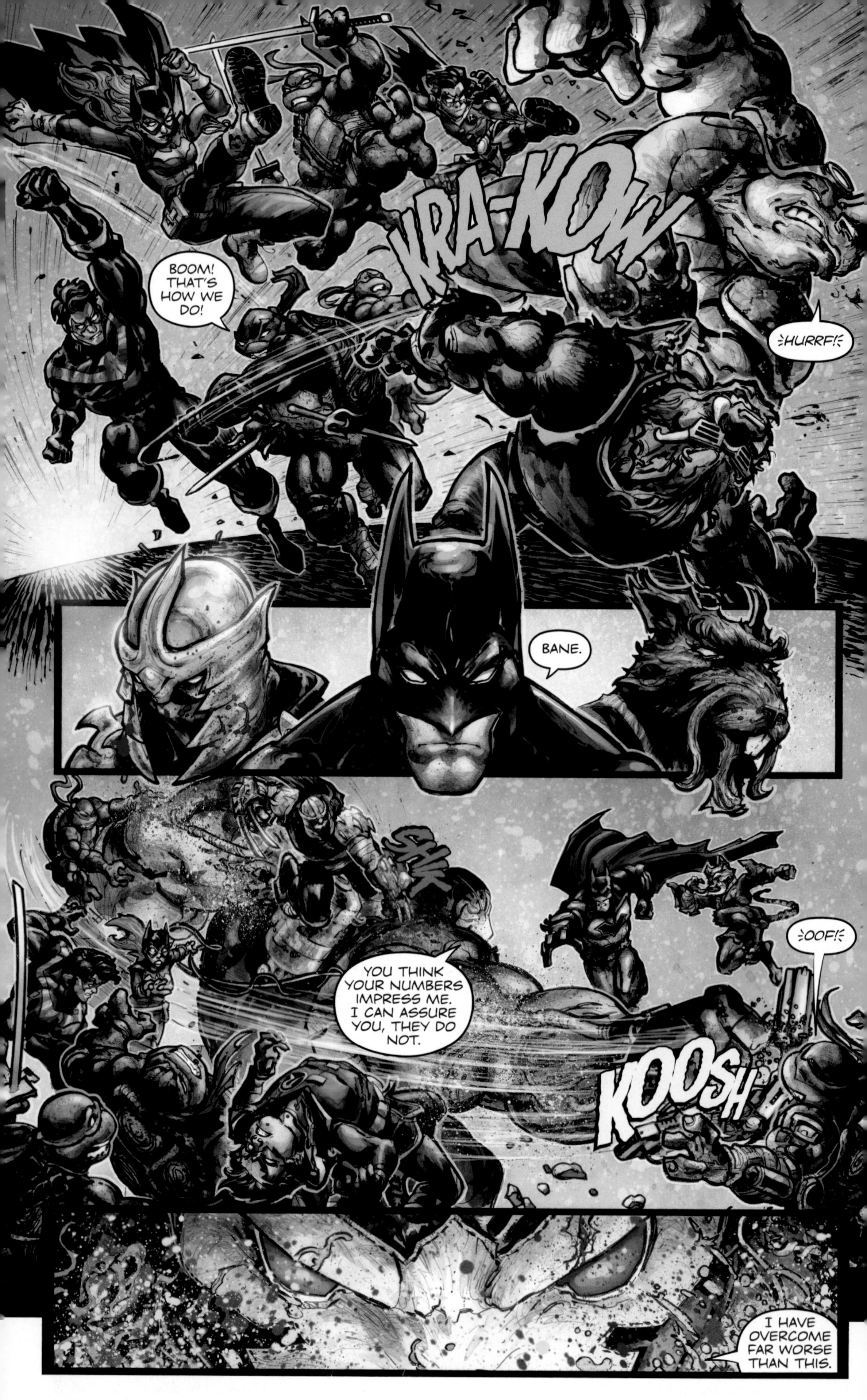
BOOM! THAT'S HOW WE DO!
KRA-KOW
HURRF!
BANE.
SHNK
YOU THINK YOUR NUMBERS IMPRESS ME. I CAN ASSURE YOU, THEY DO NOT.
OOF!
KOOSH
I HAVE OVERCOME FAR WORSE THAN THIS.

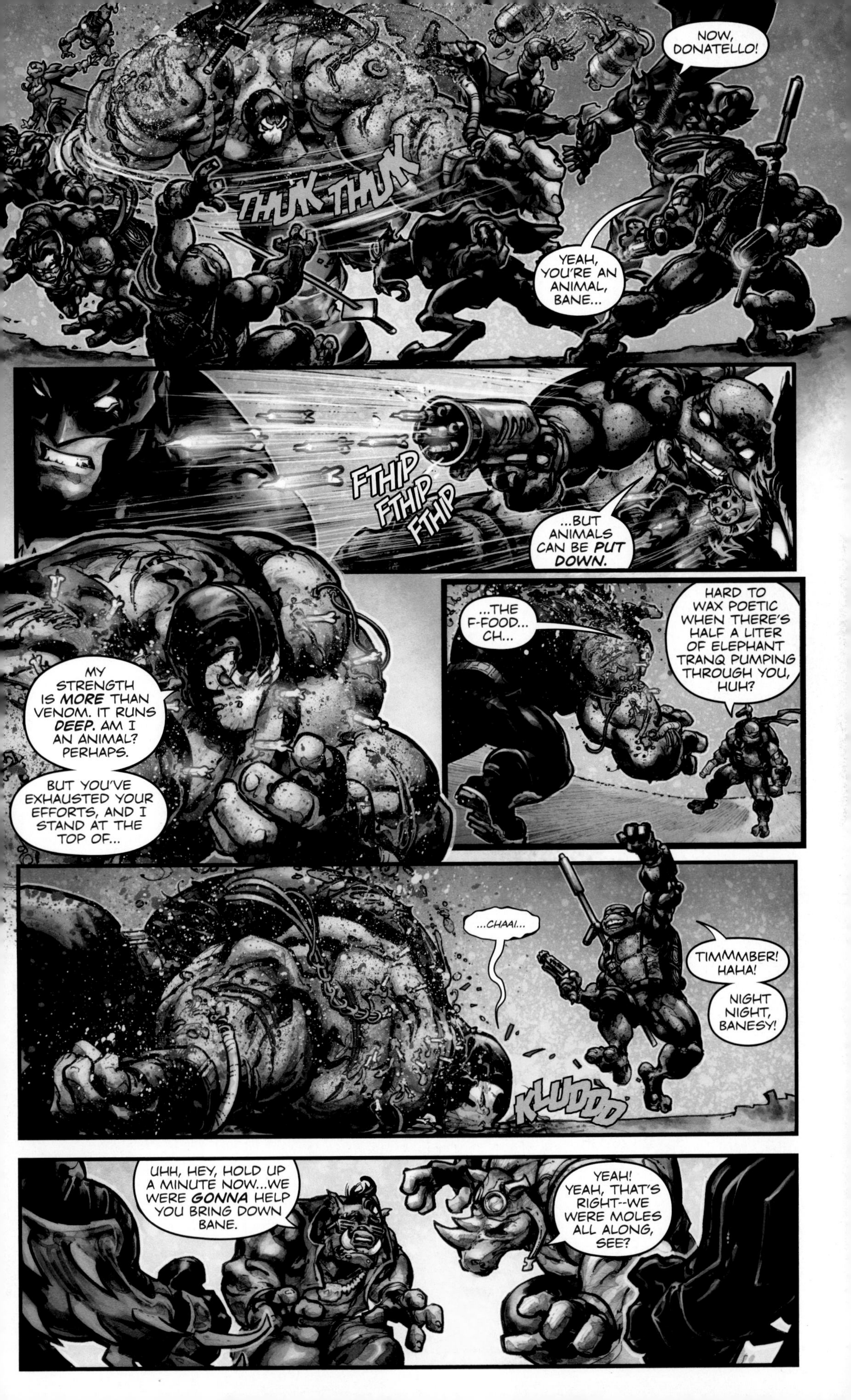
NOW, DONATELLO!
THUK THUK
YEAH, YOU'RE AN ANIMAL, BANE...
FTHIP FTHIP FTHIP
...BUT ANIMALS CAN BE PUT DOWN.
MY STRENGTH IS MORE THAN VENOM. IT RUNS DEEP. AM I AN ANIMAL? PERHAPS.
BUT YOU'VE EXHAUSTED YOUR EFFORTS, AND I STAND AT THE TOP OF...
...THE F-FOOD... CH...
HARD TO WAX POETIC WHEN THERE'S HALF A LITER OF ELEPHANT TRANQ PUMPING THROUGH YOU, HUH?
...CHAAI...
TIMMMBER! HAHA!
NIGHT NIGHT, BANESY!
KLUDDD
UHH, HEY, HOLD UP A MINUTE NOW...WE WERE GONNA HELP YOU BRING DOWN BANE.
YEAH! YEAH, THAT'S RIGHT--WE WERE MOLES ALL ALONG, SEE?

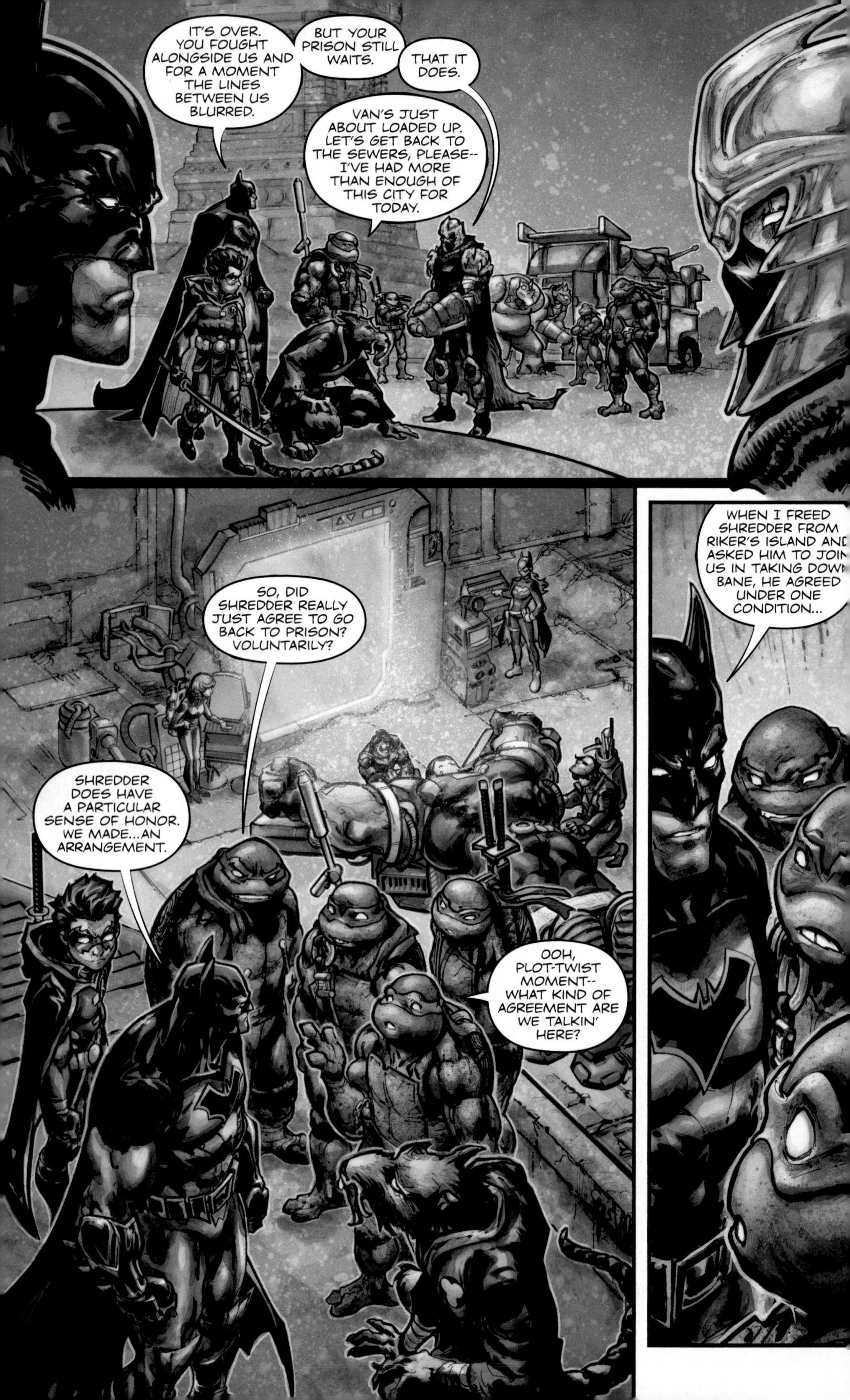
IT'S OVER. YOU FOUGHT ALONGSIDE US AND FOR A MOMENT THE LINES BETWEEN US BLURRED.
BUT YOUR PRISON STILL WAITS.
THAT IT DOES.
VAN'S JUST ABOUT LOADED UP. LET'S GET BACK TO THE SEWERS, PLEASE-- I'VE HAD MORE THAN ENOUGH OF THIS CITY FOR TODAY.
SO, DID SHREDDER REALLY JUST AGREE TO GO BACK TO PRISON? VOLUNTARILY?
SHREDDER DOES HAVE A PARTICULAR SENSE OF HONOR. WE MADE...AN ARRANGEMENT.
OOH, PLOT-TWIST MOMENT-- WHAT KIND OF AGREEMENT ARE WE TALKIN' HERE?
WHEN I FREED SHREDDER FROM RIKER'S ISLAND AND ASKED HIM TO JOIN US IN TAKING DOWN BANE, HE AGREED UNDER ONE CONDITION...

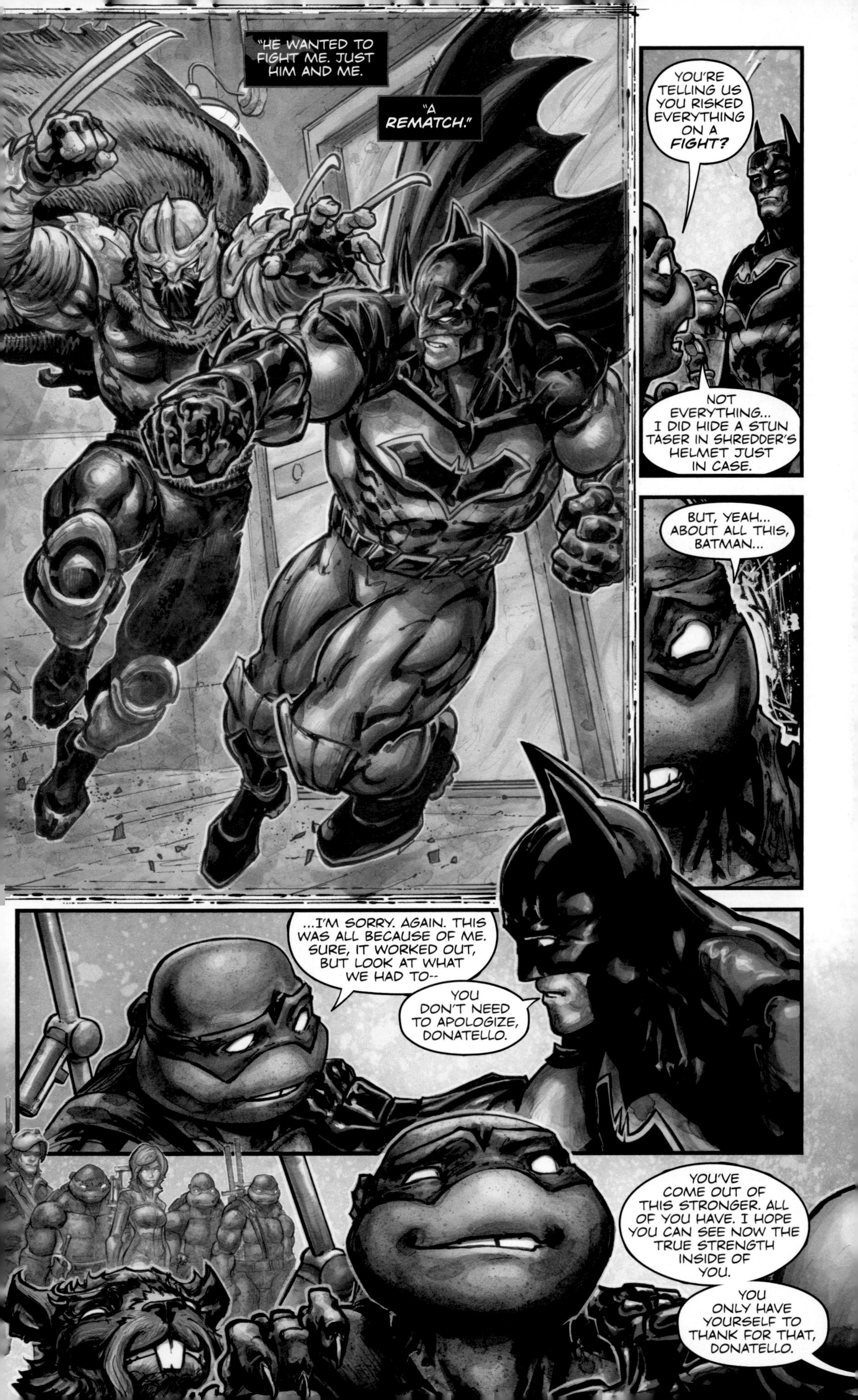
"HE WANTED TO FIGHT ME. JUST HIM AND ME.
"A REMATCH."
YOU'RE TELLING US YOU RISKED EVERYTHING ON A FIGHT?
NOT EVERYTHING... I DID HIDE A STUN TASER IN SHREDDER'S HELMET JUST IN CASE.
BUT, YEAH... ABOUT ALL THIS, BATMAN...
...I'M SORRY. AGAIN. THIS WAS ALL BECAUSE OF ME. SURE, IT WORKED OUT, BUT LOOK AT WHAT WE HAD TO--
YOU DON'T NEED TO APOLOGIZE, DONATELLO.
YOU'VE COME OUT OF THIS STRONGER. ALL OF YOU HAVE. I HOPE YOU CAN SEE NOW THE TRUE STRENGTH INSIDE OF YOU.
YOU ONLY HAVE YOURSELF TO THANK FOR THAT, DONATELLO.

WELL, THIS IS GOOD-BYE, SQUIRT. DESPITE BEING A HUGE PAIN IN MY *SHELL*, YOU'RE NOT *ALL* BAD.

NO. WE ARE *NOT* HAVING A "MOMENT." REMOVE YOUR UNREASONABLY SHAPED HAND FROM ME, OR I *WILL* TAKE YOU DOWN.

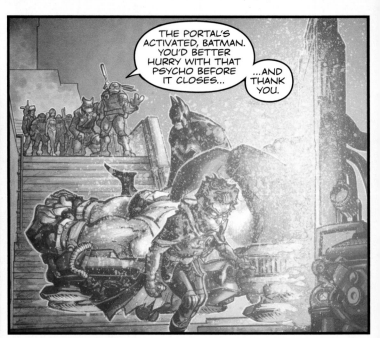

THE PORTAL'S ACTIVATED, BATMAN. YOU'D BETTER HURRY WITH THAT PSYCHO BEFORE IT CLOSES...

...AND THANK YOU.

TAKE CARE OF YOURSELVES.

UNTIL NEXT TIME.

LATER THAT EVENING...

HUH. WHAT'S THIS?

WHOA. HEY! GUYS! GUESS WHAT I'VE GOT?

IT'S BATMAN'S "*TRAINING PROTOCOL*." ALL OF HIS ROBINS DO IT. "FOR A LITTLE EDGE IN YOUR WORKOUTS, DONATELLO."

Donnie,
True strength comes from within.
But this Robin training program can't hurt.

UHH, YOU'RE GOING TO SHARE THAT WITH US, TOO, *RIGHT?*

DONNIE? DONNIE?!!

THE END... FOR NOW!

BATMAN/
TEENAGE MUTANT NINJA TURTLES II
COVER GALLERY

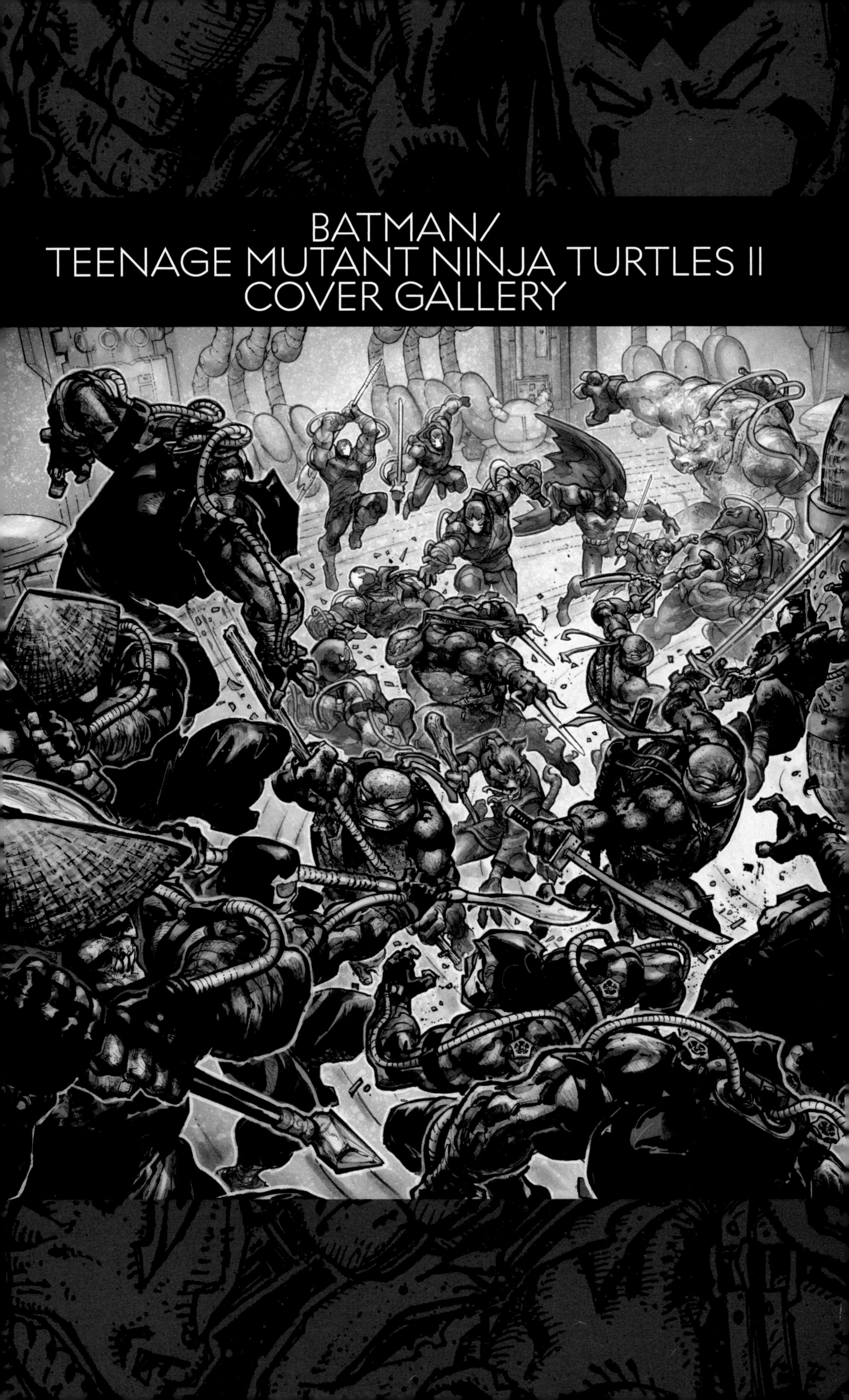

BATMAN/TEENAGE MUTANT NINJA TURTLES II #1
cover by FREDDIE E. WILLIAMS II and JEREMY COLWELL

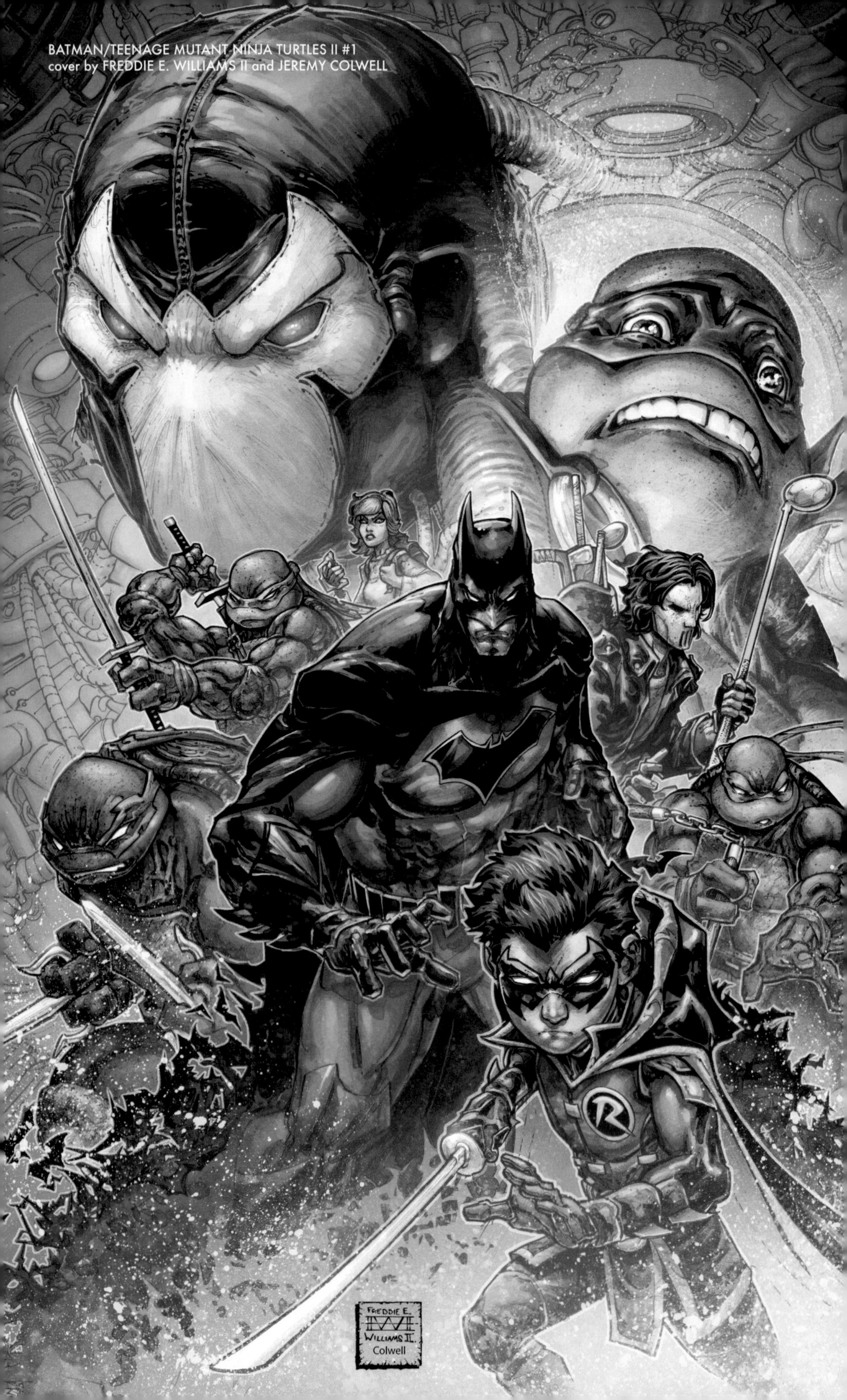
FREDDIE E.
WILLIAMS II.
Colwell

BATMAN/TEENAGE MUTANT NINJA TURTLES II #1 variant cover by KEVIN EASTMAN and TOMI VARGA

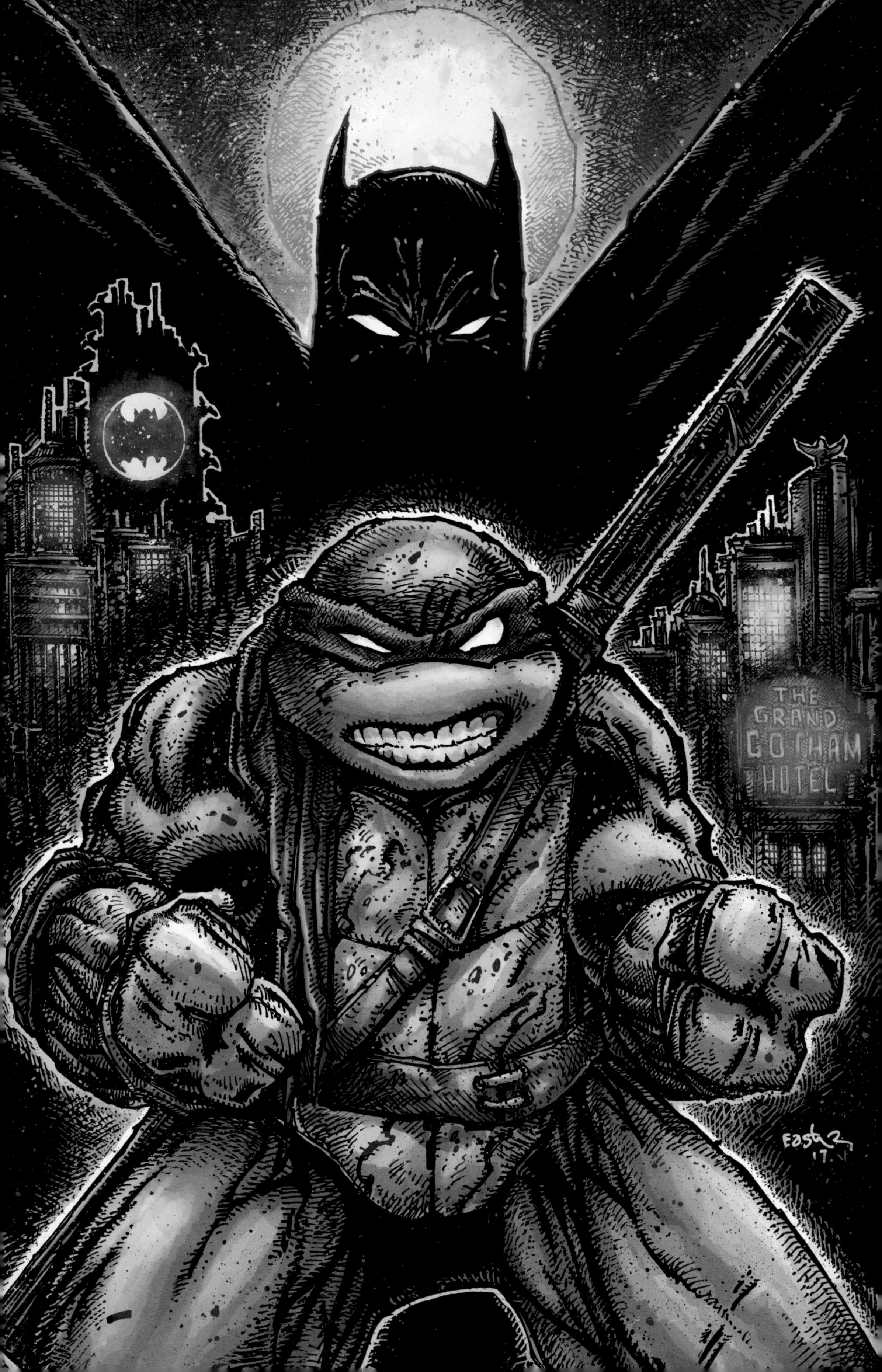
THE GRAND GOTHAM HOTEL

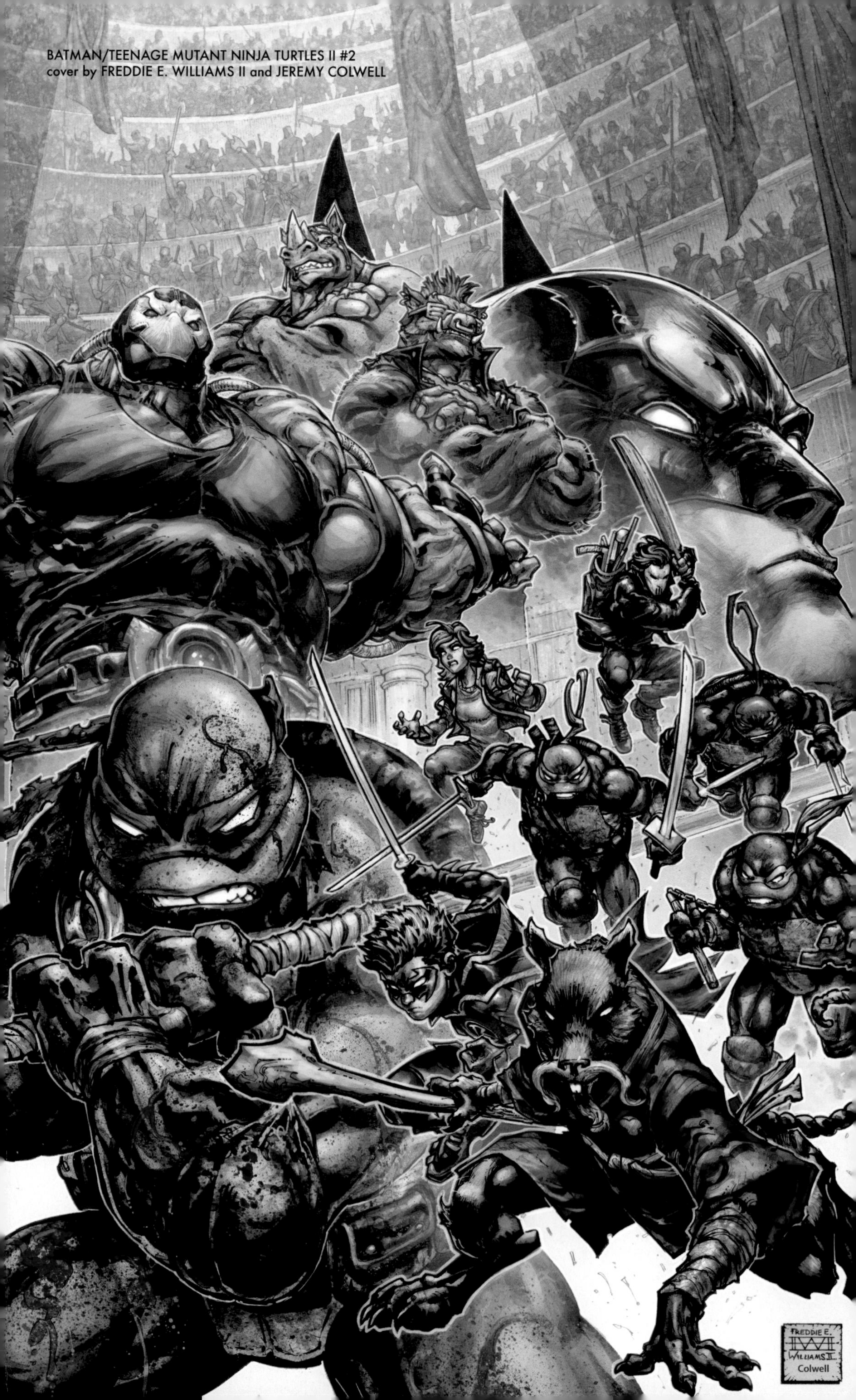
FREDDIE E.
WILLIAMS II
Colwell

BATMAN/TEENAGE MUTANT NINJA TURTLES II #2
cover by FREDDIE E. WILLIAMS II and JEREMY COLWELL

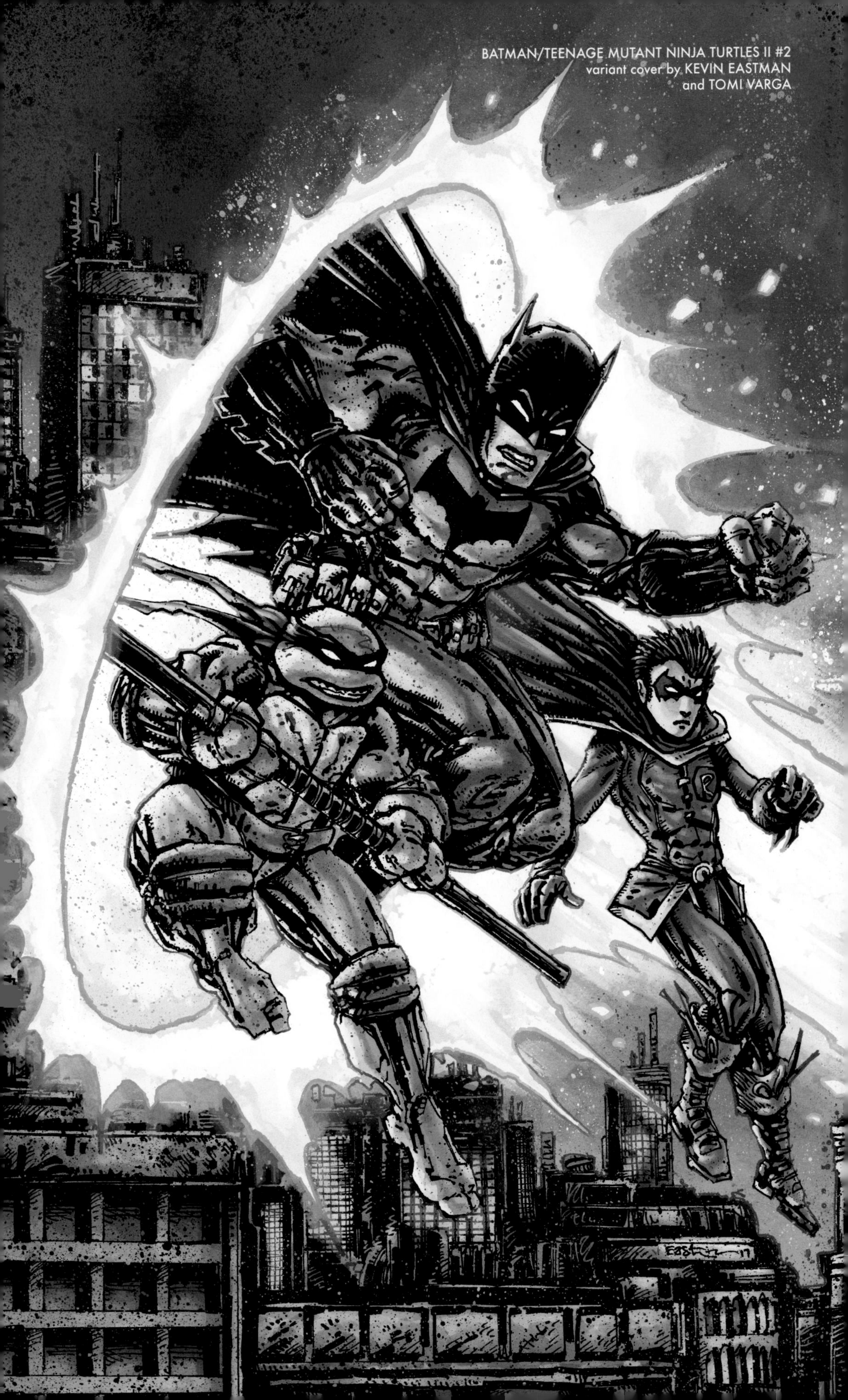

BATMAN/TEENAGE MUTANT NINJA TURTLES II #2
variant cover by KEVIN EASTMAN
and TOMI VARGA

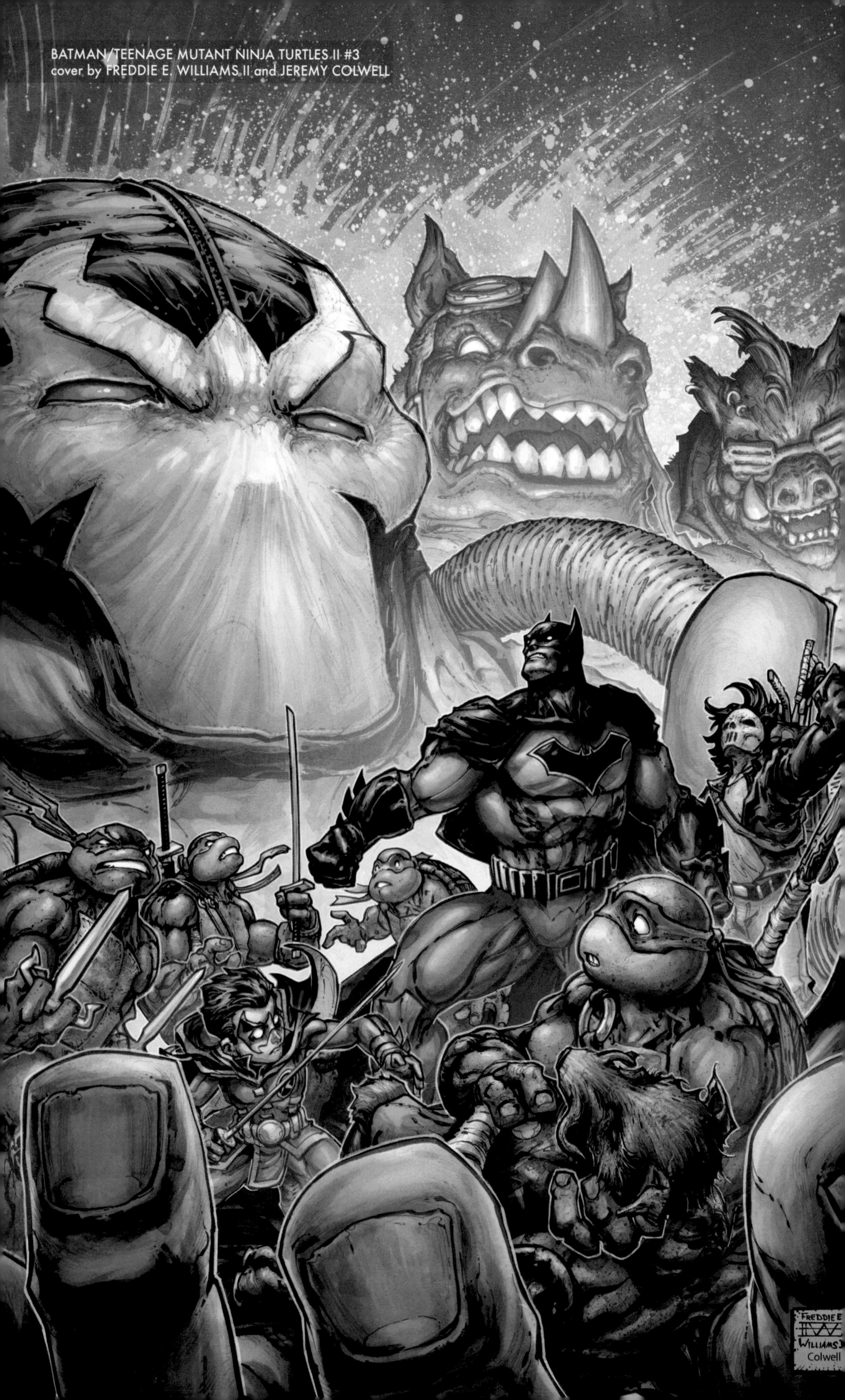
Colwell

BATMAN/TEENAGE MUTANT NINJA TURTLES II #3
cover by FREDDIE E. WILLIAMS II and JEREMY COLWELL

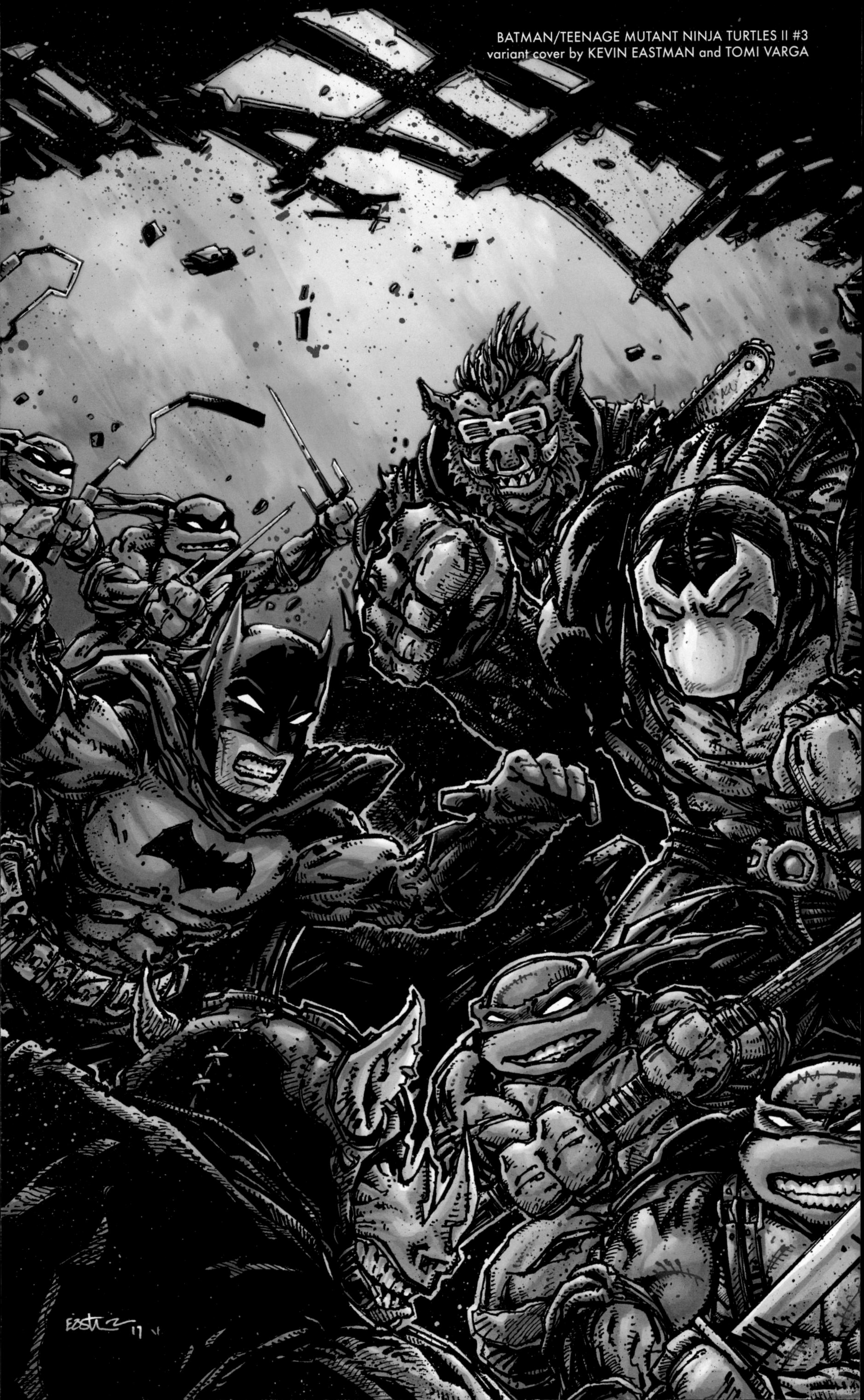

BATMAN/TEENAGE MUTANT NINJA TURTLES II #3
variant cover by KEVIN EASTMAN and TOMI VARGA

BATMAN/TEENAGE MUTANT NINJA TURTLES II #4
cover by FREDDIE E. WILLIAMS II and JEREMY COLWELL

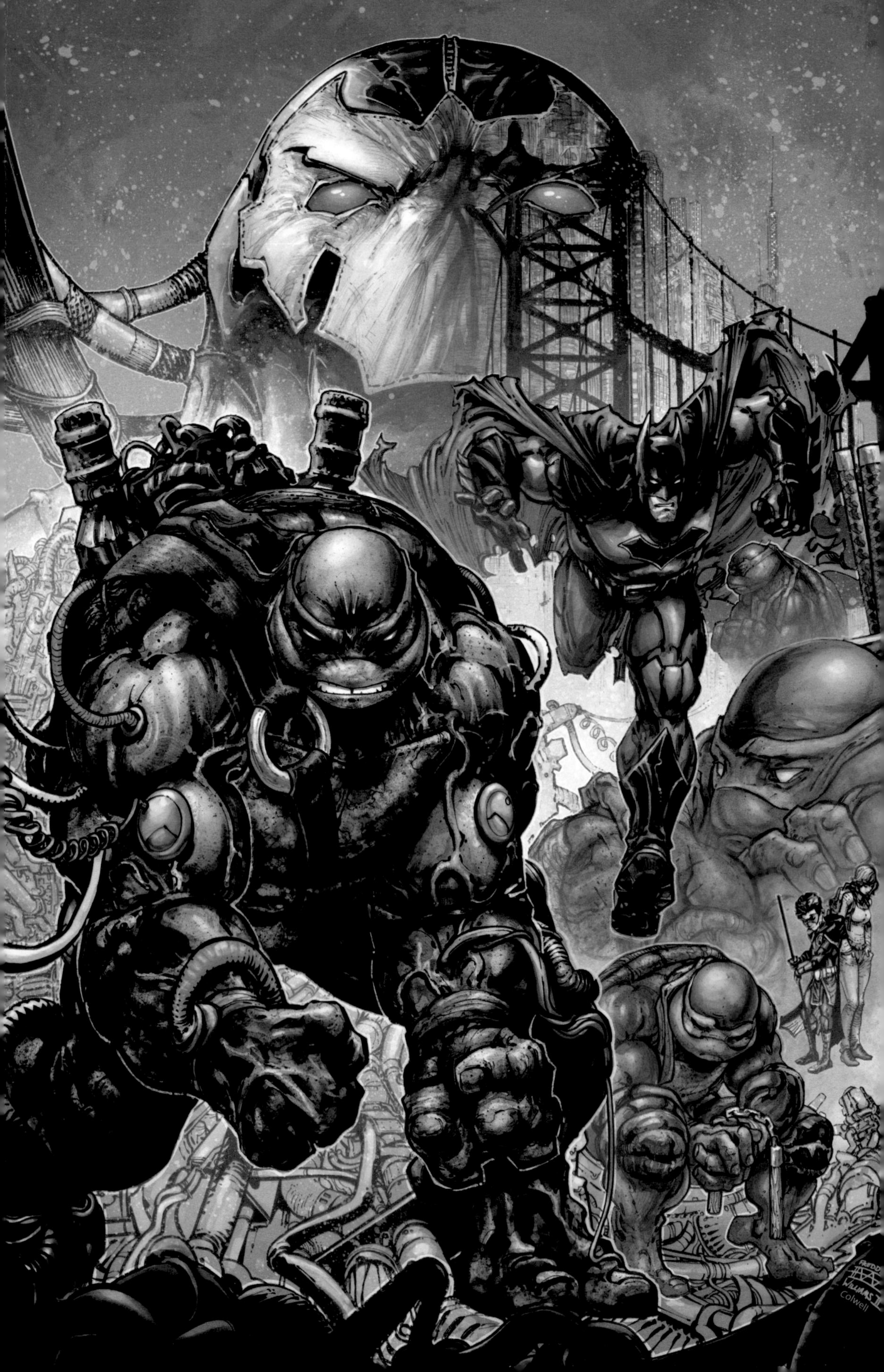
Colwell

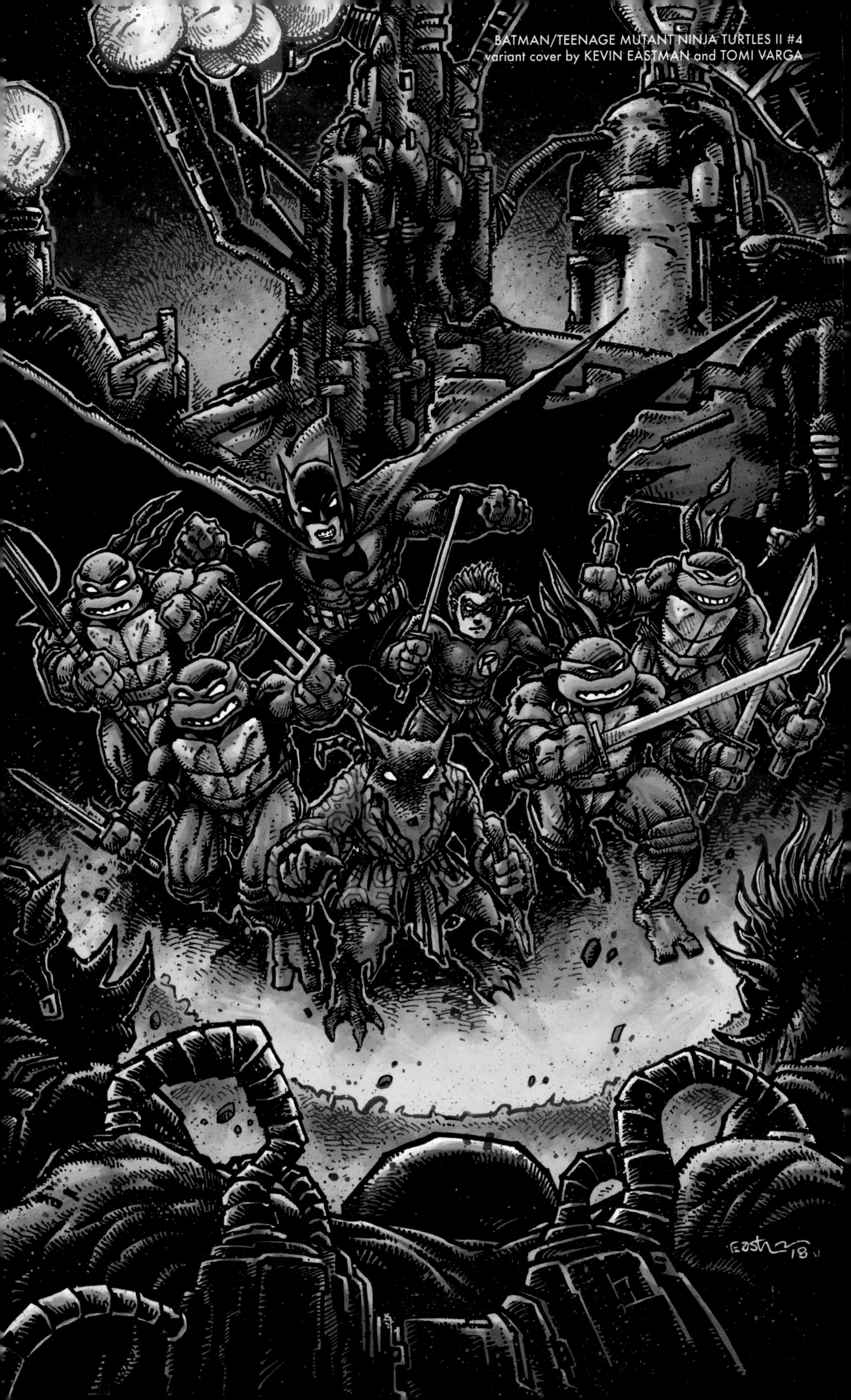

BATMAN/TEENAGE MUTANT NINJA TURTLES II #4
variant cover by KEVIN EASTMAN and TOMI VARGA

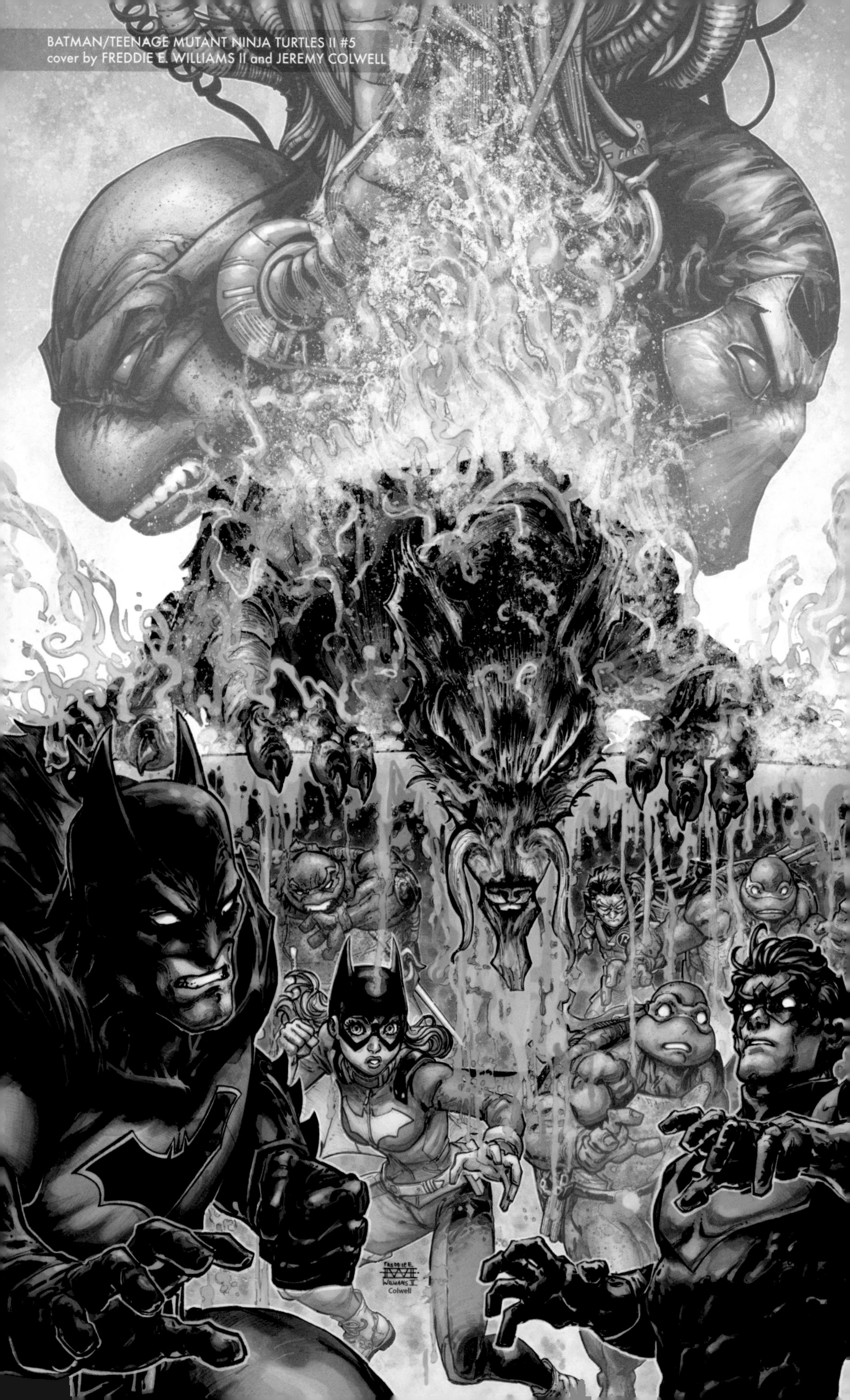

BATMAN/TEENAGE MUTANT NINJA TURTLES II #5
cover by FREDDIE E. WILLIAMS II and JEREMY COLWELL

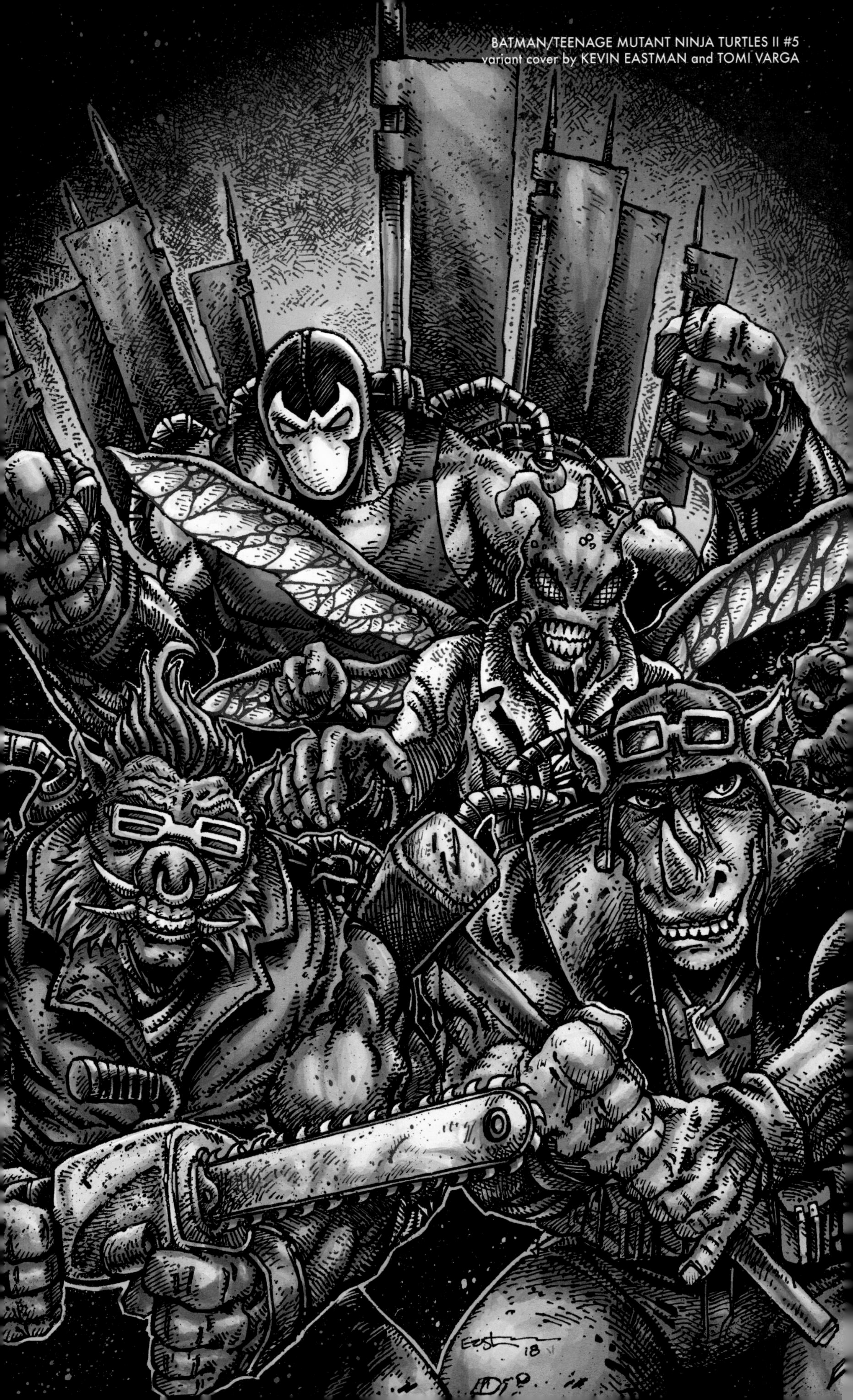

BATMAN/TEENAGE MUTANT NINJA TURTLES II #5
variant cover by KEVIN EASTMAN and TOMI VARGA

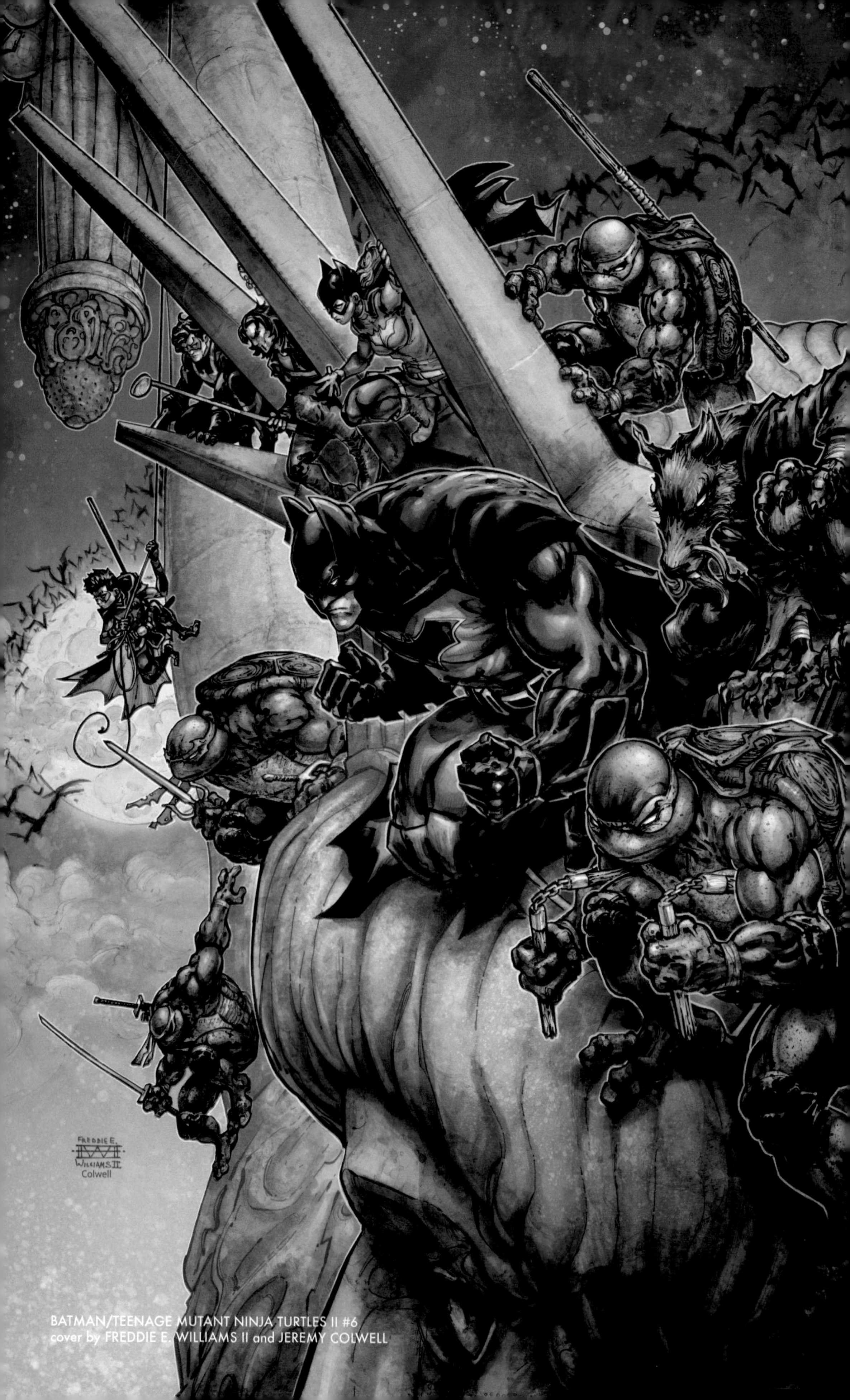
FREDDIE E. WILLIAMS II
Colwell

BATMAN/TEENAGE MUTANT NINJA TURTLES II #6
cover by FREDDIE E. WILLIAMS II and JEREMY COLWELL

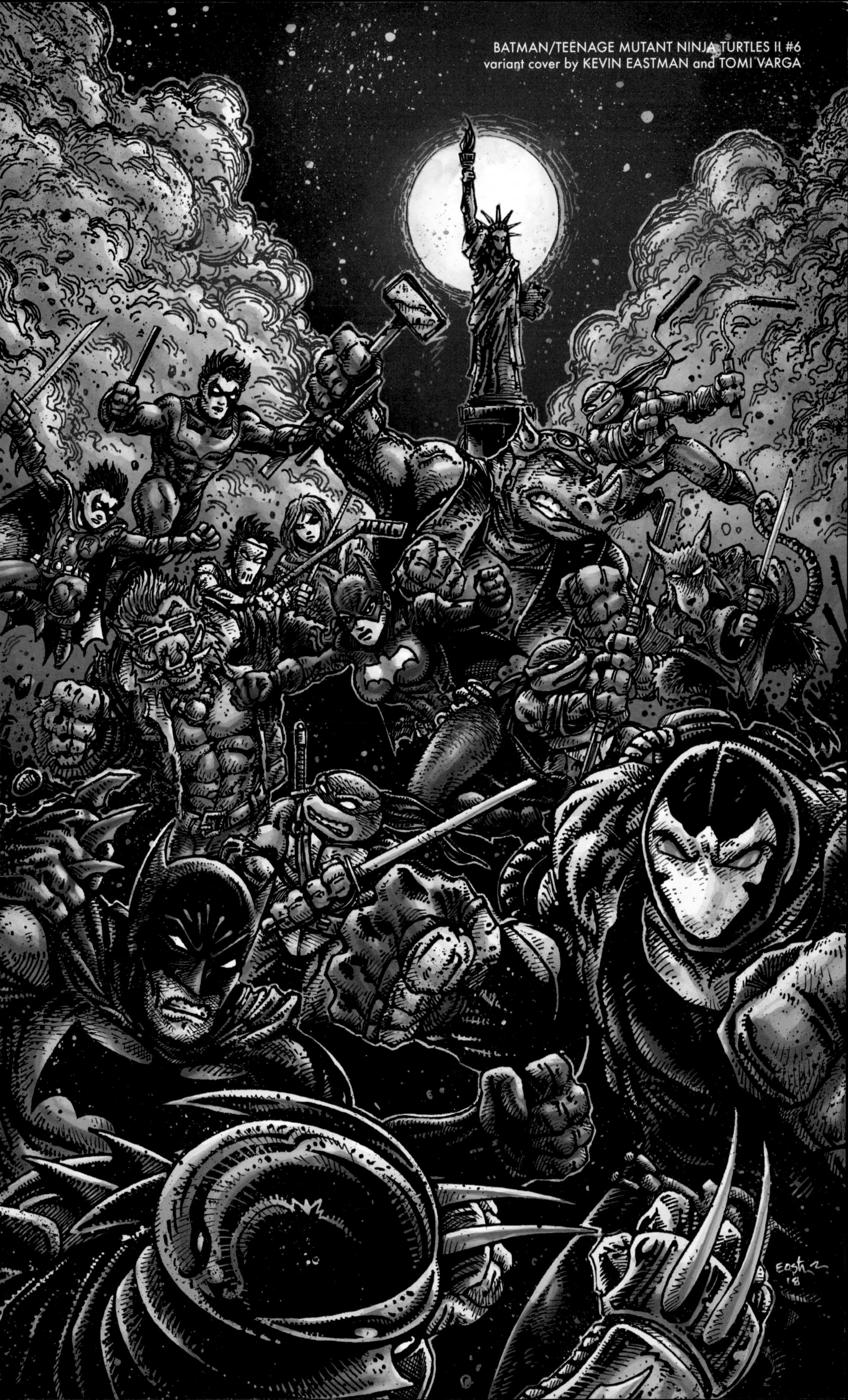

BATMAN/TEENAGE MUTANT NINJA TURTLES II #6
variant cover by KEVIN EASTMAN and TOMI VARGA

SKETCHBOOK

All sketches by Freddie E. Williams II

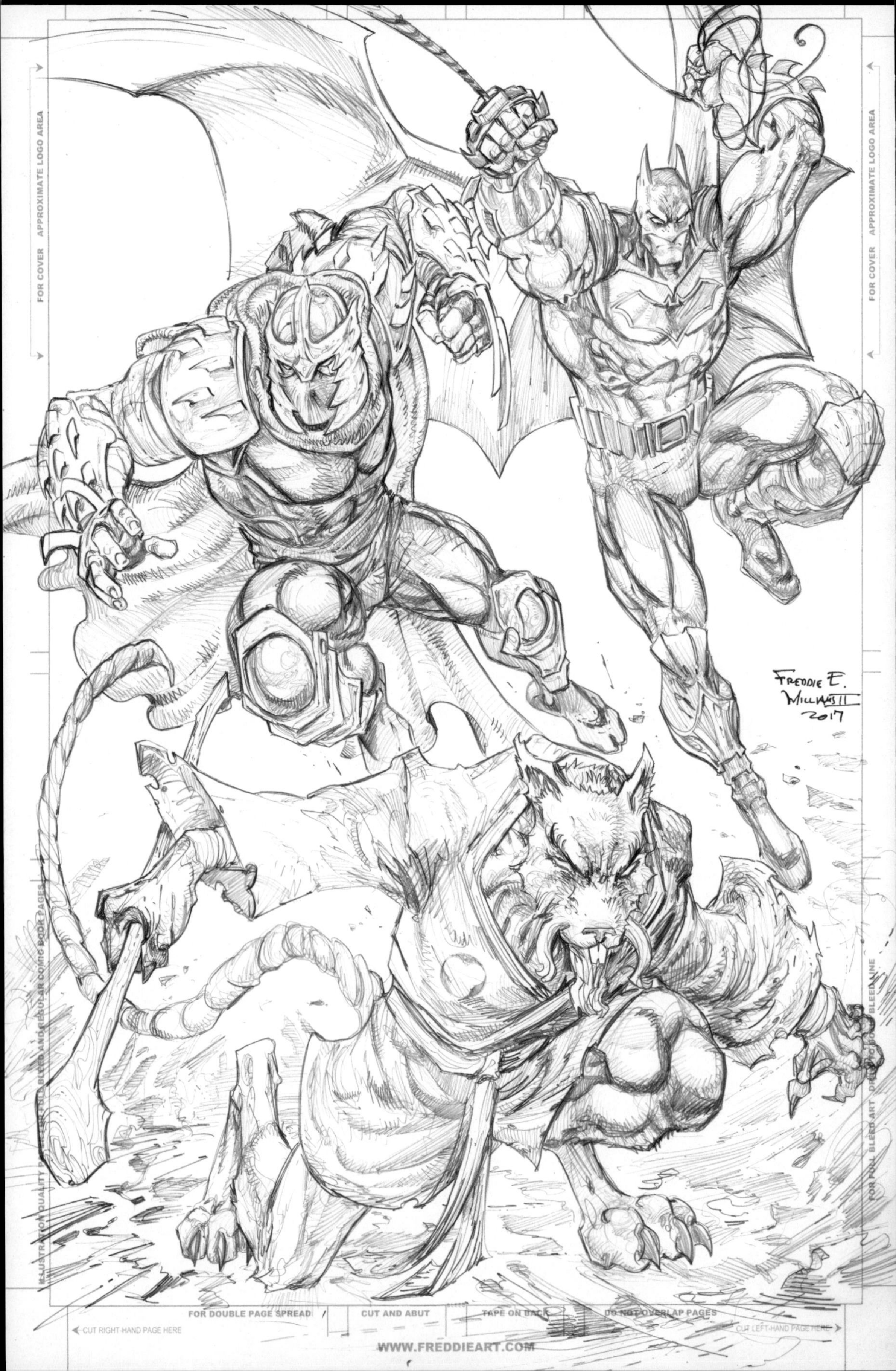

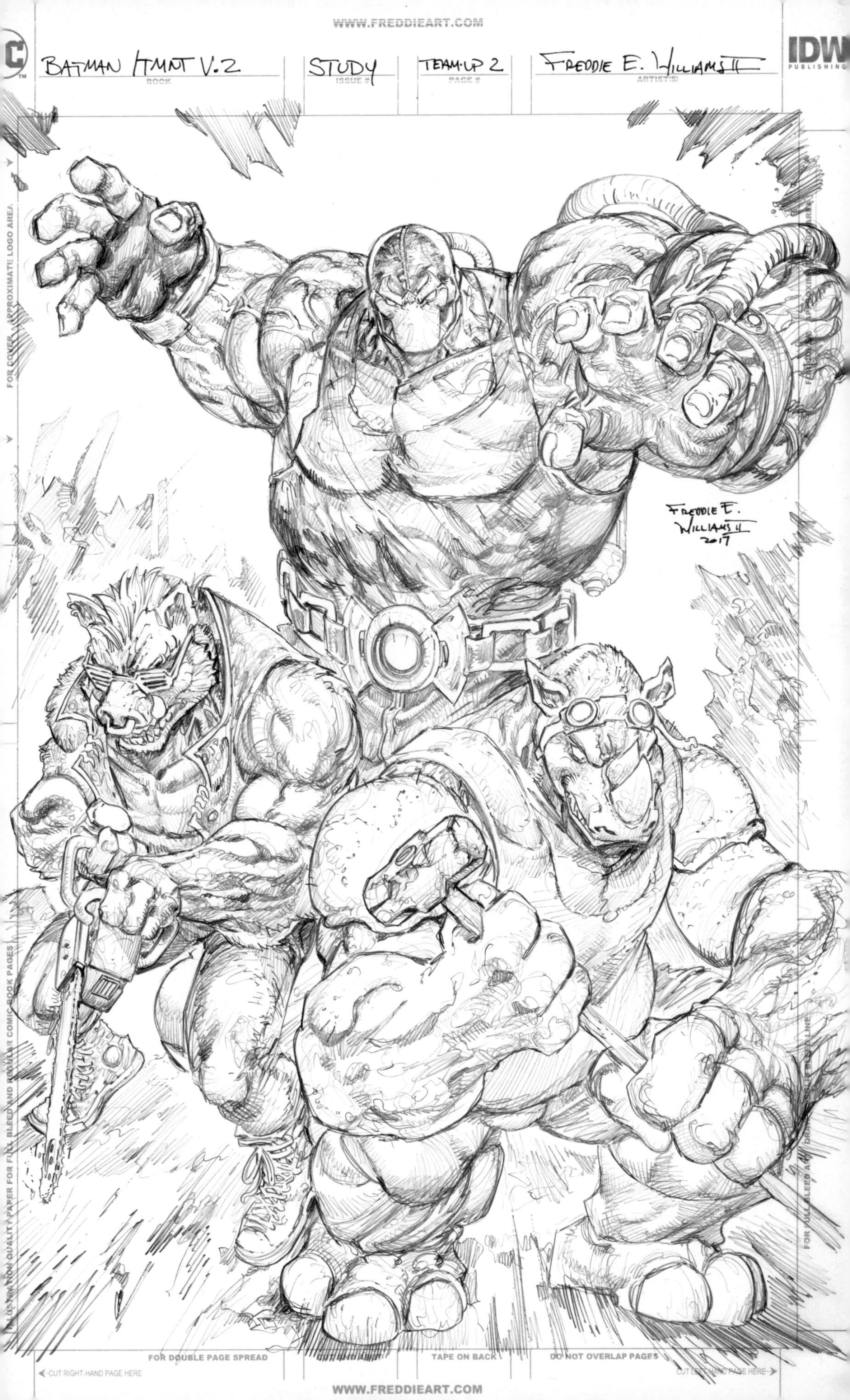
WWW.FREDDIEART.COM
BATMAN/TMNT V.2
BOOK
STUDY
ISSUE #
TEAM-UP 2
PAGE #
FREDDIE E. WILLIAMS II
ARTIST(S)
IDW PUBLISHING
FREDDIE E. WILLIAMS II 2017
FOR DOUBLE PAGE SPREAD
TAPE ON BACK
DO NOT OVERLAP PAGES
CUT RIGHT-HAND PAGE HERE
WWW.FREDDIEART.COM

BATMAN / TMNT V.2 (BOOK) | STUDY (ISSUE #) | BATMAN (PAGE #) | FREDDIE E WILLIAMS II (ARTIST(S))

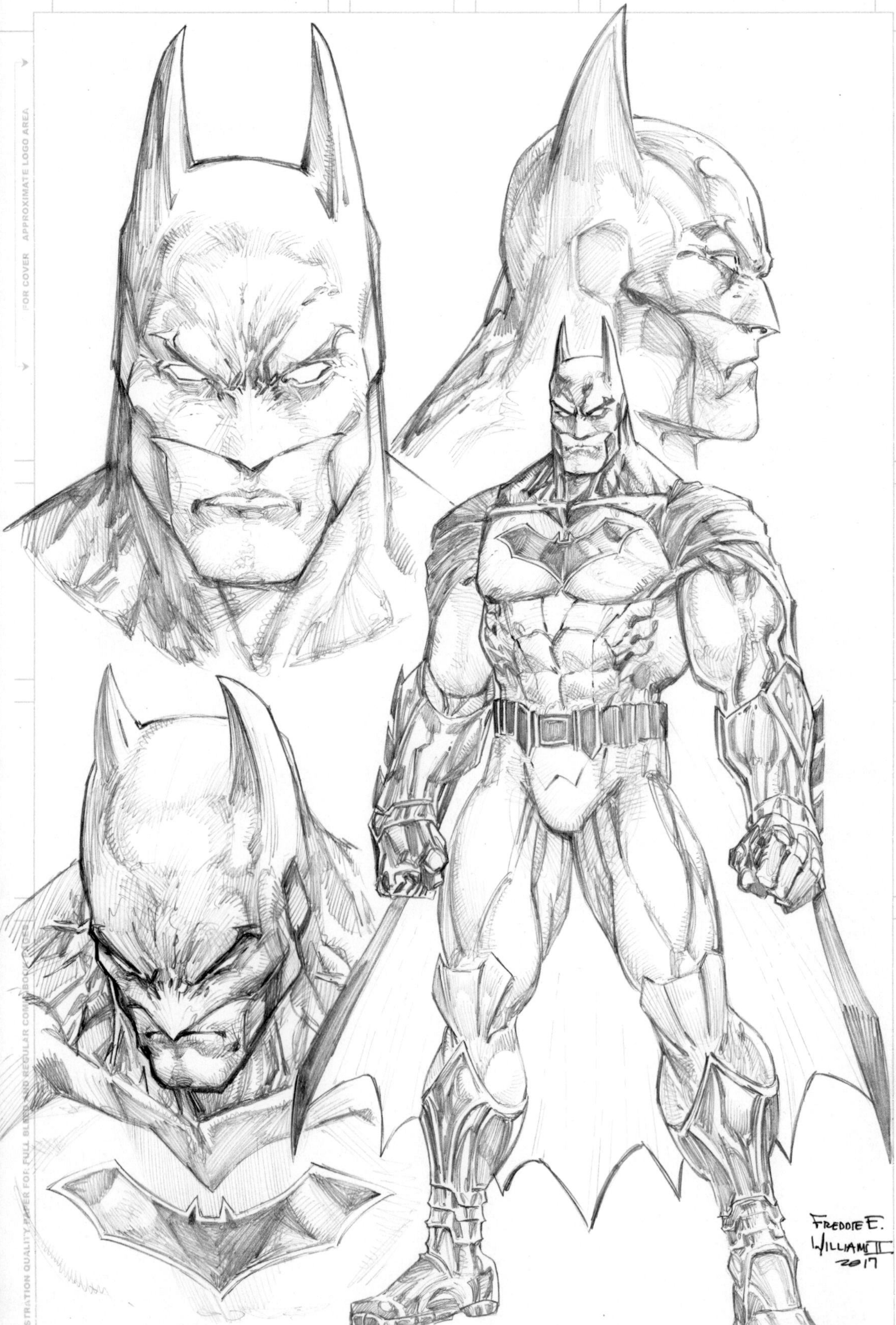
FREDDIE E.
WILLIAMS II
2017

BOOK	ISSUE #	PAGE #	ARTIST(S)
BATMAN / TMNT V.2	STUDY	ROBIN	FREDDIE E. WILLIAMS II

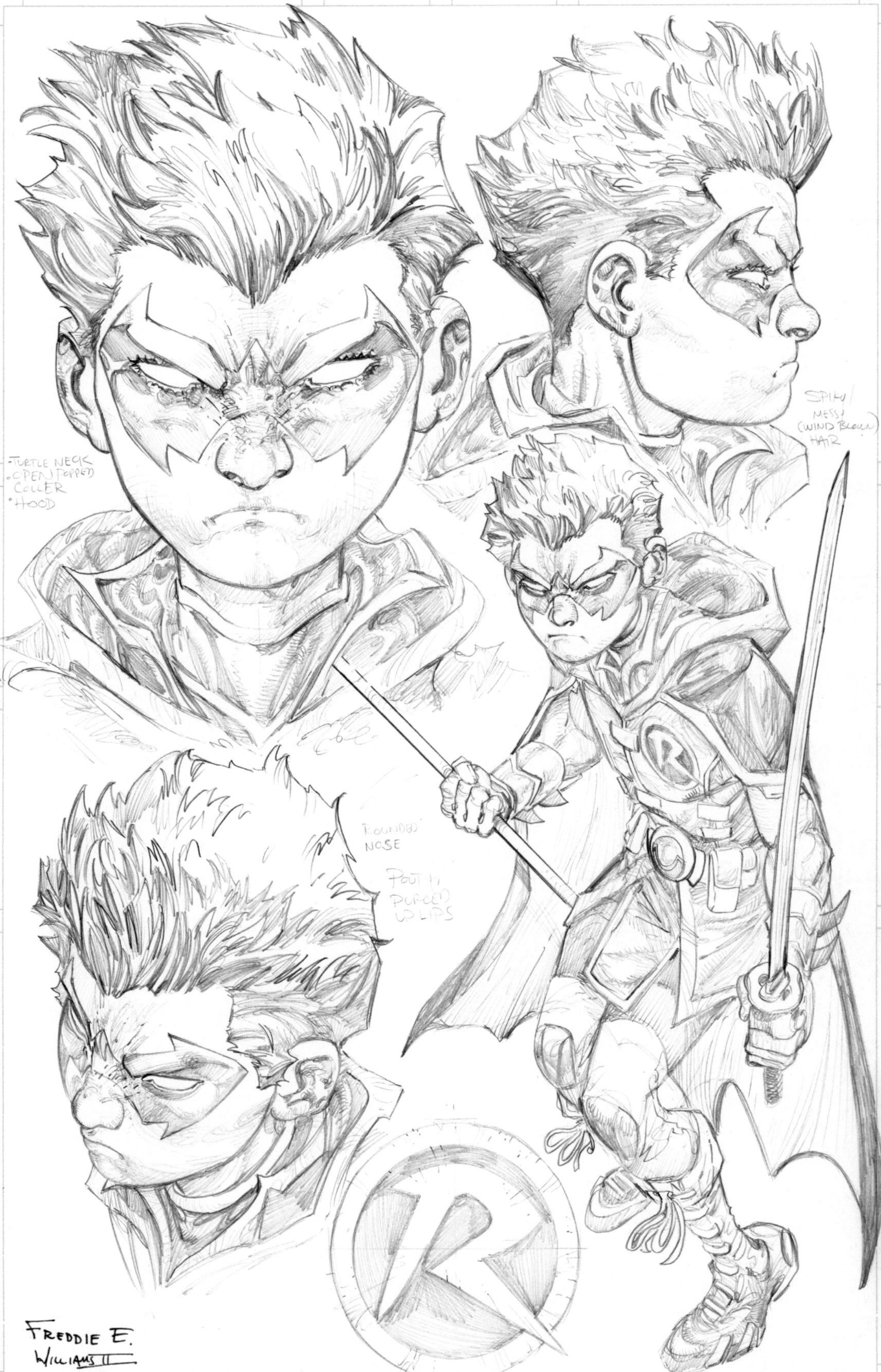
-TURTLE NECK
-OPEN POPPED COLLER
-HOOD
SPIKY MESSY (WIND BLOWN) HAIR
ROUNDED NOSE
POUTY, PURSED UP LIPS
FREDDIE E. WILLIAMS II
2017

WWW.FREDDIEART.COM

Batman/TMNT V.2 — BOOK
Study — ISSUE #
Bane ① — PAGE #
Freddie E. Williams II — ARTIST(S)

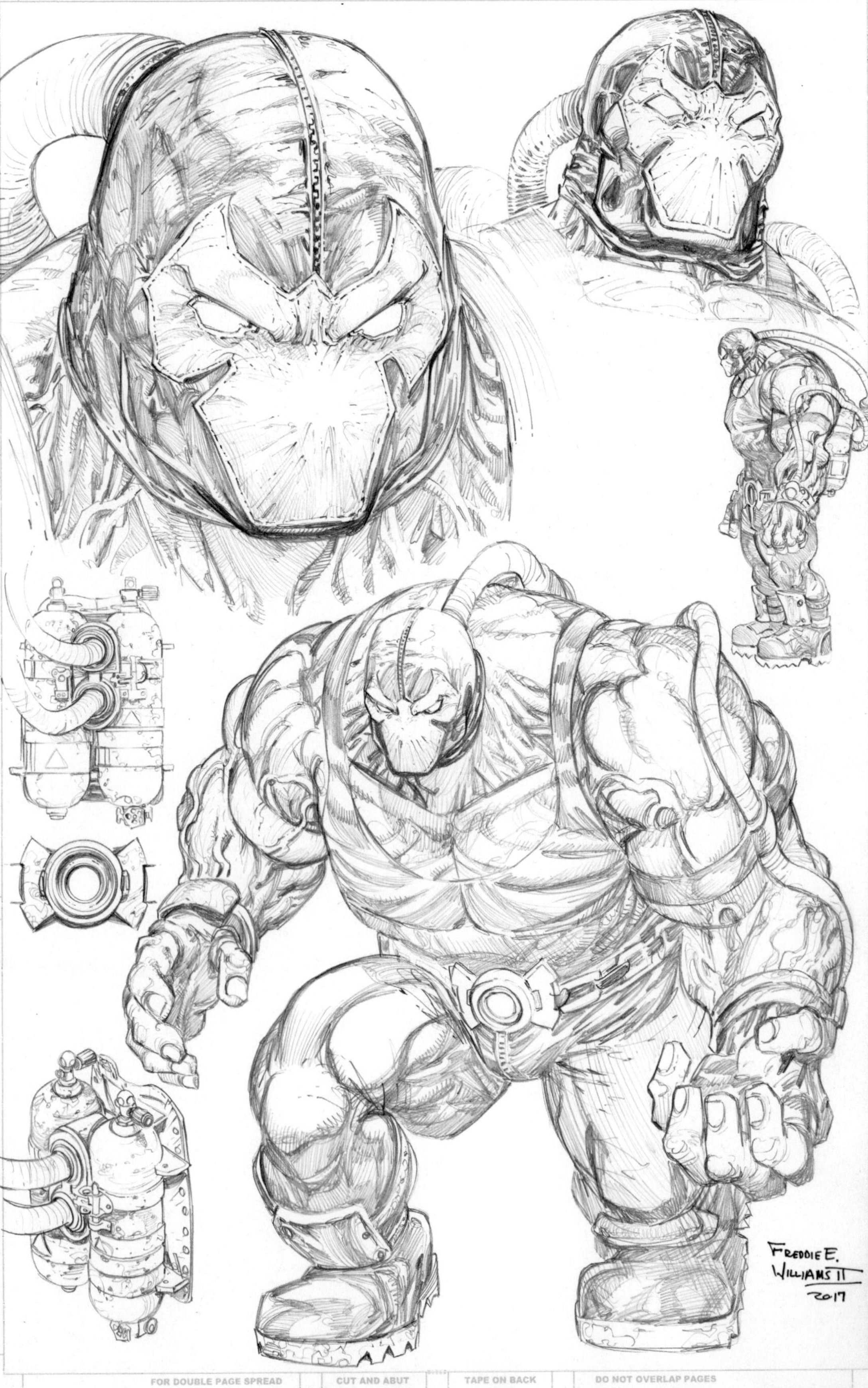
Freddie E. Williams II
2017

FOR COVER APPROXIMATE LOGO AREA

ILLUSTRATION QUALITY PAPER FOR FULL BLEED AND REGULAR COMIC BOOK PAGES

FOR FULL BLEED ART DRAW TO SOLID BLEED LINE

FOR DOUBLE PAGE SPREAD | CUT AND ABUT | TAPE ON BACK | DO NOT OVERLAP PAGES

CUT RIGHT-HAND PAGE HERE

CUT LEFT-HAND PAGE HERE

WWW.FREDDIEART.COM

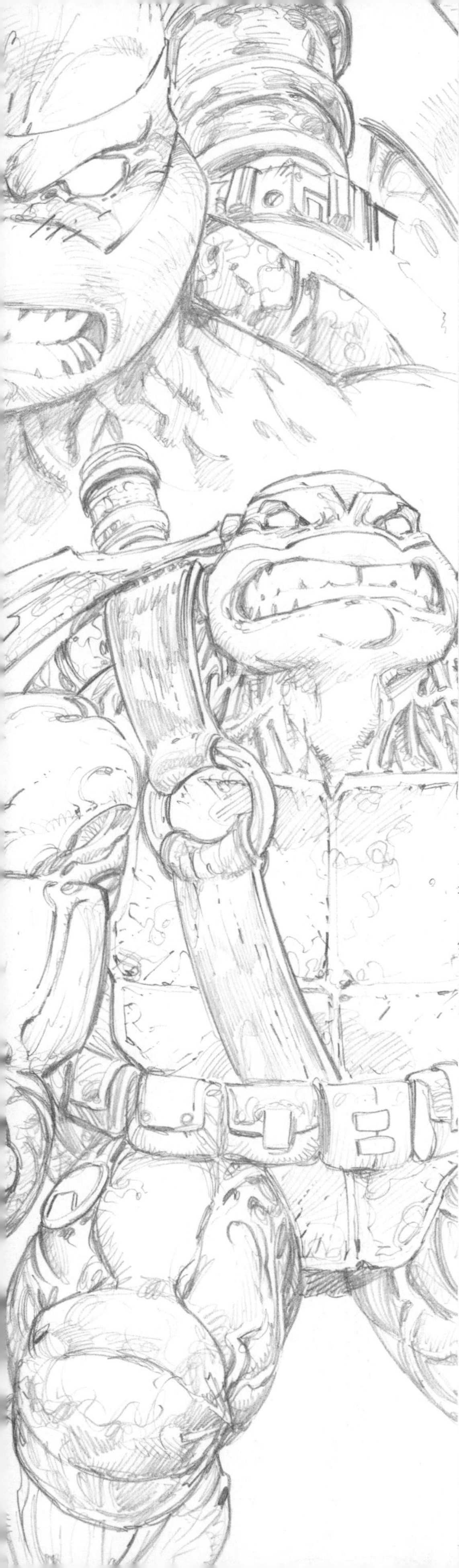

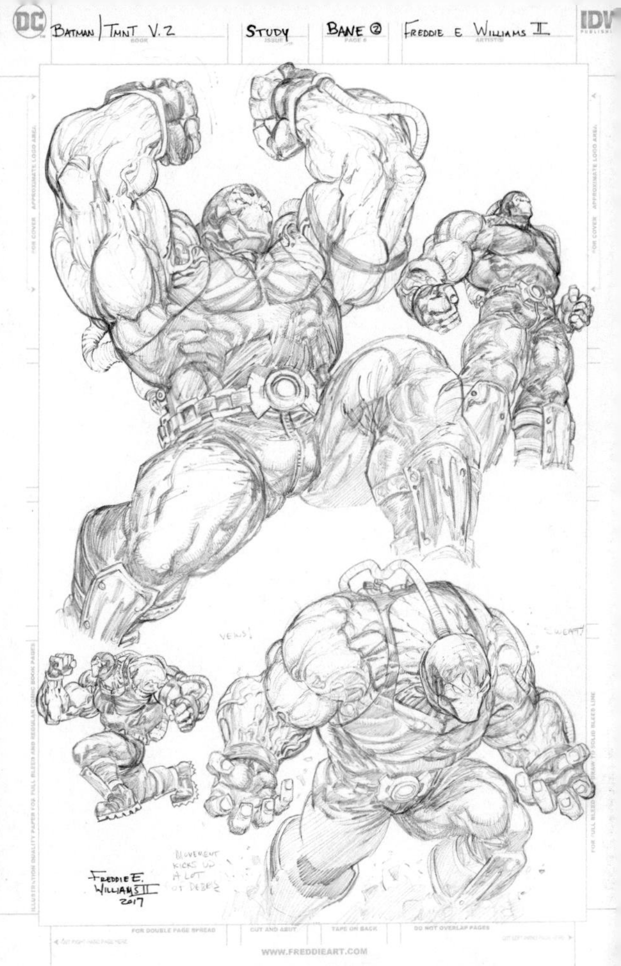

BATMAN / TMNT V. 2
STUDY
BANE ②
FREDDIE E WILLIAMS II
VEINS!
SWEAT!
MOVEMENT KICKS UP A LOT OF DEBRIS
FREDDIE E. WILLIAMS II 2017

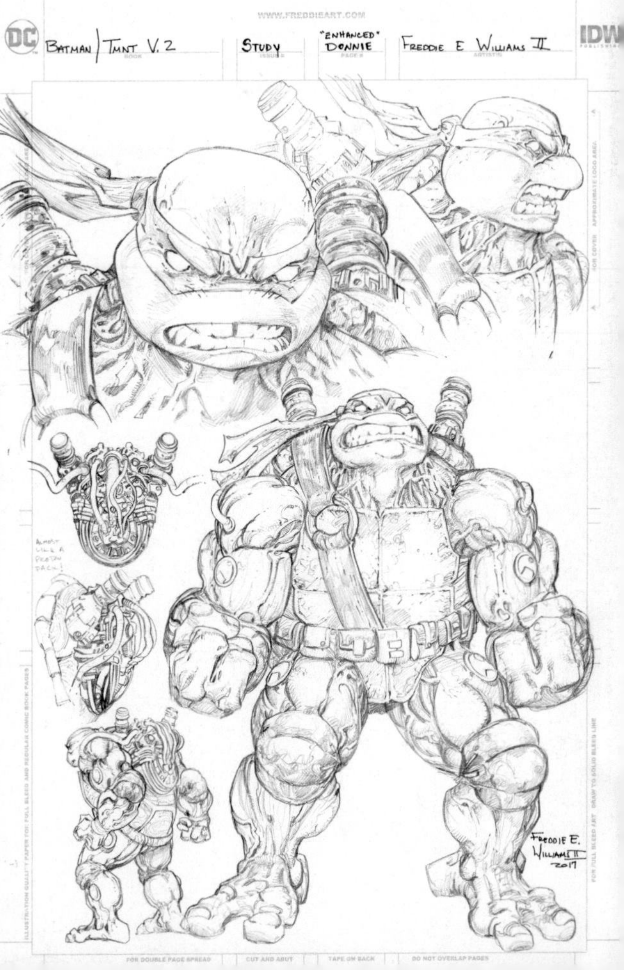

BATMAN / TMNT V. 2
STUDY
"ENHANCED" DONNIE
FREDDIE E WILLIAMS II
ALMOST LIKE A PROTON PACK!
FREDDIE E. WILLIAMS II 2017

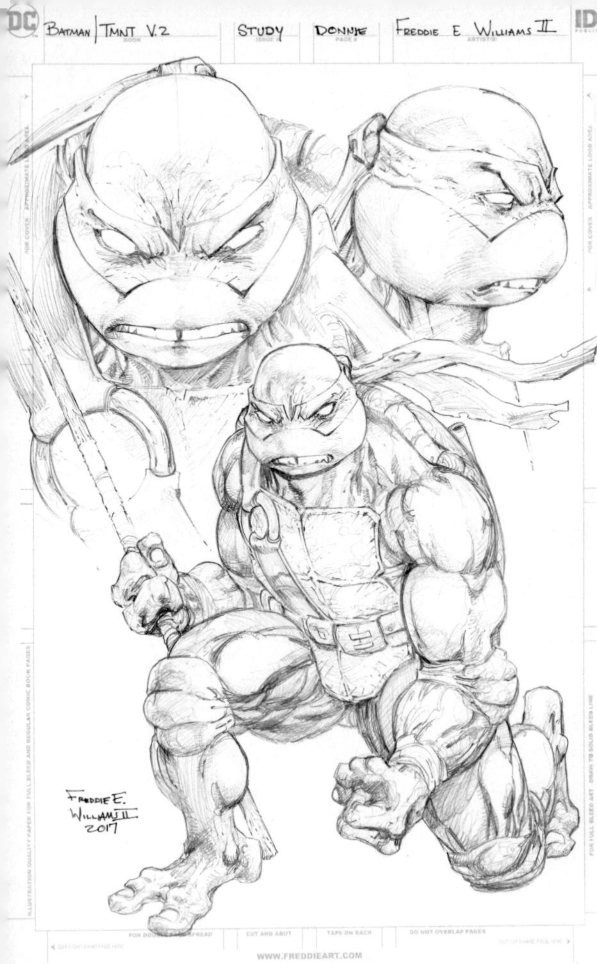

BATMAN | TMNT V.2
STUDY
DONNIE
FREDDIE E WILLIAMS II
FREDDIE E.
WILLIAMS II
2017
WWW.FREDDIEART.COM

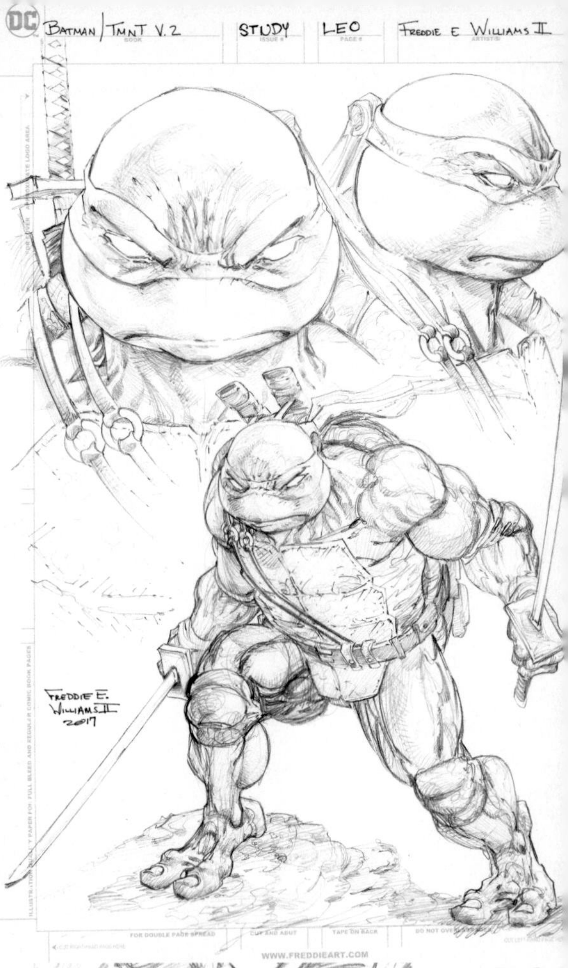

BATMAN | TMNT V.2
STUDY
LEO
FREDDIE E WILLIAMS II
FREDDIE E.
WILLIAMS II
2017
WWW.FREDDIEART.COM

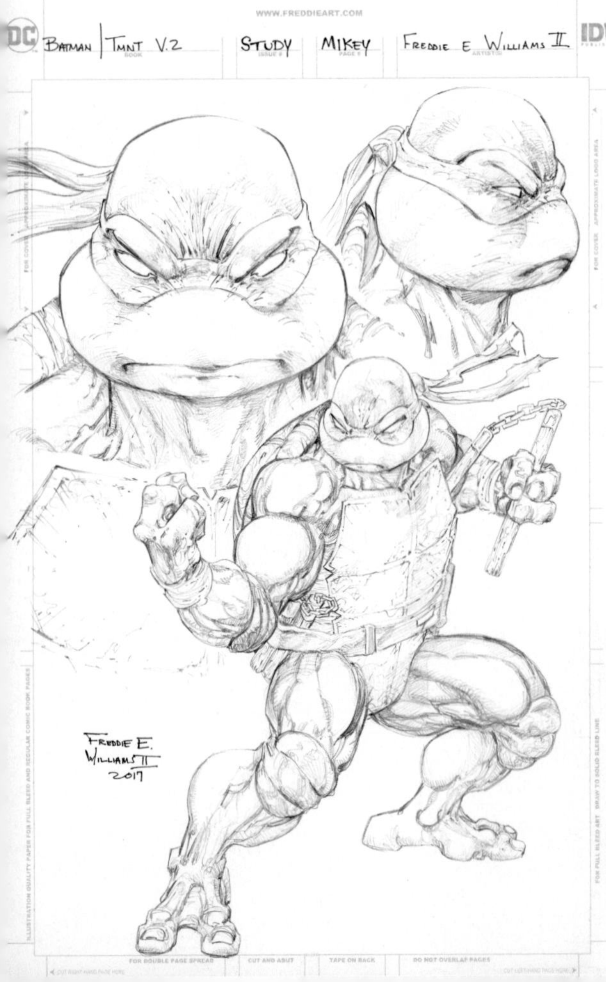

WWW.FREDDIEART.COM
BATMAN | TMNT V.2
STUDY
MIKEY
FREDDIE E WILLIAMS II
FREDDIE E.
WILLIAMS II
2017

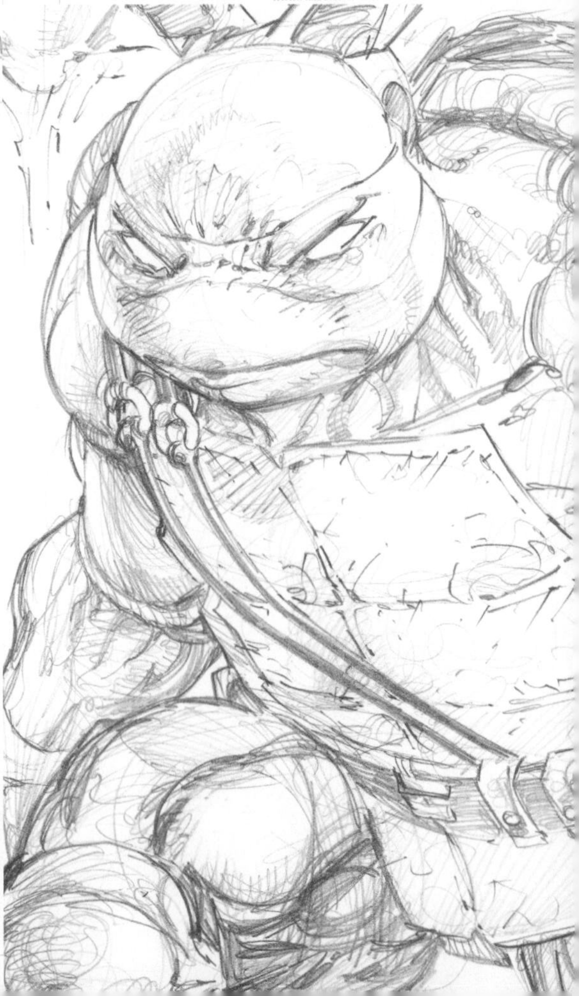

Batman | TMNT V.2

Study

Raph

Freddie E. Williams II

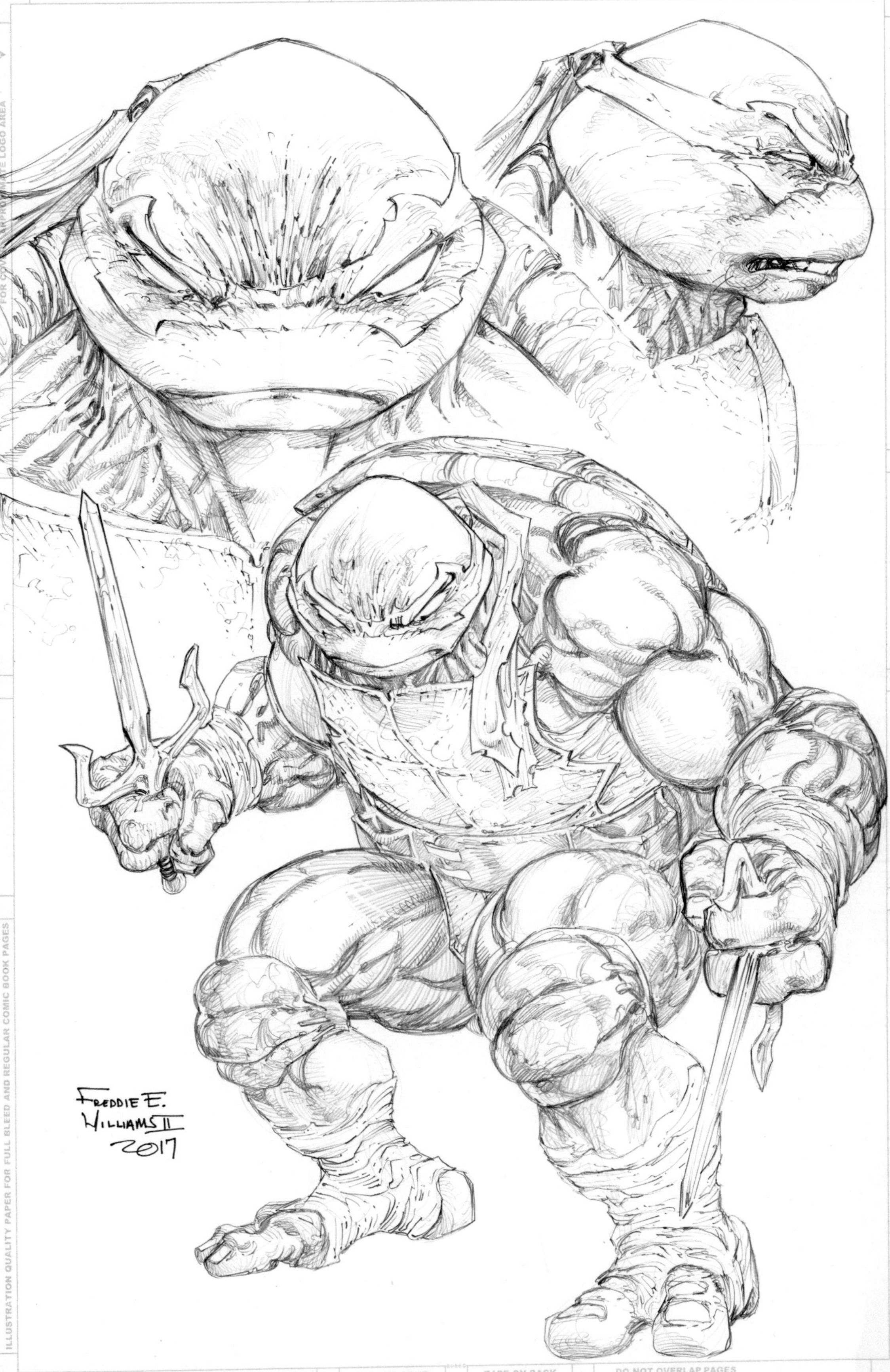
Freddie E.
Williams II
2017

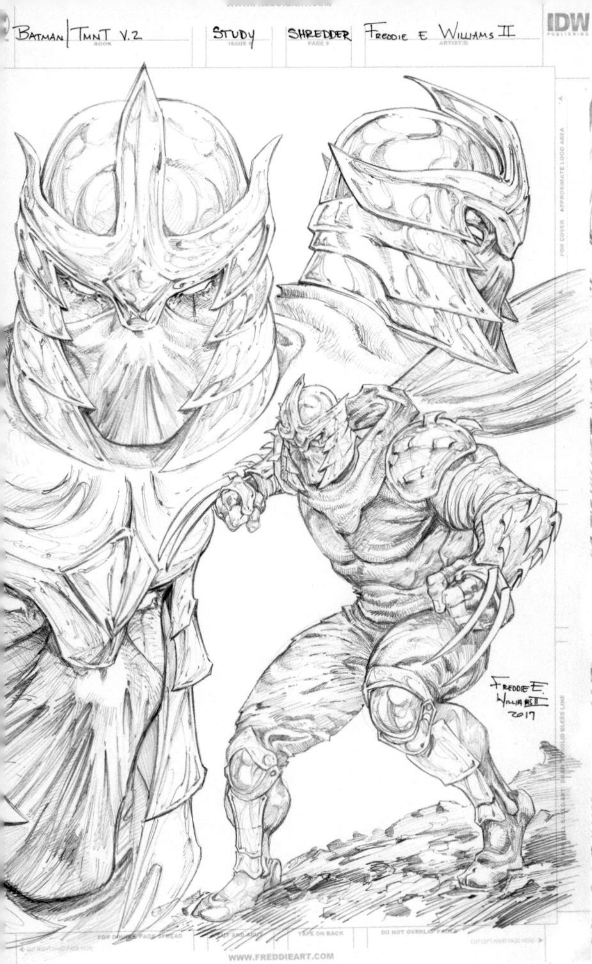

BATMAN | TMNT V.2
STUDY
SHREDDER
FREDDIE E WILLIAMS II
FREDDIE E. WILLIAMS II 2017
WWW.FREDDIEART.COM

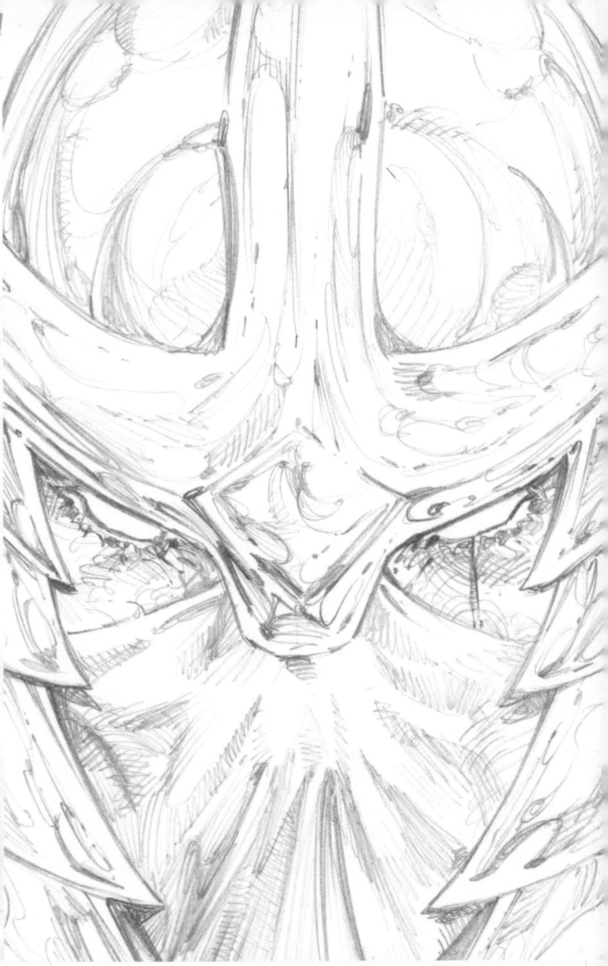

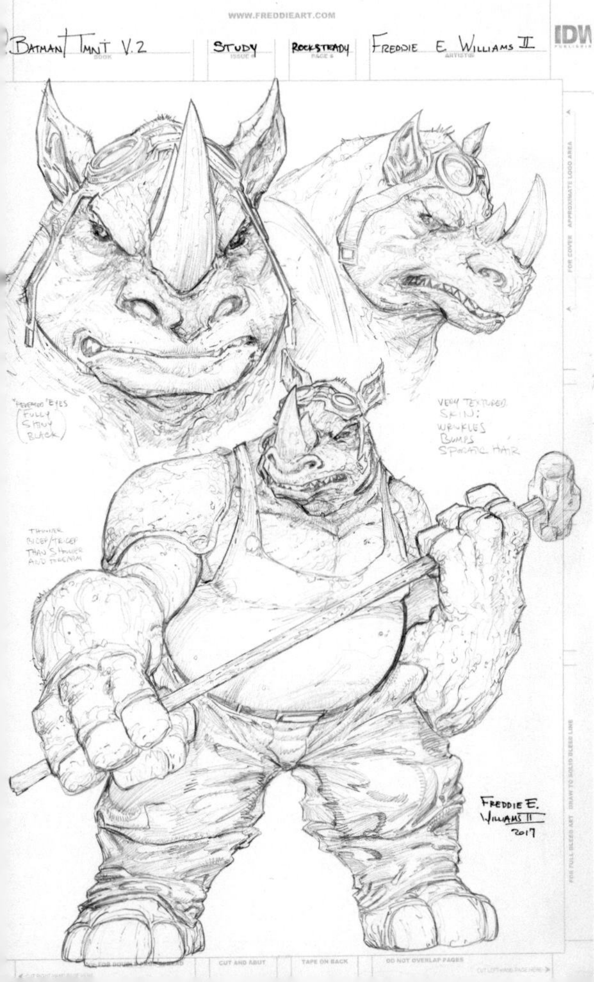

WWW.FREDDIEART.COM
BATMAN | TMNT V.2
STUDY
ROCKSTEADY
FREDDIE E WILLIAMS II
FULLY SHINY BLACK
VERY TEXTURED SKIN: WRINKLES BUMPS SPORADIC HAIR
FREDDIE E. WILLIAMS II 2017

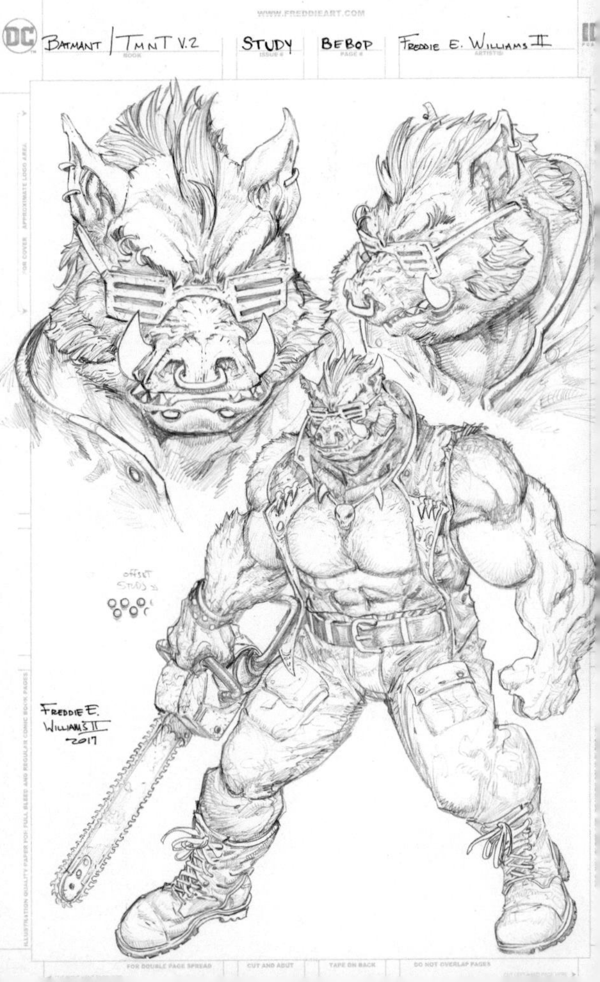

WWW.FREDDIEART.COM
BATMAN | TMNT V.2
STUDY
BEBOP
FREDDIE E. WILLIAMS II
OFFSET STUDS
FREDDIE E. WILLIAMS II 2017

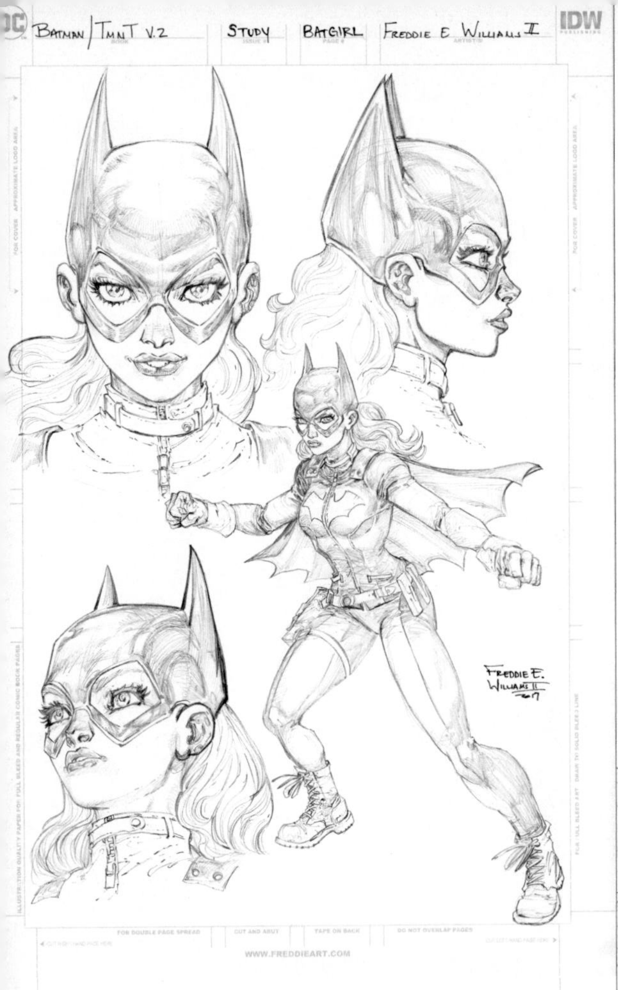

BATMAN / TMNT V.2
STUDY
BATGIRL
FREDDIE E WILLIAMS II
IDW
FREDDIE E. WILLIAMS II 2017
WWW.FREDDIEART.COM

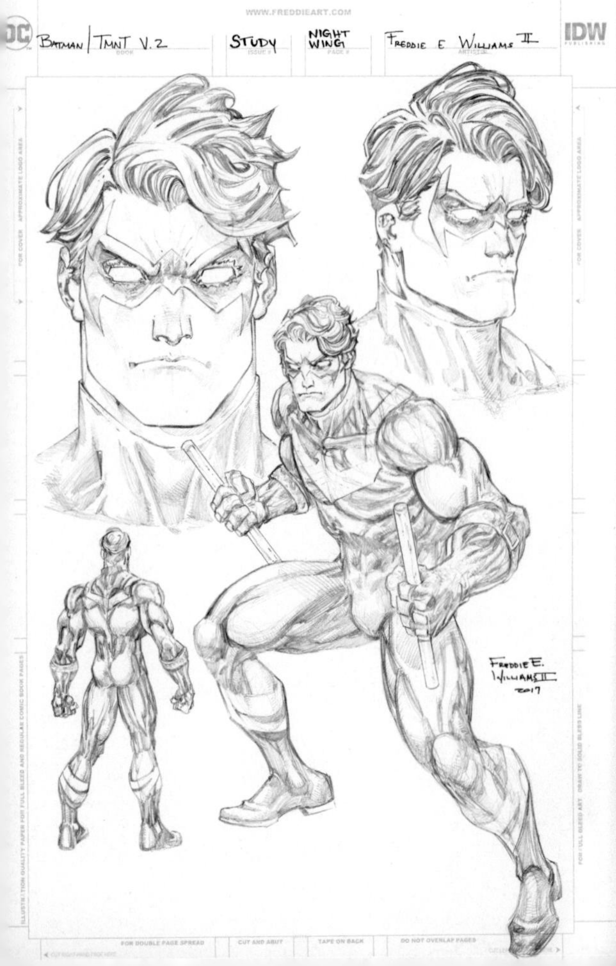

WWW.FREDDIEART.COM
BATMAN / TMNT V.2
STUDY
NIGHT WING
FREDDIE E WILLIAMS II
IDW
FREDDIE E. WILLIAMS II 2017

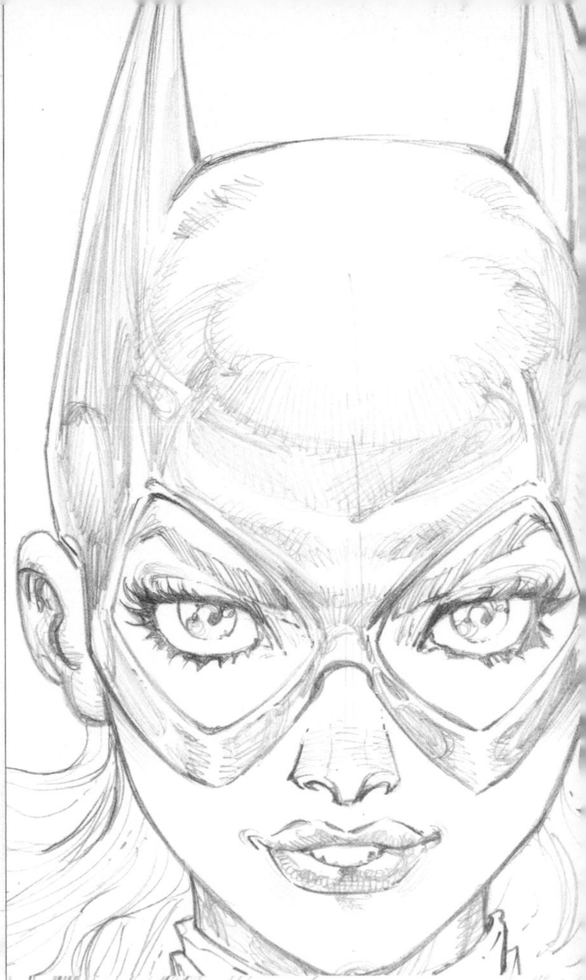

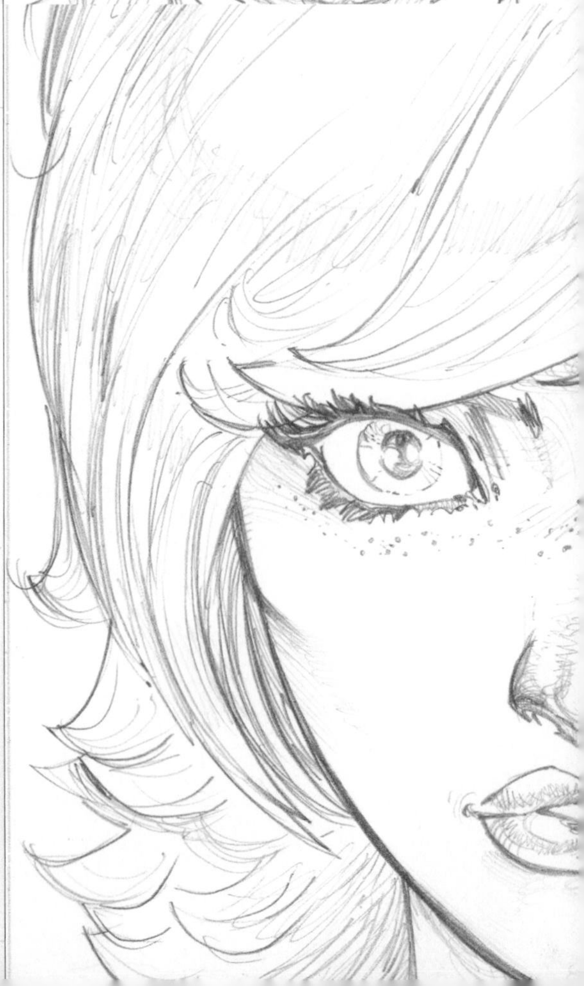

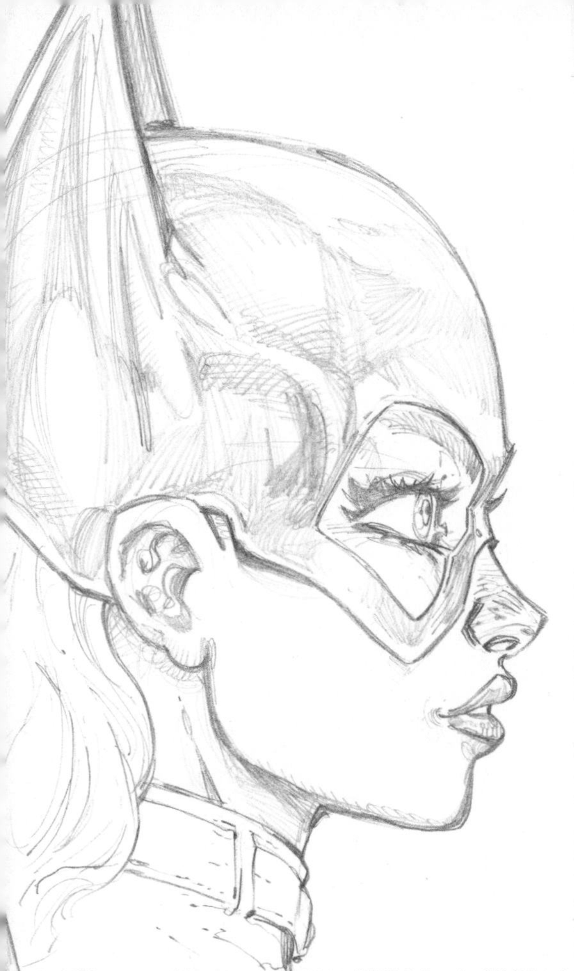

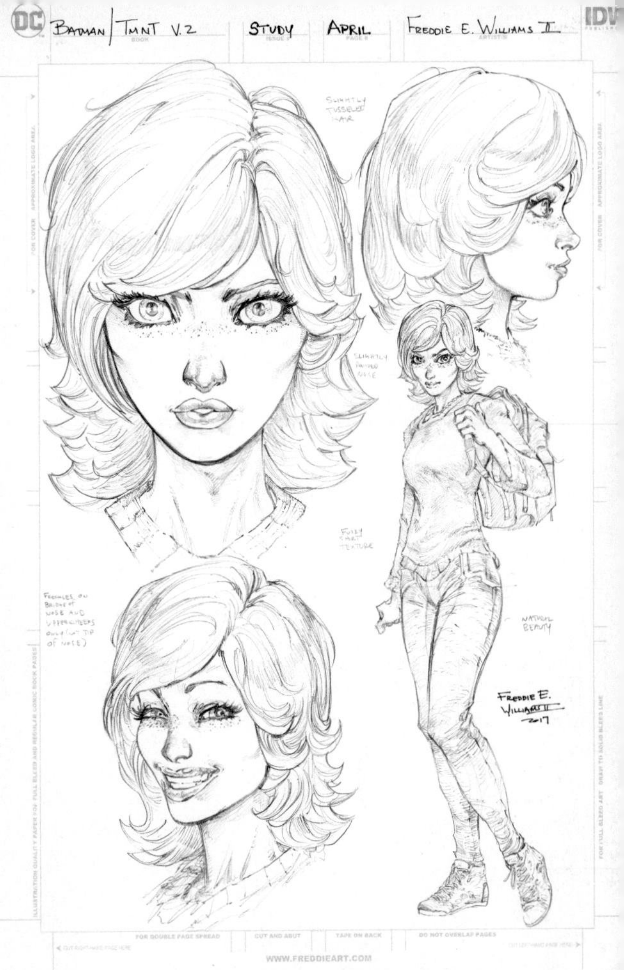

BATMAN / TMNT V.2
STUDY
APRIL
FREDDIE E. WILLIAMS II
SLIGHTLY TUSSELED HAIR
FUZZY SHIRT TEXTURE
NATURAL BEAUTY
FREDDIE E. WILLIAMS II 2017
WWW.FREDDIEART.COM

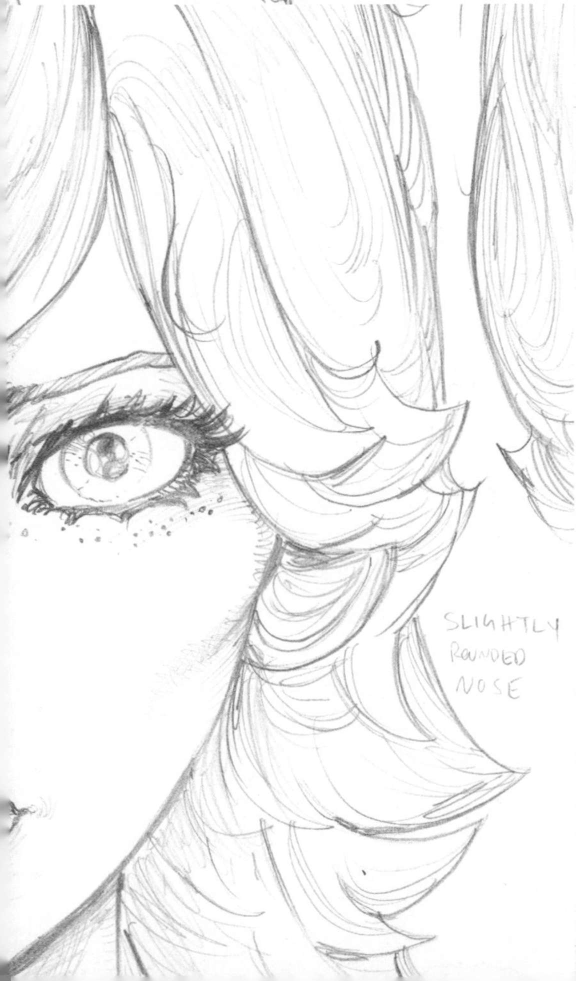

SLIGHTLY ROUNDED NOSE

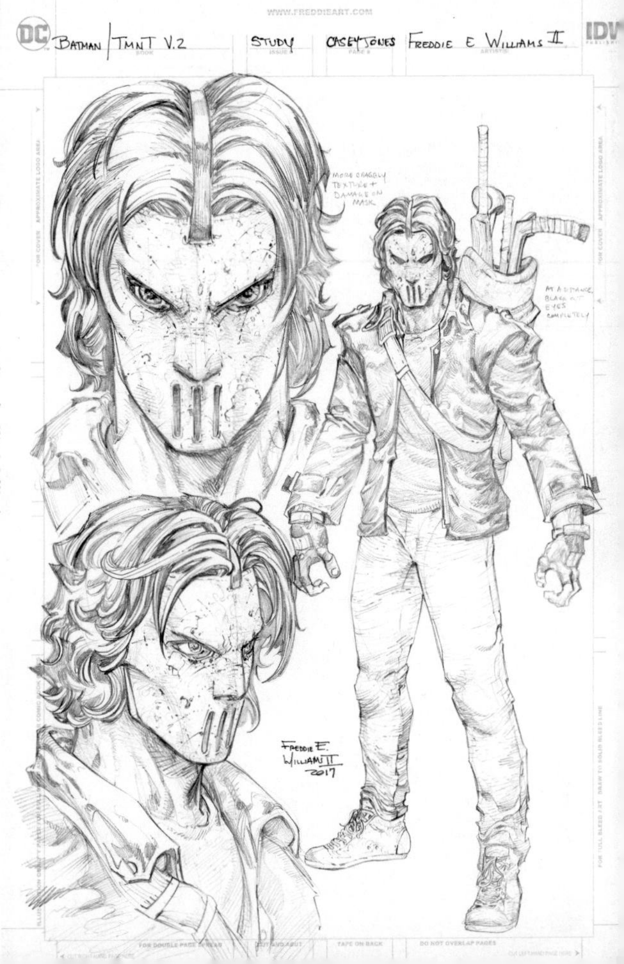

BATMAN / TMNT V.2
STUDY
CASEY JONES
FREDDIE E WILLIAMS II
MORE CRAGGLY TEXTURE + DAMAGE ON MASK
FREDDIE E. WILLIAMS II 2017

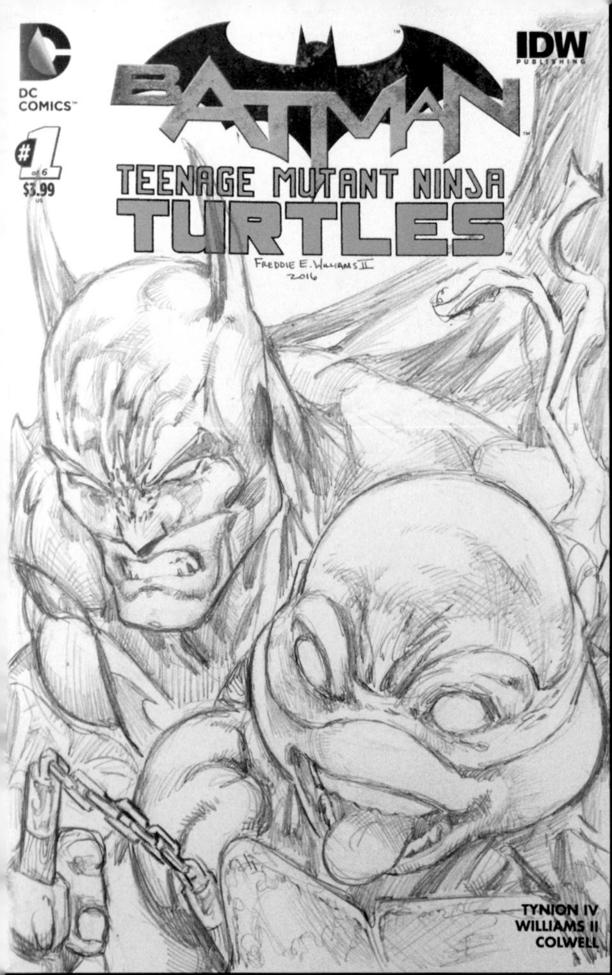
DC COMICS
IDW PUBLISHING
BATMAN
#1 of 6
$3.99 US
TEENAGE MUTANT NINJA
TURTLES
Freddie E. Williams II 2016
TYNION IV
WILLIAMS II
COLWELL

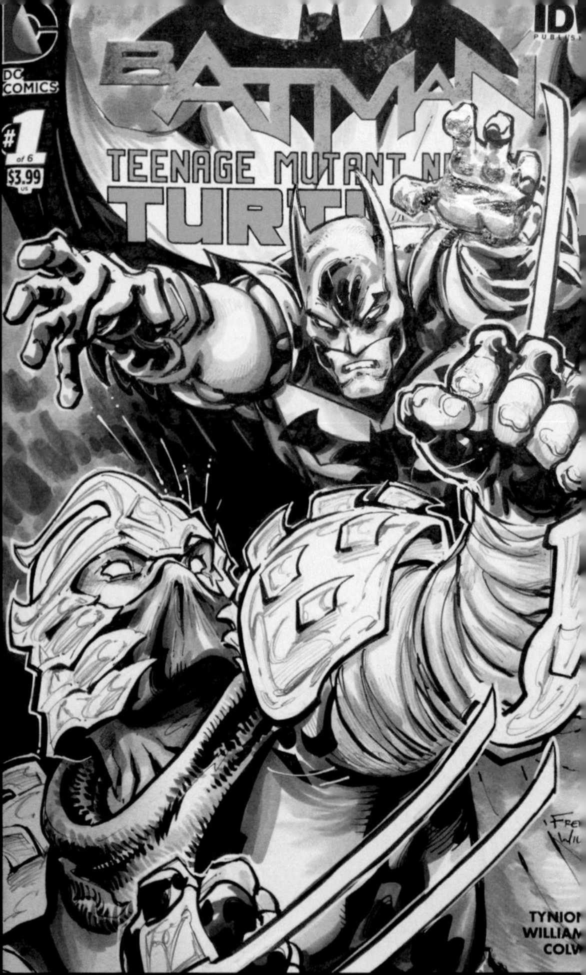
DC COMICS
BATMAN
#1 of 6
$3.99 US
TEENAGE MUTANT
TUR

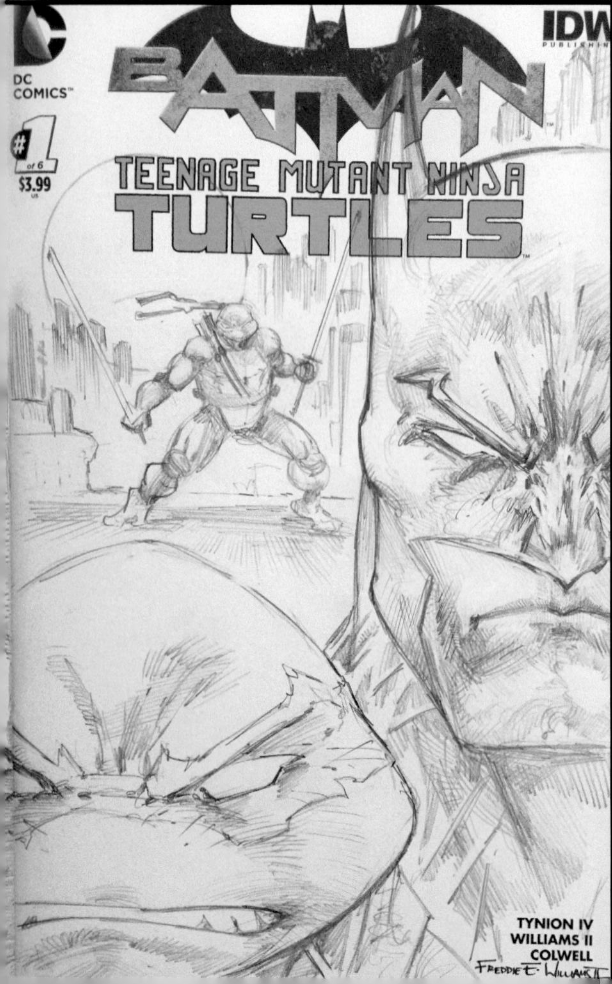
DC COMICS
IDW
BATMAN
#1 of 6
$3.99 US
TEENAGE MUTANT NINJA
TURTLES
TYNION IV
WILLIAMS II
COLWELL
Freddie E. Williams II

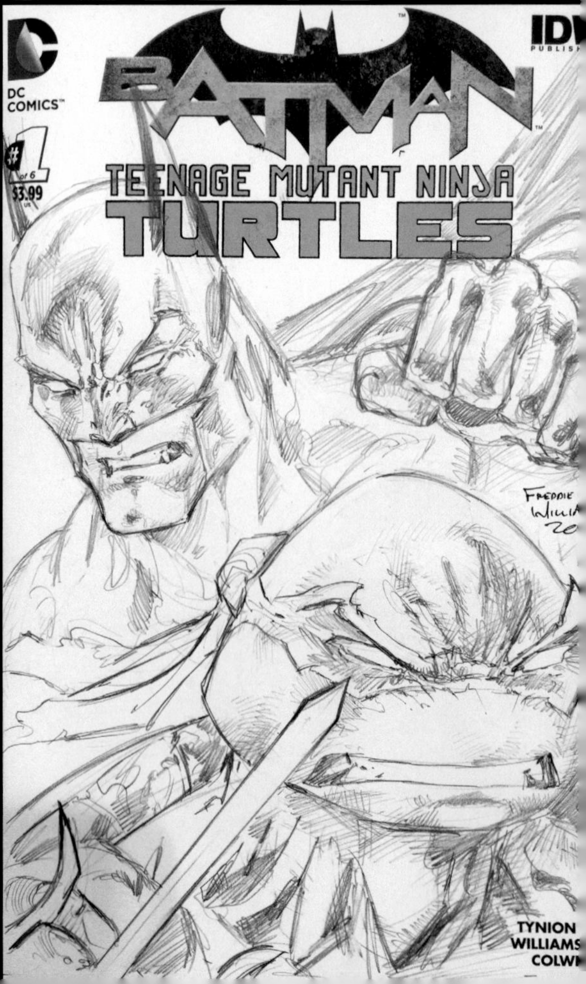
DC COMICS
BATMAN
#1 of 6
$3.99 US
TEENAGE MUTANT NINJA
TURTLES

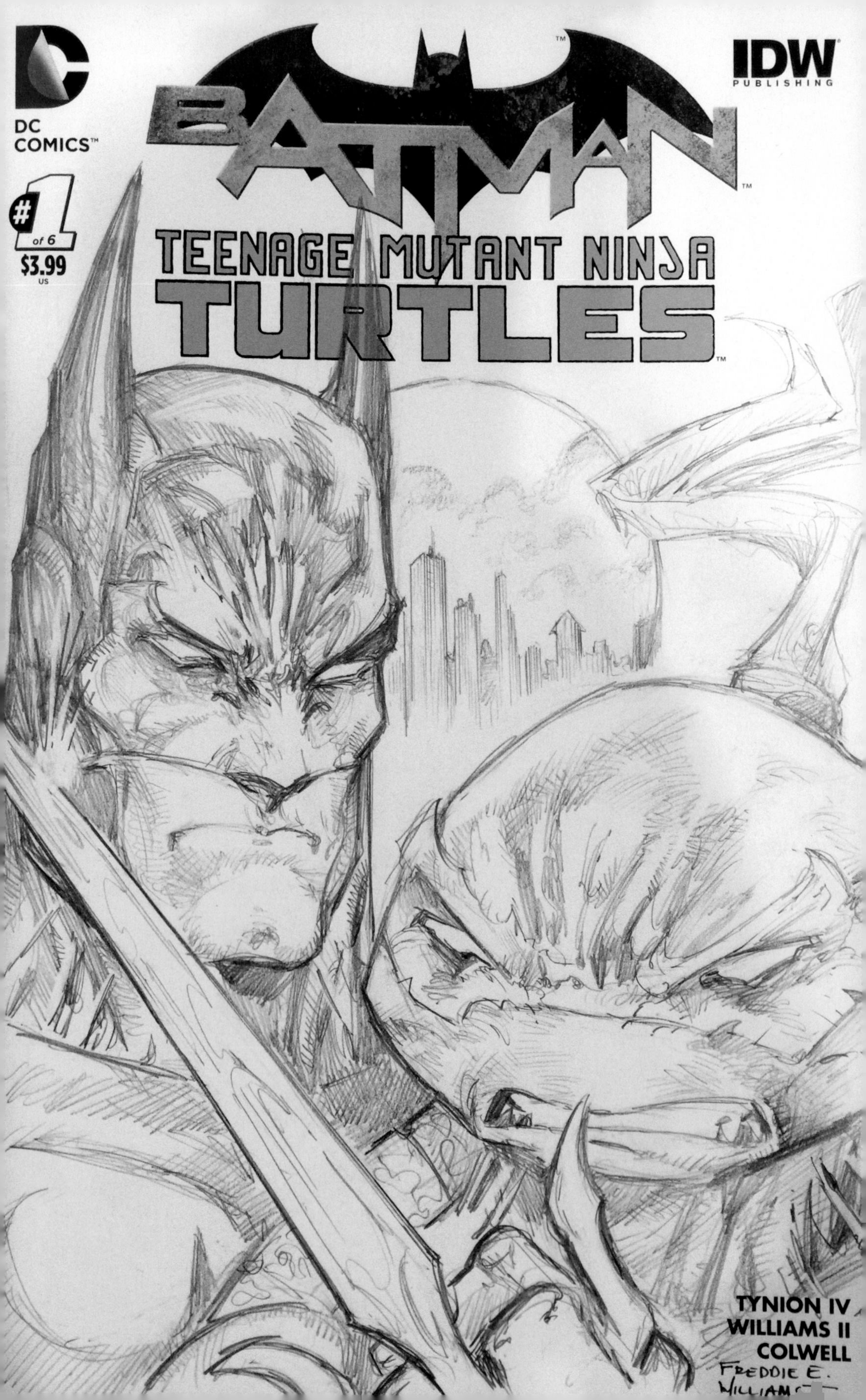
DC COMICS™
BATMAN™
IDW PUBLISHING
#1 of 6
$3.99 US
TEENAGE MUTANT NINJA TURTLES™
TYNION IV
WILLIAMS II
COLWELL
FREDDIE E.

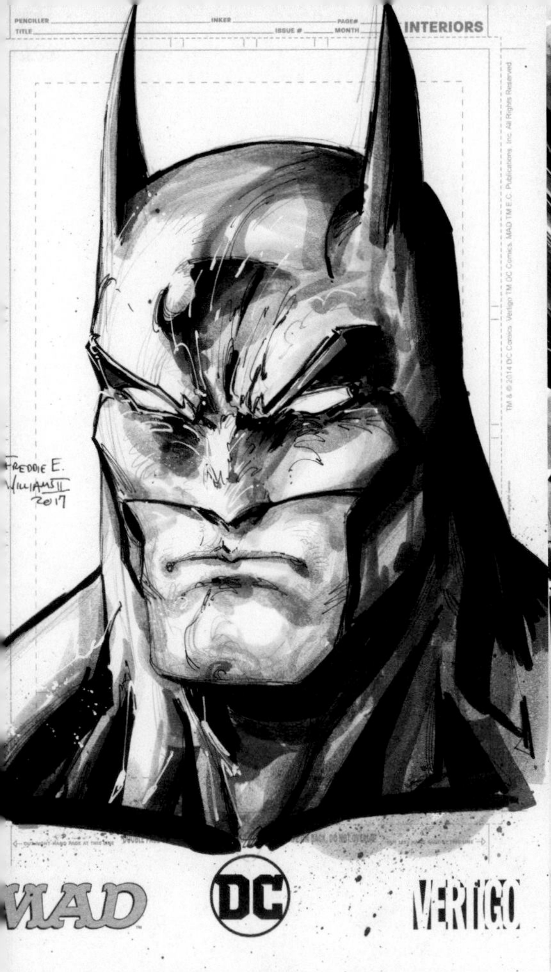
INTERIORS
FREDDIE E.
WILLIAMS II
2017
MAD
DC
VERTIGO

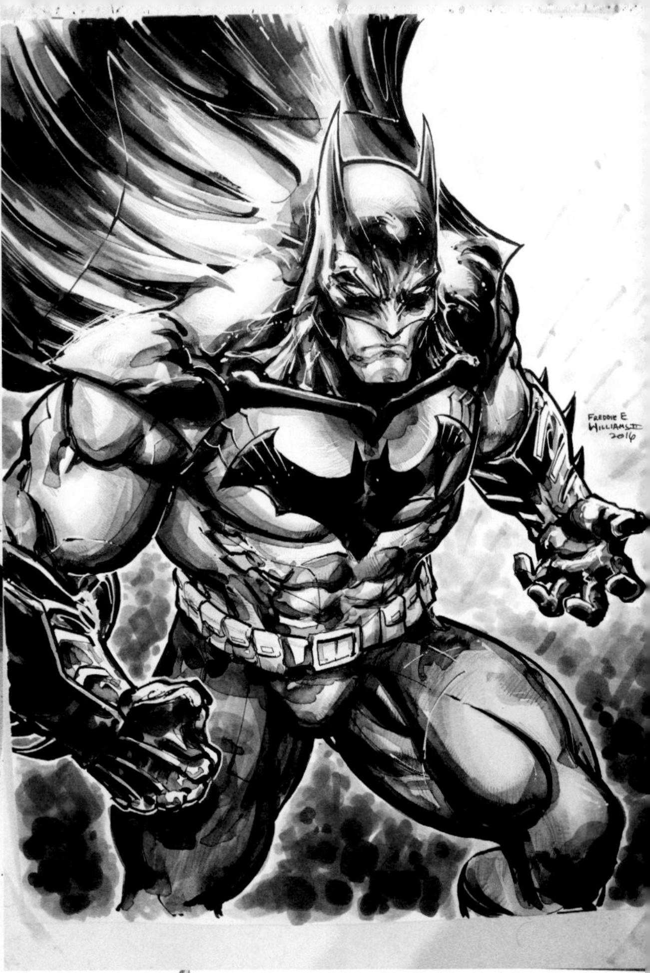
FREDDIE E.
WILLIAMS II
2016

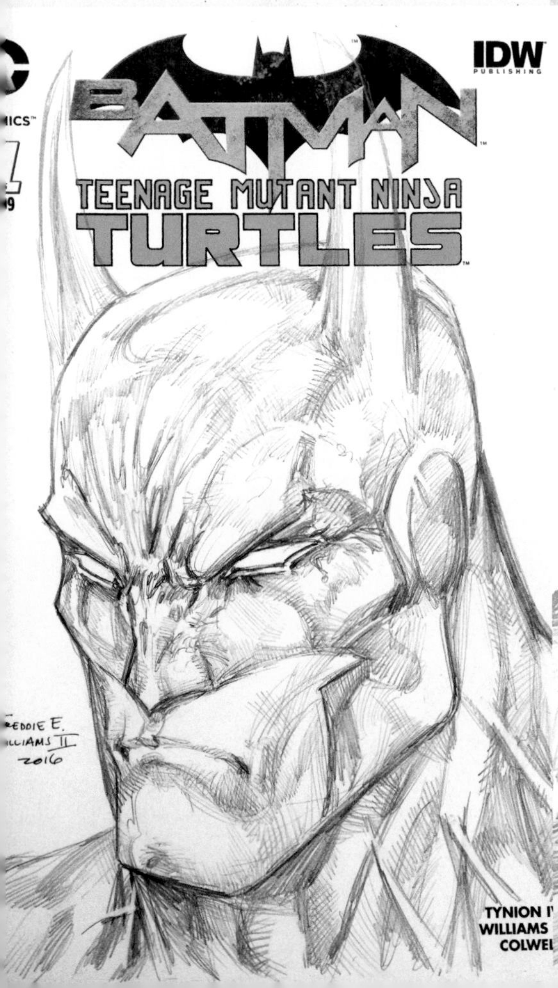
IDW
PUBLISHING
BATMAN
TEENAGE MUTANT NINJA
TURTLES
WILLIAMS II
2016
TYNION IV
WILLIAMS

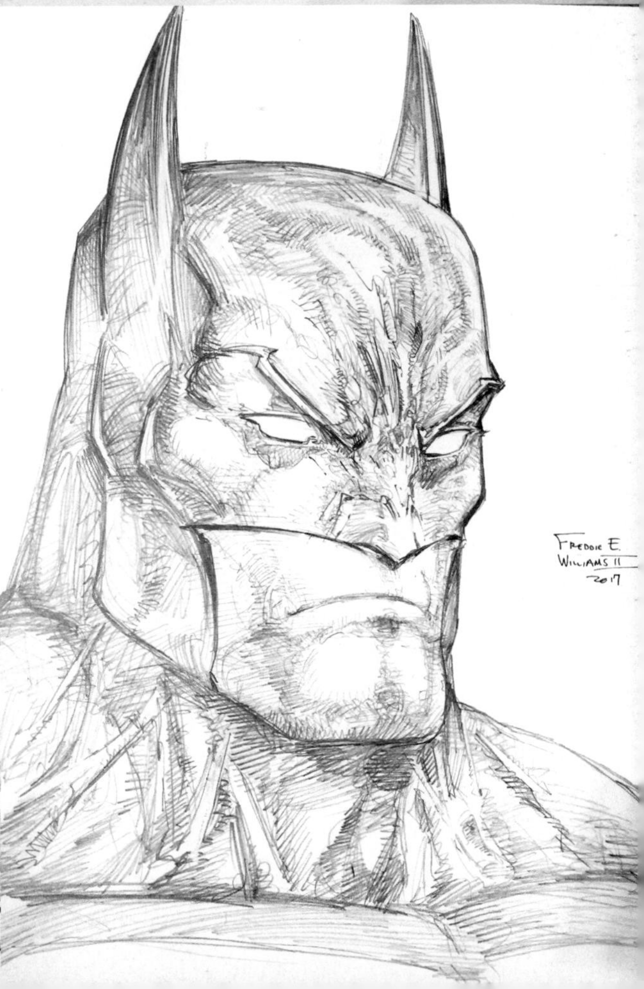
FREDDIE E.
WILLIAMS II
2017

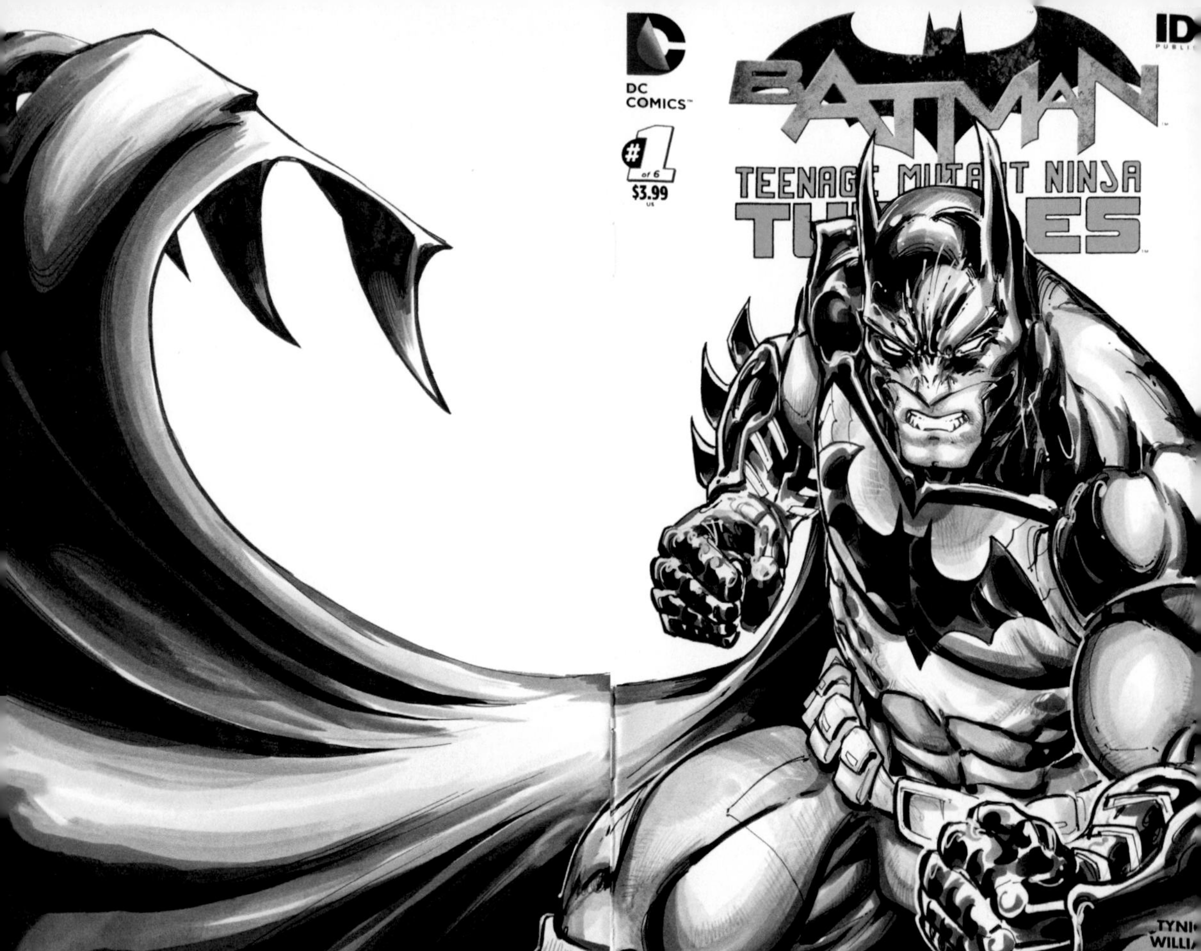
DC COMICS
#1 of 6
$3.99
US
BATMAN

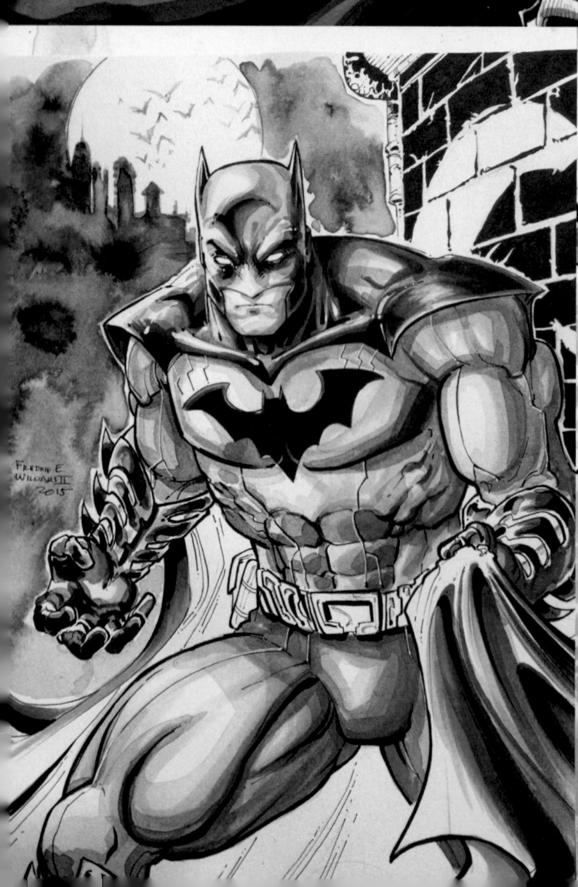
FREDDIE E. WILLIAMS II 2015

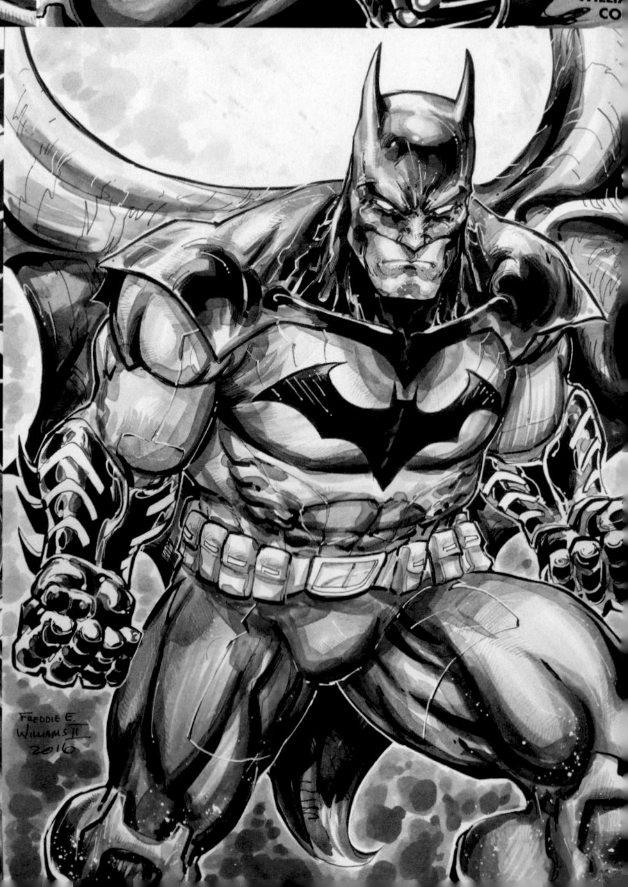
FREDDIE E. WILLIAMS II 2016

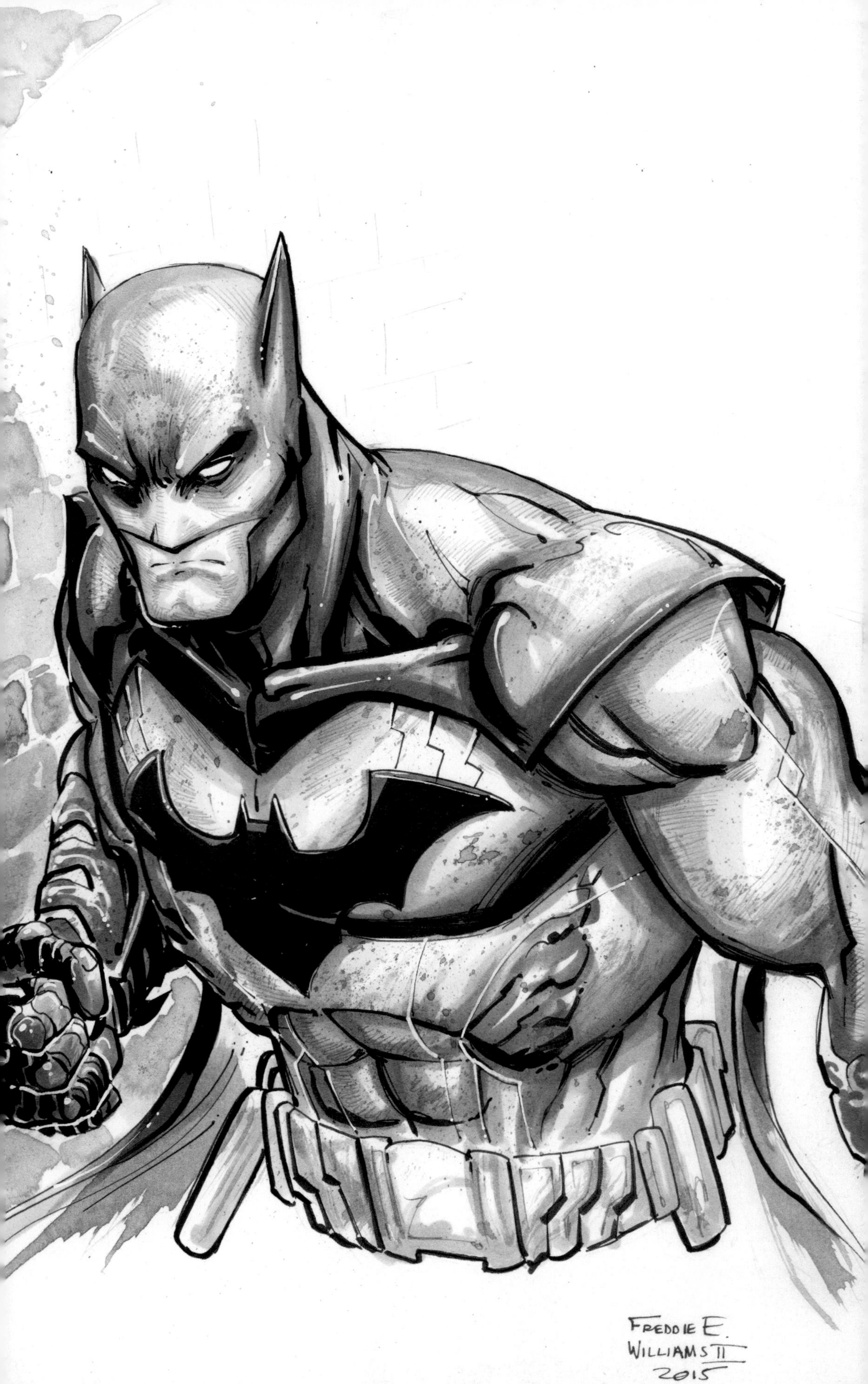
FREDDIE E.
WILLIAMS II
2015

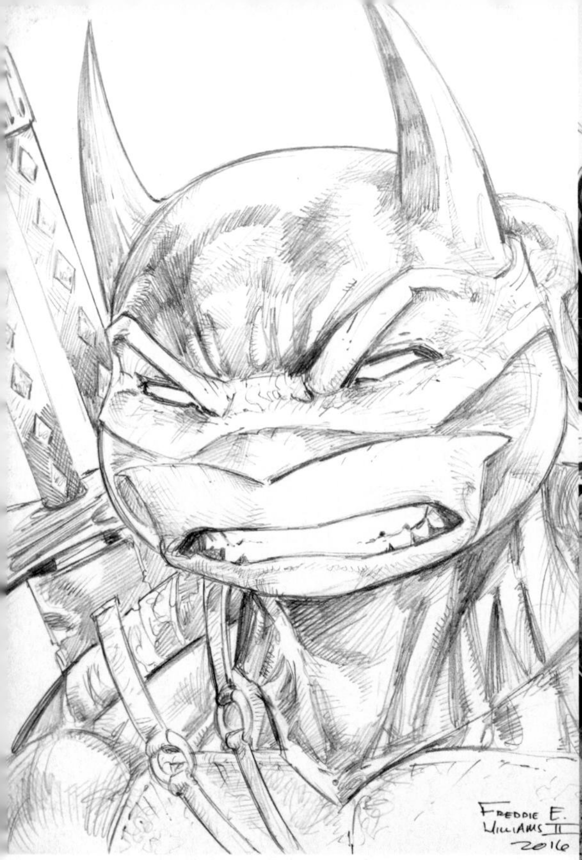
FREDDIE E.
WILLIAMS II
2016

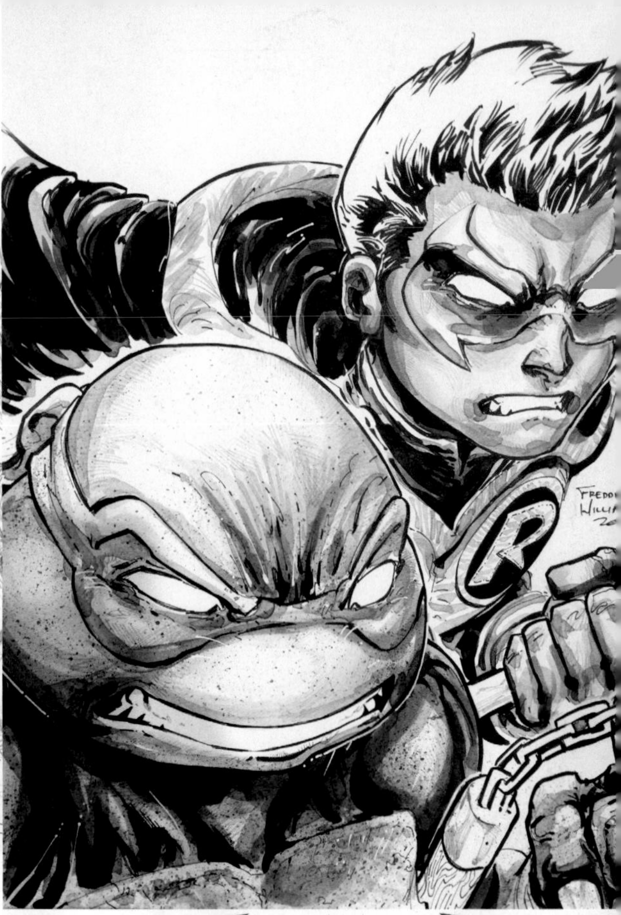

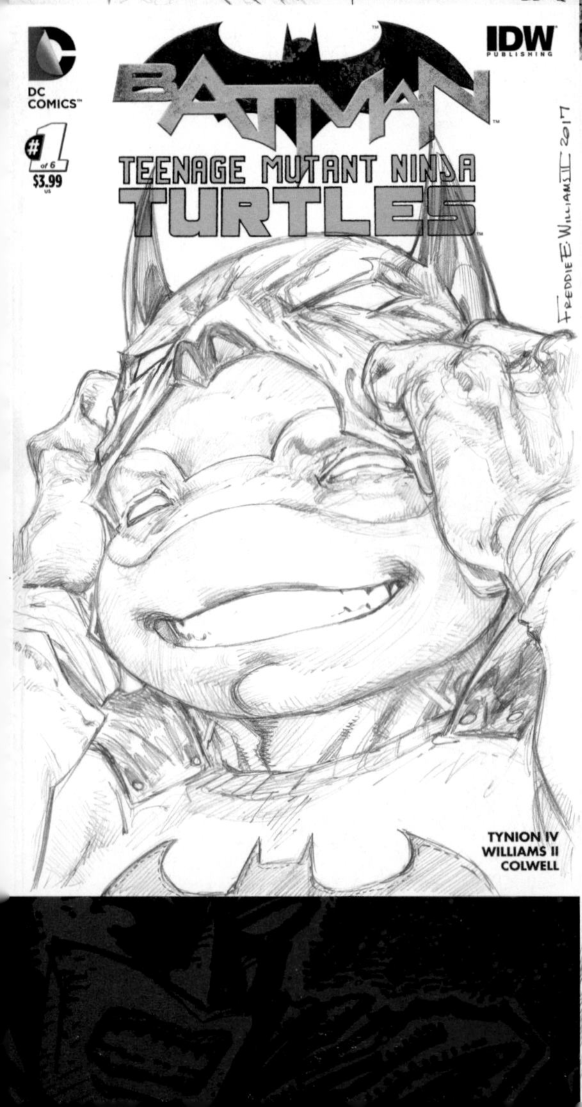
DC COMICS
IDW PUBLISHING
BATMAN
#1 of 6
$3.99 US
TEENAGE MUTANT NINJA
TURTLES
FREDDIE E. WILLIAMS II 2017
TYNION IV
WILLIAMS II
COLWELL

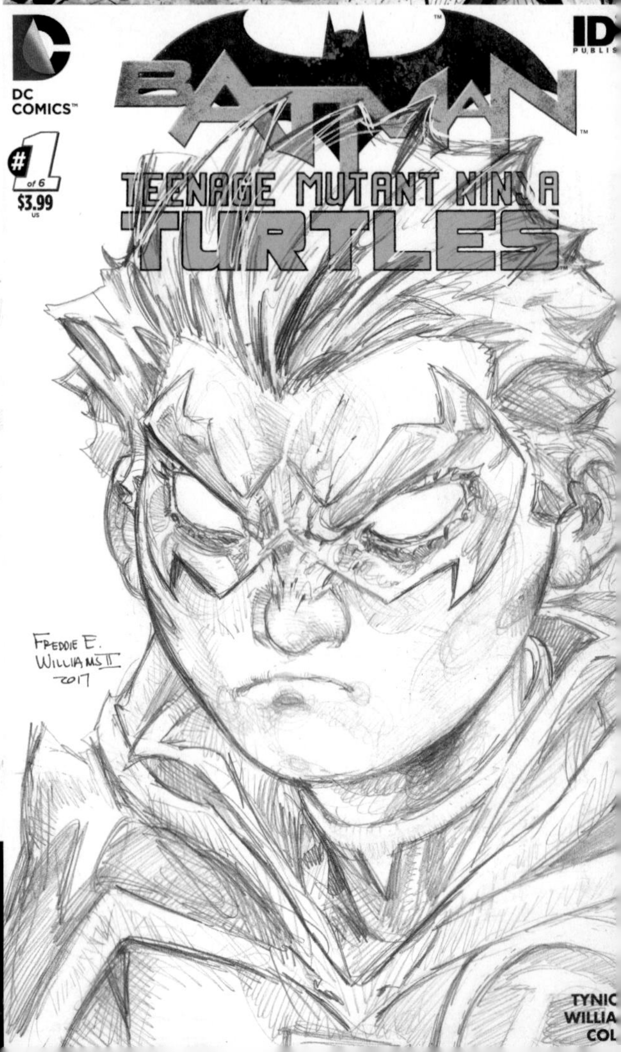
DC COMICS
BATMAN
#1 of 6
$3.99 US
TEENAGE MUTANT NINJA
TURTLES
FREDDIE E.
WILLIAMS II
2017

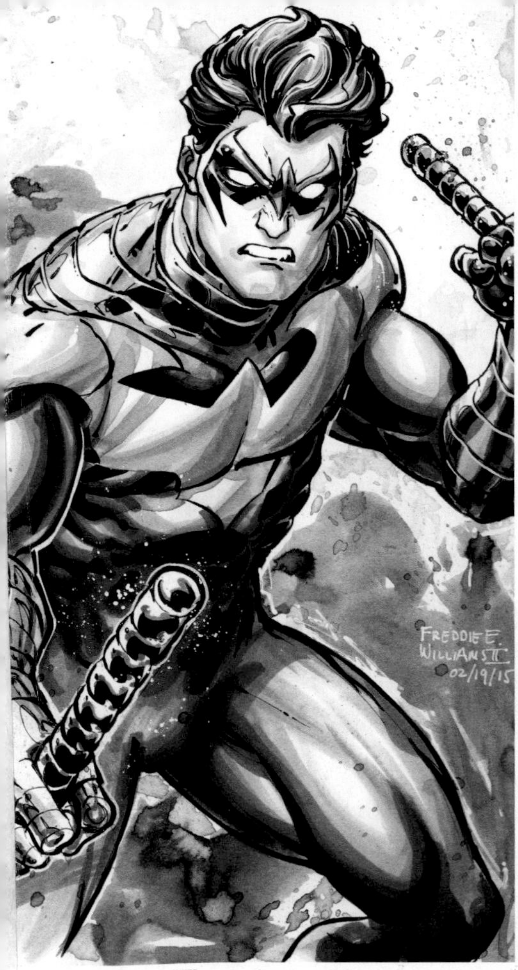
FREDDIE E. WILLIAMS II 02/19/15

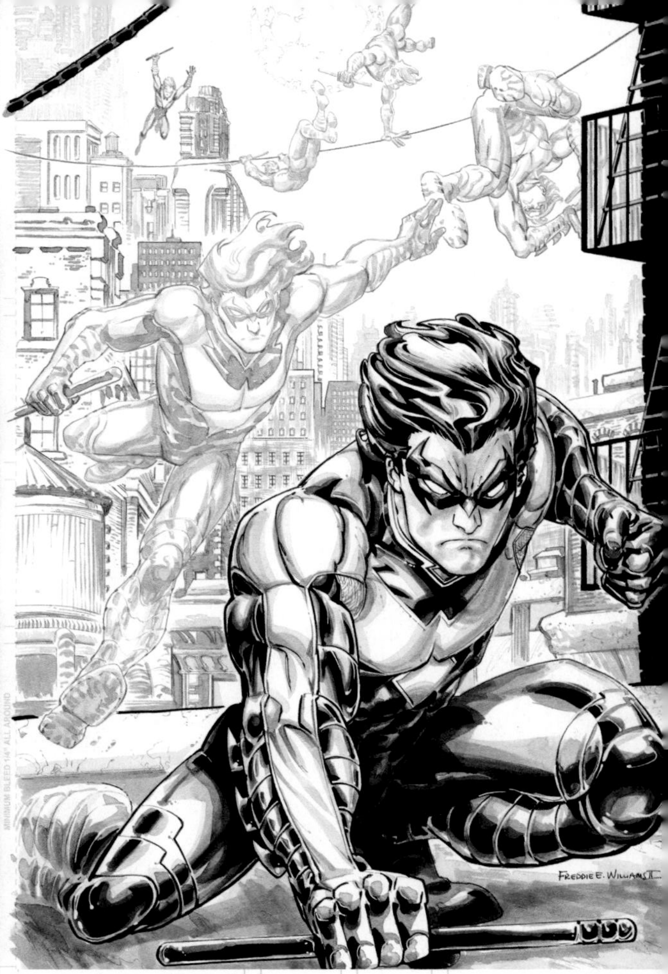
FREDDIE E. WILLIAMS II

INKER PAGE# ISSUE # MONTH INTERIORS

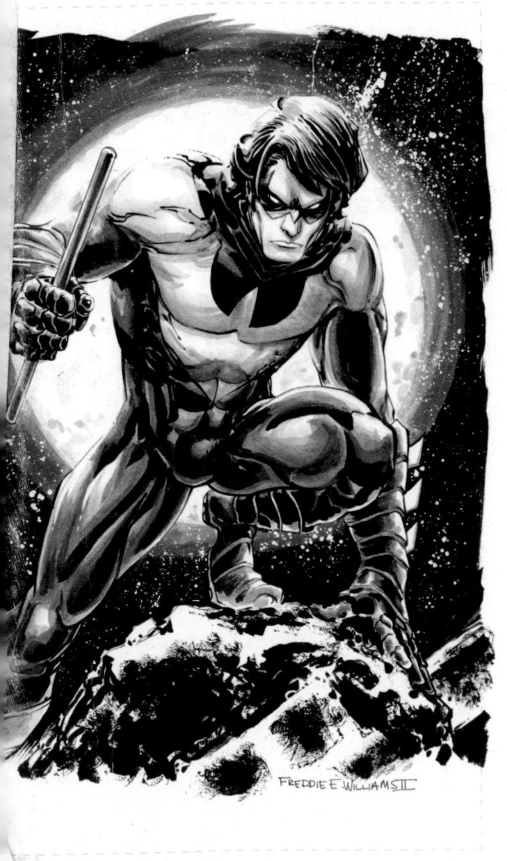
FREDDIE E. WILLIAMS II

MINIMUM BLEED 1/4" ALL AROUND

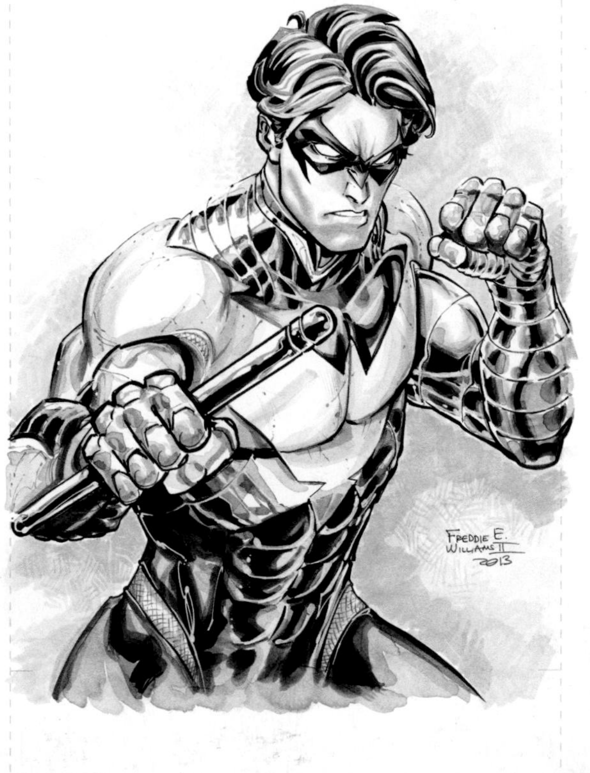
FREDDIE E. WILLIAMS II 2013

LIVE AREA

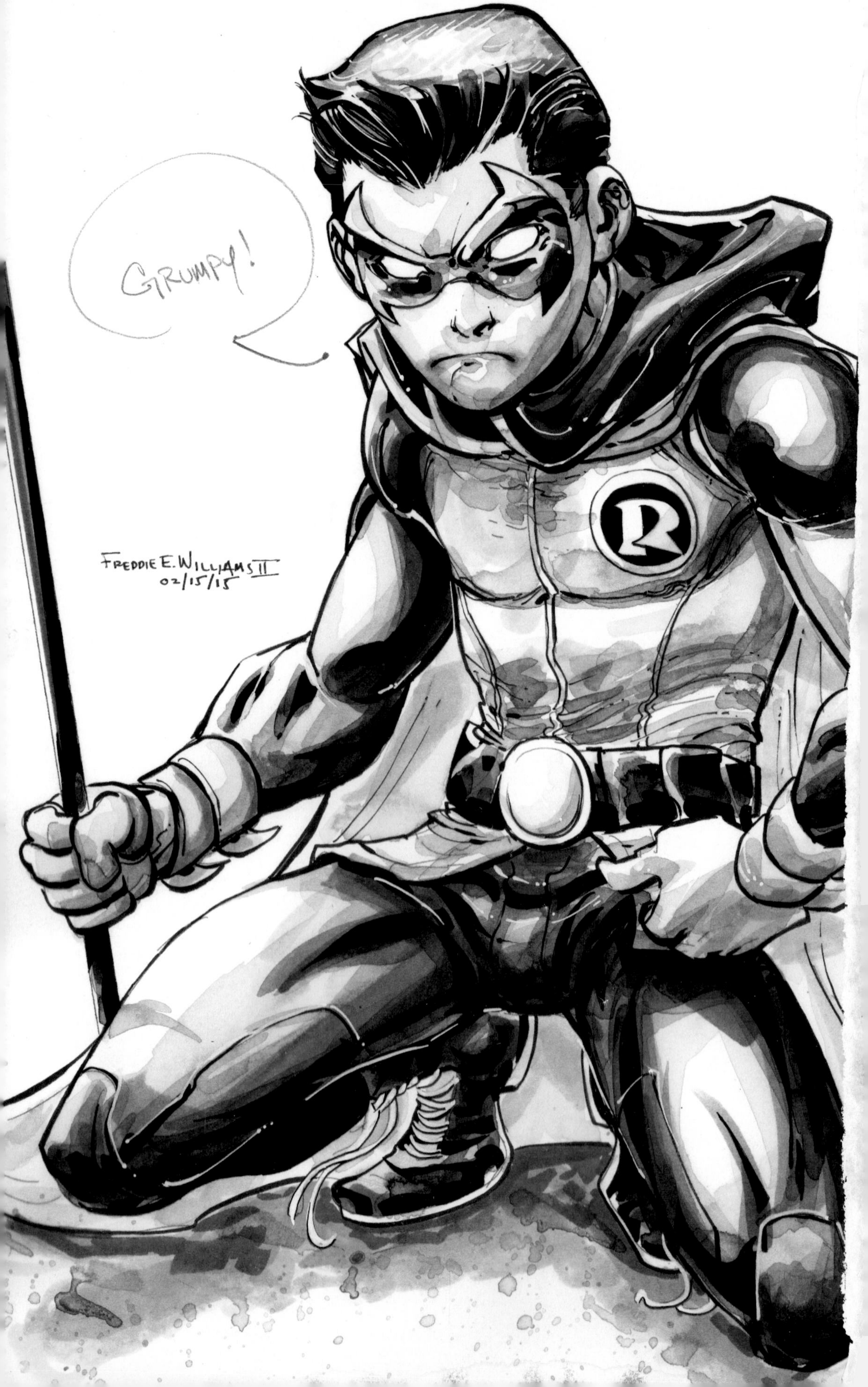
GRUMPY!
FREDDIE E. WILLIAMS II
02/15/15